# People vs. Government:
# The Responsiveness of
# American Institutions

# People vs. Government:

# The Responsiveness of

# American Institutions

*Edited by Leroy N. Rieselbach*

INDIANA UNIVERSITY PRESS

BLOOMINGTON & LONDON

Published in Canada by Fitzhenry & Whiteside Limited,
Don Mills, Ontario
Manufactured in the United States of America


Library of Congress Cataloging in Publication Data

Rieselbach, Leroy N
People vs. government.

Includes bibliographical references.
1.   United States—Politics and government—1945–
—Addresses, essays, lectures.   2.   Representative
government and representation—United States—
Addresses, essays, lectures.   I. Title.
JK271.R464   1975   320.9'73'092   74–379
ISBN 0–253–34340–2 Sept. 18, 1975

The average American is just like the child in the family. You give him some responsibility and he is going to amount to something. He is going to do something. If, on the other hand, you make him completely dependent and pamper him and cater to him too much, you make him soft, spoiled and eventually a weak individual.

RICHARD M. NIXON

# Contents

# People vs. Government:
# The Responsiveness of
# American Institutions

# Introduction:

# An Unresponsive America

*Leroy N. Rieselbach*

This book was conceived a couple of years ago in malaise, a disquiet that many of us felt as we looked back on the recently concluded decade of the 1960s. Something, it seemed, was profoundly wrong with America; her institutions—social, economic, political—seemed unable to cope even marginally with crises that threatened to overwhelm them. The old democratic adage of Abraham Lincoln—"government of, by, and for the people"—seemed in clear and present danger of becoming only a cliche. The citizens of the nation seemed incapable of getting hold of their own affairs; their institutions seemed out of reach and out of touch. Societal structures seemed unresponsive and in need of reform.

Governmental unresponsiveness seemed at the heart of the matter. The acts of the policy-making institutions from the presidency on down appeared to have little or nothing to do with popular needs or desires. Central to the concerns of the authors represented in the following pages is the sense that somehow, in some ways, social, economic, and especially political institutions should react to and take account of the needs, wishes, and preferences of the citizens that the institution is to serve. That is, those who govern can legitimately be expected to serve the interests of those they govern; the latter should be in a position to hold the former accountable and to punish leaders who lead in unacceptable directions.

Yet the issue is not so simple as the ideal of citizen control of institutions makes it seem. The concept of "the people" masks numerous uncertainties: who makes up "the people"? Do "the people" really know what they want? Can average citizens dictate to their leaders, or even give them sound advice? It is not at all clear that some form of head counting, of plebiscitory or participatory democracy, would lead to policy decisions any more beneficial than our institutions gave us in the 1960s. What does seem clear, however, is that during the last decade responsiveness in American institutions was in short supply. Some social structures seemed to be incapable of responding; others responded insufficiently; still others have responded to narrow, self-serving interests rather than to the needs of larger numbers of citizens.

The catalog of events leading to this dismal conclusion is lengthy and deeply disturbing, involving almost all major facets of the society. To start at the top, Lyndon Johnson, elected president on a peace platform, involved the nation in a costly war in Indochina which became increasingly unpopular as victory became more clearly unattainable. At least partly flowing from his policy's failure, the president's performance in the 1968 primary elections led him to conclude that his best position was on the sidelines and he abandoned the reelection contest. His party, meeting in a convention more notable for the demonstrations and devastation in the streets outside than for the debate and discussion within, selected Hubert Humphrey to carry its damaged standard. Throughout the ensuing campaign, Humphrey sought, with seeming embarrassment and substantial dissimulation, to walk the unsteady course between the Johnsonian supporters of our Southeast Asian adventure and the liberal critics of the war.

The electorate, however, preferred Richard M. Nixon, with his "secret" plan to disengage the nation from the Vietnamese quagmire. And while the newly installed Republican administration did move to reduce American involvement in the war, it moved very slowly and with digressions from its avowed course, such as the mining of

Haiphong harbor, an invasion of (or incursion into) Cambodia, and the Christmas bombing of North Vietnam. The pace at which termination of the war proceeded, two steps forward, one step backward, was not sufficient to satisfy the public or the Congress, both of which grew increasingly uneasy with the continuation of a military venture of little apparent value in a distant corner of the world. It was more and more perceived that the chief executives of the United States had led the nation into an economically expensive and politically divisive war which, if it was not lost, was most unlikely to be recorded as a singular triumph.

Looking from the White House up Pennsylvania Avenue toward the Congress revealed a similarly troubling picture. Not only had the national legislature's long-standing deference to executive initiatives in foreign affairs resulted in tardy congressional response to questions about the Vietnamese conflict, but the lawmakers' reluctance to assert themselves on the domestic scene also seemed more pronounced at decade's end. Congress retained considerable constitutional authority, but appeared psychologically constrained, if not immobilized; to an increasing extent senators and representatives seemed to prefer the political safety of "going along" with presidential leadership to the greater risks of attempting policy-making initiatives of their own. Federal solutions to the pressing problems of the day—environmental protection, crime, poverty and welfare, education, and the like—seemed slow to develop and ineffectual if and when implemented.

Neither did solutions to these problems seem likely to emerge at the state and local levels; these governments had substantial problems of their own. Malapportioned legislatures and weak executives, forced to operate within antiquated constitutional structures and on the basis of archaic tax systems that produce inadequate revenue, simply did not seem up to responding satisfactorily to the state and local manifestations of the same difficulties that bedeviled the federal government. State capitols and city halls, like their Washington counterparts, seemed at a loss when compelled to confront issues of welfare reform and finance, highway construction, the need for expanded hospital and mental health facilities, crime control, educational development and costs, and on and on. Here, too, the problems were easy to identify, were discussed openly, and were left un-resolved or haphazardly handled; again, the needs of citizens seemed largely unmet.

Nor did it appear that the elected branches of government, the executives and legislators at the national, state and local levels, were uniquely unresponsive among American institutions. Other societal instruments appeared equally culpable, equally removed from the influence of broad-based citizen preferences. The administrative cadres, the personnel of the myriad agencies and bureaus of the federal departments, seemed less attuned to the public than to the private good. Far from serving as fearless regulators in the "national interest," the increasingly large federal agencies looked more and more like the partners of the very interests they were charged to supervise.

Similarly, the judicial-legal system, long a stout pillar in the supporting structure of American society, began to seem in danger of collapse. Procedurally, the court dockets were crowded, entailing long delays before those accused could be tried before a jury of their peers. Concern about crime—flowing from student and urban unrest, symbolized by Berkeley and Watts—led law enforcement officers to propound doctrines like "preventive detention" and to propose "stop and frisk" laws, undercutting the long traditions of civil rights. The courts themselves, and particularly the Supreme Court as "final arbiter" of the judicial system, became increasingly politicized and consequently increasingly controversial. The myth of judicial impar-tiality (and infallability) was more frequently challenged; the series of decisions advancing school desegregation and legislative reappor-tionment, eliminating public school prayer, and outlining and ex-panding the rights of criminal defendents led those opposing such rulings to resort to politics to overturn them. The struggles over Richard Nixon's nominations to the Supreme Court of Clement Haynsworth and G. Harrold Carswell graphically demonstrated how ideology as well as judicial competence had influenced appoint-ments to the nation's highest court: ideological forces sought to place their partisans in a position to dominate constitutional interpretation at the highest levels.

At the opposite extreme, in the streets in the nation's cities, the image of the police as guardians of the citizen's safety came to be questioned. "Police brutality" became the cry of those challenging the traditional authority of the men in blue; "lily white" local constabularies were accused of excluding from membership the very groups with which they came into daily contact; investigatory panels such as the Knapp Commission in New York City uncovered corruption of unimagined proportions within the ranks of the "city's finest." Repressive techniques, sale of favors and favoritism, and generally inequitable application of the laws charged to the police led to citizen-officer tensions, violence, and the slogan "off the pigs" echoing through city streets. Observers were compelled to wonder about the fairness and justice with which law enforcement was conducted at the local level.

Even the military, that bastion of order and regularity, had come under ferocious attack, both from within and from the civilian world outside. Largely as the result of the unpopular Vietnam conflict, which it failed to "win," the armed forces have been subject to closer scrutiny than at any time in recent history. The My Lai "massacre," for which only Lt. William Calley was convicted, suggested that there was a dehumanizing element in contemporary training, an element which the old "war is hell" cliche could not explain or justify. Racism within the service led to riots aboard ships at sea. Military men were revealed profiteering from PX operations. Internally, dissent and demonstration erupted where they had been virtually unknown previously. Service men chafed under restrictions that compelled them to remain short haired and clean shaven; they published underground papers protesting the services' roles in Indochina; some officers refused to carry out their orders, while others who did were murdered ("fragged") by their own troops. Many found rest and relaxation in smoking pot or using harder drugs. The old image of the American military as disciplined and dedicated seemed irrevocably shattered.

This parade of horrors, White House and other, however overstated and underdescribed, inspired this book. These events demonstrated that public policy often moved in directions contrary to the desires of substantial citizen interests. The authors of this book were, early in the present decade, worried but not despairing; we were unhappy but not unhopeful, and we undertook to prepare a series of essays detailing our critiques and advancing our reform proposals.

And then came Watergate! What for us had been a problem became a crisis. The abuses revealed by the several Watergate investigations showed with an unimagined clarity how unresponsive American institutions were and how much they needed reform.[1]

The problem of responsiveness deepened while we wrote our essays. The change of language, the shift of symbols, from responsiveness to crisis of confidence or credibility or even corruption indicates only that the manifestations have altered, not that the problem has been replaced. American institutions have not responded to deeply felt and widely perceived citizen needs and interests. As they have failed, more and more people, and especially the better educated and the more affluent, have lost confidence in them.[2] Watergate, and all its attendant scandals, has merely served to illustrate unmistakably the extent to which some institutions can be used for private instead of public good. The basic questions remain: How, if at all, can our social structures be made responsive? How can they be made to serve more effectively and efficiently the needs of a greater number of citizens?

In sum, a set of critical essays conceived in dissatisfaction were actually written at a time of extreme national difficulty. Watergate and related matters have not only confirmed a diagnosis made when this volume was planned but also have made dramatically clear that the illness is a good deal more serious than we had originally believed. Our prescriptions may remain the same but the malady they are designed to treat may be more resistant than we once believed. Because this book is still, despite the latest symptoms of disease in American institutions, fundamentally reformist rather than radical, there are few, if any, suggestions for major surgery in the pages that follow. Rather, as academic social scientists are accustomed to do, we assume that our institutions are in theory workable and we point to ways which in practice those institutions might be made to work better.

We recognize that the abuses so dominating the news in the mid-1970s may lead many to conclude that reconstruction and not reform should be the order of the day. This is indeed a moment of despair; an opinion survey conducted in late 1973 for Edmund Muskie's Subcommittee on Intergovernmental Relations of the Senate Committee on Government Operations contains much disturbing data. Regard for societal institutions seems minimal. The executive branch, the locus of Watergate, fared worst; only 19 percent of a cross-section of American citizens expressed a "great deal of confidence" in the executive branch of the federal government; only 18 percent displayed a similar faith in the White House. The Congress did not fare much better: the Senate was the object of great confidence for 30 percent of the respondents while 29 percent felt similarly about the House of Representatives. The Supreme Court was more highly regarded, with 33 percent of the sample professing high confidence in it. Disenchantment was not limited to the national level, for state government (24 percent expressing high confidence) and local government (28 percent) were not accorded notable enthusiasm. Of the institutions considered here, local police (44 percent high approval) and the military (40 percent) received most plaudits, still short of a majority of the citizenry. The populace, in short, seems "down" on the institutions of society.[3] Nonetheless, we reject drastic change, preferring to propose reform which if successful should restore institutional performance, and with it popular evaluation, to acceptable levels. We prefer, in the short run at least, to tinker with our institutions in hope of reviving them.

The essays that make up this book reflect the views and concerns of a number of scholars and all focus on the common problem of responsiveness. The concerns mentioned in this introduction suggest the broad outlines of the problem while the chapters that follow spell out the details of these charges, assess their validity, and propose reforms where they appear needed and promising.

Thus, Eckart and Ries outline presidential opportunities in foreign and domestic affairs and indicate that recent presidents have favored the former over the latter when allocating resources and have, within the latter, favored the rich at the expense of the poor. The national executive, they argue, responds to power and privilege rather than to the dispossessed, to producers rather than consumers; he prefers to manipulate rather than inform the populace. The problem, however, may rest less with the presidency than with the broad social, cultural, economic, and political system within which the institution is embedded. Wealth will prevail as long as the values of the affluent dominate societal decision making. Change the nominating and electoral procedures so that candidates independent of the status quo can win office and the probability is increased that a president responsive to different interests will occupy the White House. In sum, the authors assert, "presidents are not the cause of our maladies"; without societal alteration any executive will espouse the values of the dominant social interests and act consistently with them. The president follows society, though he is its "leader," and it must lead him in new directions.

In looking at the lower levels of the executive branch, the federal bureaucracy, Salamon and Wamsley make a similar argument: bureaucrats are responsive, but they respond to the "powerful" not the "broad mass of citizenry." Agencies, charged with administering programs in an environment essentially hostile to regulation and bureaucracy, seek support to ensure survival; they often gain it ironically from the very interests they are obliged to oversee or from the legislative allies of those interests. Far from controlling their clients, agencies may be captured by them; administrative survival dictates a greater need for cooperation with clients than for stern control over them. Such a description, needless to say, hardly describes all agencies, but the pattern occurs often enough to engender questions about bureaucratic responsiveness. Similarly, concern with self-protection leads agencies to create internal organizations that are so stable, so predictable, that they cannot respond to claims forcefully pressed even from the most powerful outside interests. Thus, bureaucracy is buffered from broad interest by cozy client-centered outlooks and by comfortable organizational routines; it remains inaccessible to too many segments of society.

If broad-based but unorganized and under-financed groups and interests find access to the executive branch difficult and focus instead on Congress, they will find simultaneously greater opportunity and greater difficulty. As I seek to point out in my essay on Congress, those with ideas or programs to pursue on the one hand have multiple entry points to a decentralized legislature; through local representatives, the committees, party leaders, and others, they can register their complaints and push their policy proposals. But on the other hand, Congress, through its collective reluctance as well as its institutional incapacity, has had considerable difficulty in making its will prevail against a determined executive. Though responsive in many ways, Congress is often immobilized, and I propose a series of structural changes and some institutional tinkering that coupled with a greater determination on the part of the legislators might serve both to preserve existing responsiveness and to generate greater capacity to act on behalf of citizens' interests.

To consider state and local government indicates that there may be truth in the old adage about governments closer to the people being more responsive. Weber finds that despite numerous handicaps burdening state and local governments—old and outmoded constitutions, lack of professional expertise, and inelastic tax and finance arrangements—they are surprisingly responsive, at least on one subset of policy matters: that is, there seems a good fit between citizen preferences and government actions. Remove the barriers—provide more flexible tax systems, free local units from tight state controls, modernize constitutions, and so on—and popular proposals may become public policy still more easily.

In direct contrast to electoral politics, which are assumed to be by nature responsive, the courts and legal system are judged by different standards. In a host of activities, from interpreting the Constitution to policing the streets, the judicial and legal institutions are expected to be fair, impartial, and rational. At the same time, it is beyond doubt that the people making such determinations, being human, will act according to their own values. Whether or not the outside observer finds their actions responsive will depend in large part on whether he shares the premises on which the choices rest. As Claude points out in assessing the Supreme Court, that body is judged by the legal profession for the coherence of its judicial decisions. The high court also has a responsibility to the public for "the constitutionality of public policy." To balance these tasks will not always be easy, given the need to adapt the law—overruling precedent or explaining away earlier rulings where necessary—to altered social, political, and economic circumstances. The Court, possessing the power of judicial review by which it decides what the Constitution means, has shown it can respond to widely felt needs; decisions on desegregation, reapportionment, prayer in the public schools, obscenity, and abortion indicate the degree to which the courts "follow the election returns"—or at least are swayed by the spirit of the times. Claude, sympathetic to this general tendency, sketches some suggestions for sustaining and extending judicial responsiveness.

Responsiveness to these same citizen interests may, according to Ostrom, be absent in large central city police forces in America: "Ghetto residents feel they are receiving too few of the services they need and too much repression." Police and citizens view each other warily, with the former increasingly isolating themselves from the latter. Tightly organized, hierarchically controlled policy bureaucracies further separate the force from the citizens, and the leaders from the rank-and-file officers. Efficiency, in short, cuts into responsiveness and vice versa. To enhance responsiveness, Ostrom argues persuasively for use of small-scale police units, either independent of, or separate within, large centralized departments. Her argument parallels Weber's assessment of state and local governments: smaller units, closer to the people, may well be more responsive to the people.

The armed forces, like the police, have long appeared to epitomize the value of centralized hierarchical chains of command. How, Sherman asks, can the military with "its traditionalism, rigid career patterns, respect for order and regimentation, and dedication to martial values" be responsive to civilians, leaders and citizens alike? The creation of a permanent, standing army (sustained for years by the draft) coupled with the erosion of the power of Congress to declare war (the recently enacted War Powers legislation notwithstanding) or to control effectively the operations of the military through statutory or budgetary mechanisms has led policy to be managed by an executive-military alliance, often beyond the reach of civilian control. The judiciary, Sherman argues, constitutes one means for a more democratic control; despite some hesitation, the courts have begun to move to review military actions, particularly those which infringe upon the civil liberties of persons within the armed services. Together with structural changes designed to promote political control by civilian officials in the executive and legislative branches, judicial activism may lead to a more responsive military establishment.

These institutions, then, while responsive to important power centers, all seem to suffer from a lack of responsiveness to other important social interests—the poor, the powerless, the enlisted man, the minority. If policy-making institutions are unresponsive, it should not surprise us to discover that the policies they produce are not responsive. Although, as Caldwell makes clear, environmental policy is in some ways anomalous, it is nonetheless an area which engenders political controversy. The goals toward which the environmentalists work may be anathema to corporate executives (and the union members they employ), seeming to be fundamental challenges to the dominant business ethic. Indeed, institutional and social failure to respond to ecological arguments led to the environmentalists organizing to compel some sort of response. The passage in 1969 of the National Environmental Policy Act testifies to the force that the environmental movement was able to generate. That legislation joined the issue, basically between producers and consumers, and from its passage the struggle has been to strike a balance between the incompatible desires to use and to preserve scarce resources —energy, land, and the like. The feeling of the protectionists that the existing agencies of government have failed to respond, or have served producer rather than preservationist interests, has led them to seek judicial guardianship of their interests in the courts. Over the longer run, environmentalists seek to bring about institutional adaptation that increases responsiveness to their own sentiments and policy preferences.

Thus, the core of the complaints about American institutions, practices, and policies is that they have been unresponsive or have responded to the wrong interests. We believe that analyses of other facets of the social order—the foreign policy establishment or urban governments; business, religious, or educational organizations; policies relating to welfare, energy, or taxation—would produce similar evidence of no or only partial responsiveness. We do recognize that the preferences of the greatest number may not always be right or make good public policy, but we hold that all points of view are entitled to be heard and that those lacking clout have had too much difficulty in gaining consideration by those who make the important decisions. It is our hope that the reforms proposed in these pages could redress the balance, permit pluralistic politics to go forward less restrictedly, and serve to make American political, economic, and social process more responsive.

Moreover, we cannot blithely assume that Gerald Ford's accession to the presidency will resolve these problems. At best the change, whatever its short-term psychological impact on popular confidence, may restore the status quo ante. The pre-Watergate situation, as noted, had already raised serious doubts about institutional responsiveness, doubts which remain independent of the occupant of the White House. In the long run, change of mood or change of style will not increase responsiveness, will not restore confidence. Reform remains vital, and the issues raised here remain to be met and resolved.

# The American Presidency

*Dennis R. Eckart and John C. Ries*

It is obvious that the presidency has grown enormously in power over the past forty years. In the eyes of many, this power has been gained at the expense of other institutions of national government, especially the Congress. The rate at which the presidency is aggrandizing itself has accelerated during recent years. At least until 1965, all but a few conservatives applauded these trends. Reformers more often than not proposed to solve problems, whether of governmental efficiency or of domestic and foreign concern, by increasing still further the power of the chief executive. Not so today. Presidential aggrandizement is condemned because of its effects on both foreign and domestic policy, but more importantly because of its implications for popular government and presidential accountability. This view is held almost unanimously by academicians and intellectuals, is gaining widespread acceptance among journalists, and is heard expressed more and more frequently by the common man, especially if he happens to be a member of a minority group.

What accounts for the shift in evaluation of the power of the presidency? The simple and obvious answer is also probably the correct one: more and more people disapprove of the uses to which presidential power has been put. What people want is the wise and beneficial use of power. Until recently only a few populists, anarchists or radical conservatives among us accepted Lord Acton's dictum, "All power tends to corrupt and absolute power tends to corrupt absolutely." In light of the sordid events surrounding the Watergate affair, there are now few, if any, who do not. Despite the cynicism caused by the revelations suggesting that President Nixon's appointees engaged in burglary, illegal wiretapping, forgery, perjury, bribing and otherwise tampering with witnesses, destroying evidence, accepting bribes, conspiring to involve federal agencies in illegal actions, and then trying to cover up the entire mess, most who criticize the power of the presidency are making a judgment about the ends that presidential power is serving.

One need not look hard or far to find criticisms of what the president is or is not doing. These criticisms are most frequently focused on the lack of responsiveness of the presidency. We shall attempt to summarize and evaluate these charges. However, we also intend to examine the assumptions on which such charges are based, namely, that the president is really powerful and could do "good" if only he would. We also wish to reexamine the presidency in light of Lord Acton's and the American populists' and conservatives' distrust of all concentrations of power and privilege.

Among the most persistent and persuasive indictments of presidential responsiveness are these:

- Abuse of his power in foreign policy, not only by ignoring the sentiment of the people but also by usurping the constitutional powers of the Congress.
- Failure to use all of the powers available to him in redressing domestic problems.
- Failure to provide the national leadership that can come only from the office of the chief executive, as a result of his being hopelessly out of touch with the aspirations and hopes of those who are not receiving the benefits of our society—whether they be racial and ethnic minorities, consumer advocates, environmentalists, women, or those who reject the materialism, nationalism, and conformity demanded by those who occupy positions of power and prestige.
- Favoritism, if not outright corruption, in government, leading straight to the door of the White House, as well as a pattern of misleading, if not lying to, the public.

We shall examine each of these in turn.

## The Charges of Presidential
## Unresponsiveness Considered

*Foreign Policy.* Whatever the intentions of the framers of the Constitution, presidents have always exercised overriding power in matters of foreign policy. Cloaked by custom and sanctioned by the Supreme Court, presidents have deployed United States armed forces, suspended civil liberties, controlled the economy, and invaded foreign countries in the name of national defense. However unfettered the power of the president might be, until the end of the Second World War strong forces restrained his exercise of discretion in foreign affairs. First and foremost among them was our tradition of isolation and nonintervention in the affairs of others. Although at times these norms were observed in the breach, especially in Central America, they served as a real and substantial limit on presidential action. Second, and relating to the first, was our aversion to large and standing armies. Presidents simply could not do much because they lacked significant military means. To embark on a major military adventure, the president had to seek Congressional approval in order to create the necessary forces. And so presidents did in 1812, 1844, 1900, 1917, and 1941. For good or for ill, these impediments to the unrestrained exercise of his "unfettered" powers were brushed away in the aftermath of the Second World War.

With the advent of the Cold War, nuclear weapons, and space technology, the preconditions for the existence of a large, standing military force were established. The Cold War also provided the justification. In the face of an "international conspiracy" under the direction of the Kremlin, single-mindedly committed to the conquest of the world in the name of Communism, the United States had to have the capability to deter aggression globally as well as the forces to meet and counter such aggression should deterrence fail. The strategy of deterrence justified, indeed required, military forces in being and at the ready. Not again would America be allowed the luxury of mobilization. The industrial might of the Arsenal of Democracy would not serve to prevent the 180 Communist divisions deployed in the new Communist buffer states from sweeping across "Free Europe." The newly independent countries of Southeast Asia stood helpless before the combined might of Moscow and Peking. And the creation of a Soviet nuclear capability in the early 1950s, together with Soviet deployment of a long-range bomber fleet and demonstrations of intercontinental ballistic missiles in the latter part of the same decade, meant the continental United States had lost its immunity from attack.

From the time of the North Korean invasion of the South in 1950 to the threatened collapse of the South Vietnamese government in the face of Viet Cong and, apparently, North Vietnamese forces in the summer of 1965, there was no serious debate about the assumptions upon which American military policy was based. The only arguments concerned the nature of the military threat—there was little if any doubt that the threat was both real and imminent. Had we overprepared for the nuclear threat and neglected our non-nuclear capabilities? Had we assumed that aggression would be overt, as in Korea, and underestimated the threat of subversion and guerrilla war? These were the only kinds of questions debated.

The importance of these post–Second World War developments lay in the removal of the previous restraints on the exercise of presidential discretion. During these years and extending down to the present, the commander in chief has had at his disposal the forces to involve the United States in a great variety of military adventures. Furthermore, he also enjoyed a consensus that, especially in the case of nuclear threats or attack, he would have to act without observing the constitutional requirement of seeking a congressional declaration of war. Technology was seen as having rendered that check on presidential exercise of power anachronistic. Furthermore, few doubted that a president would act in any fashion inconsistent with national security or unlikely to receive congressional approval were there time to seek it.

Although the Cold War ideology and the logic of modern warfare served to make the Congress a contributor to the atrophy of its responsibilities for the "common defense," such systemic forces do not dictate how a president should exercise his new, truly unfettered discretion. Different incumbents have met similar circumstances and have interpreted them differently. President Eisenhower refused to create crises when he might have done so over Taiwan, Indochina, Germany, Hungary, Suez, and Korea (again). And he refused despite a dogmatic and moralistic secretary of state. President Johnson, on the other hand, created a crisis over the shelling of our warships in the Gulf of Tonkin, and President Nixon created a crisis in order to invade Cambodia in 1970 and to mine Haiphong Harbor in 1972. The point is that a president can create crises and thereby mold public opinion, but he need not do so. He can put critics on the defensive, even silence them, by alluding to his superior knowledge and by withholding, in the name of national security, information that might prove embarrassing. But he need not do so.

The resulting power of the president to act as he judges appropriate without serious limitation by either Congress or public opinion is awesome. The Harris poll reported that by early 1972, 79 percent of the national public wanted the United States out of Vietnam. President Johnson decided not to seek a second term because of the divisions in the nation resulting from his policy toward Vietnam. In his inaugural address, President Nixon promised to end the war, and he was reelected for a second term while the war continued (although the prospects for a cease-fire did seem real enough by October 1972). The manner in which the president was able to accomplish this seemingly impossible feat is instructive. He substituted firepower for American manpower in Vietnam. By mid-1972 there were only 26,000 U. S. troops in Vietnam, but there were 20,000 flyers in Thailand and aboard ships, dropping 1,000 tons of bombs a day along the Ho Chi Min Trail, 300 tons a day on Cambodia, 300,000 tons daily on South Vietnam itself, and the equivalent of twenty Hiroshima-size atomic bombs on the North after the resumption of bombing in the spring of 1972. Furthermore, the president promised to end the draft. By the two acts, reducing American casualties and reducing the threat of conscription, he succeeded in diverting a good deal of public attention from the war and in cutting most of the ground from under the critics of his war policies. As Secretary of Defense Melvin Laird commented, "The American public understands the difference between addition and subtraction."[1] These steps seemed to blur even his critics' memory of the president as the man who watched a football game while youthful protestors staged a demonstration against the war in the nation's capital and who referred to the protestors at Kent State University as "bums."

The president further molded public opinion by traveling to

Peking to "normalize" relations with China and shortly thereafter ordered the resumption of bombing of North Vietnam and the mining of Haiphong Harbor. He then signed a historic strategic arms limitation treaty in Moscow, but afterward, through his secretary of defense, informed the public that we must now undertake an increased level of arms expenditures to offset the effects of the agreement and to provide him something to bargain with in future arms limitations negotiations! His capacity to manipulate public opinion, silence critics, and command enormous military might have made it possible for the president to talk of peace while he waged war.

A major issue at stake, in this apparently Orwellian world in which war is peace, is the extent to which the fault (1) must be laid at the door of the White House as an institution caught up in a web of structural forces that determine the exercise of presidential discretion or (2) must rest largely on the conscience of the incumbent. There are important structural forces working to push the president —any president—along the route taken by Presidents Johnson and Nixon.

Perhaps the most important is our moralism as it affects military policy. Fundamental to our political culture is the belief that we are a peace-loving people who fight not when we are merely provoked but only when our cause is just. To settle for less than "victory" is to compromise with evil, to dishonor ourselves and our war dead. Overlaid on this moralism is the Cold War mentality we have been taught so carefully and thoroughly for more than a generation. The world is split in half—a free half and a Communist half. Good nations are those that stand by us in the face of the Communist threat, whether they are dictatorships or democracies, whether they are corrupt or honest, whether they share our moralism or have to be bribed through military and economic aid. Until recently, the only acceptable trade with the Reds was in epithets and there could be no communication with mainland China. Taiwan was China. These belief patterns, which have been constantly reinforced, serve as powerful forces that both direct and limit the exercise of presidential discretion. But vague or general structural limitations do not eliminate presidential freedom to act. President Nixon did travel to China. He signed an arms pact with the Soviet Union in Moscow. He welcomed Marshall Tito to Washington, D. C. But he continued the war in Vietnam for four more years, blaming his critics for his failures and the "enemy" for not giving up!

Another powerful structural force operating is a self-serving defense bureaucracy. All organizations seek to maintain themselves and to grow. In the name of deterrence, the U. S. Department of Defense successfully maintained a claim on national resources at approximately 9 percent of the gross national product from the Korean buildup until 1965. Currently it receives about 6 percent. A "defeat" in Vietnam would undermine the legitimacy of the military itself, hence its ability to thrive and grow. General Westmoreland was sure he could "win" in Vietnam in 1967 if only he were given more troops. Heavy conscription rates expanded American ground forces in Southeast Asia to more than half a million men. It is interesting to note how the military sought to protect its position when escalation failed to produce highly favorable results. The war became increasingly unpopular, and the military reluctantly acted to remove itself from troublesome activities. After years of holding on to the draft, the military supported the end of conscription. It has accepted the shift in battlefield tactics away from ground forces to reliance on air power. It has devoted more attention to the problems of deterrence and the implications of arms limitation, basing claims for continuous high budgets on the need to modernize our retaliatory equipment (for example, the air force's B-1 bomber and the navy's Trident submarine).

Indeed, the military tied its acceptance of the arms limitation treaty to congressional approval of these new weapons systems. Along with presidential advisers who accept either the Cold War ideology or the need to secure our national values through military might (or both), the defense bureaucracy exerts major influence on the exercise of presidential discretion.

Finally, there is the defense-aerospace industry and its employees. Decisions to let contracts for new weapons and to manufacture munitions affect the employment of hundreds of thousands as well as the earnings of major corporations. The economies of entire sections of the country have been depressed by failure to receive or continue contracts. And pressures on the president are not limited to votes in the quadrennial election. Congressmen, governors, mayors, union leaders, party activists, and campaign contributors from the affected areas are quick to bring all their political resources to bear on the president to enlist his action in support of their economic interest.

Despite these very real and strong systemic forces pushing him in the direction of continuing a forceful, militant, and military approach to foreign affairs, the president cannot be absolved from responsibility for his actions. Eisenhower promised to end the Korean conflict, if elected. And when elected, he did. Johnson campaigned on a peace platform. He did not have to escalate the war in Vietnam but he did—within six months of being inaugurated. One might argue it is easier for a former war hero to resist the pressures of the previously considered structural forces that operate on the presidency than for a man such as Johnson, who was uncertain about foreign affairs and felt uneasy in handling them. Perhaps so, but certainly President Nixon, avowed anti-Communist and foreign policy hardliner, would be equally resistant to such pressures. Neither his convictions nor his reputation deterred him from making the opening with China or from signing an arms agreement with the Soviets. If the military establishment was neutral about the former, it certainly was not enthusiastic about the latter.

One simply cannot escape the conclusion that the president has choices, despite the structural or systemic forces working on him. He has enormous power and substantial discretion in its use. The incumbent cannot escape judgment about its use. Whatever the rhetoric about nailing the coonskin to the wall or "peace with honor," the president must bear on his conscience the consequences for the Vietnamese, for our relations with other states, and for the domestic inflation, dissention, and casualties which accrued from continuation of the war after the electorate voted in two elections for the candidate promising peace. The structural forces are accomplices, not causes.

### The President and Domestic Policy

Many aspects of recent domestic policy have been inexorably tied to our foreign and military policy. The last two presidents were apparently convinced of the political inexpediency of financing the war by asking for new taxes. There was only one other way to meet the costs, namely, by ignoring pressing domestic needs. The money needed to pursue the war was provided through inflation and by cutting domestic programs. The "Great Society" was the first domestic casualty of the Vietnamese War. A few further examples will serve to make the point. President Nixon's stance was always for fiscal "responsibility," for making the government and its programs "pay their own way." In February 1970, when he presented the first budget developed by his administration, he said, "I have pledged to the American people that I would submit a balanced budget for 1971. This is particularly necessary because the cost of living has been rising rapidly for the past five years. The budget I sent to you today . . . fulfills that pledge."\* At the end of that fiscal year the president had a deficit of \$23 billion! In the next fiscal year, the deficit was another \$23 billion. The deficit for fiscal year 1973 was \$14.3 billion. Furthermore, between 1969 and mid-1973 the national debt increased by 20 percent and the wholesale price index rose almost 40 percent. These deficits and the rate of inflation were not the result of seeking to have both guns and butter. They were the costs of buying guns.

In 1970, President Nixon proudly announced that for the first time in two full decades the federal government would spend more money on human resources programs than on national defense. Furthermore, he pointed to an increase of over \$6 billion for programs in education, health, manpower, veterans' benefits, and income security. It sounded good; however, the latter consisted, of course, of social security and unemployment insurance, and the \$6 billion increase referred to consisted of mandatory increases in these programs. Pretense became a mockery when subsequent supplemental military expenditures were occasioned by additional escalation; and succeeding years of the Vietnamese War saw major reductions in domestic expenditures. In February 1970, the president vetoed an HEW appropriation because it would spend on schools \$1.1 billion more than he thought proper. He failed to mention that he was asking, for weapons, \$5.6 billion more than Congress was willing to appropriate. In 1971, the Office of Budget and Management im-

\* The quoted statements of public officials as well as the examples used to illustrate the arguments of this and the next section of the chapter draw heavily from editorials and feature articles of *The New Republic.* We acknowledge our debt to that journal and its authors as well as express our gratitude for their insightful reporting of national affairs and public policies.

pounded almost one-third of the money approved for housing but approved an increase of $1 billion for the Pentagon. In the spring of 1972, the administration proposed a $6.3 billion increase in defense spending (bringing the level up to a proposed $83.4 billion) in the face of a projected (in the spring of 1972) $30 billion deficit. Amid the shambles of his own budget, the president vetoed a $1.8 billion increase in HEW-Labor appropriations, citing it as "the perfect example of the kind of reckless federal spending that cannot be done without more taxes or more inflation." Meanwhile the General Accounting Office issued a report revealing cost overruns of $28.7 billion for seventy-seven military weapons systems. The Pentagon was proposing to replace Polaris submarines with a new model, the Trident, at an estimated cost of $1.4 billion apiece. Secretary of Defense Laird said that it was "essential" to build an antimissle defense for the nation's capital at an estimated cost of $8.5 billion. And, to replace our B-52s, the air force has been touting the B-1 bomber for which the research and development costs (excluding production costs) are estimated to be $2.7 billion.

And there is no end in sight. According to the Brookings Institution, the defense budget will be $100 billion by 1977 and, according to the Deputy Director of Defense Research and Engineering, $112 billion by 1980. Even at the present level ($78 billion), it is twice as much as is spent by all levels of government on primary and secondary education and eight times as much as government and industry spend to reduce water and air pollution.

Domestic budgets and programs depend upon and continue to take second priority to military expenditures. Because the domestic needs are great, the price of war is that much greater. But the effects are massive budget deficits and mounting inflation. Inflation is a cruel tax on the already meager purchasing power of the poor as well as on the fixed incomes of the elderly and the disabled. Health, education, manpower training, the environment, housing—indeed, all the programs aimed at redressing domestic problems and needs have been conscripted in the service of the Vietnamese War and national defense.

In his first address to Congress after his inauguration, President Ford carefully justified a continuing high level of defense expenditures while promising to reduce unnecessary federal expenditures as a counter to inflation. The implication was obvious: once more, domestic programs would be sacrificed in the name of "national security."

Although presidential acts to control inflation help prevent the poor from falling further behind, continued unwillingness to maintain or expand domestic programs effectively prevents the poor from making important gains. The United States is the world's wealthiest nation, yet one in nine of its citizens is poor. Of the one in eleven who are black, most are concentrated in central cities surrounded by a curtain of zoning. Within the curtain, blacks watch employment opportunities move out along with the white population to the suburbs. Left behind are decaying housing stock, high density, poor schools, and crime. Of course it is the poor who are the greatest victims of crime. Three successive presidential commissions have pointed out that one in seventy ghetto dwellers is a victim of a mugger, assailant, or rapist, in contrast with the one in ten thousand so victimized in the population as a whole. Yet presidents speak of law and order. In 1968, 58 percent of the white population earned $8,000 or more, but only 32 percent of the nonwhites did so. Twenty-nine percent of all black families are below the poverty line, but our presidents preach the work ethic to them. Blacks are 12 percent of the college age population, but they are only 6.5 percent of the high school graduates and 3 percent of the college students. Yet presidents speak of equal opportunity.

Not all economic problems are so race-related. The simple fact is that our political system reinforces and perpetuates a class structure characterized by gross inequities little changed over the last several decades. In 1915, the lowest 65 percent owned 5 percent of the wealth. The top 2 percent of the population owned 35 percent of the wealth. With regard to disposable income, the picture in 1915 was similar. In 1970, the bottom fifth of the population received an unbelieveably low 3.2 percent of the national income. The next lowest fifth received 10.5 percent, while the top 1 percent received 6.8 percent (twice as much as the bottom fifth). The top 1 percent also owned 25 percent of the national wealth, including 72 percent of the corporate stock, 47 percent of bonds (including virtually all tax-exempt state and local bonds), 24 percent of notes and mortgages on real estate, and 16 percent of all real estate itself.

It is difficult to state these points dramatically enough. Total personally owned wealth amounts to $4 trillion, which would be, on the average, about $20,000 for every citizen or about $70,000 for every family, yet only one family in twenty-five actually does own that much. The economy produces about $800 billion in personal income, or $14,000 per family, but only one family in four receives that much. Both our economy and our laws reward ownership of wealth more than labor, and ownership is concentrated in the hands of a few. Tax policies discriminate in favor of unearned income that stems from the ownership of capital. Special interests receive the greatest form of welfare of all, through exorbitant depletion allowances, overgenerous credits for investment and accelerated depreciation, tax havens in phoney agricultural enterprises, schemes for transforming legitimate income into privileged capital gains, and tax exempt bonds. The total dollar amount of "welfare" for the rich is beyond the wildest dream of the most radical advocate for the poor. It is estimated to be $77 billion annually.

To illustrate, farmers see large food-processing corporations making huge profits, not to mention the recent apparent collusion and windfall profits of grain traders, now referred to as the "great grain robbery of 1972." The national government paid almost $6 billion annually in farm subsidies, but 80 percent of these funds went to only 20 percent of the farmers—for the most part to agribusinesses and to those with the largest farms, including a few congressmen. In 1969, the wealthiest 7 percent of farmers got 40 percent of the subsidies. The poorest 50 percent received 9 percent. The landless farm workers, of course, got nothing. Indeed, the largess of the national government in paying wealthy farmers to withhold land from production cost farm workers jobs. While presidents promise a return to parity prices and farm prosperity, farm workers are still denied the protection of a minimum wage.

The national government underwrites bank loans for Lockheed in the amount of $250 billion. Secretary of Commerce John Connally rationalized the action as follows: "We feel that the impact that the demise of this company would have would be of such proportions that it ought not be permitted in the interest of economic survival of the nation." Concern for and commitment to the survival and well-being of industrial giants has become so strong that in May 1971

Arthur Burns of the Federal Reserve Board sought $2 billion in federal guarantees for corporations whose failure was deemed (by exactly whom is not clear) harmful to the national economy. One can only wonder about how the owners of the 10,000 small businesses that fail each year react to this peculiar commitment to the free enterprise system.

Clearly, rich people's welfare is much nicer to receive than poor people's welfare. Quite a picture can be painted: no ceilings set, no means tests, no social workers, and no danger of cutbacks or reductions in the welfare rolls of the rich. Letting your money earn your income certainly beats working. There is no nasty boss, no need to be competent, and no loss of income from sickness, accident, or old age. And above all, the way the deck has been stacked it is very unlikely that many of the middle class (and probably impossible that any of the low-income class) will ever manage to accumulate enough capital to compete with the investments of the very rich. On the other hand, the nonrich seem reluctant to see the privileges of the wealthy limited in any way, either because of the remote chance they themselves may take part in them some day or because they accept them as the "natural order of things."

However great, the enormity of the inequities in the distribution of wealth and income in our society receive little attention from the media and inappropriate action from public officials, particularly the president. We are not suggesting that the president, who is the chief initiator of economic policy, is personally responsible for such inequities, because clearly he is not. We do maintain, however, that he is unresponsive to demands for remedial change. Instead, he acts to reinforce the present maldistribution.

Consider, for example, Nixon's position on taxes. In the 1972 presidential election, he promised no presidential tax increase (although he did suggest that a congressional tax increase might be necessary). Given the steady rise in military spending and the existence of mandatory domestic programs, something had to give if he were to hold down tax levels. Obviously that "something" involved domestic programs such as those for manpower training, educational reform, welfare reform, and so on. For example, in January 1973, the president ordered an eighteen-month freeze on federally subsidized housing.

Regarding taxes already in existence, Nixon followed his predecessors in refusing to propose major changes that would make the
tax structure more equitable. Currently, income earned from labor
is penalized, compared with income earned from capital. The taxes
paid by a family of four vary enormously, depending upon how the
income is earned. Consider three families, each with a total income
of $10,000. If the income is earned in wages, as is the case with most
middle- and lower-class families, tax payments would be approximately $950. If, on the other hand, the earnings come from capital
gains (from sale of property or stocks, for example), which is characteristic of only the upper economic strata, the tax would amount to
about $98, or one-tenth the amount paid by the wage earner. If the
income of the third family is derived from clipping coupons on state
or municipal bonds, the tax is zero! Only the income of the very top
of the economic strata comes in this fashion.

To hope for major reforms is to ignore the ideology that under-
girds our national political economy and guides all changes in tax
rates. The tax cuts of 1965, 1969, and 1971 were completely consistent with that ideology: they increased the special privileges of those
who own capital and productive facilities, in the name of increased
productivity. Economic health and financial well-being has been
defined as a problem of growth and productivity. The way to make
all people better off is to increase the privileges enjoyed by the few.
No wonder that among the "silent majority," there is a taxpayers'
revolt and resentment of those receiving welfare. It is they, the
marginal through the middle-income families, who have been taxed
to support the war in Vietnam and who continue to provide welfare
for the poor. Tragically, their anger is misdirected. It would be more
properly focused on those who have managed to shift the burden to
taxes away from themselves in the name of "free enterprise" and "the
sanctity of capital."

The much-heralded revenue-sharing programs will not solve
any of these problems precisely because those who pay the taxes
generate the revenue to be shared. First conceived when projections
of national growth indicated an excess of federal revenues over expenditures, revenue sharing was to distribute the resulting "divi-
dend" to states and localities. But that was before the Nixon administration accumulated $80 billion in federal deficits as the method of

financing the Vietnamese War. Nor should Congress escape blame, in view of its willingness to cut taxes, especially for those who, through the magic of modern fiscal policy, supposedly will contribute to increased productivity and, thereby, increased revenues. But the stark question remains, who will pay for revenue sharing? Mostly wage earners.

Regarding other types of domestic legislation, Nixon's rhetoric was conservative even though his legislative program tended to continue in the vein of the previous administration but with reduced appropriations and without vigorous backing during the various phases of the legislative process. Perhaps the best example of the president's unwillingness to fight for his own legislative proposals was the now-defunct Family Assistance Plan. Early in 1971, the president announced welfare reform to be his first priority. The bill that was finally reported out to the Senate during the last two weeks of the session was written by the conservative members of the Finance Committee, and, although it would put a floor under family income, it would have lowered the incomes of most welfare families—a dubious reform. Liberal members of the Finance Committee organized a group of thirty-two Democratic senators who would support the bill if the White House would agree to a series of compromises in it. Nineteen Republicans urged the president to accept these compromises. During negotiations, the president was organizing support for his first-priority program with statements such as "I advocate . . . getting more people off welfare rolls" and "Most of us consider it immoral to be lazy or slothful—even if a person is well-off enough not to have to work or deliberately avoids work by going on welfare." The president's final comment on the proposed compromise, by then endorsed by his own secretary of health, education, and welfare, was that it was ". . . the wrong step because it would substantially increase the cost of welfare and move in the direction that I think the country does not want and that I believe would not be in the interests of the welfare recipients themselves."

Evidence mounts convincingly in support of the charge that presidents tend to slight the domestic needs of the nation. However, once again one must address the question of the extent to which his actions are deliberate choices based on his own values and priorities or are the inevitable result of structural forces operating on the presidency. Certainly, important structural forces affect presidential behavior in the domestic arena. Without attempting to be exhaustive, we give several of these forces closer attention here. First, there are fiscal constraints. None of Ford's three immediate predecessors actively attempted to get significant increases in the federal share of public assistance benefits. However, their inactivity was based not on principle but on fiscal constraints, so throughout the Kennedy-Johnson years the emphasis was on rehabilitative services rather than redistribution.[2] More recently, Nixon's proposal for a $2,400 income guarantee would have cost an estimated $5.9 billion. A small increase to $2,800 per family would raise the net cost to $9.3 billion.[3] National budgets would not accommodate such programs.

A second important structural factor involves psychological orientations toward domestic policy. Nixon was probably correct in arguing that a Family Assistance Plan is not the direction in which the country wants to move. In Congress, for instance, key members also share a belief in the work ethic and over the years they have focused on reforming the welfare system rather than on redistributing wealth. The compulsory work program in 1965 called the Work Incentive Program (WIN) was a congressional measure—not a presidential initiative. Moreover, the House Ways and Means Committee was solely responsible for the so-called freeze on federal sharing in cases of absent fathers under the Aid for Dependent Children legislation enacted in 1967.[4] Also, the results of two separate national opinion surveys (1969 and 1972) demonstrated that a majority of Americans regard the poor as being themselves responsible for poverty and therefore oppose such new programs directed toward eliminating poverty as guaranteed family income.[5]

Public attitudes toward welfare reform only reflect the prevailing American ideological perspective toward public policy. This perspective is a curious blend of liberal and conservative political thought. Liberals and conservatives alike accept (or at the very least are unwilling to admit the existence of) the basic class structure of our society and, to a greater or lesser extent, its accompanying inequities. They differ only in their views about the role of government in ameliorating the worst abuses. Conservatives resist governmental efforts to rectify inequities on the grounds that bureaucrats will bungle the job. They place their trust in the market place and are willing to accept any resulting inequity. Liberals would solve the problem by pouring billions of dollars and thousands of bureaucrats into housing, health, antipoverty, and welfare programs to compensate for rather than to end the inequities. And, interestingly, there are both liberals and conservatives among the major critics of the presidency—conservatives because the president has spent too many billions and created too many bureaucrats, liberals because he has not spent enough.

A radical, on the other hand, in the tradition of Thomas Jefferson or of American populism, distrusts all concentrations of power, whether in the private or the public sector. He distrusts bigness itself precisely because it tends to result in the concentration of privilege and the victimization of the consumer and the powerless. A radical, therefore, would be critical of the entire structure of power in public and private affairs in America today. He would note how trivial have been shifts in the distribution of income and wealth. He would object to the workings of our political system which have preserved these inequalities.[6]

Not surprisingly, the prevailing liberal-conservative ideology diverts attention from inequity and enshrines growth as the panacea for national ills. This ideology was articulated clearly by John K. Galbraith when he said, "It has become evident to conservatives and liberals alike that increasing aggregate output is an alternative to redistribution or even to the reduction of inequality. The oldest and most agitated of social issues, if not resolved, is at least largely in abeyance, and the disputants have concentrated their attention, instead, on the goal of increased productivity."[7]

The argument implicit in this ideology is both simple and fallacious. When productivity is increased, everyone gets more. Those who do not share directly by earning higher wages do so indirectly through welfare payments, unemployment benefits, old age and survivors insurance, and other similar programs. Thus if everyone is getting better off, people won't care too much that there are inequities in the distribution of wealth.

This line of reasoning might be plausible (provided of course one did not feel that relative deprivation is as important as any absolute measure of deprivation), except that all do not share proportionately in the benefits of increased productivity. In addition to inflation, which erodes the real additions to income and the purchasing power of lower-income groups, and racism, which still discriminates against blacks and browns in job opportunities and occupational mobility, there is our tax structure. As noted above, under our political and economic system, increased productivity does not resolve the problems of redistribution; it merely perpetuates inequality in income and wealth. Moreover, current governmental programs have little, if any, redistributive effect. In fact, the lion's share of public money for welfare benefits the nonpoor rather than the poor. Social insurance and educational programs consume 70 percent of all public welfare expenditures. Finally, the income share of the poorest 20 percent of American families has remained stable since the Second World War. Therefore, the overall effect of governmental payments to the poor has been one of income constancy; they have simply prevented further erosion.[8]

In summary, given the predominance of liberal-conservative ideology in American society, it is clear that the president can draw upon a large pool of individuals and groups to support his actions mirroring the prevailing ideology. He is relatively safe in ignoring pressures from the bottom and lower middle to make fundamental attacks on basic institutions.

## The President and the Structure of Power

As important as ideology may be, other structural conditions, which set major limits on what presidents can or cannot do, appear even more salient. Here we refer to the distribution of privilege and power within the formal institutions of government as they relate to the distribution of privilege and power within our national economy.

Consider first the distribution of power and influence within the Congress. Legislative power is not exercised by Congress as a corporate body. Rather, all aspects of legislation are delegated to committees and subcommittees, of which there are approximately 115 in the House of Representatives and 144 in the Senate. These committees have a division of labor which tends to reflect the industrial sectors of our society, e.g., forestry, mining, oil, agriculture, banking and currency, various forms of commerce, shipping and transportation, aeronautics, and so forth. The leadership of these committees is primarily determined on the basis of seniority and chairmen have a large measure of discretion in such matters as appointment of subcommittees, assignment of bills to them, and setting committee agendas and schedules as well as appointment of members to the committee itself. Power to legislate is scattered among members of a rather special class of congressmen: those who manage to get reelected regularly, that is to say, those from relatively safe districts in which elections are not tightly contested. Stated differently, leadership in legislation is exercised by those men least vulnerable to electoral pressures. Indeed, links between the electorate and the leadership of Congress are further weakened because the same conditions maintain with respect to House and Senate (as opposed to committee) leadership. The Speaker of the House and the Senate majority leader are also selected on the basis of seniority. In the absence of formal links of responsibility to the electorate, the major forces working on congressional leaders are the conditions of maintaining or increasing (depending upon the degree of personal ambition) the power they already have. These conditions rarely force a man to be either an innovator or a statesman in approaching policy matters. They usually force a man to follow the counsel of former Speaker Sam Rayburn, "If you want to get along, go along."

As mentioned, committee chairmen have a good deal of influence in the assignment of new members to their committees. They tend to want persons who will accept the particular subculture and norms governing their committees. Furthermore, it is in the interest of members of Congress to be assigned to committees that will assist them in their reelection. Urban congressmen want to be assigned to those committees which have jurisdiction over urban programs, so that by their participation in the committee's work they can make a case for reelection. The situation is similar among members from agricultural districts. The mutual needs of committee chairmen and congressmen reinforce the likelihood that committees will be composed of members sharing similar backgrounds, interests, and values. Furthermore, those interest groups whose security and well-being will be affected by a committee also have a stake in committee assignments and seek to influence them. It therefore should be no surprise that most of the members of the Agriculture Committees come from farm districts or states and are themselves actively engaged in farming or related activities. Almost all the members of the House Merchant Marine and Fisheries Committee come from districts having major seaports and related industries. The House and Senate Interior Committees are composed primarily of Westerners whose constituents are concerned with reclamation, grazing, timber, mineral rights, and water resources. This pattern is typical.

The division of labor among committees is neither clear nor stable. A bill dealing with any substantive matter which also has implications for the organization of an executive agency might end up either in the Committee of Government Operations or in one of several committees concerned with the policies involved. The absence of a clear division of labor among committees results only in part from the fact that many program areas cut across the jurisdiction of several administrative agencies and therefore involve those congressional committees which oversee them. The lack also serves the needs of congressional leadership, interest groups, and administrators. Leaders can increase or at least promote their power by assigning a bill to a committee that is likely to produce the outcome which they want. Interest groups and administrators have several arenas in which they can seek to pursue their desired outcomes. There is a great incentive for all three to cooperate, or at least avoid direct conflict.

The final characteristic of congressional structure having important consequences for the relation of public to private power and privilege is the complete separation of legislation from revenue raising and appropriations. Each house has one committee to consider revenue bills and another one to consider appropriations. Each of these committees is separated from those that deal with substance, that is, setting goals and approving programs. Stated dramatically, the purposes and directions of the national government are scattered among some 200 committees and subcommittees and at the same time are kept removed from decisions about how much money will be spent to pursue them, which decisions in turn are kept removed from decisions about where the money will come from. The president may present an integrated national program to Congress, but Congress is unable to accept or act upon an integrated national program. All, including congressmen themselves, admit the irrationality of the practice, but virtually every Congress since 1946 has refused to make any serious changes. The reasons are rather obvious. To increase the capacity of Congress to act as a corporate body would increase the power of the congressional leadership at the expense of committee chairmen. Furthermore, it might well benefit the president, in that his ability to deal with interest groups, congressional leaders, and administrators would be increased.

Similar structural conditions exist within the national executive branch. Administrative agencies are created by Congress and reflect Congress, that is to say, the industrial structure of our society. They are best seen as personifications of the values of speical interest groups in America. They represent the tangible, formal, and legitimate manifestations of the victories won by organized special interest groups or coalitions of such groups in their fights to secure, promote, and preserve their well-being. A few examples will help clarify this point. Early in our national history, Alexander Hamilton, the spokesman for fiscal integrity as a vital precondition for a flourishing commerce, succeeded in getting the national government to assume responsibility for the Revolutionary War debt accumulated by the Continental Congress. The group of persons for whom Hamilton was spokesman, calling themselves the Federalists, were also concerned about the soundness of money in order to assure payment of debts as well as to facilitate commerce. They wanted a national currency guaranteed by the national government. The instrument for achieving their purposes was the Treasury of the United States, headed by Hamilton and established in 1789, the year in which the first Congress met. This Congress was dominated by the Federalists and they quickly set about making sure their values would be secure by creating federal departments whose purposes were to implement them.

Admittedly, Federalists constituted an overwhelming majority of the political activists during the first decade after the Revolution. Their power might have been contested but it was never seriously challenged. However, the pattern they followed would be adopted by others who were merely powerful, not representative of majority opinion. And the pattern is that national politics is the preserve of those who are already powerful, socially or economically.

Perhaps the most extreme example of the extent to which a national governmental agency embodies the interests and values of special interest groups is the U. S. Department of Agriculture. Although agriculture had been the largest sector of the American economy since the time of first colonization, farmers did not organize into economic and political interest groups until after the Civil War. Organization arose along with the development of commercial farming and in response to enormous fluctuations in market prices as well as to exploitation by the railroads. Farm organizations multiplied and became more militant during the depression of the early 1870s. During the next half-century they succeeded in obtaining government programs to meet their needs for promotion and technological advances as well as to regulate those economic forces perceived as the causes of agriculture's economic problems. In addition to the Department of Agriculture and its many subagencies, which provide everything from farm credit to agricultural research and development, the Interstate Commerce Commission was created in response to demands of organizations of farmers for regulation of railroads—a major exploiter of farmers. Despite the declining importance of the agricultural sector of the economy since the turn of the century and the decreasing farm population, national budget outlays for agriculture amounted to $5.9 billion in 1968, fifth among the categories of domestic spending. A further measure of agriculture's continuing political power, despite its relatively declining importance to the economy, was the exemption of raw agricultural products from the wage-price freeze in the summer of 1971. This action was taken despite a projected decrease in livestock production for 1972. The exception was a deliberate decision to permit a raise in beef and hog prices the following year—a presidential election year. Interestingly, in 1972 the price of grain was 44.1 percent higher, the price of livestock was 22.4 percent higher, and the cost of eggs was 25.8 percent higher than in 1971. Then there was the "great grain robbery" of 1972. Agriculture's ability to get what it wanted from government and to maintain its privilege despite its declining importance may be explained in large part by the existence of a huge cluster of organizations in the national administrative machinery, for the most part within the Department of Agriculture, whose entire reason for being is promotion of agriculture.

One can continue enumerating organized producer groups and the national agencies created to preserve and promote their values either directly through subsidies or promotional activity or indirectly by regulating a competing or threatening interest group or set of groups. In every instance, agency charters and subsequent legislative extension or contraction of their scope is justified in the name of the "public interest." And so it is, in the same sense that was suggested by Charles Wilson, president of General Motors, who told Congress that what is good for General Motors is good for America. This Adam Smithian conception of national policy would indeed be good for America, providing all interests had equal access to governmental institutions and were equally able to articulate and implement their values. However, such is not the case. Concentrated economic interests are uniquely capable of exploiting the fragmentation of national political structures. They enjoy the benefits of organization and money: information, expertise, capacity to fight for what they want over long periods in a variety of arenas, and ability to reward supporters and punish opponents by dispensing campaign contributions and other tangible rewards. Those who are successful in having their values embodied in legislation and federal agencies are those organized around a producer interest—those who build highways and space shuttles; those who drill for and produce petroleum; those who cut down trees for lumber; those who fish, farm, or mine commercially; and those who manufacture goods and provide services.

The great success of producer-oriented interests in exploiting their advantages can be clearly seen in a brief review of the record of the 92nd Congress. There was no action on no-fault auto insurance and health care and tax reform got nowhere. Neither regulation of strip mining nor gun control laws were acted upon. Efforts to create a Consumer Protection Agency were dropped. Such bills would have limited the privileges of powerful interest groups.

Consider some recent presidential actions. In 1971, President Nixon created the National Industrial Pollution Control Council to "allow business to communicate regularly with the President, the Council on Environmental Quality, and other government officials to help chart the route by which our cooperative ventures will follow." In 1971, he also established the National Business Council for Consumer Affairs, to allow "businessmen to communicate regularly with the President, the Office of Consumer Affairs, the Federal Trade Commission, the Justice Department, other government agencies

. . . which are directly concerned with consumer affairs." These are neither isolated nor unusual examples.

If all groups enjoyed such privileged access to the legislative committees that enact the rules to govern them and the executive agencies charged with implementing these rules, perhaps the system would produce more equitable outcomes. However, such is not the case. Consumers, or those who wish to preserve the environment, or those who seek a redistribution of the national income have a more difficult time. And for good reasons. They lack the organization, financial resources, existing formal governmental institutions as well as the ideology and leadership skills enjoyed by producer-oriented interests. All consumers fare poorly, but consumers of lower socioeconomic status fare the worst—especially those who consume welfare, public housing, public transportation, medical care, job training and placement, and the like. Scarce societal resources are not allocated according to any collective determination of national interest, need, or want. Rather, they are allocated on the basis of the ability of an interest group to establish privileged access to government.

The creation of an environmental agency and the passage of strong enabling legislation aimed at reducing pollution have been frequently cited as the beginning of the end of the structure excluding consumer interests from the national government. Perhaps so, but the evidence to date is not reassuring. Producer-oriented interests are chipping away at both the agency and the legislation. As power-using companies, auto makers and other industries are beginning to feel the full impact of the clear air standards, for example, they are beginning to call on their friends in Congress and the administration to get the agency to reduce its standards. It has already done so for the auto industry, and its administrator is considering going to Congress to ease some of the requirements of the Clean Air Act of 1970. Much of the pressure on the agency came from the White House itself, where producer interests seemed to enjoy both welcome and support. Senator Percy of Illinois, a spokesman for the proposed Consumer Protection Agency, couldn't even get an audience with the president, but Bryce Harlow, representing Proctor and Gamble in opposition to it, could. The administration supported the supersonic transport as well as the Alaskan pipeline. The ultimate irony is that the consumer, not the industry, will pay for whatever protective action is taken, in the form of higher prices for the products of polluting industries. Furthermore, the Nixon administration consistently asked for and spent less on environmental quality than Congress was willing to appropriate. Nixon regarded such expenditures as inflationary. In addition, his spokesmen pointed to our limited technical capacity to deal with pollution. Meanwhile we see our industry and business transform the countryside into a desolate tangle of concrete, ticky-tacky subdivisions, stripmined moonscape, and silt-filled reservoirs. Our land and water are being poisoned with pesticides, herbicides, mercury, fungicides, lead, boron, arsenic, and other toxic compounds. Each year our environment must absorb 142 million tons of smoke and fumes, 7 million junked cars, 20 million tons of paper, 48 billion cans, and 26 billion bottles. Truly, the product of our technological genius is garbage—heroic piles of garbage. And presidents tell us we lack the technical capability to cope with it!

In any event, we are not yet prepared to view the Environmental Protection Agency as a deviation of any consequence from the structural patterns that characterize our national political system, a pattern of symbiosis between governmental agencies and Congressional committees on the one hand and producer-oriented interests on the other. It costs money to gain and maintain an elective office. Former Senator Fred Harris of Oklahoma described the process as follows. Owners of wealth who wish to preserve or extend their privileges contribute to campaigns (frequently to opposing candidates when there is no incumbent) in return for subsidies, tax breaks, and protection against reform. The structure of the economy will not reform itself; it needs a political shove that is not forthcoming because of the power of the wealthy to buy off the politician. Federal agencies need budgets, favorable legislation, and political support if they are to survive, let alone prosper. In return for carefully considering the interests and needs of those they regulate or serve, agencies receive support before Congress at appropriations time and when agency manpower levels are considered. The system is functional for the parties concerned. Congressmen enchance their capacity to remain in office, groups promote their interests, and agencies insure their survival. Everyone benefits except the ordinary citizens. Or, if they do benefit, they do so in the sense intended by Charles Wilson of General Motors.

The structure of our national political system ensures the continued privileges of producer-oriented interest groups within the system. Perhaps colorful but certainly no overstatement is the acid comment of TRB in the *New Republic:* "Washington is a harem full of special interests, and Congress is the Grand Eunuch guarding the seraglio"[9] Imagine the annoyance of the president of a national dairy association who had to explain to a naive member why the association had contributed more than $500,000 to the president's reelection committee immediately after the secretary of agriculture had reversed himself over a two-week period and agreed to raise the price support for milk 27 cents per hundredweight (worth hundreds of thousands of dollars to the industry): "We must have friends in government. . . . Whether we like it or not, this is the way the system works."

On the basis of such evidence as there is to judge the matter, we can only conclude that the president is so caught in a web of ideology and a network of symbiotic relations resulting from the penetration of our political system by producer-oriented interest groups that no incumbent, whatever his political philosophy, could do much about it. In short, the causes are structural, not the responsibility of incumbents who choose not to use their power in positive directions. In domestic affairs, the president's power is greatly diminished. He is a victim. The most a man of less conservative instincts can hope to do is exploit opportunities when they present themselves, as Franklin Roosevelt did in the 1930s and as Lyndon Johnson did in 1964. But most opportunities are missed because most incumbents endorse those very structures which limit their office in domestic affairs as well as accept their supporting ideology. But further discussion of opportunities and incumbents will be reserved for later sections.

## Presidential Leadership

It would be grotesquely artificial to treat the role of the president as a leader separately from his actions in foreign and domestic policy. Hence, this section extends and comments on what has already been said. As with so many words in politics, *leadership* has many uses, not all of which are consistent. President Truman has been hailed as a leader because of his unwaivering commitment to the political, economic, and military revival of Western Europe in the face of apparent Communist threats of overt aggression and internal subversion. Eisenhower was also seen as a leader, but for quite different reasons than was his predecessor and by quite different sorts of persons. To them he seemed a reassuring combination of a war hero and a father figure able to lead the country through the perils of the Cold War. Kennedy brought wit, warmth, charm, and vigor to the White House. He articulated a vision of energy, purpose, and devotion which many Americans found irresistable. Finally, there was Johnson, who after his ascent to the presidency, translated much of the vision of Kennedy's domestic affairs into the legislation and early programs of the Great Society. While the differences among them are enormous, these four incumbents shared one quality. Faced by different circumstances, each in his own way developed a rhetoric and a stance "consistent with emerging needs," to use the words of Professor Richard Neustadt. Truman educated us to our international responsibilities. Eisenhower struggled mightily to have us adjust to the role of a superpower willing to share its nuclear technology (to a point) and to come to terms with our Soviet antagonist. Kennedy began to call our attention to the need for positive international leadership, and Johnson sought to address problems of poverty and racism. The foregoing statements are not intended to be judgments, however tentative, of the performance of these four incumbents. Rather they are to suggest that whatever the meaning of *leadership* in the presidency, it need not be tied to successful programs and action, but it must be tied to a style and (or) image of commitment to goals that address and educate the public to an emerging need, regardless of the existing degree of consensus regarding that need. Leadership must confront contemporary issues and contexts, must involve setting goals, and must be committed, at least, to positive action. Leadership may be conservative, but never negative or passive.

America has almost unbounded potential to solve or at least greatly mitigate many national problems such as poverty, racial inequality, and pollution. Without national leadership, however, such potential seems destined to lie dormant. Whether deservedly or not, public expectations for national initiative generally focus on presidential leadership. Rather than responding to public expectations that he alter the status quo for better ends, President Nixon seemed intent upon retrenchment. And before his accession to higher office, President Ford was never known for leadership or innovation.

While different observers might point to widely varying contemporary issues to demonstrate the failure of presidential leadership, we would like to discuss just two of them. The first grows out of the increasing intolerance of dissent and an accompanying repression of those who articulate uncomfortable or unpopular views. These tendencies are also closely related to race and minority aspirations. The second deals with the need to give content to political freedom (freedom of choice or opportunity) by establishing the economic preconditions for exercising that freedom (the problems of economic inequality discussed above).

In 1968, Richard M. Nixon campaigned on two principal issues, law and order and ending the war in Vietnam. Elected, he continued the war, at times escalating it, and at the same time condoned harsh treatment of those who were merely protesting his failure to act in accordance with his own statements. He repeatedly went so far as to blame his critics for his own failure to secure a cease-fire and an American withdrawal from Southeast Asia. Despite the findings of presidential commissions that problems of crime were intimately tied to problems of urban deterioration, poverty, unemployment, and racism, he blamed crime on "permissiveness" and the serious "hamstringing" of police forces by the Supreme Court. He would solve the problem by appointing "strict constructionalists" to the Supreme Court and by more wire tapping, preventive detention, and spending on police. But even more disturbing is the extent to which the president played upon the anxieties, fears, and prejudices of many citizens with respect to law and order as well as to Vietnam. Some examples will serve to amplify this point and provide a basis for relating it to the issues of presidential leadership.

Law and order has become a code phrase that refers to a "counter-conscience," according to Professor Herbert L. Packer of Stanford.[10] Packer feels that the phrase embodies a hostility to Supreme Court decisons that have "judicialized every step in the criminal process and [equalized] the opportunity of all criminal defendants, regardless of their financial means, to offer effective challenges to the process." Also, the phrase expresses a belief that the underlying causes of crime are not related to urban and central city decay and other domestic problems, especially poverty, but instead are the consequences of permissiveness. "Law and order" rejects notions that the rise of the drug culture and the increasing use of marijuana are symptoms of despair with regard to the capacity of our society to govern itself and live up to the ideals it articulates, and sees them rather as evidence of moral decay in individuals, especially the young. It also denies any legitimacy in the dissent of the young and intellectuals to the Vietnamese War and brands such dissent as either lawlessness or lack of patriotism, or both. Finally, it represents a feeling that black and brown aspirations are unrealistic because they are being pushed too hard and too militantly. "Law and order" has become a code phrase for oversimplified notions of what is wrong in our society. And as is true of most code words, it blinds, even deceives; it does not illuminate or educate.

President Nixon not only formulated contemporary foreign and domestic problems in these simplistic terms, he at times condoned and occasionally encouraged public action in such an oversimplified and dangerous view. His attorney general contended that he had "inherent power" to wiretap without a warrant in the case of suspected domestic subversives (happily, this position was rejected by the Supreme Court in a unanimous decision written by the president's own appointee). Deputy Attorney General Richard G. Kleindienst opposed parade permits for antiwar protestors during the inauguration in 1969. He ordered the phones of senior officials in the administration tapped in the name of "national security," including ironically, members of the staff of the president's assistant for national security affairs. The wife of the attorney general philosophized to a reporter[11] that "any time you get somebody marching in the streets it's catering to revolution. It started with the colored people in the South. Now other groups are taking to the streets. . . . Man has been given his freedoms to a greater extent than ever, and that's quite wrong. Adults like to be led. They would rather respond to a form of discipline." Previously she had told a TV interviewer: "As my husband has said many times, some of the liberals in this country, he'd like to take them and change them for Russian Communists." In a postelection interview in 1972, the president said, "the average American is just like the child in the family, you give him some responsibility and he is going to amount to something. If on the other hand you make him completely dependent and pamper him and cater him too much, you are going to make him soft, spoiled and eventually a very weak individual."

Newspaper reporters have been sentenced to jail for failing to reveal their news sources and a Harvard professor was for a time imprisoned because he failed to identify his scholarly sources of information to a grand jury. The Justice Department sought to indict the *New York Times* for publishing the Pentagon Papers. Federal grand juries indicted Daniel Ellsberg and Anthony Russo for their part in releasing the papers. The Watergate hearings then revealed direct White House involvement in a break into a doctor's office to gain access to Ellsberg's psychiatric files (conceivably in order to gain information to discredit him). Although the "political" trials which began in the middle sixties almost invariably failed to result in convictions (it is as hard to prove conspiracy as it is easy to indict for it), in the view of the Department of Justice, they were successful. They discouraged radical activists by diverting their energies and their resources from protest to self-defense.

Former Vice-president Agnew attacked the media for one-sidedness while the Federal Communications Commission refused equal time to war opponents who wished to rebut the recruiting pitch of the military. The dissenting opinion of one of the commissioners, Nicholas Johnson, is worthy of note: "Today, one branch of the federal government ignores the orderly complaints of its citizens and rules that another branch of that same government, the U. S. Army, can propagandize without preserving for the young their First Amendment right to self-defense." Opponents of military service, he said, "are now left with nothing but the recourse of demonstrations and draft-card burning to attract the largess of the news media's televison cameras." Demonstrators are then faced with municipal police, frequently untrained for crowd control, rather arbitrary definitions of unlawful assembly, and the blows of truncheons.

When legitimate forms of petition and redress are denied, many young men of conviction resort to the only forum left—the streets.

Street demonstrations are disbanded all too frequently in the name of "law and order" and protestors are abused, sometimes beaten, and arrested. Whatever the intentions of law enforcement agencies, the courts, and the Justice Department, they are cast in the role of forceably repressing the expression of dissent.

This situation can be considered together with President Nixon's statement that "under no circumstances will I be affected whatever by it" (referring to the dissent expressed by the Vietnam Moratorium of October 15, 1969). And when he went on to say that if only he had more support from the nation, "the enemy then will have the incentive to negotiate," he was condoning the repression of dissent. In his 1972 campaign, the president condemned the "self-righteous moral judges of our society," and pledged himself to "respect and reflect the opinion of the people themselves." Which people was he speaking of? Those who agreed with his policies, approaches, rhetoric, and programs? The answer is suggested by his lament before a group of wives of prisoners of war that the opinion leaders of the country—the media and intellectuals—failed to support him in his decision to resume the bombing of North Vietnam and to mine Haiphong Harbor in the spring of 1972.

Consider what the black man saw when he looked to the president for leadership.[12] He saw the president nominate a man to the Supreme Court who in a political campaign a score of years earlier asserted, "I yield to no man, as a fellow candidate or as a fellow citizen, in the firm, vigorous belief in the principles of White Supremacy, and I shall always be so governed." He watched his president sign a Voting Rights Act, but only after vigorously lobbying to dilute its provisions. He saw 29 percent of black families below the poverty line and white unemployment dropping while black unemployment rose. He looked in vain for the benefits of "Black Capitalism." He saw hardening of the color line that restricts housing for blacks to the inner city, 24 percent of black housing labeled substandard by the Bureau of Labor Statistics, and a Justice Department failing to vigorously prosecute discrimination in housing. He saw appointed to the Justice Department a man who said, "We're going to have to change things here basically from [former Attorney General] Clark's approach. I absolutely disagree with the theory that you can upgrade the poor by giving them things like better housing.

The liberal idea is wholly without substance. . . . I don't believe in education for most people. Teach them how to use a lathe and let it go at that." He also observed a man appointed to head first the Civil Rights Division and later the Law Enforcement Assistance Administration who maintained his membership in the lily-white Order of the Eagles and resigned only upon public protest.

The black man saw President Nixon opposing bussing and vowing to seek a constitutional amendment to end it if he could not get the legislation he wanted from Congress. He watched the president welcome a delegation of "hard hats" to the White House while refusing to meet with the Caucus of Black Congressmen. He saw the president ignore and at times disown the recommendations of one presidential commission after another dealing with the root problems of racism and poverty. Finally, he saw the president vetoing or refusing to spend what Congress had appropriated for programs dealing with domestic problems, in the name of "economy" and fiscal "responsibility," while billions were spent to continue the war in Southeast Asia, embark on new adventures in space, build new military weapons, and subsidize the aerospace industry. Is it any wonder that black confidence in the White House and the entire national government diminishes? President Ford clearly had a long way to go in overcoming years of distrust when as one of his first acts in taking office he met with the congressional black caucus.

Nor does the problem end with apparent indifference to the genuine needs and problems of minority groups. Blue-collar workers, those with incomes between $5,000 and $10,000, also have very real grievances. Their income as skilled workers frequently peaks out just when their expenses are burgeoning. They are among those most hurt by the invisible tax used to finance the military, inflation. Their own education is limited and they cannot afford to send their children to college. Their work has lost status; college graduates get both the respect and the pay. They are the ones subjected to the travail and the disruption of social transition. It is their neighborhoods and schools that are the first to be integrated. They pay a disproportionate share of the taxes that provide the revenue for welfare, family assistance, skill training, and other programs needed by minority groups. At the same time, blue-collar workers are the ones whose own jobs are threatened when minority citizens begin to climb the employment and income ladder. And President Nixon callously played upon their circumstances, anxieties, and fears with the code phrase "law and order." Appallingly, the presidency exacerbated racial tensions in recent years. Nixon particularly (whether intentionally or not) mobilized blue-collar resentment and focused it on minority groups and college youths and encouraged the widespread belief that it is minority groups who constitute the welfare burden (which is not true—most welfare recipients are white) by implying that they lack the "work ethic," are lazy, and prefer the dole to employment. He apparently approved of a social and economic structure that not only makes occupational mobility difficult but also places heavy tax burdens on the marginal worker to pay the costs of welfare for the poor. He then exploited the anxieties of the marginal man when assessing the state of domestic affairs. In his nationally televised speech October 21, 1972, the president said that those opposed to "income redistribution," to bussing, and to employment quotas ought not be charged with selfishness, bigotry, or racism. These values, said he, are "values to to to be proud of—values that I shall always stand up for when they come under attack." To such depths did the leadership possibilities of the modern presidency fall under Nixon.

Albert H. Cantril and Charles W. Roll, Jr., in *Hopes and Fears of The American People*[13] made the startling finding that concern for national unity, political stability, and law and order jumped from 1 percent in 1959 to 15 percent in 1971. Furthermore, they found that an alarming number of citizens blame unrest on young people and minority groups rather than on our political and economic system. And the president adroitly focused these anxieties on those who seek social, economic, and political justice rather than on any basic faults in our system of national governance. The credit or the blame for these developments must clearly go to Richard Nixon. There are no systemic forces that make a president mobilize anxieties as the solution to the problems of domestic and foreign policy. The failure of a president to teach the public that opposition to higher taxes and expenditures for domestic programs is often selfish, that resistance to bussing for school integration is frequently bigotry, and that there is an element of racism in most of the resistance to employment quotas[14] is a disastrous and unpardonable failure in leadership.

This failure was compounded by his reelection campaign during which Nixon spoke of the old virtues such as the work ethic and peace with honor while exploiting prejudices with such code phrases as no quotas, community schools, free choice in housing, and strict construction of the Constitution.

### Corruption and Deceit

Corruption and veniality of one form or another apparently are the inevitable companions of power and politics. All societies are plagued with corruptable individuals who misuse the trust placed in them for their own self-enrichment. The political history of our own nation is replete with instances at all levels of government of patronage, nepotism, kick-backs, and the exploitation of public authority for private gain. However, recent years have seen not merely a continuation of abuse of power in public office but the rise of two forms of corruption different in degree if not in kind from previous forms of abuses. The first is dishonesty or lying in the name of national interest or national security. This form of corruption we label *dishonesty for "reasons of state."* The second has grown out of the increasingly close ties between politics, elections, and monied interests in our society. This second form of corruption we label *corporatism.*

The conduct of international affairs has never been characterized by "open covenants openly arrived at," as the idealism of President Woodrow Wilson would have it. Statesmen have always thought it necessary to maintain a greater or lesser degree of secrecy in order not to reveal their intentions too clearly to an opponent and thereby lose a possible bargaining advantage. Authoritarian societies have generally been considered to have some advantage in the international arena because of the greater possible secrecy in their governments. However, our society has been subjected to an increasing amount of both secrecy and manipulation in the name of "national interest and security," despite its norms of public disclosure, popular participation, and honesty in dealing with the media and the population at large. Probably the best illustration of this trend came during the Kennedy administration immediately following the Cuban missile crisis of 1962, when Assistant to the Secretary of Defense Arthur

Sylvester announced that "news" was a weapon in the Cold War and defended the right of the national government to deceive the public when, in the opinion of administration spokesmen, the national interest called for it.

An even more blatant instance of deception occurred during the election campaign of 1964. A major pillar of Lyndon Johnson's campaign for reelection was his repudiation of candidate Barry Goldwater's "blood and iron" solution to the perceived Communist menace in South Vietnam. Johnson's subsequent landslide victory must be attributed at least in part to public rejection of the major escalations advocated by his opponent. Subsequently, the Pentagon Papers revealed that at the very time Johnson was basing his campaign on opposition to a military solution in Southeast Asia, he was authorizing the planning of massive United States intervention with men, weapons, and money, which eventually took place in the following summer.

Four years later, candidate Nixon properly argued against the return to office of an administration that had four years to extricate us from Vietnam but had failed to do so. He pledged us "peace with honor" and implied that he could achieve both in short order. He then proceeded to escalate the war even more, while continuing to speak of peace and blaming his political opponents for his failure to achieve a settlement. But even that bit of chicanery was less odious than his callous exploitation of the wives of prisoners of war and those missing in action. If it was necessary to continue the war in order to rescue their loved ones (a troublesome bit of logic in itself), it was also inevitable that more men would be lost and taken prisoner, the longer the war continued. At times the administration's practice of Orwellean "double-think" reached the point of justifying the continuation of the war in the name of these victims of its madness.

Presidential dishonesty reached such heights as blatant attempts to deceive Congress about our aid to countries such as Pakistan and Thailand, senseless slaughter of civilians in South Vietnam, bombing of the dikes in North Vietnam, and, revealed most recently, about the secret air war in Cambodia. Caught in such deception, the administration seemed to be beyond shame and attempted to justify its actions. For at least the past twelve years or so, presidents acted as if deceit, deception, and lack of moral leadership were an inevitable concomitant of affairs of state. Many people apparently came to accept deceit and deception on the part of the president and his spokesmen. Most ignored and many accepted the president's intervention in the case of Lieutenant Calley when he was released from the stockade and confined to his quarters pending his appeal for the conviction of more than one hundred murders at My Lai. So used to double standards are we that little general outrage was expressed when Air Force General Lavelle was allowed to retire on a $25,000 pension ($23,000 of which is tax-exempt because he was declared 70 percent disabled!) after admittedly disobeying orders governing the rules of engagement for aircraft in Vietnam.

With respect to the second type of corruption, corporatism, all too frequently it has been written off as mere "veniality." Unfortunately, the basic problem goes much deeper. Our entire national government has come to be penetrated by producer interests in the economy, and not only are national politics and policy bought and sold but the process is made legitimate in the name of participation and federalism. The price paid since the 1930s to get industry to accept positive governmental action with respect to the economy has been to permit industry to participate in its own regulation. Conflict of interest has become a greater good in the political process. When producers are given access to those who regulate them, when their participation in policy making is made legitimate, when they are courted for the contributions they can make to the election of candidates to political office or the support they can give administrative agencies, it is hardly surprising that they treat the government with contempt and accept bribery and corruption as a way of life.

"Corruption is as American as apple pie," writes Lewis Stone, vice-president for economics of Harris, Upham and Company in the brokerage house's *Monthly Investment Letter* of October 1972. Stone continues, "People as a whole don't care about the broad social issues, or even specific scandals such as the Watergate incident, or the campaign contributions, or the Russian wheat and soybean sales, or the *undoubted corruption that is inherent* in the American political system" (emphasis added). Sad to say, Mr. Stone is probably correct. The public made no outcry, the media were silent, and the president stood aloof—in the face of evidence linking the attorney general to a deal with ITT over antitrust action and contributions to the Republican national convention; in the face of links between those who eavesdropped on the Democratic national chairman's office and the Committee to Reelect the President and the White House staff itself; in the face of Richard Nixon's chief fund raiser in 1968 becoming secretary of commerce then moving back to the fund raising role in 1972; in the face of exchanges of personnel between the governmental agencies that negotiated the grain deal with the Soviet Union and the traders who were to handle the sale; and in the face of dairy industry contributions to the president's campaign after the secretary of agriculture reversed himself and increased the price of milk. And what is one to make of the indictment, resignation, and in some cases conviction of the president's closest advisors, members of his personal staff and cabinet, his vice-president, and, finally, the resignation of the president himself? Their complete lack of repentence and continued efforts to justify their action in the name of the very principles they had so shamelessly violated should be a cause for alarm, not mere cynicism.

Nor can one castigate President Nixon alone. Was it a coincidence that the Justice Department dropped action on the IRS indictments of Representative Adam Clayton Powell after he announced his endorsement of Eisenhower's reelection in 1956? Was the shift of defense contracting to the Northeast, especially Massachusetts, during the incumbency of Kennedy and then to Texas under Johnson pure chance? Perhaps, but the evidence in both academic and journalistic literature linking producer interests to national policy and politics appears sufficient to justify the tentative judgment that indeed "corruption is as American as apple pie."

In the first instance, corruption for reasons of state, the burden of justification would appear to lie with the incumbent. Whatever the real and justifiable need for secrecy in the conduct of foreign and security policies, there is nothing in the nature of that policy itself and the structure of our society which forces a president to go to the limits reached by Johnson and Nixon. In arrogantly ordering the most massive bombing of the war when peace talks faltered before Christmas 1972, Nixon acted without consulting or informing anyone—including Congress. There is nothing inherent in the office to make an incumbent deceive, manipulate, or misinform the public. Responsibility must rest with the conscience of the man.

In the second instance, the consequences of corporatism, the fault lies not with an incumbent but with the structure, with the system of governance which has evolved. Few would challenge the integrity of Dwight Eisenhower, but he was powerless to prevent the exploitation by monied interests of the structure of our political system which enables them to corrupt both men and laws. And poor Ike suffered the ultimate embarrassment of having such corruption creep into his own office and compromise his hand-picked assistant, Sherman Adams. Beginning with the Philadelphia convention when the "democratic excesses" of the Articles of Confederation were rectified by men of substance from agriculture and business, from religion and government, right on down to the present practice of appointing representatives of business and industry to assist the government in developing and implementing the policies to govern them, producer-oriented interests have dominated our political system. Such men are accustomed to governing as a matter of right and willing to buy what they want when they cannot obtain it by other means. In short, the corruption of corporatism is essentially structural in nature.

### The Prospects of Reform

Throughout this chapter the term *responsiveness* has been used frequently. A discussion of reform requires a clarification of its meaning. In our view, definitions of presidential responsiveness are value judgments about the policies or political outcomes produced by the exercise of presidential power. If one likes what presidents do, they are "responsive." If one does not like what they do, they are "unresponsive." Precisely because there are different patterns of values in our society, there are different criteria for judging presidential responsiveness. From a radical perspective, a president is responsive only when he understands the extent to which those who are on the lower rungs of the socioeconomic ladder—consumers and minority groups—have been cruelly exploited by existing patterns of foreign and domestic policy. Responsiveness calls for more than mere recognition of these conditions, it calls for action to redress them.

Liberals and conservatives, on the other hand, use a different yardstick for judging presidential responsiveness. Both persuasions are critical of the exercise of presidential power. Both have been exasperated with our Vietnam policies, but for differing reasons. Conservatives criticized the last two presidents for being unwilling to take the necessary military measures to "win" the war. Liberals criticized them for their failure to withdraw our forces immediately and completely. Conservatives are worried about the rapprochement with the Soviet Union and the People's Republic of China. Liberals applaud and consider these steps long overdue. Conservatives worry about compromises to our national security which may result from the Strategic Arms Limitation agreement. Liberals not only applaud the agreements but advocate large reductions in defense spending. Conservatives are skeptical of social legislation and poverty programs. Liberals advocate more of them. Conservatives criticize court decisions that strengthen the rights of the accused and advocate more resources and discretion for police. Liberals applaud these decisions and demand more open-end, external review of police actions.

Generally, liberals advocate retrenchment and less emphasis on military power in coping with other states and more positive interventions by government domestically. Conservatives tend to advocate continued reliance on military might and have always been skeptical about the efficacy of governmental intervention in the domestic market place. Truly, among both liberals and conservatives there is a range of values and a range of judgments about the responsiveness of any particular presidential position or program. But in every case, judgments about presidential responsiveness are precisely that—judgments.

These varying value judgments about the president, his policies, and their consequences are reflected in perceptions as to the worth and effectiveness of the formal institutions of government. Conservatives, generally critical of positive action by government in domestic affairs, have been critical of the strengthening of the office of president, especially the enormous build-up of staff during the past two decades which has accompanied the growth of domestic programs and bureaucracies. Generally, they approve of the existing pattern of economic power and privilege in our society and therefore place greater faith in that institution which tends to reflect it, the Congress. Historically, congressional dominance in national policy has meant fewer initiatives by the national government. Presidential dominance has meant more new departures and expansion of the national government's role. Liberals favoring such directions have supported strengthening the presidency and favor presidential ascendancy over Congress.

The reversal of the liberals as a result of Vietnam is instructive. They have criticized not only our policy but also the institutions that they perceive as responsible for it—the president and the formal organization that surrounds him. They clamor for Congress to assert itself, to reduce the discretion and leadership role assumed by the presidency and its staff. The lesson is clear: The driving force behind judgments about presidential responsiveness and the appropriateness of the various institutions of the national government are judgments about policies and their outcomes.* If one likes what the president articulates, advocates, and does, one judges him to be responsive and the institutions of his office and his power with respect to other institutions such as Congress to be appropriate and proper. If, on the other hand, one does not like what he sees happening, he takes the opposite view. There is no definition of *responsiveness* free from political ideology.

Since both liberal and conservative political ideologies accept the socioeconomic structures that underlie and condition our political system, they tend to underestimate the extent to which these structural factors shape and limit the discretionary power of the presidency. Or, stated positively, they tend to believe the president could "do good" (as each of them defines the "good") if only he would, or if only some of the formal institutions of government were adjusted. There are several kinds of forces which tend to reinforce such a view of presidential discretion. The first is primarily political-institutional. There is a tendency to confuse the truly impressive power of the national government with the power of the chief executive himself. Because of the Constitution, judicial extensions of the national powers therein, as well as both the need and willingness of the national government to exploit modern technology in the face of an increasingly complex domestic and international milieu, the national government does indeed have formidable power at its dis-

---

* We are indebted to our colleague, Paul Halpern, for stressing the relationship between judgments about the structure of the presidency and judgments about policy outcomes.

posal. However, as we have argued throughout this chapter, its power is fragmented and scattered. It cannot be concerted toward a predefined set of national priorities or goals. Americans' blindness about the extent to which the already powerful have penetrated the structures of our political system stems precisely from both their acceptance of a class structure within our society and their acquiescence in defining away problems of distribution of its benefits. This blindness is reinforced by normal human anxieties that cause us to want to believe there is someone running things, someone who controls. We find it difficult to accept the chaotic character of the real world; and the possibility that no one is really in control is unthinkable for most of us. Hence we have constructed a socio-psychological organizational chart of national politics, at the top of which is the president. He is someone to blame if things go badly (by our lights) and someone to praise when things go well. We attribute to him almost superhuman power. He has more and better information than others. When he does something that appears unwise, it is not because he used bad judgment—it is our fault that we do not see the superior logic of his actions. If he continues to act unwisely, it is because he is evil and is abusing his power.

Such myths are dangerous because, in the manner of self-fulfilling prophecy, they tend to create some of the conditions that are assumed to already exist. If presidents are treated as though they are all-powerful, they may try to act that way. If the media treat them as unapproachable, they may become unapproachable. And from the standpoint of those who enjoy true power and privilege in our society, what could be better? Criticism of the consequences of their exploitation of the political system is directed not at them, but at the president!

We have devoted considerable attention to the existence of a socioeconomic structure that directs and constrains presidential action, not because we believe it completely determines what presidents will do but because insufficient attention has been given it in both the academic and popular literature concerning the presidency. We put forward no deterministic theory of presidential action. On the contrary, ours is a multi-causal theory of presidential responsiveness. The values, style, and personality of incumbents are vitally important in explaining presidential behavior. Factors inherent in the situation are also very important. Nixon's commitment to "peace with honor" in Vietnam, his emphasis on moral decay and permissiveness as the causes of crime, and his willingness to make overtures to China and pursue the arms limitations agreement with the Soviet Union all had to be accounted for by his values, his sense of history, and his concept of the role of a president, as well as by situational factors. His stances and actions surely told us as much about the man as they did about the sociopolitical structure of America.[15] However, structural characteristics discussed throughout this chapter set a context and framework, define boundaries and limits, and in some instances (especially in domestic policy), set the direction of any incumbent of the office.

For the purposes of this study, emphasis on the structural characteristics of American national politics is especially important because they must be carefully taken into account in any proposed reforms intended to overcome or offset the patterns of unresponsiveness characterizing the modern presidency. For example, many liberals advocate both strengthening Congress and weakening the institutional presidency as a guard against a repetition of Vietnams and Watergates in the future. If such a redress of power could be achieved, it would likely be accompanied by other consequences quite unacceptable to liberals. Given the extent to which producer-oriented interests have penetrated Congress, increases in its power with respect to presidential initiatives in foreign policy are likely to be accompanied by increases in the power of Congress to block domestic initiatives undertaken by presidents. In light of the dominance of conservative forces in the national legislature, liberals should be very wary of efforts to reduce the formal powers of the presidency. When one does take into account the extent to which systemic forces in our society shape and constrain the presidency, one quickly recognizes the extent to which they are the tap root of many of the instances of presidential unresponsiveness discussed earlier in this chapter.

If only presidents conceived of themselves as committed to redressing the inequities of distribution of income and ownership within our society, then domestic programs might not be sacrificed in the name of national security, then domestic programs could seek redistribution of economic power and not merely the compensation of the poor for their plight, then the presidential office might not be so out of touch with the aspirations of the dispossessed, and there would probably be fewer incentives for presidents to cover their lack of concern for domestic needs with a veil of deceit and (or) corruption. The problem is, of course, what types of reforms are likely to lead to a presidency that is so oriented? In judging reforms, two criteria are important. First, are the reforms likely to lead to the preconditions of a redistribution of power and privilege in our society? Second, are they likely to succeed in the face of the concerted opposition of those whose positions will be undermined in the process? Few reforms meet these two criteria, but unless they do, they are mere institutional tinkerings, not reforms at all.

From a radical perspective, a fundamental reorientation of the presidency depends upon accompanying fundamental changes in other parts of the system. Those who hold this view argue that social problems such as those discussed in previous pages are inevitable consequences of the structure of American political and economic institutions. One cannot expect the problems to disappear unless there are major changes in these institutions.

Major systemic changes appear highly unlikely at the present time. Individual leaders and groups who currently are flourishing under existing conditions lack the motivation to initiate fundamental changes. But could citizen groups initiate and carry out such modifications? Many have pointed out that an alliance among small farmers, consumers, students, blacks, Chicanos, environmentalists, women, and unorganized labor would be logical and natural—that is, among those who are not receiving the benefits of the existing distribution of power and privilege in our society. Unfortunately, as of this writing, their differences outweigh their common plight of powerlessness. Furthermore, those benefiting from the status quo, in and out of government, have always used the courts, the law, the police, the media, education, control over employment—and frequently enough, military force—to discredit or destroy those who would alter existing patterns. Start with the Alien and Sedition laws of the nation's early years and work right up to recent political trials, jailing of newsmen for failure to reveal their sources, and the "accidental" shooting of student protestors. We have always repressed radical views when they have reached the point of organized expression.

There never will be any fundamental change as long as existing liberal and conservative views dominate. "Kooks" working outside the political system—such as, for example, the suffragettes earlier this century, the freedom riders of the 1960s, and contemporary "hippies" and "peace-freaks" or "eco-freaks"—are the engines of what little change has taken place. But note how slow and marginal such changes are. In the long run, the solution lies in the dynamics of our class structure itself as it responds to changes in the situation. If present inequalities continue to be exacerbated by a war economy, if the tax burden of the middle and lower classes is not eased, if the aspirations of minority groups are not given more legitimacy, then the preconditions of fundamental change will continue to exist. These latent conditions might become manifest and active if triggered by a sharp economic downturn, an international crisis, or an eruption of race tensions.

Unfortunately, the direction of any change is far from clear. There is equal probability that the outcome could be electoral fascism or implementation of the economic preconditions of realizing true political equality. Without such triggers, there is no reason to believe present trends toward corporatism will not continue until our political institutions are completely dominated by business interests.*

Given the unlikelihood of fundamental changes, what are the probable consequences of and prospects for reform measures of more limited scope? In discussing limited proposals calculated to increase presidential responsiveness, it is useful to specify first the desired outcome and then consider ways in which that outcome might be achieved. There is but one overriding goal: reducing the advantage of wealth in determining the outcome of elections and the content of public policies. Wealth provides all of the ingredients of successful electoral politics and exploits as well the fragmented institutions that create and implement national policy. The presidency must be tied more closely to and made more dependent upon those not now enjoying the bounty of our economy.

One challenging possibility would be to open up the electoral

* These comments about some of the conditions of fundamental change have been influenced by the work of Kenneth M. Dolbeare and Murry J. Edelman, *American Politics: Policies, Power and Change* (Lexington, Mass.: D. C. Heath, 1971), chapter 17.

process with the expectation of reducing the influence of wealth over the selection of the president and therefore over the larger political process. Political parties, for instance, are closed instruments of selection. Normally, they operate to screen out candidates who are ideologically outside the mainstream of American politics. In recent years, several proposals for reforming the process for selecting the president have been suggested or actually implemented. Foremost among them were the McGovern Committee reforms.

In many respects the McGovern Committee reforms of the Democratic party and its national convention are far more important than the fact that McGovern's success in the primaries led to a Democratic convention controlled by delegates pledged to him. These reforms assured that state delegations would better reflect the composition of the state parties. They opened up the state party structure. Those who attacked the reforms because they also produced a candidate who went on to suffer one of the greatest electoral disasters ever to befall a Democratic candidate are confusing two issues that must be kept separate. The important issue is that the reforms made it possible for those who had previously been denied access to party office and influence to participate in party policy and the nominating process. The overall effect was to alter (temporarily, at least) both the structure of influence and the balance of interests within the party. The less important issue is that in 1972 most of the new delegates were chosen from among McGovern supporters because McGovern had won so many state primaries. In future years, there will be different candidates, but (providing the reforms are not completely undone) those who previously had been denied a voice in party councils will still have representation. Although the process of party reform is much farther along among the Democrats, the same pressures are building among Republicans.

A second electoral reform proposal would obviate convention reforms, for it would replace the convention system and statewide primaries with nationwide primaries. Regrettably, the winners of the latter system would not be champions of redistribution and social change but wealthy or well-endowed Olympians. As Herbert Alexander points out, candidates would need sufficient money and stamina for two national campaigns rather than one. The effect would be to reinforce the ability of political contributors to dominate elections. Candidates with little initial financing would be unable to parlay individual primary successes into new financial contributions for use in later primaries.

Related reform measures that might help compensate for the weaknesses of nationwide presidential primaries are those designed to limit or restrict ways of getting, giving, and spending political contributions. Such efforts have a dismal history of failure. The ingenuity of monied interests to circumvent new restrictive laws as soon as they are passed seems as boundless as the capacity of legislators to enact reforms which favor incumbents. When the civil service reform movement prohibited assessment of governmental employees, focus shifted to contributions from corporations. When corporate contributions were forbidden, gifts from wealthy individuals such as stockholders or corporate officers increased. When direct contributions from the rich were restricted or insufficient, program books, fund-raising dinners, and special events attracted more donors.

Another alternative would be to have the national government underwrite the costs of all candidates for national office—presidential, senatorial and congressional. Even the most utopian of reformers would admit that such financial support could not be limitless. The support would probably need to be up to some maximum, for example, one half or some other fraction of the cost incurred by the successful candidate for that particular office in the two preceding elections, in the case of general elections. Similar restrictions might be placed on primary candidates with some minimum number of petitioners in support to qualify for federal support.

Such a reform would certainly increase the number of candidates, serious and otherwise, in both primary and general elections. At the same time it would not entirely neutralize the advantage of those who can count on the support of the wealthy. However, it would permit dramatically greater participation by those now precluded from candidacy because of their lack of wealth. One could hardly begin to predict the ultimate consequences of such a radical reform in electoral finance. Since more candidates would appear, sponsored by many more groups (from the ideological right as well as the ideological left), elections might well become much more ideologically oriented and electoral conflict increased. The consequences of so opening up the process of recruiting candidates and conducting elections is almost impossible to predict, but that it would *open them* is beyond doubt. For that very reason, such a reform is well worth considering, costing out, and analyzing carefully.

The success of such a reform would have to be tied to a more careful reporting of campaign expenditures. Great strides in this direction have already been taken by recent Congresses. Public interest groups should continue to place great pressure on the strict implementation of the existing reporting laws which in themselves contain the seeds of further reform. As the patterns of financial support for presidential and other national candidates unfold, beginning with the 1972 elections, there is greater opportunity for the average voter to begin to understand the advantage enjoyed by producer groups as well as the intensity of their involvement and their efforts to manipulate the vote. The disclosures regarding expenditures in behalf of the propositions on the California ballot in June and November 1972 are already having such an effect. For the first time, the average citizen has been given dramatic evidence of the lengths to which producer groups are willing to go to avoid diminution of their privileges despite benefits for the state at large.

It is difficult to be optimistic about the success of such a radical reform as national underwriting for national elections, however logical it would seem to equalize access to electoral office. Since one of the most likely consequences of such a reform is a Congress and a presidency slightly less beholden to and dependent upon producer-oriented interests (and their money), these groups can be expected to oppose such a reform vigorously, citing the possible diminution of the major national parties' role in developing consensus on issues, the emergence of either nonserious or extremest candidates, and the dollar costs. Furthermore, most of those now in elective office could be expected to resist such a reform because it would tend to reduce the advantage an incumbent has in gaining support from the interests with which he is in regular contact.

Hence, this reform meets only one of our two criteria. It has a strong probability of shifting the advantage of election finance away from established interests to those now denied access to office because of their lack of wealth, association with a producer interest, or their minority status in the society. However, with respect to feasibility, the possible virtues of this reform are also its vices. To the extent established interests perceive this change to be threatening, they can be expected to use their privileged access to both the presidency and Congress (and the national political parties) to defeat it. On the other hand, there is increasing public acceptance of governmental financing of campaigns. Popular support rose from 25 percent in 1938 to 58 percent in June 1973. In September 1973, 65 percent of those queried in a Gallup Poll favored exclusive governmental support of presidential and congressional candidates and the prohibition of all private contributions. Despite the uncertain outcome, it is our conviction that the reform is worthy of serious consideration, study, and debate. The seeds of reform are always slow to mature, if they mature at all, and it is time this seed is planted. Whether or not it lives to maturity, only time will tell.

A final electoral reform measure to be considered here is the perennial proposal to abolish the Electoral College and weight votes everywhere equally in a direct election of the president. The present workings of the Electoral College are sufficiently mystifying to most voters to provide grounds for believing the thing itself may discourage many voters from participation. If it were removed and individual votes clearly had equal weight in electing presidents, so that individual votes might make the difference in close elections such as those in 1960 and 1968, the 35 to 40 percent of the electorate who do not participate in presidential elections might have more incentive to do so. Studies of voter participation make it clear that nonvoters are precisely those at the bottom of the socioeconomic ladder and (or) members of minority groups. On the one hand, all measures that would promote their participation should be given careful and favorable consideration on grounds of democratic principle and in hope that such measures will make the president more dependent upon their support and thereby more responsive to their needs. On the other hand, the most obvious drawback of this proposal is that it would reduce the electoral impact of large urban states—the main political bases for the poor, the unemployed, those suffering from air pollution, and so on.

Electoral reform measures discussed above are concerned with increasing political participation and reducing the advantage of established interests over legislative and executive decision-making processes. There are, of course, alternatives for arriving at these outcomes. Reforms dealing directly with Congress are discussed elsewhere, so we limit our proposals to those directed at the national administration. Among the most promising would be to undertake on a national scale what has already proven so successful at the state level, namely, legal assistance regardless of ability to pay. Indeed such successful state ventures (like, for example, California Rural Legal Assistance) might well serve as the building blocks of a national organization. They have made available to the poor what the rich have always had, competent legal advice about how to alter the environment in ways as to promote their interests. Such "environmental alteration" ranges from making sure that administrative agencies are living up to their own standards in treatment of the poor to challenging administrative rules that adversely affect the economic and political opportunities of the poor, in the name of the due process clause of the Fifth Amendment and the equal treatment clauses of various national legislative enactments and of the Fourteenth Amendment. In short, to provide the poor with some of the advantages of information, expertise, and capacity to manipulate policy and administrative agencies now enjoyed by the wealthy.

Again, there is a serious question of the feasibility of congressional subsidy of a program designed to offset some of the privileges of those who now control Congress. However, precisely because of the success of the state programs, largely funded by the Office of Economic Opportunity, and because of the quality of these programs —upon investigation they have been found to have been characterized by the highest standards of legal professionalism—they have developed large constituencies that stand a chance of putting enough pressure on Congress to transform these state programs into a national one. Once again, however, one cannot be sanguine about the willingness of Congress to implement such a radical shift in the structure of power in our society.

One might properly wonder why we have not included a discussion of reforms concerning the staffing and structure of the presidential office, the character of the national personnel or budgeting process, use of cabinet or relations with executive departments and, especially, with Congress. We omit consideration of such proposals because of our conviction that without systemic changes (that is, reducing the privileges of wealth) and unless the presidency itself can be more closely tied to the dispossessed, such reforms are literally meaningless. Reforms that will make the presidency more responsive must change the environment in which the presidency operates. Presidents are not the cause of our maladies nor does the burden of reform rest on that office.

No reforms of the party system or the nominating process, much less of the presidential office alone, will make the president more responsive to the dispossessed of our society unless they are accompanied by changes in our entire political and economic system. And frankly, we are not at all sanguine that such changes will be brought about through reform. Our economic system will not reform itself, and government, because of the extent to which it has been penetrated by powerful groups within the economy, is not likely to rise above its present narrow conception of self-interest in order to do what governments are supposed to do—govern—let alone do what democratic governments are supposed to do—govern in the interest of the many. Despite our misgivings, we advocate reform because of our fear that present conditions, if not radically changed, will continue their drift toward corporatism and repression, accompanied by the specter of violent revolution and even more repression.

No single reform will make it possible for those now exploited by the distribution of power and privilege in our society to gain their rightful place. Indeed, if history is any teacher, most reforms fail to achieve their intended results. Invariably, they produce as many problems as solutions. Perhaps the commitment to reform as a process is as important as any immediate results. Once taken, the road to reform is endless and its destination is unknown, as the 1960s have taught us. When Mrs. Rosa Parks refused to give up her seat on a Montgomery bus in 1955, few blacks could have imagined that her act would precipitate a dynamic process that would not only change their own self-image but would affect the consciences of all Americans. Women's liberation was taken as a joke in the beginning, but no one laughs at the consequences of the antidiscrimination sections of the 1964 Civil Rights act, the court-initiated revision of state antiabortion laws, or state ratifications of the Equal Rights Amendment to the Constitution. The protest movements have not only illuminated the inequities of our system of power and privilege to the nation at large but they have had greatest effect on the victims of inequity, who no longer accept their condition as either "the natural order of things" or "inevitable."

We understand little about the ultimate impact of the protest movements on those it has touched directly. About the only certainty we have is that the protests have changed people's understanding of themselves and of our country—with what ultimate consequences, we know not. Travelers taking the journey of reform can only hope to get to know themselves. Perhaps that is what America needs more than the dreams of utopia, whether formulated by liberals, conservatives, or radicals.

# Congress:

# After Watergate, What?

*Leroy N. Rieselbach*

In one of his better-known songs, Bob Dylan noted that the times, they are a-changin', and he particularly warned senators and congressmen that they'd better move with the times or they would be moved by the battle raging outside their walls. But what Dylan summed up in a few pungent lines, others were busy elaborating. His song repeats a theme, played with diverse orchestrations and multiple variations, that critics, both social and political, have sounded more and more frequently as this century progresses: For a multitude of reasons, Congress is not equipped to cope with the crises of the modern age. Innumerable problems create substantial discord, while Congress, so the argument runs, is content to deal with these tumultuous times in conventional fashion, using the same organizational structures and practices so often found wanting in the past.

The specifics of the critics' charges are by now, even without the cacophony of the Watergate affair, a familiar refrain. As the history of American involvement in Indochina demonstrates, the national legislature has relinquished to the executive the power to wage war, almost whenever and wherever he chooses to act. Presidents, from Eisenhower to Nixon, determined, virtually unrestrained, the nature of the country's participation in the Vietnam War. Most other aspects of the nation's foreign actions, especially in the areas of military strategy and defense posture, are now formulated beyond the purview of Congress; the president and the pentagon have reduced the legislature to a minor role in world politics.

Domestically, the story is much the same. Congress has not kept pace with changing national needs; it continues to employ an outmoded division of labor that leaves critical issues firmly in the hands of small numbers of lawmakers, ostensibly experts, who remain steadfastly in tune with the status quo. For example, friends of the oil industry, entrenched on the Senate Finance and House Ways and Means Committees, have preserved that interest's favorable tax loophole, the oil depletion allowance, against the onslaughts of those pushing for a more equitable distribution of tax burdens.[1] Similarly, other vested interests, within and without the legislature, have prevailed. Congress has not responded sufficiently to the environmental crisis; crime still abounds in the land; poverty has, if anything, become more widespread; inflation has eroded the purchasing power of wage earners; a host of discordant notes continues to be heard in this country and the national legislature has not, to date, been found in the vanguard of those seeking to bring harmony to American life.[2] The Congress has not responded to the changing times, its antagonists claim, because it is not organized to deal effectively with contemporary problems. Congress, in short, has abdicated its responsibility; it has relinquished to the presidency and to the bureaucracy the role of chief conductor of public affairs.

This widely-proclaimed decline of the legislature is neither inevitable or irreversible. Congress still possesses the constitutional and statutory means to have a major impact on the formation of public policy. It retains the power to declare war and to appropriate money to sustain the military. It holds the power to authorize major domestic programs and to fund them. If it has not employed these powers, it is because most lawmakers have chosen, rationally or otherwise, to defer to expertise, to permit others to make decisions that they as elected legislators could choose to make for themselves. Thus the song of reform is in the air; the call is to "strengthen" the Congress, to restore its initiative in both foreign and domestic policy.

Yet reform, in and of itself, is often a siren's song, seductive in the short run, but fatal over the long haul. Reform, to make sense, must have a focus; reformers must look to some vision of a preferable state of affairs and must seek to channel change toward that goal.[3] Contemporary critics have different visions of American politics in general and Congress in particular; some place their trust in the executive branch while others put their faith in Congress to bring about desirable political results. This essay will explore some distinctly different views of what the legislature can or should do. We begin by indicating some criteria by which to evaluate congressional performance and then use those criteria to describe the current legislature, to outline systematically some reform proposals, and finally to project a possibly useful vision of a more desirable state of affairs.[4]

## Some Evaluative Criteria:
## Responsibility, Responsiveness,
## and Accountability

What should Congress do? Should the legislature call the tune? Should it blend its efforts harmoniously with those of the executive? Should Congress act as a stern critic, sounding a loud alarm when executive leadership moves in unsatisfactory directions or when bureaucratic performance is unacceptable? Should Congress relinquish its policy ambitions altogether and rest content to transmit popular opinion to those who actually render decisions? There are three alternative vantage points from which to begin an assessment of Congress, each of which yields differing answers to these questions.

*Responsibility.* The first criterion, responsibility, focuses on problem-solving. An institution is responsible to the degree that it provides reasonably successful policies that resolve the major problems committed to it for solution. The emphasis of the responsibility criterion is on speed, efficiency, and, of course, success. Can Congress as a decision-making institution produce policy that deals promptly and effectively with national problems? If, as many critics of Congress believe, the answer to this query is burdened with negatives, then reform proposals to improve the *product* of the legislative process are clearly in order.

*Responsiveness.* Responsiveness, the second criterion, emphasizes *process* more than product. To be responsive, a decision-making center like a legislature must listen to, and take account of, the ideas and sentiments of those who will be affected by its policy decisions or pronouncements. It must appear to provide an open channel of communication with those it influences. In other words, it must take heed of, and respond to, the preferences of its constituency. If it does not, the third criterion comes into play.

*Accountability.* An institution like Congress will periodically face those to whom it is responsible for a judgment upon its record. If the decision-makers are found wanting, the "rascals" can be "turned out," removed from office. The contrast between Congress and the Supreme Court makes the point clearly. Justices of the Supreme Court, once appointed, are protected by life tenure and are difficult to dislodge; congressmen must soon face the voters and can be denied reelection. Thus, the legislators must calculate the popular response to their actions (or lack thereof), or risk loss of position and power.

Note that these three criteria of evaluation—responsibility, responsiveness, and accountability—are by no means mutually exclusive; they overlap. The principle of accountability operates regardless of whether we judge performance by product or process, efficiency or representativeness. However it is displeased, the electorate can vote legislators into early retirement. Similarly, at least in theory, it is possible for decision-makers to be both responsible and responsive; they can move rapidly on the basis of full consultation to adopt workable policies. Richard Nixon, in effect, made such a claim for his administration's handling of the Indochina War.[5]

In practice, however, there seems considerably more potential for a clash between responsibility and responsiveness. The stress of the one on efficient problem-solving conflicts with the other's concern for registering the viewpoints of a multitude of groups and interests. To delay while collecting a wide variety of sentiments, organized as well as random, may require a long pause, during which the problem may grow worse or potentially effective solutions may become obsolete. But to act while the problem remains fresh and tractable may foreclose the opportunity for concerned citizens to form and air their opinions before some line of policy is pursued. It is unlikely that any institution, however accountable it may be, can always be both responsible and responsive; at least, it appears likely that more than minor tension will exist between the two qualities.

In any event, assessment of Congress' place in the American political process will require some judgment as to the degree to which any criterion should dominate the assessment. The desirability of particular reforms will depend, to a considerable extent, upon which vision of Congress the observer holds. Is Congress to be preeminently a responsible policy-maker? Or should it yield its decision-making functions and concentrate instead on serving as a conduit for popular opinion? Is it sufficient that the citizenry retain the power to hold its national legislature accountable? More realistically perhaps, is there an optimum "mix" of responsibility, responsiveness, and accountability that will permit Congress to survive and to work well?[6] It is these issues that the remainder of this essay addresses.

### The Contemporary Congress:
### A Critical Assessment

Before speculating about the future, it may be well to note the current state of legislative affairs. How well does Congress do at present? Baldly put, the arguments advanced here, subject to subsequent elaboration, are: (1) Congress is, at best, only imperfectly responsible; especially in foreign relations it has yielded much of its decision-making authority to the executive branch. (2) Congress is modestly responsive; it does listen, but it does little or nothing to seek out the voices of those who do not come knocking on its door. (3) Congress is held accountable far more in theory than in practice, an unsatisfactory situation that is not entirely the fault of the legislature itself. If these propositions are true, and the evidence for them seems persuasive, then there is ample opportunity for reform; the legislature's performance can be improved on all fronts.[7] But reforms designed to improve performance in one area may have unintended and unanticipated repercussions on another front.

Nor do Congress' present troubles seem momentary aberrations. On the contrary, its basic structures have undergone only modest alterations in the past half-century. The 1911 "palace revolution" in the House of Representatives that overthrew Speaker Joseph Cannon marks the beginning of the modern era. Since then, with the single exception of the Legislative Reorganization Act of 1946, the main outlines of congressional organization and procedures have evolved slowly until in recent years the situation has become almost static.[8] The major elements have been intact for some years.

In general, Congress has become "institutionalized;"[9] year after year the same men operate in the same setting using only slightly modified operating procedures. The congressional *modus operandi* is one of fragmentation and decentralization, with authority and influence widely, but not necessarily equally, dispersed among the 535 senators and representatives. Many legislators have some direct and immediate impact on congressional decisions. In such circumstances, congressional politics becomes coalition politics, as proponents of various proposals seek through bargaining, compromise, negotiation, or "logrolling" to assemble fragments of political power into winning coalitions, to produce sufficient strength to move a bill ahead at successive stages in the legislative process in each chamber, eventually to the president's desk in the White House.

The sharing of power in Congress, which results in decision by bargain and compromise, is a product of many conditions. In the first place, the electoral process in America stimulates independence of central authority in those who successfully run the gamut and win seats in Congress. Electoral triumph, especially in the smaller House districts, is almost surely the product of the individual efforts of individual candidates, running with only modest assistance from national political party organizations. A candidate may have to survive a difficult primary fight, a bruising general election struggle with the opposition, or in some cases both. To do so, he will have to create his own campaign organization, design his own strategy, raise his own funds, and put together his own electoral coalition.[10] No wonder that most legislators pay prime attention to their districts, "where the votes are" that ultimately decide their fates. Incumbents learn the ropes and begin each reelection effort with more substantial advantages over their challengers. Few sitting congressmen are turned out of office, but enough lose every two years to reinforce the inclination of the survivors to count their constituents and to resist national, centralizing forces which might jeopardize electoral security.

The internal organization, formal and informal, of Congress sustains the individual legislator's independence. The use of specialized standing committees as the chief agents of decision-making constitutes the major decentralizing force in Congress; the committees are relatively free of restraint, are autonomous, and what they decide is often what the parent chamber will decide. Committees are the repositories of congressional expertise; each has a virtual monopoly on legislative specialization in the area of its jurisdiction. Nonmembers are prepared to defer to committee expertise, to accept committee recommendations; they expect, of course, reciprocal deference in their own special areas.

The committee, then, is a highly independent body with substantial influence over legislative activity. Its chairman is the single most important member of the panel; though chairmen wield their powers in various strengths and degrees, most are able to shape what their committees do. Because a chairman is often able to sustain his own view, or some close approximation of it, within his committee, and because the reciprocal deference noted above leads Congress mostly to ratify committee decisions, the fragmented, divided character of legislative authority becomes clearly visible; in short, committee actions are very often synonymous with legislative action.[11]

By contrast, the political parties in Congress, which might centralize legislative authority, are weak. The party leadership—the Speaker of the House, the floor leaders, and the whips—has few genuine sanctions with which to enforce discipline on the disparate party membership. As noted, electoral realities lead legislators to vote their districts rather than the party line where tension between the two occurs. Committee considerations—the use of seniority to select committee leaders; the protection of the panel's expertise and power—often militate against supporting the party. Party leaders are not without some bases of influence, but their resources rest on persuasion rather than compulsion; the leadership can seek to persuade the rank-and-file to go along, but cannot compel cohesion within its membership. While parties are often successful in generating considerable discipline, on balance, it seems evident that they generally lack the power regularly and effectively to countervail the centrifugal forces of electoral and committee realities.

Congressional rules and procedures contribute directly to the fragmented, decentralized character of the legislature. The rules institutionalize and protect arrangements that require a bill to move past many "veto points," institutional decision-points at which a bill must succeed or die. They define and defend committee jurisdictions, insulating the committes from outside pressures, making it unlikely that the committees will be circumvented, and keeping the major decisions safely inside the committee. The Rules Committee in the House and the rule of unlimited debate, the well-known filibuster or cloture rule, in the Senate are among the much discussed procedures which serve, among other things, to buttress the position of legislative minorities. Without discussing the many other intricate rules that might be cited,[12] it is clear that congressional procedures operate to sustain a set of power relationships with multiple centers of influence, and in so doing, contribute to making bargaining the dominant way of resolving conflicts in Congress.

Finally, like any other organization, Congress operates within a context of uncodified but easily observable mores and practices that color its activities. These informal traditions, or norms, foster a diffusion of power. Senators and representatives alike are constrained to specialize substantively on a small number of subjects, to defer to one another's expertise, to treat each other courteously, and in general to get along within the system. This "legislative culture" permits each lawmaker to try to carve out a niche where he can exert some influence over congressional decision-making. Many are successful and achieve some fragment of power, even at the cost of forfeiting any authority beyond their little preserve.

To repeat, Congress is a highly decentralized, fragmented institution. The committee structure, the formal rules and procedures, and the informal norms and expectations work to diffuse authority widely, although in no sense equally, among the lawmakers. Many legislators become important in some corner of congressional activity. Negotiation and compromise become the chief style of decision-making in Congress; bargaining provides the only viable method of assembling the fragments of power into coalitions capable of moving legislation ahead. The political parties, a possible centralizing force, have been incapable of overcoming these divisive forces. In consequence, and in the absence of other alternatives, the coalitional character of congressional politics has survived without serious challenge in recent years.

Policy-making becomes a slow, complicated process. To enact policy, those in favor must move their legislation through a subcommittee, a full committee, the Rules Committee in the House, and out onto the floor where a majority vote is required for passage. If the process can be repeated in the other house and all the inevitable differences in the two chambers' versions of major bills can be resolved in conference committee, then and only then will the new policy, or modification of an old policy, be *authorized*. If money is necessary to implement the program, as it most often is, then the entire process must be repeated, with *appropriations* legislation moving through the Appropriations Committees rather than the standing, substantive panels. It is the need to move across, around, or over these imposing hurdles that gives congressional politics its distinctive, coalitional character. To assemble a winning coalition at each of these stages, and to do so in a permissive and individualistic environment of shared power, requires bargaining skill and patience which must be sustained over considerable periods of time.

Given this picture of congressional practice, it is not surprising that the national legislature has been judged deficient on *responsibility* grounds. Congress is simply not capable of acting efficiently in any but the most unusual circumstances. Such extraordinary situations occur, as they did in the early New Deal period and during 1964–65, when exceptional series of events conspired to give one party in Congress both overwhelming majorities, which make the weakness of party discipline tolerable, and extra incentives to advance a major legislative program.[13] But ordinarily, conditions are far less propitious. Where the control of government is divided, with one party controlling the presidency and the other holding a congressional majority (as has been the case for twelve of the twenty-two years since 1952), prospects for cooperative lawmaking are substantially reduced. Even where the president and the congressional majority share a common party label, responsible lawmaking seldom follows, for nominal majorities show a decided tendency to evaporate when the roll is called. Thus, policy-making in Congress dribbles from slow, painstaking negotiations, which often cross rather than follow party lines.

This is especially apparent in domestic affairs, where Congress retains much of the policy-making authority. It is no doubt true that, even on the home front, the president proposes while Congress disposes, but the end result regularly bears the imprint of legislative deliberation and decision. Indeed, Congress seems to prefer to respond to presidential initiative, to demand that the chief executive set the national agenda. Congressional criticism is commonplace when the lawmakers feel that the president is slow in coming up with a legislative program. Once that program is forthcoming, however, the legislators are more than willing to alter its proposals dramatically or to reject them entirely. Numerous struggles—against Richard Nixon's efforts to reorganize the executive branch; to abolish the Office of Economic Opportunity[14]; to impound funds properly appropriated; and to extend broadly the doctrine of "executive privilege," by which he sought, pleading "national interest," to deny congressional access to information—amply testify to the legislature's ability to resist and defeat undesired presidential initiatives.

Where Congress is prepared to substitute its own for the executive's priorities, it provides a target to those who criticize it on responsibility grounds. As suggested above, the congressional process is something less than efficient. To assemble a winning majority takes time; accommodations to many independent power holders must be made. Thus, the critics can point to extended hearings, lengthy sub- or full committee executive "mark up" sessions,[15] long periods of delay, and, in the Senate, unlimited debate as evidence that the legislature cannot act decisively. While these critics do not always recognize that time may be the essential ingredient in legislative decision-making, that delay may permit action in a specific compromise settlement, their essential argument is sound: Congress does often move ponderously. Furthermore, the negotiated agreements that emerge, able to command a majority, tend to be modest in scope. Proposals for major change are often jettisoned in the search for a winning coalition; they must be sacrificed to secure the support of critical power holders.[16]

In sum, in domestic matters, where Congress' influence is highest, its output is neither radical nor rapid. Congress seems in no hurry to respond to interest groups or executives, but prefers to develop its own domestic programs in its own way and at its own pace. Needless to say, those who see responsibility as demanding more efficient development of more imaginative and innovative solutions to pressing national problems find congressional performance unsatisfactory. There is, in truth, considerable merit to their argument: in ordinary times, Congress seldom generates dramatic departures; rather it gives shape and substance to the ideas of others and does so over extended periods.

With respect to foreign relations, the situation concerning congressional responsibility is even less satisfactory. Over an extended period, the president has capitalized on a number of advantages—his power as the commander in chief, vastly greater resources of information and technical expertise, the Supreme Court's *Curtiss-Wright* decision that the president is "the sole organ of the nation" in international relations, and most importantly the recognition by Congress that its mode of business is often inappropriate in the foreign sphere. These have permitted him to seize a dominant position vis-a-vis Congress, which has come to defer to presidential expertise in military matters. The Armed Services Committees have become, in Dexter's phrase, "real estate" panels,[17] concerned with the management of military installations and content to leave the more critical issues of military strategy and procurement to Pentagon generals and White House executives. Diplomatic initiatives, such as President Nixon's rapprochements with China and the Soviet Union, have been executive in initiation and conduct. Tariff agreements are negotiated by the executive under broad congressional delegations renewed and extended at regular intervals. Wars, the ultimate in international relations, have come under total presidential control; the two most recent ones, in Korea and Indochina, did not receive the constitutional blessing contemplated in the provision requiring congressional approval in the form of a declaration of war.

This is not to say that Congress cannot influence American foreign policy. Control over the purse strings permits the legislature, if it chooses, to deny funds for policies initiated by the executive. The increasing unpopularity of the Vietnam conflict generated numerous proposals to cut off money for that war. Only in the last days of American involvement, in early summer 1973, did Congress succeed in forcing the president's hand at all. In June, eight years, more than 40,000 dead and 250,000 wounded, and $100 billion expended after its initial effort, the legislature tacked a provision cutting off funds for bombing in Cambodia to a 3.3 billion dollar supplemental appropriations bill, needed to enable the federal government to keep operating in the new fiscal year beginning July 1. President Nixon vetoed the bill and the House sustained his action, but lest the government go out of business, the president accepted a compromise and signed a second supplemental bill prohibiting spending for military purposes in Indochina without legislative approval after August 15. But on the whole, it seems incontrovertable that the substance of the nation's Indochina policy—from its inception in the Eisenhower and Kennedy administrations to the end of direct American involvement during Nixon's term—embodied the executive's rather than Congress' policy choices.

Likewise, Congress could have, but has not, reclaimed the power to set tariffs or to designate some independent agency to negotiate trade agreements. The legislature has tried, with only modest success, to keep closer tabs on military matters by insisting that funds for weaponry be authorized on an annual, not a long-term basis.[18] The lawmakers have affected the shape of the foreign aid program; they have reduced it in size through major cuts in the president's fund requests and they have altered its scope through a reallocation of money between military and economic varieties of aid. Yet, when all is said and done, the president is central and Congress peripheral in foreign policy making. Responsibility for America's international relations rests in the White House not on Capitol Hill.

The public tendency to focus policy responsibility on the president rather than on Congress, in short, seems to have some justice to it. The legislature is not preeminent in policy-making much of the time, and where it is, it leaves its mark only after an extended period of deliberation and debate. Congress has not been the responsible initiator of public policy; rather it has been the molder and legitimator of policy originating most often outside of the legislative chambers.

When the spotlight shifts from responsibility to *responsiveness,* Congress appears in a considerably better light. What appear to be its defects on one front become its advantages on another; its vices become virtues. The very openness, decentralization, and bargaining style of decision-making which seem to critics to inhibit responsible policy choice, appear to be the stuff of responsiveness or representative concern. The necessity of moving slowly and waiting for policy to emerge guarantees time for those with a stake in the outcome of legislative deliberation to communicate their sentiments. The multi-stage process of lawmaking provides points of access to legislators, identifies the places where outside pressures may be brought to bear. Congress, for its part, has been more than willing to listen to what nonmembers have to say.

To put it another way, Congress has ample opportunity, and regularly seizes the chance, to attend to messages from interested parties, including the president, interest groups, and public. As noted earlier, the legislature voluntarily depends on the president to set its agenda; it responds to executive initiatives. Moreover, the president has at his disposal what Neustadt has called his "power to persuade,"[19] which he employs to prod Congress to act affirmatively on those initiatives. The president can use his popularity and prestige to influence lawmakers; it is difficult for them to resist a popular and determined leader. He can argue on the merits of an issue, using speeches, press conferences, special messages, and his ability to command general attention. He can focus on party loyalty, appealing to partisan interests. He can deal with the appropriate congressional committee by sending his chief aides and experts to testify at hearings; by courting the important committee members, especially the chairman and ranking minority member; or by accepting amendments in order to gain votes. He may use personal contacts to win over crucial individuals—committee chairmen, party leaders, influential members. If he can secure the support of such leaders, they in turn may use their levers of influence to persuade their followers to back the president.

To the extent that his constituency differs from those of the lawmakers—and the differences between the president's national orientations and the supposedly more parochial perspectives of the representatives of the states and districts have been widely noted— the president will introduce into legislative deliberations points of view that might otherwise not be heard or at least be less forcefully expressed. He may also, by means of "executive privilege," keep information out of legislative hands.

In such situations, the president's ability to do favors, to provide goods and services, constitutes the force behind his persuasive power. He can veto bills to the advantage of some legislator or in other ways use his influence over pending bills to help the man he wants to influence. He may also make use of this patronage power, offering to appoint political associates of a congressman to federal posts to help the legislator solidify his local political situation. The president can, in addition, give or withhold election aid; he can, if he chooses, endorse congressional candidates, pose for pictures with them, or make personal appearances in their districts. If he is highly regarded, such electoral assistance may be of great benefit. While it is never clear precisely to what extent these means of persuasion are used— bargains struck are not likely to be explicit or widely publicized— these advantages do enable the president to work from a position of some strength to influence congressional decision-making.[20]

The legislature is also responsive to the views of organized interests which move in and about the halls of Congress. The law-makers are often deeply involved with representatives ("lobbyists") of such groups in working for mutually desired legislation. Yet this is not to argue, as do some observers, that pressure group activity is decisive in lawmaking. Indeed, the best and most recent evidence suggests that the interests do not call the legislative tune (and do not really pay the piper either); rather they work collaboratively with, and sometimes at the request of, sympathetic congressmen.[21] They lend support to developing coalitions, working to pass or to block bills as seems appropriate.

Specifically, the lobbyist seeks to establish free and open lines of communication with members of Congress in positions to help promote his group's cause. These channels enable him to secure a hearing for the views he wishes to present. Only if he can "make his pitch" can he hope to exert any influence at all. Thus, much of his activity is designed to sustain his access; he may, in fact, run a service operation designed to supply information, manpower, and contacts to lawmakers working for the views he seeks to promote. The pressure group, in sum, belies its name; it is a coalition partner rather than an irresistible force in the legislative process.[22]

Even such low key tactics, relying on friendship and trust rather than pressure or threats, provide groups and their representatives with ample opportunity to present their opinions. They appear regularly, as witnesses, at committee and subcommittee hearings; they exploit whatever access they have to present research findings and documentary evidence directly to the relevant legislator or members of his staff. Through such channels, group postures become known to the lawmaker, and often at a time when his own position has not yet crystalized. In some cases, however, the group provides only data which reinforce the legislator's existing judgment; it introduces no new perspectives. In any event, if responsiveness means open and operative channels of communication, Congress is responsive, at least to organized interests.

And here, of course, lies the rub. While the national legislature does hear and have the opportunity to respond to the views of business, labor, agriculture, veterans, and the professions—those with the means to hire or create active lobbying organizations —other interests, in stark contrast, go unheard and unheeded. For one thing, access is unequally divided, communications links are unequally available, because of the decentralized character of the congressional process. Many groups will have some access, but some will have ties to important leaders while others can reach only the rank-and-file. More importantly, some interests—the poor, the blacks and consumers come readily to mind—with views well worth hearing are inadequately organized. Lacking experience, adequate funds, and know-how, they may be unable to present their positions effectively. What the legislator hears may be far from the full story; his intake of information will depend on what messages are being sent as well as which available communications he chooses to hear.

One other audience, the unorganized public, provides a focus for legislative attention. Too often, individual citizens do not present their views. Congressmen do not accept the executive or lobbyists as the "voice of the people." They attend to the polls, seeking a general sense of popular sentiment. They attend, perhaps more closely, to opinions of their own constituents, as expressed in conversations, in letters, in newspaper columns and editorials. Some, recognizing the imperfect character of these sources,[23] commission their own opinion polls; others rely more on intuition, on their sense of what their constituents believe. In truth, for most lawmakers reliable information about their constituency's sentiments is not available; they do not really know what the "folks back home" feel on any but the most dramatic issues of the day.

Yet there is considerable incentive to heed constituents' views. The legislator, in the absence of clear data on district opinion, remains uncertain about whether his actions will affect his prospects for reelection. Thus, before he acts, he will take into consideration local realities, including his own feelings—however intuitive they may be—about what this constituents elected him to do in general and what they would want him to do in certain specific circumstances. All this provides no clear guide to action, but it does seem to require each congressman to think about possible local repercussions of his behavior. This ensures some policy linkages, though clearly imperfect ones, between Washington and the local communities.

On the whole, then, Congress does moderately well in responding to, in representing, a variety of interests. The legislature cannot avoid getting messages, often loud and clear ones, from the executive; indeed Congress demands such communications. Interest groups also abound, using their access to transmit their views to senators and representatives. The legislator finds those views helpful and may solicit them where they do not come forth readily. Lawmakers also feel the need to gauge local sentiment; they seek to head off possible disapproval by taking citizen opinion into account. Moreover, as noted, Congress's decentralization and fragmentation, the slow pace of its bargaining, guarantee opportunities for access and time to transmit messages. Congress can and does hear many voices during its deliberations.

Yet the national legislature is by no means perfectly responsive, completely representative. In one sense, it can never meet these criteria fully, for in resolving conflicts it must respond favorably toward some interests and less satisfactorily with respect to others. On all fronts—executive, group, individual—congressional responsiveness can be improved and, not surprisingly, these defects have become the targets of reformers seeking to enhance the responsiveness of Congress.

These same defects, especially those involving popular indifference to the legislature, also go far to explain the fact that Congress is held *accountable* only imperfectly. Accountability, citizen control of Congress through the ballot box, depends upon at least three factors to operate meaningfully. First, those making the judgment, the citizens, must be aware of their legislators' behavior. Second, the citizen must have some views of his own, some set of goals for which he expects the legislator to work. Third, if legislative behavior and citizen preferences don't match, there must be some way to express dissatisfaction; that is, the citizen must have available a candidate with whom his views do coincide. Such a viable alternative may be found in the primary of the incumbent's political party or in the general election. In truth, these conditions are only poorly met in modern America. No one of them finds much more than an approximation in reality. It is highly unlikely that all three exist in more than a small minority of instances. Absence of the requisite conditions leads inexorably to the conclusion that accountability operates only at the margins of legislative politics.

Lack of these conditions for accountability permits congressmen to act free of popular check on all but the most dramatic and emotional issues.[24] This is true because, in direct contrast to condition one, the citizenry is on the whole unaware of the major details of legislative behavior. Polls continually reveal that large proportions of the population cannot name their elected representatives. The complexity of the congressional process, with its myriad decision points, remains beyond public grasp. The meaning of even the most public act, the roll call vote, is not widely understood. Voters are not aware of the possibilities for taking many sides on an issue in a decentralized organization like Congress. Legislators can act in inconsistent ways, working against a bill at one stage, in committee for example, but voting for it later at the roll call. Such behavior will allow them to be all things—friend *and* foe—to all bills, and immeasurably complicates the citizen's task of understanding congressional politics. Nor do the media of communication offer much help. Understandably, the single chief executive is more "newsworthy" than the plural legislature. Dramatic events in Congress are the exception not the rule, and coverage of the legislature is modest, even in the best media. Detailed consistent coverage of individual congressmen is nil. In short, the citizen who wants to follow legislative politics has a hard time knowing what his representative is up to in Washington.

In addition, and in contradiction to condition two, citizens who try to be attentive are rare. The voting studies amply demonstrate that ballots are seldom cast on the basis of issues but on "party identification"—a voter's habitual commitment to a major political party—and the candidate's "image."[25] While there is some reason to believe that the 1950s were the nadir of issue orientation[26]—the "bland leading the bland"—it is doubtful that the concern in the 1960s for issues and performance involved enough people or has continued in sufficient strength to give us the informed electorate needed to hold our lawmakers truly accountable. The rejection of presidential candidates who sought to offer choices, Goldwater in 1964 and McGovern in 1972, seems to have had more to do with their "unsuitability" in the eyes of the electorate than with any detailed awareness of their specific views (though the former may flow from the latter). If this is true for highly salient presidential contests, it is even more so for less well publicized legislative races. There is adequate reason to believe that choices in congressional elections seldom reflect detailed awareness of the candidates' positions on issues.

Finally, in practice, the third condition necessary for accountability is not entirely satisfied: there is not always a candidate with whom the citizen agrees who can be substituted for the incumbent whom he opposes. In part, this flows from the fact that the voting population is relatively uninformed. If the citizens know neither what the incumbent does in Washington nor what the major issues are in any campaign, they are unlikely to be given a campaign focused on those matters. Even where there is a clear substantive contrast between incumbent and challenger, the lack of effective competition between parties in most districts precludes the challenger from winning.[27] Moreover, even where the voters have and recognize clear electoral choices, it is highly unlikely that one set of views will gain ascendence in Congress. Voters in one set of districts may choose liberals over conservative incumbents, but the reverse will occur in enough other constituencies that the composition of Congress varies little from year to year. In fact, there is little turnover in legislative seats at all.[28] In recent decades fewer and fewer congressional seats actually have passed from one party to the other; more than two-thirds of the seats have stayed Republican or Democratic without change.[29] Thus, putting all these pieces together, even where there is a choice between ideologically distinct candidates, electoral realities—the advantages of incumbents and the lack of genuine interparty competition in most districts—deny the minority candidate any real chance of election. Whatever change there is in Congress reflects what happens in about a hundred or so highly competitive districts; since these districts seldom shift uniformly to one party or the other, each succeeding Congress looks very much like its predecessor. These relatively modest changes in composition are seldom sufficient to change the ideological outlook of the entire legislature.[30]

Thus, this assessment of the contemporary Congress—a decentralized institution which diffuses authority and which reaches decisions only through a time-consuming process of negotiation and compromise—shows the legislature to be something less than ideal in responsibility, responsiveness, and accountability. Congress simply is not equipped to be responsible on a regular basis; its organization and procedures are not designed to allow efficient and rapid formulation of policy. No wonder that Congress has delegated much of its policy-making power to the president, especially with respect to international relations. Only the Indochina War and Watergate have provided much incentive for it to flex its muscles and to try to recapture its lost authority. The legislature's performance is better with respect to responsiveness. The same structural shortcomings which inhibit responsibility encourage it to be representative. Many groups—but not all, and particularly not those lacking in money and skill—can find the time and the locus in the legislature to present their views before policy is enacted. Finally, Congress is held accountable in that elections are held every two years and dissatisfied citizens can retire its members. In practice, however, the citizens regularly lack the intellectual sophistication and/or the electoral opportunity to exercise meaningful popular control over public policy. Thus, whatever the criteria employed, critics of all persuasions find Congress wanting. Each set, from its own particular vantage points, has specified reform proposals intended to make the legislature a "better" institution.

## The Future Congress:
## Some Alternative Visions

What constitutes a "better" Congress is, of course, the central question. Each would-be reformer proposes changes intended to move the legislature toward a particular vision of that Congress should be, depending upon what values are being upheld—responsibility, responsiveness, accountability, or some combination. The important point is that reforms designed to promote one value may have costs in another. Here, we will note some major reform proposals and assess their potential impact on legislative practice.

*Responsibility.* There exist two quite distinct perspectives on the appropriate way to achieve congressional responsibility—one which subordinates the legislature to the executive, one which envisions congressional supremacy—but the common element in both is a desire to centralize legislative operations. Each vision points to fragmentation of power, to multiple centers of decision-making authority, as the vice which prevents Congress from efficiently formulating public policy. Each, on its own terms, seeks to bring some order out of congressional chaos; each seeks to make it easier for Congress to act promptly and effectively. Each proposes reforms that, as we shall see, reduce political responsiveness.[31]

The propresidential proposals, often the pets of liberals (at least before Nixon), suggest that the gradual emergence of the president as chief policymaker and administrator is both inevitable and desirable. Congress, in this scheme of things, would devote its energies to nonpolicy activities, such as overseeing the executive branch, to insure that the agencies and bureaus conduct their affairs in keeping with the goals of policy. It would serve as a "service" agency for citizens, to provide the populace with a point of contact with government. In short, Congress would concede lawmaking to the president, occasionally modifying his proposals but largely legitimizing them. Legislative attention would be directed instead to policing the bureaucracy and serving the citizenry.

Frequently, and especially among academics, the "executive dominance" notion is incorporated in a broader political (and constitutional) reform movement, the "responsible two-party system."[32] This scheme would centralize the policy making process through disciplined political parties. The British parliamentary arrangements provide a model of the sort of beneficial order that these reformers envision.[33] The president, like the prime minister, would possess, through his leadership position, the ability to win approval for and to control the implementation of his preferred programs. He would have the virtually guaranteed support of Congress, for the legislator, given his dependence in the new order on powerful political parties, could oppose the executive only upon pain of terminating his political career. The independent legislator would no longer be the control mechanism in the system: the electorate would punish poor performance by voting the party responsible out of office. Congress would become a part of the party "team," accountable en masse.

Strengthening the presidency, whether or not as part of a new, invigorated party system, would entail specific alterations both in the electoral system by which legislators are selected and in the internal operations of Congress. Electorally, the reformer would undercut the independence that current practices instill in the contemporary legislator. This might be accomplished by the oft-proposed, never seriously considered extension of lawmakers' terms of office to four years in the House and eight years in the Senate. All congressmen would be selected simultaneously with the president, and presumably would be obligated to him, because they would owe their electoral success to his efforts more than to their own.

Lengthening congressional terms might encourage loyalty to the White House, but would in no way compel it, especially if the election produced a president of one party and a legislative majority of the other. Thus, the party responsibility reformers desire to guarantee party, and in consequence, presidential government. In effect, new, centralized national party committees would control the fate of their own congressional candidates. The powerful party organizations would control campaign finance and would manage a national campaign on national issues. If the ultimate power to control nomination to Congress—to exact loyalty pledges in advance or to deprive the recalcitrant legislator of his seat—rested with the president and his national committee, then he, like the British prime minister, would have a virtually certain congressional majority in support of his program.

The propresidential reformers also propose many alterations in the internal dynamics of congressional operations, all intended to promote executive control and to reduce the ability of various minorities to block the movement of the president's program through Congress. Most importantly, these suggestions seek ways to curb the present independence and autonomy of congressional committees. One suggestion is to curb the powers of the panel chairman to enable a majority of committee members to control his behavior. Often proposed is a set of rules, carefully adhered to, that would permit the majority to call meetings, place items on the agenda, and bring matters to a vote even against opposition from the chairman. Some committee majorities do currently possess such powers, but they are often loath to use them in view of the chairman's available sanctions. If, however, the perquisites of the chairman—his ability to establish subcommittees and appoint their chairmen, and to manage staff and committee funds, for instance—were reduced, the rank and file should be more willing to challenge him. If the president could command a panel majority under such circumstances, he would be able to move his proposals through the congressional committees.

A second method of gaining control of the committees, and a more basic one in the view of those fostering executive supremacy, would be to ensure that the chairman continued to wield substantial authority, but did so as a party loyalist. This would, of course, require abandoning the selection of chairman by seniority, which guarantees that the majority party member of the committee with the longest continuous service on the panel automatically becomes its chairman. Indeed, the seniority custom (it was never a formal rule) has been weakened in principle if not in practice; it is now possible to place someone other than the most senior congressman in the committee chair, although it hasn't been done yet. By 1971, both parties in the House had decided that they could choose chairmen by criteria other than seniority; both empowered their party caucuses to vote on whether to accept the recommendations of the party committees-on-committees as to who should be the chairmen and ranking minority member of each panel.[34] A hint of change reached the Senate in 1973 when the Republicans adopted a proposal which had committee members electing the ranking member from among their own number without regard to seniority; no deviations from seniority in fact occurred when the new process began. Nonetheless, the breach in the seniority principle is likely to have considerable impact in the future. It will most certainly cause chairmen and ranking minority members to be more open to and solicitous of those who may vote to deprive them of their seats of power. It may also afford the president an opportunity to seek to remove from their positions senior lawmakers who oppose his legislative program.

Either way of curtailing committee autonomy—through placing a loyalist in the committee chair or through reducing the powers of the chairman over his panel—correspondingly elevates the legislative parties at the expense of individual power and local considerations. Reformers propose that party leaders should assume the role of "president's men" on Capitol Hill rather than act as legislative emissaries to the White House, as they do now. Party agencies should also be devoted to advancing the president's program. The caucus should control committee assignments, for example, rewarding the faithful and meting out punishments to the disloyal. Policy committees should be able to set forth party positions, subject to review and ratification by the full party membership, and in Congress should be empowered to schedule party-sponsored bills for prompt floor consideration. If parties were able to control the nominating process, these other changes might make them into powerful organizations capable of steering executive programs through the legislature.

The reformers seeking to speed executive policies down the congressional path would like to change the rules of procedure as well. Here, too, the goal is to remove the threats to administration programs posed by minorities, entrenched at particular veto points within the present decentralized system. In the House, the chief focus is the Rules Committee, and the major suggestion is to reinstitute and make permanent the twenty-one-day rule which permits the Speaker, over committee objections, to call up measures for floor consideration after the bill has been in committee for more than twenty-one days. The provision has proven successful in facilitating the movement of legislation to the floor on the two occasions on which it has been adopted, most recently during the 89th Congress (1965–66). But in each instance it did not survive renewed conservative strength and was stricken from the rules. Another proposed procedural change, applicable to all committees, would alter the discharge rule, by which a bill may be extracted from a recalcitrant committee. Needed at present are the signatures of 218 legislators, a majority of the full chamber; the suggestion is to reduce the requirement to some more readily attainable number, such as 150. Such changes would reduce the ability of the committees to block passage in the full chamber of measures favored by majorities, including presidentially-directed majorities.

On the Senate side, the reformers' main target is the obvious one: unlimited debate, the filibuster, and the cloture rule. They want to foreclose the possibility that extended debate will prevent a vote on a bill commanding majority support. To control debate, they suggest eliminating various dilatory tactics and distracting procedures,[35] leaving more time to deal with substantive legislation; limiting the amount of time any Senator can hold the floor; requring that debate be germane to the issue at hand; reducing the opportunity to mount a filibuster[36]; and, finally and most importantly, altering the cloture rule to allow a smaller majority—either 60 percent, or a simple majority (50 plus 1 percent) of those present and voting—to terminate debate. Each of these changes would curtail the ability of a minority to tie up the Senate to defeat specific bills.

One other potential presidential weapon is often discussed in this context: the item veto. Presently the chief executive must accept or reject a bill in toto; given an item veto he could strike out single provisions without having to reject an entire bill. Such a move would cancel one legislative strategy for asserting congressional initiatives, that of including a few items opposed by the chief executive in legislation containing major programs he favors, on the assumption that he will accept a few undesirable provisions rather than risk losing major matters of central concern.[37] Executive impoundment, the refusal to spend funds that Congress has appropriated, has been employed, especially by the Nixon administration, as a partial substitute for the item veto. The legislature has responded angrily and taken its case to the courts; although the Supreme Court has yet to rule on the issue, numerous lower court decisions have held the administration's practice to be unconstitutional.

All these suggestions, whether adopted wholly or in part, singly or in combination, would basically alter the position of Congress in the national political process: fragmentation of power would be diminished and centralization created; committee independence would be restricted, the parties strengthened, and the rules altered—all to permit executive leadership to carry the day. The executive would dominate national parties and, through them, the legislature. By controlling finances, the parties would control congressional nominations and legislative careers. Each party would nominate its presidential candidate, each would run on a clearly defined party platform, and the voters would select that program that best suited them. The victor would be virtually guaranteed a legislative majority to enact his policies; the centralized, party-managed Congress would do his bidding.

This scenario can be labeled a responsibility-accountability vision. Such arrangements would be responsible because, through them, effective solutions to pressing problems could be efficiently and promptly produced, and would be subject to accountability because the voters could replace a governing party with an opposition which persuasively claimed that it could do more and do it better.[38] The cost of all this, as noted would be loss of responsiveness. With Congress subordinate to executive-dominated political parties, the channels of communication by which many groups currently inform and influence the legislature would disappear or become mere formalities. Congress would not be able to respond to citizen and group sentiments or translate into policy major ideas that contradicted the majority party's platform. Citizens and interest groups would have to seek the president's ear. While he would no doubt have to calculate public reaction to his initiatives he would nevertheless have virtually unlimited authority to chart the country's course for four years (or six, if Richard Nixon's recent proposal for a single, six-year presidential term were to be adopted).

There is a second, less widely discussed, concept that focuses, to some extent at least, on responsibility—the congressional-supremacy position. It is the mirror image of the executive-dominance proposal. It seeks to establish Congress as the dominant force in national politics. Often called the "literary" or "whig" theory, it would have the legislature exercise all powers in all areas; the president, by contrast, would have considerably less initiative and would commit himself substantially to the execution of congressionally determined policies—efficient administration in keeping with legislative intent.[39]

To establish congressional supremacy would obviously require many reforms. One possibility would be to centralize legislative operations, in ways not unlike those proposed by proexecutive forces, but with the power relation with the White House reversed, so that Congress would call the shots rather than respond to presidential leadership. Yet in reality few critics, even those most favorably disposed toward Congress, have gone so far as to suggest that legislative dominance is desirable or even workable. Even members of Congress, understandably unsympathetic to subordinating the legislature to any branch, do not seek to master the executive. Rather those who hope for a resurgent Congress want only to redress the balance, to stem the historical flow of authority to the president, and to reassert the coequality of congressional perspectives. In short, the critics of executive dominance envision a situation in which governmental decision-making is responsive to the sorts of interests only Congress is capable of representing adequately.[40]

*Responsiveness.* The prolegislative reformers, while they do not seek to subordinate the executive, do value both responsiveness and congressional power. Their intent is to make the legislature a meaningful participant in policy formation, to put Congress in a position to assert its own priorities, even over executive opposition, without resort to excessive centralization. Their ideas, if implemented, would "democratize" the legislature; they would diffuse authority more widely than it is at present. Such developments would in turn intensify the current use of bargaining as a way of resolving conflict in Congress.[41] There would be more influence wielders to accommodate in any legislative settlement, and more access points necessitating additional communications channels for extra-legislative interests to use in urging their particular proposals on Congress.

Those who promote congressional responsiveness and power vis-a-vis the president share particular views on electoral politics and congressional structures and procedures. Procongressional forces stand firm against reapportionment and any effort to impose national, disciplined political parties. Indeed, the very "localism"— concern for local as opposed to national interests—deplored by believers in executive dominance is a positive virtue for the backers of legislative power. Reapportionment, even to reflect simple population equality, and the subscription to a national party's platform, compelled by the party's ability to inflict electoral defeat, would minimize the representation of diverse interests, especially those geographically dispersed or otherwise incapable of being represented on any basis determined by population.[42] Thus, it is desirable to have an election system not unlike the present one, in which each candidate is free to build his own organization, raise his own funds, take his own position on the issues, and appeal to whatever groups he deems appropriate; in this way the widest possible array of differing viewpoints will find expression in Congress.

With respect to the internal operations of Congress, those favoring legislative resurgence seem relatively well satisfied with existing arrangements, resisting efforts to reduce committee autonomy, to impose centralization by strengthening political parties, or to foster both objectives through changes in the rules. Thus, they oppose proposals to alter the seniority system or the basic powers of committee chairmen. Some recent changes in committee practice seem compatible with a concern for responsiveness. The impact of the enacted but thus far insignificant changes in the seniority practice are, as noted, ambiguous. It is true that the election of committee chairmen might provide an entering wedge for a disciplined majority to gain control of the panels. Such a result, however, seems unlikely unless chairmanship elections are linked to a general centralization of legislative authority, an improbable development. Therefore, under current conditions, modification of the seniority principle seems most likely to diffuse power further, to give majorities the ability to replace or control reluctant chairmen, and thus, to enhance responsiveness.

Similarly, recent changes in the process of assignment of Congressmen to committees seems, at first blush, to spread rather than concentrate influence in Congress. For some years, the so-called "Johnson Rule," initiated during Lyndon B. Johnson's tenure as majority leader, has guaranteed each Senator one major committee post before any colleague can receive a second choice assignment. In 1973, House Democrats took a step in this same direction; the party caucus formally divided the committees into "exclusive" panels (Appropriations, Rules, Ways and Means) whose members can serve on no other committee, "major" bodies to which each representative (except those on exclusive committees) will have one and only one assignment, and "minor" committees. These formulas go far toward providing every member with a place on a committee with jurisdiction over important legislative business. At the same time, however, the House Democratic Committee-on-Committees (actually composed of the party's Ways and Means delegation) began formally to include the party leadership—the Speaker, the majority leader, and the caucus chairman. While the leaders have always had some informal influence over the committee assignment process, they now have direct involvement. Such participation might but need not be a move toward centralization; it is unlikely that the leaders would seek to dominate the assignment process.[43] In short, committee assignments at present seem to contribute to diffusion of legislative authority and thus to the Congress' responsiveness.

The pro-Congress reformers see possibilities for strengthening the committees, in general and relative to the executive, without impairing their autonomy. More and better staff resources and increased information will help the panels formulate and promote alternative programs. More professional staff, capable of sophisticated research and analysis, would strengthen the committees' policy-making ability. Providing the minority with its own independent staff would allow it to state its differences with the majority more clearly and persuasively.[44] Similarly, improved committee procedures—more open, less carefully stage-managed hearings; increased opportunity for deliberation; reduced constraints on rank-and-file members' participation—should permit airing of additional points of view. More useful reports might grow out of improved hearings and extended consideration and, in turn, if circulated to the full chambers well in advance of floor treatment, might help to raise the quality of debate. Such changes in committee practice, promoting wider participation and fuller discussion, could make Congress more responsive and more effective in opposing the executive.

Concomitantly, the congressionalists' faith in open, autonomous committees leads to a distrust of centralized political parties and resistance to means designed to achieve them. Such things as strengthened party caucuses or policy committees would reduce the chance for various interests out of favor with party leaders to be heard or to exert influence; centralized parties might move too quickly, running roughshod over minorities deserving of a say. Accordingly, congressionalists want the political parties in Congress to remain loose confederations that do little more than facilitate legislative organization. The recent enlargement of the Senate Democrats' steering committee, which makes committee assignments, could cut in either direction: it might permit other points of view to be heard in the assignment process, or, if the new members supported the leadership—the majority leader chairs the steering committee—it might give the party additional control.[45] In general, however, few congressmen seem anxious to yield their cherished independence to the political parties.

Similarly, the pro-Congress forces seem as satisfied with the basic procedural and structural organization of the legislature as they are with autonomous committees and weak political parties. To be sure, they would prefer fuller debate in the House of Representatives and more unrestricted opportunity to propose amendments; such changes would permit a wider range of views to find expression. But they resist reform that might alter the fundamental character of Congress, opposing changes in Rules Committee power in the House or the rule of unlimited debate in the Senate that might mute minority voices or restrain minority power. The rules should, from their point of view, continue to protect decentralization of authority; current practice enhances responsiveness.

Simultaneously, without fundamental change in legislative organization or procedure, the pro-Congress reforms seek to reassert legislative prerogatives in the face of what they see as a dramatic shift toward presidential domination of policy-making. The problem is particularly acute in foreign affairs where legislative supremacists have long sought to redress the imbalance of power between the branches; in 1954 they came within a single vote of achieving the two-thirds majority in the Senate necessary to pass the so-called Bricker Amendment to the Constitution. The proposal was designed to limit presidential discretion in foreign affairs; to curb the practice of making arrangements with foreign countries through executive agreement, which bypass the Senate's right to give advice and, especially, consent to treaties.[46]

These efforts, though following a somewhat different tack, reached fruition in 1973. Frustrated by a general inability to influence the conduct of the Indochina War significantly and emboldened by the Nixon administration's Watergate embarrassments, Congress passed, over a presidential veto, a War Powers bill, limiting to sixty days the chief executive's authority to commit military forces to combat without explicit congressional approval. Such legislation surely reestablishes Congress as a force to reckon with in military affairs, though it is not at all certain that the legislature would actually seek to cancel military action that a president asserted to be in the "national interest."

Budgetary reform is a second area in which the legislature has sought to reassert its authority and increase its capacity to influence policy. Impartial observers as well as critics agree that Congress has failed to exercise its power of the purse effectively. Consequently, the president has justified impounding appropriated funds as necessary to sustain fiscal responsibility. If Congress is to reclaim effective participation in budget making, reform is essential; to improve the quality of its financial decisions, the legislature must equip itself to make those decisions wisely.[47]

Under present procedures, the president submits a single unified budget, but Congress, through its Appropriations committees, splits the program into a dozen or more bills which are given separate, unrelated treatment. At no point does the interested lawmaker have occasion to see how the total budget looks and to compare total proposed expenditures with available revenue.[48] Rather, the full picture is not visible until all appropriations measures have been passed; the last bills in the series become major targets for reduction as the sums already committed begin to mount. What is cut at one point can, of course, be restored later in supplemental appropriations bills, an opportunity that may encourage cuts for partisan effect, since such reductions need not permanently impair desirable programs. What is needed—to reduce Congress' competitive disadvantage when facing executive experts in the narrow confines of the latter's specialization and to give the legislature the opportunity to set its own spending priorities—is to coordinate, centralize to some degree, the congressional consideration of the budget.

Recognizing the need to put its houses in order, Congress created a Joint Study Committee on Budget Control in 1972 and, in the following year, that panel recommended legislation intended to restore parity between congressional power and executive influence. This proposal, enacted in 1974, creates special budget committees in the House and Senate, a single joint staff, and a congressional budget office composed of skilled experts well-versed in the use of computers. The committees are to report out a resolution, on which the full chambers would have to pass and eventually agree, setting an overall ceiling on federal spending and defining the maximum that could be spent within various subareas of the budget. A reconciling resolution would be passed, if needed, to cover any altered circumstances that might develop; a tax surcharge could be considered at the end of a fiscal year to make up any deficits that might occur. When fully implemented in 1976, the new provisions will make Congress able to match the executive branch Office of Management and Budget in expertise and, thus, to set its own spending priorities confidently. The president might disagree with congressional allocations and conflict would surely follow, but the struggle would be fought on terrain more favorable to Congress than any in recent years.[49]

But this sort of change may not offer a gain in responsiveness. On one hand, such reforms may enable the congressional point of view to prevail against the president's in the allocation of funds; legislative decisions, as responsive choices, might well reflect sentiments other than the executive's. On the other hand, the reformed budgetary process may cut into the power of the congressional committees. The substantive panels should remain open and responsive since they will continue to authorize funds through a process of negotiation, but they may be seriously constrained by the overall spending ceilings imposed by the new budget committee. That is, they will have to bargain about a limited sum and can not accommodate multiple interests simply by increasing the total funds allocated. The most responsive sort of bill, the "something-for-everyone" logrolling type, should be severely restricted. In sum, the new budgetary system should strengthen Congress as a whole in its struggle with the executive, should make the ultimate outcomes more responsive to congressional preferences, but at the same time may lead to internal centralization with the new budget committees exercising authority now held by the standing committees and subcommittees.

The reservations of some congressmen, particularly as reflected in the unwillingness of the committees to yield any of their budgetary authority, has led Congress to move against the executive practice, increasingly used in recent years, of impounding monies Congress has authorized and appropriated. The 1974 Budget Reform Act also includes provisions designed to curb the president's ability to impound funds. If the chief executive defers spending, either house can compel expenditure of the funds by passing a resolution to that effect. If the president seeks to terminate programs or reduce total spending, he must persuade both houses to rescind the previously-enacted appropriation within forty-five days; if the chambers do not act, he must spend the funds.[50] Such legislation should enable Congress to assert its own spending priorities and diminish the countervailing executive power to spend selectively.

Most legislative supremacists see additional possibilities for strengthening Congress. As the previous discussion indicates, the lawmakers could profit from better staff and more information. Increased staffing has much to recommend it. Additional manpower could generate and analyze new data; the lawmaker would get careful research support, based on reliable information. Members of the House might gain from having available a specifically designated legislative assistant comparable to that provided senators. In general, more aid might improve both the lawmakers' ability to act rationally and to confront executive branch specialists.

Yet enlarged staffs, however attractive in theory might not in practice enable the legislature to challenge the president more meaningfully; indeed, some skeptics hold that additional staff would create additional burdens rather than alleviate present ones. More employees might discover new areas for attention and so create new demands on the already overcommitted time and energies of legislators. Too large a staff might convert a lawmaker into an office manager, to the detriment of his policy-making tasks. Without proper supervision, staffers, especially investigators, might be tempted to engage in unrestrained partisanship and to neglect data-gathering, idea-generating duties.

A second and related set of proposals seeks to improve the quantity and the quality of information available to Congress. Insufficient and unreliable data often make it difficult for legislators to oppose bureaucratic experts; the congressmen may feel obliged to defer to the specialists. Executive privilege—by which the president can, in the "national interest," decide to withhold information from Congress—and national defense requirements limit the data available. Interbranch competition and suspicion lead executive personnel to enlarge the areas in which they feel they must not release information. Moreover, the executive is able to put its own construction on events in a way that minimizes legislative opportunity to advance alternative proposals: the executive briefs the press and other mass media in "off-the-record" or "not-for-attribution" sessions, releasing only that information it deems advisable to reveal, interpreting what it does make available to suit its own purposes. In addition, news, appropriately structured, can be "leaked" to the media.

Beyond this dependence on the executive as the source for data, however incomplete or slanted, the nature of Congress itself contributes to the legislature's information deficit. A decentralized institution with numerous centers of autonomous power, each with lines to different information sources, leads to data being fragmentary, uncoordinated, or often unavailable; data are collected in one place, for one set of purposes, and simply not made accessible to other congressmen in other locations with other purposes in mind. These problems contribute to placing the individual lawmaker in a situation where he must often make decisions on complex and controversial issues with minimal information, less even than he might get with a modicum of difficulty, less certainly than he would need to decide with some acceptable degree of "rationality."[51]

Two sets of proposals to remedy this grave defect in congressional deliberation and decision-making have emerged. The first and most pragmatic seeks to remove current impediments to gaining information and to expand the presently available data sources. For one thing, Congress has begun to move against the "executive privilege" doctrine, seemingly stimulated by the Nixon administration's aggressive use of the notion[52] and especially by the furor over the Watergate tapes and other executive documents. Legislation is pending that would restrict and regularize the use of executive privilege. If enacted, the law would require executive personnel to appear on demand before legislative committees, if only to claim the privilege; would require a formal, written presidential statement to invoke the privilege; and would enforce the request for information by mandating an automatic cutoff of funds for a noncomplying agency. Such a bill would place the burden on the executive to justify withholding information from Congress.[53]

In the meantime, other steps are possible. Additional staff—for individual members or for committees—for research purposes would help produce additional data. More funds for existing agencies such as the Legislative Reference Service of the Library of Congress or the General Accounting Office would enable them to investigate on more fronts and with greater depth and diligence. Learning experiences for legislators—foreign travel, visits to federal installations, time to read and money to buy books, for example—might be provided. Extended use of outside consultants or congressionally created task forces, comparable to those that the president has employed for many years, has been suggested, as has the establishment of a "congressional institute of scholars" or some similar "university-type organization."[54] All such ideas seek to enlarge the assistance in data-gathering and interpreting available to the lawmakers.

Far more basic, and seemingly considerably more promising in the long run, is a second set of proposals urging Congress to harness computerized information-storage and retrieval systems for legislative purposes. Such techniques may be necessary simply to stay abreast of the executive, notably the Defense Department, which has pioneered use of electronic equipment in making policy. Adjustment to the new technology thus may well be imperative if Congress is to survive; without adaptation in this sphere, the legislature may find its information deficit too severe ever to make up. A relatively simple and inexpensive congressional information-processing system is by no means out of reach.[55] With little difficulty, each lawmaker could have on his desk a terminal, linked to a central computer, that he could use as he chooses to call for information on topics of interest to him. It is important that the legislator be able to choose what he wants to know; his freedom to specialize, to follow his own inclinations, would not then be impaired; he would run little risk of being overwhelmed by information useless to him. His options, dictated by political and value considerations, would remain open; the information system would be the lawmaker's servant, not in any sense his master.

Information storage and retrieval of this type could aid congressional policy-making in numerous ways. For instance, the often arduous task of discovering the existence, content, and location of bills of interest could be vastly simplified. A "legislative history" could be complied and stored in the computer; at any time a lawmaker could get an up-to-date status report on any measure. He could avoid being caught off guard, work up his own position before he had to act, and reduce his dependence on word-of-mouth assurances from experts, party colleagues, or house leaders. He would be in a far better position to interject his own views into congressional deliberations. Computerized information retrieval might also provide data on lobbyists (who they are, whom they represent, what legislation they are interested in, where to reach them, and so forth); on actions taken by the executive branch; on the results of studies undertaken by the Legislative Reference Service, the General Accounting Office, or the various committee staffs; or on the contents of present law. The ready availability of information, from these and other sources, would enable congressmen to make policy choices based on considerably more data than now seem to enter their calculations.

In all these ways, then, Congress can be strengthened relative to the executive. Through passage of the War Powers bill, it has begun to reassert its control over foreign affairs. Budgetary reform, especially if linked to improved information resources, should permit the legislature to take full advantage of its power of the purse to impose its own financial priorities. In the long run, creation of new resources—expert staffs and better information—may prove more fundamental in permitting Congress to have its way, even in the face of stiff executive opposition. Increased legislative power, reflecting views that differ from those of the executive, would obviously contribute to a more responsive policy-making process.[56]

The vision of the pro-Congress reformers, in sum, consists of a decentralized, responsive legislature capable of determining public policy and making its choices stick against executive opposition. A resurgent Congress could, as a responsive institution, listen to a diversity of interests and blend them more or less harmoniously into legislatively determined programs that would compete on equal terms with executive preferences. Such competition, the interplay of roughly equal branches of government, should enhance the responsiveness of the entire policy process.

The realization of such a vision, should it ever come to pass, would of course, be at the expense of responsibility. The more Congress is capable of frustrating the president, the greater the possibility of deadlock, The greater the need to reach agreements through bargaining, whether within the legislature or between Congress and the executive, the less likely it is that the resulting policy will be bold or imaginative. Moreover, the greater the number of interests that any policy settlement must accommodate, the greater the possibility that any decision will be slow in coming. Thus, a fully responsive process, open to all points of view and marked by multiple channels of communication, might produce policy of the "too little, too late" variety, overtaken by events and outstripped by history.

*Accountability.* Whether executive or legislative supremacy seems preferable, accountability—the opportunity for the governed to pass judgment on the performance of those who govern—remains desirable, complementing either responsibility or responsiveness. As noted earlier, accountability sustains responsibility in a straightforward fashion. The electorate chooses between two political parties and in so doing gives the winner both a mandate to govern and the majority to do so. The voters subsequently decide, based upon their assessment of the "ins' " performance, whether to renew that mandate or to place the "outs" in office. Their retrospective evaluation constitutes the chief check on administration behavior; unless the citizenry is prepared and able to hold its rulers accountable, the power of the government becomes virtually unlimited and unchecked.

Where responsiveness is the central concern, accountability seems both more difficult and, perhaps, less critical. A decentralized system is certainly harder for the voter to fathom; if things go badly it is more difficult to know whom to blame when the fateful decisions somehow emerged from elaborate bargaining at multiple stages of a complex process involving multiple participants. The voter must pay far more attention to be able to pin down who did what in circumstances where many participants may have had some impact on the eventual outcome. At the same time, however, where communications channels are open, citizens have possibilities beyond holding legislators accountable for completed actions. The citizen can do more than judge *ex post facto;* he can, if he chooses, use whatever access is available to him, as an individual or as a group member, to shape the outcome in advance. Thus, accountability, which remains desirable, is not the only mechanism of control; rather it is another way in which the electorate can seek to set national directions.

In either case, accountability provides a device by which the ruled can manage those whom they select to rule them, and steps have been proposed to remedy the defects, noted above, in the process. A first condition for accountability is that the citizen be aware of his representative's performance, and several steps could be taken to help generate more information about Congress, though not all of them are within the power of the legislature to take. For one thing, the mass media could provide additional congressional coverage. Admittedly, it will be difficult to endow a 535-member, two-chamber institution with the glamorous aura which automatically attaches to a single chief executive, but television and the press could do a better job. They could, if they choose to do so, give the kind of coverage accorded to the Senate Watergate and the House Judiciary Committee impeachment hearings to other important matters, for example, the details of the War Powers or anti-impoundment bills.[57] As matters stand currently, only the most dramatic events are covered and then only in the most nationally oriented press, like *The New York Times* or *The Washington Post.*

Congress can neither compel media attention nor alter its own fundamental modus operandi to accommodate media coverage, but it can, at the margins at least, make the media's task somewhat simpler. The legislature can act to expose more of its complex decision-making process to media investigation and so ultimately to public scrutiny. Much legislative activity, often the critical decisions, occurs in private, shrouded in secrecy, both in committee and on the floor. Committee meetings are often closed to the public; on the average one-third are closed sessions. Floor proceedings are often hard to follow. Obviously such secrecy, however much it may facilitate bargaining and negotiation, does little to let the alert citizen detect who does what in Congress.

Recognizing that there is merit to these charges, Congress has taken some steps to lift the curtain of secrecy. The Legislative Reorganization Act of 1970 included a provision granting permission to televise, broadcast, and photograph committee hearings at the discretion of the individual panels; the provision makes possible but does not guarantee broad coverage of hearings. In 1973, an additional step was taken concerning regular committee meetings. The House decided to mandate that all committee sessions be open unless a majority of the panel voted, in advance or at the time of scheduled meetings, to close them. At the same time, the Senate refused to go even that far; it narrowly voted down a similar proposal. Instead, the upper chamber granted each committee the freedom to establish its own rules regarding secrecy, thus putting the burden on those who would open meetings rather than on those who prefer secret sessions. The 1970 act also required the recording and publication of members' votes in committee; under the old rules only vote totals, not the stands of single members, were made public. Exposing committee voting makes more difficult the strategy that tempts some congressmen, of taking both sides of a question, one in the privacy of committee and another in public. So Congress has moved to lift the shroud surrounding committee deliberations, but it has, for the most part, reserved the opportunity to continue to meet in private when the members deem it necessary to do so.

Another step has been taken that promises to shed light on congressional operations at the floor consideration stage. Before the 1970 Reorganization Act, under certain circumstances no votes were recorded during House floor debate and decision; there could be voice, standing or unrecorded teller votes,[58] but in each instance the positions of individual legislators remained unrecorded. The act included a provision that, if twenty House members demand it, the names of those participating in teller votes must be listed as they walk up the aisles. Again, since teller votes may be decisive, especially on critical amendments on which no formal roll call vote will occur later, the reform both makes it difficult for lawmakers to hedge by taking contradictory positions at different stages of the legislative process and makes individual actions somewhat more visible to attentive correspondents and interested citizens.

Secondly, accountability requires informed, interested citizens capable of matching their own views with those of their representatives and willing to cast their vote on the basis of how the two match. Little direct reform is possible, but some current trends seem promising. Evidence from sample surveys shows that the better educated tend to be more aware of, concerned about, and knowledgeable about political affairs. Since educational levels are rising across the nation, there are more and more citizens potentially able to exercise accountability. If these voters have the benefit of better media coverage of a less secretive Congress, they may evaluate the legislature more carefully and may be able to make their electoral choices with fuller knowledge of the available policy alternatives.

Providing clear choices among candidates within single states or districts, the third prerequisite for effectively holding Congress accountable, is more problematic; little can be done to guarantee voters a choice between ideologically distinct nominees. Under an order emphasizing responsibility, this would be unnecessary: the individual candidates would be beholden to the centralized parties and the voter would merely have to form judgment as to the desirability of retaining the incumbent party. In an order emphasizing responsiveness, the parties would remain decentralized and the availability in any constituency of an opposition candidate whose policies were clearly distinguishable from those of the incumbent would depend on the uncertain operation of nominating politics in many districts.

Accountability, in short, will not easily be improved. However much the observer may wish for more media attention to Congress or for more citizen concern with the legislature and the issues it confronts, there is not much the reformer can do in those areas. About all that is possible, and Congress has moved a few steps in this direction, is to make sure that those who wish to inform themselves are not thwarted by unnecessary secrecy in the legislative branch. Greater numbers of interested citizens attuned to a more visible Congress give rise to the hope that accountability will be exercised more intelligently and, thus, more meaningfully in the years ahead.[59]

To summarize this long section: Two differing and to a degree incompatible perspectives characterize those who seek to reform Congress. On the one hand, those who put high premium on prompt, efficient solutions to policy problems seek to move toward a more centralized legislature. They are prepared to sacrifice openness and multiple channels of communication—responsiveness—in favor of effective confrontation of policy issues—responsibility. They propose numerous reforms, outlined above, and they are prepared to rely upon citizen-enforced accountability to keep the powerful executive on the track. On the other side are those equally committed to reform, who place the ultimate value on a free, open deliberative process and are prepared to endure for the sake of responsiveness a decentralized scheme of things, seemingly irresponsible, which reaches decisions only slowly and after considerable negotiation and compromise. They, too, propose a variety of reforms intended to achieve their purposes—as noted above—and they rely less on accountability after the fact, though they do not oppose it, than on the ability of citizens, individually or in organized groups, to present their views before policy formulation is completed. There is, of course, no way to choose definitively or empirically between these alternative visions of Congress; the choice ultimately must rest on the relative weight any observer assigns to the competing values of responsibility and responsiveness.

## Toward Majoritarian
## Democracy in Congress

These alternative visions are, of course, in a sense, straw men. The description of the reform proposals designed to move Congress toward greater responsibility or toward enlarged responsiveness is not intended to represent full blown, widely shared visions of a better political order; rather it is intended to represent tendencies to see either a strengthened executive or a revitalized Congress as most likely to bring about the sort of political system that particular reformers value. There remains, however, considerable dispute over the wisdom and desirability of specific changes within those general reforms and tendencies. It is unlikely that widespread agreement on any basic package of fundamental reforms will develop. Change is more likely to come, as in the past, incrementally in response to specific crises or particular problems.

In this spirit, the concluding section of this essay advances a vision of a congressional future—called for want of a better term "majoritarian democracy." These proposals could be adopted in an ad hoc fashion, but considered as a whole, they offer a useful "mix" of responsibility and responsiveness, a balance between the twin needs for deliberation and decisiveness. This modest proposal may satisfy no one; it may picture a policy-making process too slow to be responsible, too centralized to be responsive. Yet it seems clear that no fully responsible *and* responsive political order is possible. About all that can be sought, and this is the intention here, is to maximize both values.

Such a mixed pattern seems desirable because neither the proexecutive nor the legislative supremacy positions seems tenable. The supreme executive notion seems, in the wake of Watergate, to have grown out of a misplaced faith, a nâivete perhaps, in the inherent goodness of the presidency. In the 1950s it may well have been reasonable to assume, given the nature of the political forces then operating, that only the chief executive would pursue policies of internationalism in foreign affairs and "liberalism" on the domestic scene. Events of the past decade seem to have disposed of such a vision of executive nobility. The "peace candidate" of 1964 enmeshed the nation in a long, costly, bloody and, in the view of many, meaningless war in Southeast Asia, and his actions made it impossible for him to seek reelection.[60] His successor, following a "secret plan" so convoluted in practice as to defy the belief it could have been conceived in advance, greatly reduced American presence in Indochina, but found it necessary in so doing to turn back congressional initiatives for more than four years and to deceive both the legislature and the public by concealing more than 3,600 bombing sorties over Laos and Cambodia, supposedly neutral nations.

Domestically, the Watergate revelations, leading to the unprecedented resignation of the president, dramatically focused attention on the deliberate efforts of the executive to enhance its position vis-a-vis other parts of government, all in support of policies opposed by the liberal adherents of strong presidential government. The Nixon White House moved against Congress, pushing broad definitions of impoundment prerogatives and executive privilege. It set up, and revoked after only five days, a domestic surveillance unit, authorized to engage in illegal acts.[61] It created the now-famous plumbers to close leaks in the administration's information system; it moved to politicize the CIA and FBI. The Committee to Reelect the President, a White House appendage, bugged the Democratic National Committee headquarters and engaged in many seemingly illegal activities in campaign finance. Paradoxically, a conservative president, eager to reverse the growth of national power, anxious to reduce the scope of federal activity, moved unilaterally to strengthen his own ability to bring about his desired results. Liberals have found that they do not approve this use of executive supremacy; it appears doubtful that conservatives would appreciate such strength in the hands of a future liberal president. Thus, no matter whose political ox is being or may be gored, there seems good reason to avoid an undue concentration of authority in the executive's hands.[62]

Yet the arguments for congressional supremacy are no more promising or appealing. Neither a highly centralized Congress, independent of the president and capable of responsible action, nor a largely fragmented institution, totally responsive, presents a compelling vision. The former possibility seems both unrealistic—there are so many subjects that not all can be handled with dispatch—and undesirable—the same arguments that apply to a powerful presidency militate against a concentration of authority in the legislature. Dismantling the federal establishment, to permit easier congressional dominance, seems impractical. There exist too many programs, each with its own clientele, to permit easy termination; in addition, it is by no means certain that state and local governments could easily take on such burdens should they be devolved upon the federal system. The second formulation, the open institution with minorities protected at every stage of the decision-making process, recalls the sort of paralysis, the *immobilisme,* that crippled and eventually brought down the French Fourth Republic.

The situation, quite clearly, seems to demand some combination of features that maximizes both responsibility and responsiveness. What follows is one vision of such a combination, a view that proposes to wed an open, responsive deliberative stage of legislative policy making to a more decisive, responsible decision taking phase. The former is democratic and seeks to open avenues of participation for all, inside and outside Congress; the latter is majoritarian and endeavors to permit majorities, given sufficient time to form, to carry the day at the point of decision.

Before turning to the specifics of the majoritarian democracy view, I want to make it clear that what follows is in no way intended to minimize the importance of popular accountability which remains highly desirable. As discussed above, the media should be encouraged to cover Congress fully and at length, and the legislature should follow up on the recent measures that have begun to reduce congressional secrecy.[63] Any or all such steps would increase the attentive citizen's chances to discover what Congress in general and his own representatives in particular are doing. There is not much to be done to promote clear electoral choices; short of some form of centralization under executive domination, there is little likelihood that the fragmented, seemingly incoherent electoral patterns, with each race virtually distinct from every other contest, can or will be altered. At least candidates can be pressed to present their views with some specificity, enabling the watchful, issue-oriented voter to cast his ballot intelligently. In any event, greater openness in Congress and awareness among the electorate should alert legislators that what they do in Washington is observable "back home" and may have an impact on their political futures. And from the electorate's vantage point, the greater the possibilities for a meaningful accountability, the stronger the likelihood that the rulers will make more careful calculations about the desires of the citizenry. In either case, the linkage between represented and representative will be tightened and popular control of public policy will become more a reality.

Moreover, under majoritarian democracy, accountability is

only one avenue of popular involvement. During the earlier stages of lawmaking, when the policy process should be most responsive, citizens should have free and available channels of communications to present their views. They can both suggest to Congress what should be done and, later, in the polling booth, render a verdict about what was actually undertaken. To facilitate access, many changes suggested by prolegislative reformers seem worthwhile. In general, these proposals are intended to democratize Congress, to open the way for as many legislators as possible, representing the widest diversity of interests, to achieve some influence and to offer access to extra-legislative groups.

Specifically, this view favors a moderately paced deliberative stage, during which all interested parties can be heard; the chief goal is openness and accessibility. This means basically an unaltered electoral system: equitable apportionment based on districts about equal in population is desirable; campaign reform measures, spawned by the Watergate abuses, that entrench incumbents are not. The electoral process should operate to allow the widest possible latitude for candidates of differing views, speaking for local interests, voicing diverging concerns, to win places in Congress. Current practice, with its "localism," its constituency-based, individualized campaigns, should continue to operate.

Internally, the deliberative stage, if it is to be responsive, must also promote the extended presentation of multiple points of view. Such a goal entails a number of steps at the committee level. Committees would continue to be autonomous and specialized, and members should be assigned to ones where they could best serve their constituencies, represent their states and districts. Such changes as the Senate's "Johnson Rule" and the limitations on subcommittee chairmanships in the House serve to diffuse power, to create greater opportunities for junior legislators to achieve positions of some significance. More important, perhaps, and at variance with more commonly proposed reforms, committee responsiveness could be extended by instituting rules guaranteeing that the panel majority could firmly control the conduct of committee business. Under such conditions there would be less need to eliminate seniority as the basis for selecting chairmen; it is not the rule that is at the root of most complaints, but rather that the system automatically elevates the most senior majority member to a very powerful position. If the chairman was more the presiding officer, less the decisive force, the real virtue of seniority—the automatic, noncompetitive character of the choice of chairmen—might be preserved.

Such democratically governed legislative committees could perform more effectively and consider the available options more fully if information and research resources were enlarged. Extra staff, but not so many that the congressman becomes an office manager rather than a policymaker, seems likely to help; enlarged minority staff would certainly aid in ventilating additional points of view. So, too, would the creation and use of a computerized information retrieval system; legislators would be able to generate and sustain their own policy proposals to an extent impossible under present conditions. Finally, more open committee hearings—scheduled well in advance; with ample notice given to potential witnesses; and importantly with the less well organized interests invited, encouraged, and perhaps even subsidized to appear—would contribute to responsiveness.

In short, the majoritarian democracy proposal envisons that the fragmented congressional decision process will continue, with the work divided among independent, specialized committees, each deferring to others in their areas of competence. The reforms, suggested above, are designed to make sure that the widest possible range of opinion finds its way into legislative deliberations. Political parties will, likewise, continue to be substantially nonideological facilitators of organization and election. Under such conditions, legislative committees—composed of expert and well-informed lawmakers, adequately staffed, and open to the views of all interested parties—should generate responsive policy.

Such legislation, however responsive the process by which it is formulated, must have a chance not only to pass Congress but also to survive executive branch opposition. Otherwise the legislative process would be an exercise in futility, appealing only to conservative elements that take responsiveness as a means for guaranteeing inaction. Unless the national legislature can act and act in ways that do resolve problems, it is unlikely ever to serve as an effective counterweight to executive authority. Action on two fronts would be useful: internal change to permit majorities to act and statutory restraints on presidential power.

On the first front, a number of internal roadblocks should be removed, among them procedural devices that serve to protect minorities, to slow down or block entirely congressional action. The intent is to let majorities carry the day more easily than at present; what the responsive deliberative phase has produced should be voted up or down with a minimum of delay. In the House of Representatives several reforms would help guarantee greater dispatch in dealing with committee recommendations. Over-long consideration of proposals, often indulged in mainly to bury the legislation permanently, could be avoided by a more usable discharge rule; after sufficient time had elapsed for full study and deliberation, say 90 or 120 days, a discharge petition bearing 150 signatures (rather than the 218 now required) would enable bills to move to the floor for a vote.[64] A similar change in the powers of the Rules committee would be in order; most observers recognize the need for a traffic cop to regulate the flow of floor business, but trouble develops when Rules is able to block bills that the substantive committees wish to send to the floor. As a remedy, permanent adoption of the Twenty-one-day rule, twice enacted previously and twice subsequently dropped, would enable the standing committees to guarantee the full chamber a chance to pass on reported legislation; Rules could only interpose a three week delay in floor treatment. Other minor changes aimed at eliminating the use of dilatory tactics—excessive quorum calls, reading the *Journal* in full, and so on—would make marginal improvements in the House's ability, already far superior to that of the Senate, to deal decisively with pending bills.

In the upper chamber, the major target for reform is, of course, the filibuster. To ensure majority rule, Senate debate must be curtailed, and the most obvious cure is to ease the task of imposing cloture. This would entail eliminating the "morning hour," making debate germane and focused, and limiting the opportunity for filibusters—all moving the floor proceedings more quickly toward a decision. At such a point, more importantly, the "ayes" should have it if they have the votes, and the simplest way to bring this about would be to permit debate to be ended by a simple majority of those present and voting (rather than the extraordinary two-thirds majority presently necessary). Such changes, like those proposed for the House—would increase the likelihood that determined majorities could carry the Senate on behalf of the bills they favored.[65]

These bills would, of course, have to survive encounter with the president who could still veto measures and who would prevail in any confrontation unless Congress could muster a two-thirds majority in each house to override the veto. Still, there are reforms that would enhance the competitive position of the legislature and budgetary reform is the most important of them. Until Congress puts its fiscal house in order, its authority to set national priorities will remain suspect, perhaps fatally so. Unless Congress makes some concerted effort to balance income and expenditures and to justify its actions in raising and allocating revenue, the president will have the advantage in credibility when he challenges its decisions. The Budget Reform Act, if effective when fully implemented, is promising, but it does involve some costs.[66] A congressionally determined spending ceiling in line with anticipated revenue, and congressional allocation of that overall sum to various budgetary categories—all prepared with the help of substantially improved staff and information resources—should make the legislative budget a serious alternative to that of the executive.

Beyond the budget, Congress has been flirting, seriously for the first time, with many other devices to arrest the drift of policy making power to the president. Anti-impoundment legislation, requiring the executive to release funds unless the legislature agrees to his action, may enable congressional fiscal priorities to prevail if Congress wishes. Anti-executive privilege legislation, defining and regularizing the claim of privilege and compelling agencies to divulge needed information, would reduce the information deficiency under which Congress operates. The recently enacted War Powers legislation, delimiting the president's authority to commit military forces in "undeclared wars" or "police actions" without legislative approval, should restore some congressional voice to the determination of foreign policy. All these laws could help to redress the executive-legislative imbalance of power in the favor of Congress and make both branches forces to reckon with.

These changes, statutory and structural, however much they would strenghen Congress against the president, are not enough to create the kind of majoritarian democratic institution we are discussing. More subtle change, more difficult to achieve, is required: Congress must enhance its reputation as a body committed to national rather than local interests, as an institution of unquestioned integrity, able to rise above "politics as usual" to make contributions to the national welfare equal if not superior to those of the executive. Congress suffers in this regard, for it is now seen more as an append-age than as a rival of the president. When the public holds the chief executive in high esteem, it values the legislature as well; when his prestige falls, so does that of Congress.[67]

To gain public approval in its own right, competing for the attention naturally focused on the president as one person able to act dramatically and swiftly, will not be easy for the plural legisla-ture. Yet some of the possibilities for change outlined above would help. More media attention, less internal secrecy, more forceful ad-vocacy of congressional views in policy making would give citizens more of a sense of the legislature; importance in the political land-scape.

Another cause of public skepticism is a sense that lawmakers are sometimes less than entirely ethical; there have been proposals to ensure that they are as free as possible from conflicts of interest and that their actions are intended to advance the public good rather than their own financial positions. The increasing number of cases publicized of legislators engaging in illegal or unethical actions in the past decade has heightened the concern over ethics. Unless doubts about congressmen's self-serving behavior are removed, Con-gress' reputation and popular support will be eroded.

The pressures of legislative life constantly raise the ethics issue. On one hand, the citizens want their elected representatives to be beyond reproach. On the other hand, to put it bluntly, legislators need money. They must engage in virtually continuous campaigning, which is costly; some maintain residences both in their constituency and in Washington; others are caught up in the demanding and expensive social life of the capital. In addition, the lawmaking task itself creates difficulties. The notion that Congress should stay in touch with the populace requires the lawmakers to listen to the requests and importunings of many groups and organizations. It is not surprising that special interests seek to exploit this access for their own goals; in so doing they may sometimes offer inducements that fall between outright corruption—graft and bribery—and the understandable need of legislators to earn outside income.

In recent years, there have been criminal indictments against several legislators for illegal acts committed while in office. Ex-Senator Daniel Brewster (D., Md.), former House members Thomas Johnson (D., Md.), John Dowdy (D., Tex.), J. Irwin Whalley (R., Pa.), and Representative Bertram Podell (D., N. Y.) have been indicted for or convicted of corrupt practices. The Senate censured Thomas Dodd (D., Conn.) for misuse of campaign funds in 1967; the House excluded Adam Clayton Powell (D., N. Y.) following a series of legal problems, including his refusal to pay a libel judgment against him; and, in 1973 Representative William O. Mills (R., Md.) committed suicide after the publication of reports that he had received an illegal $25,000 cash contribution to his campaign. Far more pervasive, however, than these dramatic events are conflicts of interest, where a lawmaker renders judgments on matters in which he has a personal stake. How is the public to regard Congress when Rep. Robert T. Watkins (R., Pa.), with a personal interest in the trucking business, sits on the House Commerce Committee which has jurisdiction over the laws and the agency, the Interstate Commerce Commission, which regulate truckers? What should people think when Senator George Murphy (R., Calif.) receives a $20,000 annual retainer, a travel credit card, and half the rent on his apartment from a major corporation as compensation for "public relations" work?[68]

Such questions, asked more frequently of late, have encouraged Congress to act to raise its own standards of conduct. Each chamber now has a Select Committee on Standards and Conduct charged with policing the ethics of its members; but according to critics neither has accomplished much, lacking both incentive and enforcement powers to act effectively. There also exists a set of conflict-of-interest statutes, last revised in 1962, which outlaw bribery and corruption, proscribe compensation for appearances by legislators before federal agencies, ban direct contacts between congressmen as advocates and government, and prohibit receiving salary as direct compensation from an outside source for services rendered. Finally, there is also on the books a set of financial disclosure requirements intended to reveal the lawmakers' major sources of outside income and so to indicate potential conflicts of interest. These somewhat limited statutes do enable the interested citizen to discover some, but not all, of the potential conflicts of interest under which national lawmakers work.[69]

To be held in high regard, especially in the suspicious Watergate era, Congress should be, in Dwight Eisenhower's pithy phrase, "cleaner than a hound's tooth;" and critics feel that some scouring is required on the ethical front. They are unwilling to accept the present internal arrangements, especially the weak and more hortatory than enforceable code of ethics, or to rely exclusively on the electorate to control wrongdoing and punish transgressors.[70] The new campaign finance laws, an outgrowth of Watergate, may prove helpful; they will limit to a relatively small sum the amount any individual can contribute and require full reporting and disclosure of who gives what to whom. Other proposals include a more strongly worded, more thoroughly implemented code of ethics; an expanded set of conflict of interest statutes with broadened self-denying ordinances;[71] and an extension of the ban to prohibit outside compensation to cover not only direct payment for representing any outside interest before the government, but also indirect payment in the form of bonuses, stock options, and the like.

Financial disclosure laws would go far to inform the public of their lawmaker's interests. Senator Clifford Case (R., N.J.) has for a number of years pushed to require each member of Congress to reveal the donors of all gifts, including campaign contributions; to report all income from outside sources; to issue an assets-and-liabilities statement; and to record all sales and purchases of stocks, bonds, and real estate. Such disclosure, either as a supplement to, or substitute for, restrictive statutes like campaign finance acts would seem a practical way to avoid the extraordinary difficulty in identifying a genuine conflict of interest. It is certainly possible for congressmen to share viewpoints with their constituents, or some segment of them, and to act on behalf of those interests without engaging in improper conduct. Disclosure laws would have the virtue of revealing what financial stakes a member has in issues he must decide. If Congress is to compete on equal terms with the executive and to prevail in its sound policy determinations, it must be recognized as a non-self-serving body whose priorities are not suspect. Codes of conduct, conflict of interest statutes, and disclosure laws should help convince the citizenry that the legislature has nothing to hide and raise the necessary popular esteem.

A last, and perhaps most important, requisite for an independent effective Congress is the will and determination to assert its preferences and to fight for them. Critics often charge, with some justice, that too many lawmakers are unwilling to run the risks of serious commitment to policy making. Instead, they prefer to concern themselves with local interests, subordinating national concerns to comfortable provincialisms. They depend on presidential initiative to set the legislative agenda, preferring to respond rather than to propose. They tolerate congressional folkways that favor minority power and inaction over majority rule and accomplishment. They protect themselves through reciprocity and courtesy, taking credit for what goes right and avoiding blame for unsuccessful or unpopular action.

What is required, of course, is a Congress actually co-equal with the president, a legislature willing to assert its views and to accept the consequences. This would mean a psychological shift for many legislators. They must be prepared to take regular stands on national issues when local considerations might suggest some other course of action to be safer. They must eschew the "something for everyone" attitude with its reciprocity and "logrolling;" rather they must be prepared to say "no" to a colleague and, more difficult, to hear "no" said to them.[72] The congressmen must be willing to match their best efforts against the ideas of the executive and to stand or fall on the result. This requires risk-taking and, thus, political courage. It will not come easily, and there will unquestionably be electoral casualties along the way for those brave enough to try. Yet only by such an exercise of will can Congress hope to achieve parity with a powerful executive. Moreover, the congressional contribution to the resignation of Richard Nixon in no way resolves the matter; Congress must be strong even when the occupant of the White House is respected and revered.

In sum, the scheme presented here as "majoritarian democracy" envisions a system of separation of powers and of checks and balances, in the best sense of both those overworked terms. It projects a system of separate institutions, legislative and executive, sharing overlapping powers. Since events have rendered untenable the older, now seemingly naive, faith in the beneficence of the president some executive-legislative policy-making partnership has become essential. Such arrangements would include three major components:

(1) *A responsive, deliberative phase of policy-making.* A strengthened legislature, with better staff and information resources and open to all interested points of view, would sift proposals and draft legislation to deal with the major issues confronting the country. Such a careful, reflective, and open deliberative stage would raise the danger of intervals during which problems might intensify or opportunities for solutions might be lost. Yet such a price must be paid if our politics are to be based on citizen wants and needs. Moreover, the costs will be minimized if the deliberative stage is not allowed to drag on unnecessarily.

(2) *A responsible decision-making phase of policy-making.* After some proper interval, the deliberative stage would give way to decisive action. Presumably, at the given time, the legislation under consideration should be ready for the full chamber to take up. Majoritarian standards should then operate: easier discharge of committees; simpler access to the floor, especially through limitations on the Rules Committee in the House; more germane debate, especially in the Senate; elimination of dilatory tactics, most particularly the filibuster in the upper chamber. After due deliberation and careful formulation, bills should be faced squarely on the merits and voted up or down without delay. There are costs here, too; to move legislation ahead with all possible dispatch means to foreclose opportunities to defeat by indirection. Minorities can and should have a full say during the deliberative stage, but at the point of action they must be restrained; they must not be permitted to make policy by blocking a decision. The need to act, to be responsible, must override the need to represent, to be responsive. Congress must first listen carefully, then it must act, decisively.

(3) *A strengthened Congress relative to the executive.* Congressional policy making, hopefully reflecting a satisfactory mix of responsiveness and responsibility, must produce decisions that stand some reasonable chance of prevailing against presidential power. I am proposing a combination of increased statutory authority—laws to restrict the executive's use of war powers, impoundment, and executive privilege; a renewed congressional reputation, rooted in

greater openness and a clearly visible increase in ethical standards; and greater legislative determination. Enactment of such a program would convincingly demonstrate such a determination on Congress' part.[73] Throughout the entire process, the public, now better informed about the legislature, would be preparing to render judgment, to hold Congress accountable at the ensuing election.

Even though proposals such as these, if they survived close examination, could be adopted incrementally and without major constitutional alteration, the prospects for reform are not bright. The executive will, I fear, resist such changes; some legislators, reluctant to yield powers they presently possess, may also oppose them. The Watergate tragedy has perhaps provided an impetus for change: it has revealed how strong the president has become, especially in relation to Congress, and it has provided Congress the opportunity to move against a temporarily weakened executive. Thus, if anyone is attracted by the picture of a balance of power in which the Congress and the president, each representing their own constituencies and each with an independent power base, work together for responsible and responsive public policy, subject to popular accountability, now is the time to act. "The times, they are a-changing" indeed, and if the opportunity for constructive change is missed, the result could be perpetuation of a system now shown clearly to be in need of reform.

# The Supreme Court Nine:
# Judicial Responsibility
# and Responsiveness

*Richard Claude*

Public opinion surveys confirm what historians and grade school children have long professed to know: that respect for the ideals of human rights and rule of law remain high on the hierarchy of American values. The problem comes in making the ideals work. Rights work by legal writs, according to a quip by Roscoe Pound, and lawyers are in the writ business. The 1970 census reckons the legal profession to be a half-million strong. That is quite a few shoulders to cry on for those who think that their rights have been abused. Still, it is not enough. Above all, we need an impartial and independent Supreme Court. Without a judicial appeals system to harmonize federal and state regulations under the Constitution, the bench and bar would be unable to resolve controversies because the rule to be used in settling conflicts would remain in dispute. Fifty various versions could develop of the obligation of the states to the federal Constitution. As John Locke long ago observed, civil society may slip into a state of natural anarchy unless all persons, government officials as well as other citizens, "have a common established law

and judicature to appeal to, with authority to decide controversies
between them and punish offenders."[1]

At the apex of the legal profession, the Supreme Court derives
its authority and renown from its role as final interpreter of the
Constitution. It applies that document as law to cases before it. This
is essentially a law-making function which has long carried with it
the power of judicial review. That is, by tradition the Court refuses
to enforce a regulation which is, in the judgment of a majority of
the justices, forbidden by the Constitution. A law that is tested and
passes constitutional inspection, by contrast, enjoys the luster of
legitimacy. Equipped with this kind of authority, the United States
Supreme Court is a very powerful tribunal. Of all of our agencies
of government, it is perhaps the most difficult to appraise.

Such difficulty seldom deters editorial commentators from evaluating judicial rulings. For example, in 1973, when the Supreme
Court invalidated virtually all state laws limiting abortions, critics
of the decision, such as editorial writers for the *Cincinnati Enquirer,*
the *Norfolk Ledger Star* and the *Indianapolis News,* complained
about the misuse of judicial power to achieve what the Supreme
Court considered desirable social objectives. On the other hand, the
rulings in *Roe* v. *Wade* and *Doe* v. *Bolton*[2] were described by the
*Pittsburgh Post Gazette* as "compassionate," by the *Long Island News-
day* as "solidly constitutional," and by the *Christian Science Monitor*
as an "historic victory for women's rights."

Do we like what the Court is doing these days or do its rulings
distress us? Standards for evaluation are not easy to come by, even
in the complex literature of jurisprudence. Since ours is a democratic
system, nevertheless, we are obliged to judge the judges. Indeed,
according to George Gallup, we do it all the time.

For over three decades, the Gallup poll has tested public sentiment toward the United States Supreme Court and its major decisions affecting many areas of life. During the four years from 1963
to 1967, Gallup annually asked the same questions of a national
sampling: "In general, what kind of rating would you give the Supreme Court—excellent, good, fair, or poor?" Although over these
years the Court handed down some far-reaching and highly controversial rulings, American opinion remained fairly constant—and

mixed. Among those voicing opinions, about as many gave a poor or fair rating (46 percent) in 1967 as gave it a good or excellent rating (45 percent) compared to the same unfavorable (41 percent) and favorable (43 percent) categories in 1963.[3] In table 1, the columns on the right reflect marginal changes in such favorableness ratings, comparing 1968 with 1973 data by education, age, political and regional categories.

In 1967, Gallup also asked for views regarding the Court's fairness. The question was: "Do you think the Supreme Court has been impartial in its decisions or do you think it has tended to favor one group more than another?"[4] Nearly half of the American people, according to Gallup, said that the Court has lived up to the goal of impartiality in its decisions. That is, 47 percent of the national survey in 1967 replied "impartial," 30 percent said the bench showed some group favoritism, while 23 percent offered no opinion.

Some of this data is presented in the left hand columns of the table 1 where several relationships disclosed are both clear and enduring. According to the respondent categories reported in the table (they only marginally overlap), the Supreme Court was most likely to be faulted for lack of fairness and impartiality by older citizens, Republicans, and Southerners. (These are the same groups showing the highest approval in the 1973 survey.) As one 51-year-old corporation vice-president in the South put his discontent in 1967: "The Court has set itself up as an oligarchy and has imposed its social and political views on the nation under the guise of interpreting the Constitution, without regard to the wishes of Congress or the people." In 1967, younger adults were more favorably disposed. One Eastern college student interviewed by Gallup remarked: "The Supreme Court has become progressive and courageous as a full-fledged instrument of social change rather than of preservation."

The questions of whether the Supreme Court has or has not been impartial in its decisions, and whether it does or does not deserve high performance ratings point up tough problems. What can we reasonably expect of our highest judicial body? In our examples above, the corporation executive was distressed by what he perceived as judicial irresponsibility. The college student by contrast invoked some privately held standard of judicial responsiveness in

**Table 1**
Perception of Impartiality (1967) and Change in Favorable Ratings
(1968, 1973), Supreme Court

| | Perceptions of Impartiality | | | "Good"–"Excellent" Ratings | | |
| | Im-partial | Favors One Group | No Opinion | 1968 | 1973 | Change |
|---|---|---|---|---|---|---|
| National | 47 | 30 | 23 | 36 | 37 | + 1 |
| Education | | | | | | |
| College | 52 | 38 | 10 | 48 | 45 | − 3 |
| High School | 51 | 29 | 20 | 36 | 36 | — |
| Grade School | 34 | 28 | 38 | 27 | 28 | + 1 |
| Age | | | | | | |
| 21–29 | 62 | 23 | 15 | 51 | 42 | − 9 |
| 30–49 | 50 | 29 | 21 | 40 | 36 | − 4 |
| 50 & over | 38 | 35 | 27 | 25 | 31 | + 6 |
| Politics | | | | | | |
| Republicans | 40 | 35 | 25 | 28 | 40 | +12 |
| Democrats | 50 | 27 | 23 | 41 | 35 | − 6 |
| Independents | 47 | 33 | 20 | 37 | 36 | − 1 |
| Region | | | | | | |
| East | 54 | 24 | 22 | 43 | 40 | − 3 |
| Midwest | 49 | 25 | 26 | 38 | 38 | — |
| South | 36 | 42 | 22 | 23 | 34 | +11 |
| West | 36 | 34 | 20 | 40 | 34 | − 6 |

expressing approval. Each relied upon a legitimate but different touchstone. Let us analyze these concepts of responsibility and responsiveness.

## Responsibility To and For

As the scope of modern government has become extended and centralized, holding government officials to responsible conduct has become ever more problematic. Indeed, definition of what would constitute such conduct for judges and other public servants has become something of a will-o-the-wisp. Responsibility is a complex idea. The term itself is the common province of the three fields of law, politics, and ethics, each with its separate analytical standards.[5]

In the framework of all three disciplines difficulty results because we often fail to distinguish between being "responsible to" somebody and being "responsible for" some action. In discussing the Supreme Court and responsibility I shall attempt to make this distinction explicit. For example, I delineate a field of responsibility which I label *technical responsibility* whereby the Supreme Court may be viewed as answerable *to* the legal profession *for* coherent rule-making. Second, I attempt to identify the Supreme Court's *institutional responsibility to* the public at large, *for* the constitutionality of public policy. A review of some of the chief contemporary criticisms of the Supreme Court will, I believe, put us in a better position to clarify some of these aspects of responsibility.

In 1959, at a time when the John Birchers, self-appointed Southern white spokesmen, and anti-Communist zealots began their billboard impeachment proceedings against Earl Warren, Professor Herbert Wechsler helped to raise the level of public scrutiny of the Supreme Court. In his famous call for "neutral principles in constitutional law," Wechsler laid the keystone to a set of views earlier developed by J. B. Thayer and others in attempting to develop realistic standards of judicial craftsmanship.[6] Wechsler expressed admiration for the Court's responsiveness to petitioners in a number of cases but criticized the same rulings for irresponsible shortcomings. For example, the rationales offered by the Supreme Court in the school desegregation cases as well as in the "white primary" and restrictive covenant cases all failed to meet Wechsler's expectations for clarity and credibility, based upon "neutral principles"[7] His viewpoint, put briefly, is that the claims of blacks have, with undue partiality, been singled out for special compensatory treatment. He feels that if comparable claims had been made by members of other groups, the Court might not have vindicated them. According to Wechsler, the rules as formulated do not sufficiently rest on generalized principles, a prerequisite for effective social control.

But Dean Rustow of the Yale Law School has found Wechsler's views excessively abstract and says that the Harvard professor's references to "reason," "principle," "generality," and "neutrality," were employed in multiple ways, "apparently deriv[ing] from different definitions."[8] If by *neutrality* is meant the judicial impartiality that would assure that like cases be decided alike, it may be argued that neutrality is not breached simply because there are no other like cases. The three nineteenth century civil war amendments to the Constitution and six twentieth century civil rights statutes testify that the position of no other group is like that of blacks, with their history of slavery and enforced segregation.

Joining Wechsler in an attack on the craftsmanship of the United States Supreme Court of the 1950s and 1960s is Professor Phillip Kurland, one-time law clerk to Justice Frankfurter. In *Politics, the Constitution, and the Warren Court,* the University of Chicago professor acknowledges that the judicial protection of individual and minority rights is praiseworthy in the light of social change and government giantism.[9] But, he believes, the Court has failed to convince the legal profession and those upon whom the weight of the law falls that its judgments have been made for "sound reasons." Despite *Brown* v. *Board of Education,* growing masses of ghetto children remain separated in unequal all-black classrooms.[10] Public schools still serve as daily forums for forbidden devotional exercises, *Abbington School District* v. *Schemp* notwithstanding.[11] Violations of the Voting Rights Act are silently tolerated as if South Carolina had won its suit against Attorney General Katzenbach.[12] Persons accused of crime are daily questioned without the assistance of counsel and without notification of their rights as though *Escobedo* v. *Illinois* and *Miranda* v. *Arizona* had never been decided.[13] In many police precincts, warrantless searches are more common than is familiarity with *Mapp* v. *Ohio.*[14] All of this is evidence, in Kurland's critical analysis, that the Court's rulings are perceived as mere rhetoric. Deterioration of faith in the word of the Supreme Court is due, not only to the Court's failure to frame its decisions in "sound reasons," but to other flaws in craftsmanship as well. Kurland charges that the Court acts arbitrarily on the assumption that justice can be done *ad hoc* in each case. He asserts that the bench not only resolves the case before it but offers advisory opinions which do not always advise. Disregarding the needs of lawyers for clarity, some rulings give evidence of scant deliberation. Attuned more to politics than to precedent, the Court disregards *staré decisis* at will without offering adequate reasons for change.[15]

Professor Alexander Bickel is another academic critic who, like Professor Kurland, was at one time a law clerk to Justice Felix

Frankfurter. In *The Supreme Court and the Idea of Progress* Bickel argued in 1970 that the high bench had come dangerously close to exhausting its reserves of legitimacy.[16] It had done so through its lack of consideration for how its decisions would be understood and received. The effectiveness of its rulings, when universalized to the country at large, depended upon consent, upon lawyers and citizens being "convinced by the force of the Court's reliance on reasoned principle applied impartially." Instead of consent, according to Bickel, the Court faced criticism by attorneys, law professors, and judges for "erratic subjectivity of judgment, for analytical laxness, for what amounts to intellectual incoherence in many opinions, and for imagining too much history." To a tribunal he saw as hellbent on a course of reckless reform, Bickel warned: "Revolutionaries are not a reliable constituency for judges."[17]

If there is a serious point in Bickel's latter comment, it is a reminder that judges do indeed have a "reliable constituency." It is the fraternity of counsellors at law. Their day-to-day interaction with judges and their legal training fix in lawyers a set of expectations about the proper role of judicial decision making. Such expectations create a line of responsibility from bench to bar, which, for lack of a better term, we may call *technical responsibility.* If the Supreme Court owes technical responsibility *to* the bar, what is it responsible *for?* The Wechsler, Kurland, and Bickel literature, in my view, reflects a set of interests that are both legitimate (because of the permanence of the constituency of lawyers) and narrow (because the Court has other more public concerns as well). Professional requirements tend to make lawyers equate responsible action with "rational action" defined as action (1) taken in the light of full information, (2) after due deliberation, (3) not arbitrarily, and (4) with considerable consistency. Though it may be a superhuman demand, these critics call for judicial decisions at once keenly precise in formulation and thoroughly general in application. After all, attorneys earn their considerable keep through the effective counseling of clients. That effectiveness depends upon a body of unambiguous rulings illuminated, in Wechsler's phrase, by "analysis and reasons quite transcending the immediate result that is achieved," so that principles will cover cases.[18] The objective, according to Oliver Wendell Holmes, speaking before the Harvard law class of 1897, is so to fashion the law that, in the hands of the skilled attorney serving his client, it may become the art of the predictable. Said Holmes: "When we study law we are not studying a mystery but a well-known profession. We are studying what we shall want in order to appear before judges, or to advise people in such a way as to keep them out of court."[19]

The Wechsler, Kurland, and Bickel complaints, at least as I have isolated them here, are part of a professional indictment that has been voiced also within the Supreme Court itself. Mr. Justice Harlan, one year before his retirement in 1971, said: "It does not derogate from steadfastness to the concept of developing constitutionalism in the field of civil rights . . . to insist upon *principled* constitutionalism which does not proceed by eroding true fundamentals of Federalism and Separation of Powers."[20] Of course, the difficulty with this position, as with that of the academic critics, is that reasonable men will disagree about the meaning of such abstract standards as "true fundamentals" and "principled constitutionalism." Subordinating a claim of states rights to a claim of civil liberties —as in the great criminal due process cases of the 1960s which applied the Bill of Rights to the states—may be challenged on the grounds that the principle of federalism is being undercut.[21] But it is too much to say that such rulings were not rationalized by means of any principles at all. What can be acknowledged is that, behind most of these great "incorporating cases" of the 1960s stands the gravestone of a precedent overruled.

For Justice Harlan, the Court's decision of 1969 in *Benton* v. *Maryland,* applying the double jeopardy clause of the Fifth Amendment to the states by virtue of the Fourteenth Amendment, was a painful case in point.[22] In dissent, Harlan agonized over Justice Thurgood Marshall's alleged distortion of history, his cavalier treatment of the technicalities of the "concurrent sentence" doctrine, and his trampling upon the previously controlling precedent of *Palko* v. *Connecticut.* On the other hand, Justice Marshall writing for a five-man majority did invoke an unambiguous constitutional principle, albeit one antithetical to earlier ideas of federal-state relations. The overriding principle, according to dictum in the opinion of the Court, is that the Fourteenth Amendment must not be seen to apply to the states "a watered down version of the Bill of Rights." This, of course, was the view urged by Benton's lawyers. He had been tried in Maryland on charges of larceny for which he was acquitted, and burglary, for which he was found guilty. His conviction, however, was set aside under a Maryland Court of Appeals ruling which voided the requirement that jurors swear to their belief in the existence of God. Benton was then tried again, but this time he was found guilty of both burglary and larceny. Justice Thurgood Marshall said that sentencing Benton for larceny, after he had once been acquitted, violated the double jeoparty clause of the Fifth Amendment. That provision clearly covered a situation like Benton's but had previously been thought to apply only to the federal courts. In a landmark ruling, Marshall asserted that the Bill of Rights provision also applied to the states by virtue of the Fourteenth Amendment prohibition against state deprivation of "life, liberty or property without due process of law." Justice Marshall argued that the 1937 Palko precedent, leaving the states free to subject persons to double or multiple jeopardy, had been eroded by changing circumstances. In taking this position, the majority was turning its back on the tendency to equate "principle" with precedent, a kind of common law formalism which is not necessarily appropriate to the performance of the Supreme Court's institutional responsibilities as they have developed in our system.

As long as judicial review is lodged exclusively in the Supreme Court, that body must balance its technical responsibility to the legal profession with its institutional responsibility to the public. This larger duty has been the subject of considerable debate. The obligation to the public has been contemporarily defined by Chief Justice Harlan Fiske Stone as that of effecting "the reasonable accommodation of the law to changing social and economic needs."[23] Stone's view, if it may be distinguished from that of his one-time law clerk, Herbert Wechsler, suggests that due regard to crafting articulate neutral principles cannot always take precedence over judicial concern with public policy. Institutional responsibility, in this light, focuses on the obligation between the Supreme Court and the public at large. If, in the name of Stone's sort of judicial statesmanship, the Supreme Court is responsible *to* the public at large, what is it responsible for? The answer, a distinctive feature of modern American constitutional law, was supplied by Stone himself in a footnote that has become more famous that the ruling to which it was attached.

The occasion for defining a modern role for the Supreme Court was supplied in the routine review of *United States v. Carolene Products*.[24] The dispute was trivial, but it reached the Court in the critical year of 1938. Involved was a minor statute called the "Filled Milk Act." A concession to Midwest dairy interests, the federal statute forbade shipment in interstate commerce of skimmed milk compounded with any nondairy oil to resemble milk or cream. Indicted for trafficking in such milk substitutes, Carolene Products of southern Illinois argued that the act was an unconstitutional deprivation of property (in the form of interstate contracts without Fifth Amendment due process.) There was substantial precedent for this line of defence, but Justice Stone (later promoted to chief justice by F.D.R.) refused to void the law by disputing its substantive wisdom. In saying that "the existence of facts supporting the reasonableness of the legislation is to be presumed," Stone was pleading for judicial restraint in interfering with business regulation by government. At the same time, he took the opportunity to write a kind of policy charter for the Supreme Court of the future. In that now famous footnote, he virtually announced that although economic policy makers would henceforth not have to worry about possible Court vetoes, judicial review was not being foresworn. Of course, no mention was made of earlier Supreme Court clashes with New Deal economic policy or of the embarrassments of the Court packing plan. The point made in this case reviewing a minor business regulation was that judicial review was not dead. Its weight would be shifted to the field of civil rights and civil liberties. But why?

Stone wrote that perhaps there might be occasion for departing from the normal presumption of constitutionality for legislation in cases where the action in question involved a restriction on the ordinary political processes. The notion of presumptive constitutionality is grounded in the democratic theory that accountable elected officials and not the judiciary reflect current majority will; and that the transient make-up of the majority reflected in the legislature can "ordinarily be expected to bring about the repeal of undesirable legislation." The democratic process, in other words, may be relied upon to remedy unwise economic legislation. But legislation which restricts the democratic process itself is not comparably self-corrective. For example, if manipulation of electoral laws or interference with political rights of expression, petition, or assembly, impede the free functioning of the political process, then the essential premise from which the presumption of constitutionality is derived—the notion of a representative majority—cannot be said to be present. The first paragraph of the Carolene note suggests that for legislation which contravenes the specific negatives set out in the Bill of Rights, the usual presumption of constitutionality enjoyed by federal or state government action may be waived. The second paragraph indicates that the Court has a special responsibility as defender of those rights which are prerequisite to maintaining open channels for change through political processes: "legislation which restricts those political processes [whereby unwise policy is repealed] should be subjected to more exacting judicial scrutiny under the general prohibitions of the Constitution than are most other types of legislation." The third paragraph, apparently composed by Charles Evans Hughes and accepted by Stone, looked to the future in adding that the Court may:

> enquire whether similar considerations enter into review of statutes directed at particular religious . . . or national . . . or racial minorities . . . whether prejudice against discrete and insular minorities may be a special condition, which tends seriously to curtail the operation of those political processes ordinarily to be relied upon to protect minorities, and which may call for correspondingly more searching judicial inquiry.

As a turning point, a footnote may seem a modest milestone to mark constitutional change. As dictum, the lines quoted above had no legal importance to the Carolene Products Company. Stone's footnote is cited by political scientists as a tip-off to a new direction to judicial policy, and by historians as the symbolic juncture where the Supreme Court turned its back on nineteenth-century laissez-faire economics and dedicated itself to a new twentieth-century responsibility. In Gerald Garvey's incisive words: "in 1937 the Supreme Court stopped functioning as a political magic wand, propagating the illusion of the non-existence of power."[25] To lawyers, the Stone-Hughes view represented the first doctrinal challenge to the post-1937 tendency to abjure the power of judicial review altogether, and as such it marked the first formal step towards the development of judicial activism during the 1940s, 1950s and 1960s.

Debate over institutional responsibility tends to focus on the question (first set out in the Carolene footnote) of how active the Supreme Court should be and in what fields of public policy it should use its power of judicial review. In 1949, Justice Felix Frankfurter deplored the use of a footnote as the "way of announcing a new constitutional doctrine."[26] He avowed that he was unable to justify a doctrine of judicial review which arrogates to the judiciary responsibility to void acts of elected legislators and executives who have derived their powers directly from the electorate. Allied contemporary foes of judicial activism who profess the virtues of judicial restraint vis-a-vis other government agencies have been labelled the "judicially modest" by Martin Shapiro and, more gratuitously, the "Frankfurter school of judicial inertia" by Fred Rodell.[27] The most serious critique of the jurists and commentators whose ideal is judicial passivity is that they suffer from a disabling blind-spot in constitutional vision. Pointing to state responsibilities in criminal trials, they underrate the clear prohibitions of the Bill of Rights and the Supreme Court's task of preserving the integrity of the judicial process. Where they see undemocratic judicial venality in apportionment and voting cases, they fail to account for the need for some mechanism to monitor the democratic process so as to preserve continuous (and therefore everchanging) majority rule. Professing to see judicial grasping for power in discrimination cases and disputes involving the rights of the poor and the dispossessed, they fail to acknowledge legislative and executive unresponsiveness. One may speculate with Adolph Berle that the Supreme Court might have avoided entering these areas in the first place, but it cannot retreat from them now. Berle concludes that the Court "has entered, created and accepted a field of responsibility."[28]

The adherents of judicial restraint might have had a lively debate with John Marshall, as Thomas Jefferson did, over the advisability of judicial review. That question was settled, however, by the Chief Justice in *Marbury* v. *Madison* in 1803.[29] In our own day it is equally idle to debate whether judicial review can responsibly be exercised in the context of modern democracy. That responsibility has been thrust upon the Supreme Court by legislative neglect of the voteless, the poor, the powerless, and those alienated by a system which seems to them to abuse their individual rights. Into this circle of neglect, Justice Harlan Fiske Stone inserted his "Bill of Rights—political process—insular minorities" note to answer the question of where judicial review should be actively employed. It was Stone's hope that, should the Court assume such responsibilities to the public, it would also thereby become a responsive instrument in the democratic process.

## Setting the Responsiveness Agenda

Responsiveness is a complex notion little analysed by political scientists. Let me offer a formal definition. Responsiveness is the taking of nonarbitrary, pertinent, and timely action by a decisional body in reply to expressed preferences by clients, constituents, or some segment of the public.[30] This definition is admittedly somewhat mechanical: it simply attributes certain qualities to an action-reaction relationship involving, on the one hand, decision-makers with authority over a defined policy area, and on the other, petitioners with one or more grievances or requests. To satisfy the definition, eight conditions must be met. (1) Needs must be felt and expressed. (2) A decision-making body must be accessible to those expressing such needs. (3) These expressions must be taken into account. (4) Some mechanism must be available for the decisional body to discriminate according to the intensity of demands. (5) The decision-makers must be capable of a reply. (6) They must ground their reply on some justification which distinguishes the ruling from arbitrariness. (7) The reply must be pertinent and germane, if not sympathetic, to the request. (8) A decision must be timely and not excessively dilatory in resolving the conflict.

Each of the conditions noted here has risks for the effectiveness and legitimacy of the decision-making body. For example, the effectiveness of responsive judicial decision-making may decline when court dockets become so crowded that timely adjudication becomes impossible. (In the abortion cases of 1973, the problem of "standing to sue" was complicated by the fact that the gestation period was shorter than the appellate litigation period.) Moreover, responsiveness threatens the legitimacy of the decision-making body by giving the appearance of partiality—of favoring one group over another. This is so because, in keeping with the first condition stipulated above, someone or some group must express its needs. Groups which do not articulate their interests may be less fully taken into account. The risk of appearing to be less than impartial is unavoidable so long as judicial decisions affect various groups differently.

Responsiveness has always characterized the United States Supreme Court, and with it, charges of group, sectional, or interest partiality. As final interpreter of the Constitution, the Supreme Court has been placed in the position of selecting and determining the interests which the law should recognize and seek to secure. The Court has always had some interest to secure. For example, under Chief Justice Marshall (1801–35) the early Supreme Court sought to legitimize and shore up strong national unity (which was favorable to Eastern industrialization) against the disintegrative pressures of provincial states rights claims. During Chief Justice Taney's tenure (1836–64), a period of expansive population migration, the Court's policy-making supported a number of outlying regional objectives favorable to the economic interests of the West and South. By a series of late nineteenth- and early twentieth-century rulings, which sound very strange to modern ears, the Court tried to ease the country through continental growing pains by encouraging a *laissez-faire* program of rapid economic development. The beneficiaries were the alliance of Eastern factory owners, industrialists, and Western railway companies which promoted westward migration.

The redefined challenge since the New Deal days of Chief Justice Harlan Fiske Stone (1941–46) has been to balance government— strong enough at the federal and state levels to deal with unemployment and economic depression, yet restrained enough not to inhibit individual rights. The dockets of the Stone, Vinson, and Warren Courts have continued a policy of noninterference with government regulation of the economy in favor of furthering the court's potential for innovation in defining the fundamental freedoms secured by the Constitution. Debate within the Court presided over by Chief Justice Burger, as President Nixon made clear in his television nomination of Justices Powell and Rehnquist, centers on the question of how actively the Court should continue to decree change in the civil rights and civil liberties *status quo.*

Resisting the temptation to speculate prematurely about the long-term direction of the Court in the 1970s, let us concentrate on the record for responsiveness of the Supreme Court during Earl Warren's tenure as Chief Justice. Upon his retirement in 1969, Chief Justice Warren gave an unusual television interview in which he permitted questions on his Court record. When asked why he had encouraged so much controversial civil rights and civil liberties litigation, he replied that the record of judicial performance since 1953 when he became Chief Justice simply reflected the kinds of cases coming up on appeal in ever-increasing numbers. A documentary record supporting the Chief Justice's observation is etched in the rising curve of privately initiated and government sponsored civil rights and civil liberties litigation in federal courts. In 1950, a total of 192 rights violations were privately asserted, (in an additional 18 cases, the federal government was the plaintiff); in 1955, 241 private, 20 government; in 1960, 316 private, 12 government; in 1965, 994 private, 60 government; in 1970, 3,586 private, 126 government initiated suits. The "J" shaped curve described by these five year data-increments prefigure no decline in the demands made upon our 92 federal district courts. Figures for 1971 are: 4,609 private, 154 government; those for 1972 are 5,482 private, 132 government.

Why this pattern of increase? The question, though data is lacking that really bears on the causes, is nevertheless important to an analysis of Supreme Court responsiveness. Two distinct explanations may be offered. The first may be called the "social change" theory.[31] It suggests that the Court has been authentically responding to felt social needs in the political environment. The second may be labelled the "legal change" theory. It asserts that the Court has by and large invited litigation over civil rights by espousing a gratuitous program of elite-minded reform.

The social change theory sees the actions of judges more as symptoms than causes; it points to the rapidly shifting social structure to explain the increasing reliance upon courts to sustain and extend socio-political freedoms. When the population doubles, not only do assaults, boundary disputes, tax hassles, and civil rights litigation increase, but problems never before heard of must be settled. Examples include such recent concerns as the admissability of "bugging," evidence gathered without warrants by police using electronic eavesdropping; the ecological consequences of the disposal of chemical wastes; and welfare recipients' troubles made jurisdictionally complex by an increasingly mobile population. The demands for all forms of justice, civil as well as criminal, appear to multiply in geometric proportion to increases in the population. In the thirty years from 1940 to 1970, for example, personal injury cases have increased 500 percent; petitions from state prisoners seeking federal habeas corpus relief have mushroomed from 89 to 12,000. Such expansion makes judicial responsiveness a hostage to over-crowded court dockets. The danger, as Chief Justice Burger noted in his Bar Association address in 1970, is that people suffering from judicial delay "may come to believe that courts cannot vindicate their legal rights from fraud and over-reaching."

Not only has our population increased rapidly in numbers, but its profile of problems has changed as well. Since the 1920 census revealed that our population had became 51.2 percent urban, defenders of the values of rural America have been at bay, struggling to hold their former preeminence in race, religion, and politics. The needs of polyglot urban America are sharply different from those of the white, Protestant, and Anglo-Saxon countryside. For several decades, black and emigré Americans have looked for escape from peonage and former oppression, sought jobs, and aspired to better economic and social status in the cities. Where the promise of full citizenship and equal treatment proved elusive, it could sometimes be secured through litigation. The development of ethnic politics kept the constituencies of city-based politicians fragmented and hardly engendered the tolerant atmosphere required for persons of diverse races and religions to live peaceably in close proximity. But discrimination based on race, creed, color, or politics could be resisted by suits in the federal courts; which have power to punish any person who deprives another "of any rights, privileges or immunities secured by the Constitution and laws of the United States."[32] What is more, city-dwellers under-represented because of malapportioned legislatures have been given by the courts larger slices of power to press for political response to the urban problems of housing, transportation, delinquency, and social disintegration. In short, powerless citizens and voters have been behind the effort to secure through litigation equality in race, religion and representation, and their cases have come before the Supreme Court for the final disposition.

Urban problems, intensified by legislative neglect, have mapped out the major concerns that have reached the Supreme Court—fairness for persons accused of crime, rights of free expression in both politics and religion, freedom from racial discrimination, and the full weight for every vote. These areas of active judicial policy making are broken down into ten categories in table 2 below, which summarizes a dozen years of rulings. Decisions the Court thought important enough to require signed written opinions form the basis for the data in the table. It tabulates and ranks issue responsiveness in the ten areas in which the Supreme Court persistently granted more than 50 percent favorable answers to individual claims against government for each year from 1957 to 1969. The percentage of decisions favorable to a constitutional rights plea is recorded, aggregating all related decisions over twelve years. The standard deviation score answers the question, What is the range of year by year performance? It supplies an indication within each category of the extent to which the record of favorable decisions deviates above and below the average (mean) year's record. According to the theory of social change,

**Table 2**
Supreme Court Issue-Responsiveness (1957–1969)

| Rank Issue | Number | Percent Favorable | Standard Deviation | Year of Highest Court Consensus |
|---|---|---|---|---|
| 1. Rights of the Poor | 12 | 92 | 9.43 | 1969 |
| 2. Racial Discrimination | 79 | 89 | 14.77 | 1967 |
| 3. Free Association | 15 | 87 | 13.27 | 1960 |
| 4. Electoral Rights | 48 | 83 | 20.59 | 1968 |
| 5. Free Expression | 56 | 82 | 17.14 | 1967 |
| 6. Fair Criminal Process | 225 | 66 | 13.15 | 1967 |
| 7. Free Religion | 17 | 65 | 36.62 | 1960 |
| 8. Internal Security | 77 | 64 | 33.75 | 1957 |
| 9. Privacy & Government Eavesdropping | 69 | 61 | 32.64 | 1968 |
| 10. Immigration & Citizenship | 21 | 57 | 38.87 | 1957 |

the explanation for the areas of approbation and innovation reflected in the table is to be found in the intensity, diversity, and novelty of demands made upon the trial court judiciary.

A second theory of change, the legal theory, attributes the initiative in shaping change to appellate courts rather than to the populace at large. The justices of the Supreme Court perform more as stimulus to innovation than as a mere response to circumstances. According to the legal theory, Chief Justice Warren's casual observation that the Court simply "takes what comes" paints a misleading picture. The Corinthian temple in Washington does not house a panel of nine oracles passively awaiting callers knocking on the appellate doors. The Court is quite able to lend its collective ear selectively to the pleas of that segment of the population that seem to it compelling enough to deserve a hearing.

The mechanism for selection is described in the Judiciary Act of 1925, which sets out the appellate province and jurisdiction of the Supreme Court. Under its terms, when four members of the Supreme Court coalesce to support a petition for *certiorari,* the case is heard. Otherwise, entrée to the bench is denied—and no explanation need be offered. How important is this form of docket control? In the ten years from 1959 to 1968, the Supreme Court disposed of a total of 24,012 disputes; 1,394 (or 6 percent) under its original jurisdiction described by article 3 of the Constitution, 1,202 cases (5 percent) came up on "automatic" appeal; and 21,416 (89 percent) reached the high bench under its discretionary grant of *certiorari.* In nine out of ten cases, this record shows, the Court has been able to pick and choose what it would hear. According to rule 19 of the *Supreme Court Rules,* this discretionary mechanism weighs the general importance and novelty of the question, whether it raises substantial constitutional issues, whether there is conflict among intermediary federal courts of appeal, or whether the court below has departed from a controlling Supreme Court decision. Since the terms, *question of substance, decision in conflict,* and *important question,* found in rule 19 are hardly self-defining, nothing about the *certiorari* procedure is automatic.

The ability to set its own agenda spells the difference between creativity and drudgery for the Court. For the petitioner, getting on that agenda spells the difference between responsiveness and neglect.

The agenda is set by what the judges think is important. To the attorney ambitious to carry his case up the appellate ladder until he is satisfied with the result, some knowledge of the Court's issue responsiveness (as documented for example in table 2) is a significant key to the weighty phrase, *question of substance.* If he has a handle on the kinds of cases that are likely to be granted *certiorari,* he will also want to be familiar with changing trends within the Court. Inquiry along these political lines may require sophisticated analysis, in part because *certiorari* discretion since 1925 has, as a side effect, brought about a higher rate of division within the Court, a greater proportion of five-to-four rulings, and greater variability in the rate of intra-Court division.[33] Still, the flexibility enjoyed by the Court in setting its agenda does permit glimpses into what policy areas are favored by individual members. Table 3 below aggregates the ten constitutional issues from table 2, reports on the record of changing favorableness to rights claims over a 15-year period, and indicates percentage changes from the previous year. If the favorableness record may be seen (in the framework of the legal change theory) as

**Table 3**

Responsiveness Record by Year (1957–1972)

| Year | Number (categories 1–10) | % Favorable | % Change from Previous Year |
|------|--------------------------|-------------|------------------------------|
| 1957–58 | 57 | 61.40 | — |
| 1958–59 | 43 | 51.16 | −10.24 |
| 1959–60 | 35 | 65.71 | +14.55 |
| 1960–61 | 47 | 57.45 | − 8.26 |
| 1961–62 | 28 | 78.57 | +21.12 |
| 1962–63 | 42 | 80.95 | + 2.38 |
| 1963–64 | 45 | 84.44 | + 3.49 |
| 1964–65 | 37 | 81.08 | + 3.36 |
| 1965–66 | 44 | 79.55 | − 1.53 |
| 1966–67 | 56 | 66.07 | −13.50 |
| 1967–68 | 71 | 83.10 | +13.48 |
| 1968–69 | 65 | 83.08 | − .02 |
| 1969–70 | 52 | 55.77 | −27.31 |
| 1970–71 | 82 | 48.78 | − 6.99 |
| 1971–72 | 84 | 63.09 | +14.31 |

an inducement for litigants to pursue their appeals according to the predisposition of the Supreme Court, then we should expect to find evidence that the public is responding to the Court rather than the other way around.

A feature of this thesis has been examined by two political scientists, Richard Richardson and Kenneth Vines. They studied the flow of cases from district to appeals courts in three circuits for the years 1956–61. Of 649 disputes raising issues of constitutional rights in three courts of appeals, two-thirds originated in district courts where no civil rights or civil liberties claims were pressed. Richardson and Vines conclude: "These data indicate that one of the important political functions of the appellate process in the federal courts is the transformation of cases that were routine trial types in the district into cases with greater political significance as civil liberties issues."[34] It appears that the higher the litigant wishes to go in gambling on appellate relief, the greater is the inducement to up the constitutional ante. The Supreme Court, it may be argued on the basis of these facts, creates its own demand by a process of (1) designating constitutional rights cases as those raising "important" issues and therefore needful of review and (2) then acting with consistent favorableness to the rights claimants. On the supposition that consistently positive response to demands generates more demands, the Supreme Court is seen by the legal change theory as the instigator or retarder of change: at least as much a stimulus as a response.

In my view, there are winning points to both the social change theory, whose adherents tend to view the Supreme Court record of the past generation as responsive, and the theory of legal change, whose adherents see recent judicial innovation as a kind of high level ambulance-chasing. I believe, however, that a two-factor theory of social and legal change explains more, though hardly all, about the relationship between public needs and judicial solicitude. We may here suitably use the language of supply and demand. Society undergoes a set of transformations generating conflicts which require judicial services for their resolution. The Court provides the opportunity to resolve these conflicts through constitutional innovation in the fields of most intensely felt social needs. The judiciary can supply the second condition—legal adaptation—but not the first—social alteration producing new needs and demands. Pressure on the Court to accede to change is particularly great when demand is strong (stimulated, for example, by the tendency of Americans to look to the courts to solve all problems) but supply is short (deflated, for example, by legislative and executive unresponsiveness, administrative inefficiency, and governmental impersonalism). There is not room here to go more deeply into this concept, but a final distinction should be noted between short- and long-term demand and supply. Constitutional rights litigation, both civil and criminal, has climbed steadily since 1945. It has not been diminished (at least not by any short-term quantitative standards) by lapses in Supreme Court responsiveness. For example, in 1969, the responsiveness record (as defined for table 3) showed its sharpest decline in twelve years (a drop of 27.3 percent from the previous year), but the volume of constitutional rights litigation mounted constantly over the subsequent twelve months (up 60.8 percent above the 1969 docket, counting all federal district courts.) In the 1970–71 term, the number of cases affecting fundamental rights was then at its highest historical level (54 percent of the 148 cases eventually yielding written opinions). Yet the number of rulings favorable to the person asserting the constitutional right fell below the 50 percent level for the first time in twenty years (forty favorable out of eighty-two cases). In other words, civil rights litigants in 1970 and 1971, given less reason than ever to expect easy Supreme Court vindication of their claims, nevertheless pressed harder than ever for judicial relief from problems growing out of political unrest, congestion in the cities, the ferment of war, and the mobility of the people. Clearly public need and institutional accessibility are both necessary, though neither in isolation is sufficient, to ensure responsiveness.

In spite of the substantial number of rulings by the Supreme Court from 1970–74, and despite the addition of four Nixon appointees to the Court, there were few substantial changes in the law during that period. By and large, the Court did not undo earlier libertarian decisions (with notable exceptions such as *Harris* v. *New York* modifying *Miranda* v. *Arizona, Mahan* v. *Howell* loosening the one-person, one vote strictures of *Reynolds* v. *Sims,* and *Miller* v. *California* revising *Roth* v. *United States* so as to facilitate obscenity control).[35] Nor did it break new ground (except for innovative constitutional policy regarding abortion, the death penalty, and eavesdropping without warrant in national security cases.[36] Although the four Nixon-named justices were regularly united on questions of criminal law from 1970–74, clear trends did not otherwise dramatically emerge. For example, in the 1972–73 term, unanimity prevailed in nearly one-third of the decisions; division among the Nixon appointees was not uncommon, and only one out of three rulings found a conservative majority of new justices (often joined by Justice White) prevailing over the alumni of the Warren Court. The immediate impact of the four Nixon appointments seems to have been to halt the trend of the 1960s toward enlarging constitutional rights. Whatever future course the Supreme Court of the present decade takes, a continued record of responsiveness to support of fundamental freedoms will be widely expected. Whether liberal or conservative by the standard of favorableness to civil rights claims, any Supreme Court devoted to the people's rights must face a difficult question: How can it preserve the Constitution and uphold its technical responsibilities to the legal profession, while meeting popular demands for responsiveness? Trust of both lawyer and citizen are needed to undergird the Court's legitimacy and prestige.

## The Supreme Court Nine

In a James Madison lecture in 1967 at New York University Law School, Justice Abe Fortas commented: "It is fascinating, although disconcerting to some, that the first and fundamental breakthrough in various categories of revolutionary progress has been made by the courts—and specifically by the Supreme Court of the United States."[37] Reviewing the scope of the Court's accomplishments during the 1950s and 1960s, Adolph Berle has approvingly described the members of the Court as a kind of "revolutionary committee."[38] The contours of their "revolutionary progress" have been foreshadowed largely, though not wholly, by the prophetic Carolene footnote on civil liberties, democracy, and minority rights. First, the Court followed a trail initially blazed in 1925 when *Gitlow* v. *New York* enforced the First Amendment against the states.[39] In the 1960s, however, the process of applying the Bill of Rights was greatly accelerated when the Fourth, most of the Fifth, the Sixth, and the Eighth Amendments were incorporated into the Fourteenth

Amendment, requiring state adherence to due process. Second, in the political rights field, the Supreme Court has transformed itself into a kind of trustee of electoral accountability by greatly expanding the promise of voting rights and by setting constitutional and therefore nationalized standards for the conduct of elections. Finally, the equal protection requirements set by the Court during the 1950s and 1960s have loosed a flood of egalitarian litigation beneficial to "insular minorities" and disadvantaged groups. In the process, judicial decrees have laid many new obligations upon the states in the fields of discrimination, welfare rights, and equal rights for the poor. The net result is a program of legal change unmatched in American history except for the efforts of the Radical Congresses of the 1870s which worked a revolution in the arrangements of American federalism.

Revolution, or rapid change, precipitates recrimination. The Court is an easy target for a reason long recognized. When the Supreme Court assumes an activist role in bringing about social change, it unavoidably takes sides in political controversy, calling into question the legitimacy of its claim to administer "equal justice under law." Code words like *strict constructionist,* suggestions that "mediocrity deserves representation on the Court," ideologically inspired charges of "democratic centralism," are all frivolous reminders of a serious situation. It is that the Supreme Court's capacity for avoiding self-aggrandizement and partiality have come to be viewed by many with suspicion. The threat of the proposed Bricker, Dirksen, and Becker amendments to curtail Court jurisdiction or reverse its rulings show that significant numbers of legislators see the Court as a political partisan. Such "realism" also affects presidential politics. The heated debate over appointments to the Supreme Court (averaging one every twenty-two months) has had overtones of a struggle to inhibit the Court from protecting minorities whose election-year clout is considered marginal. Under these threatening circumstances, it is not enough to say complacently that judicial activism has been an effective though costly route to social change. The cost must be assessed and minimized.

By exploring the ninety-four instances of Court vetoes of federal policy up to 1965, Robert Dahl has associated periods of judicial activism with interludes of the Court's being isolated from lawmaking majorities (that is, executive-legislative coalitions). Over the long run, Professor Dahl notes, such coalitions "generally have their way."[40] He argues convincingly that, as judicial activism increasingly threatens the policies of "law-making majorities," the basis of the Court's power—its prestige—becomes increasingly visible and subject to attack. If Dahl's analysis as I have interpreted it is correct, then the principal threat to judicial activism may come from the isolation that results when the Court gets too far ahead of the other branches of government. It then becomes an easy mark for allegations impugning its most vital defense, its impartiality. The prestige generated by its record of responsiveness may be outweighed by such attacks on its legitimacy. How can the Court be even-handed in administering justice—and be seen to be even-handed—so as to preserve its legitimacy and promote its continued responsiveness? I would suggest that the task, at least in part, lies in breaking down the appearance if not the reality of the Court's isolation without compromising its independence. I will try to clarify this observation below with six specific suggestions. First, I should note that several recent broad and constructive suggestions prescribe radical revision of the role of the Supreme Court as it faces the last quarter of the twentieth century.

Rexford Tugwell has addressed himself to the Court's present vulnerability, proposing a new constitution that would sharply reduce the power of the Supreme Court to hold acts of Congress unconstitutional.[41] Theodore Lowi suggests that the Court gain public sympathy by turning on government giantism and bureaucratic abuses and, in the name of a new "juridical democracy," extending its power of judicial review to declare "invalid and unconstitutional any delegation of power to an administrative agency that is not accompanied by clear standards of implementation."[42] Adolph Berle calls for "extricating the Court . . . from the position of danger as well as honor it has acquired" by establishing a "Council of Constitutional Advisors," patterned after the Council of Economic Advisors.[43] In 1972 a special "study group" chaired by Professor Paul Freund and appointed by Chief Justice Burger presented a controversial recommendation for congressional consideration. It called for the creation of a new National Court of Appeals composed of seven judges from U. S. Circuit Courts of Appeal who would serve three-year terms. The new body would screen all cases coming to the Supreme Court, forwarding its recommendations for review (perhaps 400 annually) from among which the Supreme Court would make a final determination on which 150 or so it would hear full oral argument. Petition-denials from the new national court could not be appealed to the Supreme Court.[44]

My own suggestions are more modest. On the one hand they are predicated on my sympathy with judicial activism on behalf of constitutional rights, and on the other hand, on the frank recognition of deficiencies in the effectiveness of the Supreme Court in marshalling support, enforcement, and understanding of its decisions. Six diverse, admittedly fragmentary proposals are sketched to indicate the kinds of changes in the pattern of operations in and around the Supreme Court that may be needed to sustain public confidence in activist decision-making. Public discussion is needed about ways to mitigate the inhibiting effects on behalf of constitutional rights activism that grow when the Supreme Court becomes isolated from other branches of government and from the public.

1. My first suggestion acknowledges that the increasing volume of litigation in federal courts strains the capacity of the judiciary to be responsive to the extent that overwork and delay in decision-making may result in justice denied. For those who conclude that the effectiveness of the federal courts has been compromised by an excessive volume of litigation, it would be well to explore the appropriateness of establishing new adjunct grievance-processing institutions. The office of ombudsman is an example. As shown by experience in Denmark, Sweden, and New Zealand, and as explained by a report of the International Commission of Jurists,[45] the ombudsman cannot always handle the kinds of cases that Americans are apt to turn over to their judges. But such an officer, as yet virtually unknown in the United States, can act with remarkable responsiveness where appropriate, because he can proceed more speedily, informally, and with greater regard to the individual merits of a case. The ombudsman can be more available to the public than can the courts, in the ordinary course of events, and he must constantly respond in a nonarbitrary and pertinent, if not sympathetic manner to complaints because persuasion, recommendation and publicity, rather than compulsion, are his principal instruments.

2. My second suggestion focuses on the nagging questions raised by our recent—and continuing—military involvement in Southeast Asia. Judicial reluctance to review the propriety of our participation in an "undeclared war" was apparently promoted by the doctrine of "political questions" which is said to bar full-scale inquiry into the validity of a war in progress.[46] The judicial process is hemmed in on all sides with externally imposed restrictions. The "political questions" doctrine, however, is a judicially formulated self-restraint imposed selectively. Practical reasons support its use, such as that, for certain kinds of disputes—especially those dealing with foreign affairs—no effective judicial remedy may be devised and enforced for a given complaint. In cases raising "political questions" there may be nothing but repudiation, embarrassment, and disobedience facing a court attempting to impose injunctive relief. I would suggest, however, that in such cases, the Supreme Court seriously consider the appropriateness of supplying declaratory relief in order to isolate and define the responsibilities of the political branches to which the judiciary defers, and to forewarn all branches of the implications of failing to resolve conflict. The Declaratory Judgment Act provides that "any court of the United States . . . may declare the rights . . . of any interested party . . . whether or not further relief is or could be sought."[47] In an adversary setting, and in a case properly initiated by an interested party, the question of an unconstitutional war could quite adequately be reviewed to determine unambiguously where the Constitution, under the circumstances, lodges responsibility. If the provisions of Article 2 naming the president as commander in chief were declared sufficient to support the continued use of troops under emergency conditions, then responsibility and electoral accountability could be clearly fixed with the executive. If, alternatively, the Court were to determine that American participation in extended conflict is constitutionally baseless, then the president would be free to ask for a congressional declaration of war, thereby extending responsibility for action or inaction to every congressman facing reelection. With lives in jeopardy and liberty impaired, the nation should not again be treated to the sort of constitutional "pea and shell game" staged during the Indochina involvement in which confusion was permitted to continue concerning

where responsibility could be fixed, and all participants played a Pontius Pilate role of irresponsibility.

3. A third suggestion is for the Court to find some procedure for giving vitality to the broad civil rights powers which it has recently attributed to Congress in interpreting section 5 of the Fourteenth Amendment.[48] Given the formidable difficulties faced by the Court in gathering facts, it may occasionally be preferable to share with Congress the task of devising a program of remedies, even in connection with specific litigation. For example, when the Court sees a violation of the equal protection principle of nationwide scope, it might take the interim step of adjudicating the complaint on its merits, but announcing that it will wait a reasonable time to allow Congress to devise legislative remedies before ordering (or remanding to fashion) equity relief. To take a hypothetical example, should the Court rule in a case before it that the perpetuation of all-black schools is a violation of the Equal Protection Clause, even though they result from housing patterns and not from previous segregation laws, it could delay the inevitably tortuous process of judicially determining what the Constitution positively commands. Judicial relief could be promised after a specified period that would give the legislature time to act (something like this is already done in apportionment cases). The Civil Rights Commission has drawn up a specific set of legislative proposals to eliminate racial isolation in public schools, and in its Report of 1967, it argued that "congressional action affords greater promise for effective relief than judicial action."[49] Should Congress fail to act, or fail to develop legislation satisfactory to the Court, the Court could still act more effectively than otherwise, using the information developed by the legislature in its considerations.

That the Court cannot draw lines as precise as can legislatures seems especially clear where such districting abuses as gerrymandering are concerned. Spurred directly by the Court, Congress might well devise clear guidelines for equal, compact, and contiguous districts consistent with constitutional voting rights. When the Court has only the command in article 1, section 2 that representatives are to be "elected by the people" to justify its actions, it hazards accusations of arbitrariness were it to attempt, as Congress more convincingly might, to specify that populations of voting districts must vary no more than 5 percent above or below the state's district average for the lines to be accepted as fairly drawn.

4. Another suggestion for sharing responsibility is addressed to the executive branch. The president should present to each Congress an address on the state of civil rights and civil liberties, making such recommendations as he deems appropriate. Constitutional rights are at least as important in the scheme of American values as the topics reviewed in the "State of the Union," the budget, and economy messages of the president. In this regard, the fact should be faced that enforcing constitutional rights is costly. If school construction is a necessary part of a comprehensive program of extending equal opportunities to all, then federal financial help must be planned. The Criminal Justice Act of 1964 supplies an example of budgetary commitments on behalf of civil liberties, because it guarantees a lawyer for criminal defendants (at public expense for the indigent) and also appeals at public expense. A constitutional rights address from the president to Congress would formalize and make explicit existing executive participation in formulating rights policy. The Civil Rights Acts of 1957, 1960, 1964, 1965, and 1968, and the Voting Rights Extension of 1970 were all largely drafted in the Department of Justice. And there is more for the president to explain. *The Annual Report of the Attorney General,* with its section on civil rights enforcement, is a seldom read, poorly distributed, but very significant document for the record of accomplishment and default which it presents. The president currently has the assistance of the Civil Rights Commission to evaluate the laws and policies of the federal government with respect to the equal protection of the laws required by the Fourteenth Amendment.

A commitment to periodic review of the people's rights would enhance presidential accountability. Accountability of political officials refers not only to "electability" but to "answerability" as well. Our chief executive should be made to answer for his stands and decisions affecting civil rights and civil liberties. A president who is hostile to the freedom of the press, who has reservations about the Fourth Amendment barriers against government invasion of privacy, should be made to put his views on record so that, in making electoral choices, voters can compare rhetoric with action. Voters should not have to match the words of an attorney general, national security officer, or vice president to the deeds of the president, who after all, is the electorally accountable official. The "State of the Judiciary" address initiated by Chief Justice Burger admirably illustrates recognition for the need to give a public accounting of the progress and difficulties facing the administration of justice.

5. A fifth suggestion deals less with substance and responsibility than with appearances, which are also important. Public opinion regarding the Supreme Court is shaped less by what the Justices say than by what the newspapers and media attribute to them.[50] When a radio announcer in Virginia reports that the "Pentagon Papers Case"[51] means that military secrecy is henceforth unconstitutional, or when an Arkansas headline carries the news: "Mention of Religion Forbidden in Schools," there is cause for concern over the quality of legal reporting. There is a communications gap between the judiciary and the public. The Court must take seriously its educational role, and it, rather than the media, bears the responsibility for thinking broadly and creatively about this problem. Chief Justice Burger has been sensitive to this point, and he has experimented with precedent-breaking press conferences. There is, however, a daily need for a professional information officer, an overdue innovation in public relations. Professional accreditation for reporters who regularly cover the Supreme Court would also help in conjunction with orientation sessions for them and for "interns" from university journalism schools. Justice Fortas has publicly speculated that "if some way could be worked out to facilitate the task [of journalists], the stories that appear in the press would be more informative—particularly in the sense that they could more adequately convey to the public the substance and tenor of the Court's opinons."[52]

There has been little bold thought given to establishing effective lines of communication between the Court and the public. Television coverage of "decision days" has never been publicly considered. Available professional organizations have not been recruited to supply regular aid to the media in explaining the functions, activities, and opinions of the Supreme Court. Educationally minded organizations have not been encouraged to support innovative high school studies of the Bill of Rights and the Constitution. In the place of well developed presentation of information regarding the law, misleading media coverage of important Supreme Court rulings has been too often the standard. The result is unnecessary controversy, public lack of confidence in the courts, and impairment of the prestige and effectiveness of the judiciary.

6. The Supreme Court does not have an adequate range of reliable sources of nonlegal information regarding the consequences of its ruling. It needs better feedback. What are its present sources of socio-political information? (1) The *amicus curiae,* or "friend of the court" brief by private policy-oriented groups is one source, and the Court occasionally takes the initiative to invite briefs from interested government parties which are not litigants. (2) An administrative profile of the shifting pattern of litigation (with implications regarding the changing socio-political environment) is an important source of information statistically compiled under the aegis of the Judicial Conference of the United States. It tabulates the types and volume of federal litigation, the character of issues, the duration of trials, and the speed of disposition in all federal courts. (3) The remand of desegregation and districting litigation to lower courts has resulted in a fruitful reliance by district judges upon *amici* briefs, the use of expert testimony, and the investigative skills of special masters. (4) More informally, as Glendon Schubert has pointed out, the Court may simply rely upon procrastination, as it did in the apportionment field between 1961 and 1964, to learn from the varied experience of lower court litigation before making the push for change.[53] (5) Informational help sometimes comes from lawyers who follow the example of the famous "Brandeis brief" in supplying the bench with social and economic analysis along with an exposition of legal principles. (6) Finally, law reviews serve as a clearinghouse for law-related data; they assess the relationship of legal change to society at large, and help courts to weigh legal analysis along with nonlegal facts in exploring new policy directions.

With all of these sources of information, the social sciences are still left largely unused in shaping legal change. Responsive constitutional adjudication can no longer afford to promote broad policy reform without some adjunct support from the behavioral sciences. In recent years, political scientists increasingly have directed attention to the impact of Supreme Court decisions on grass-roots compliance and noncompliance.[54] The quality of scholarship dealing with such impact has been plagued by disputes over research techniques, but the volume of such studies has increased impressively; some way should be found to bring the best of them to judicial notice and make them more methodologically sophisticated. Commissioned research by the Judicial Conference or the Federal Judicial Center could institutionalize the valuable study of what happens to a decision when it leaves the hands of the Court. Joint sponsorship by private groups such as the American Political Science Association and the American Bar Association might better ensure published, independent impact scholarship. At a minimum, individual social scientists should remedy their ignorance about how to file a brief *amicus curiae*. While there are many public interest law firms and a few public interest economics associations, there are no public interest groups of behavioral and social scientists. Unless the Supreme Court is to retreat into a self-imposed restraint in policy-making, it must continue to study the mechanics of protecting and extending liberty. This challenge presupposes not only legal expertise of the highest order, but also familiarity with the social impact of its rulings in order to avoid overstepping practical limits upon effective legal action.

The several proposals set out above involving shared responsibility, public relations, and improved research are offered, I confess, a bit nervously. The reason is that judicial activism does not fully fit into my Platonic view of the best of all possible democratic worlds. Judicial activism might ideally give way to legislative activism, should the latter suddenly begin to operate in the field of constitutional rights. Legislatures, after all, have the superior fact-finding facilities of investigative committees, expert counsel, and the power of subpoena. But until legislatures and administrators become more responsive to the need for social justice and less preoccupied with social control, the responsibility for active vindication of the people's rights should remain a staple of our judicial system. Not since the time of Oliver Wendell Holmes has the philosophy of judicial restraint given strength to humanitarian and progressive causes. As long as that remains true, judicial activism should be constantly reviewed for public approval and continuously refined by standards of effectiveness. With rare exceptions, such as the contrast between the Sit-in Cases[55] and the Civil Rights Act of 1964, we seldom face a choice between a Supreme Court muddling toward innovation and legislatures dealing with it expertly. The standard choice has been between the Supreme Court responsively acting to remedy instances of the unconstitutional *status quo* and no other body acting responsively at all.

# The Federal Bureaucracy: Responsive to Whom?

*Lester B. Salamon and Gary L. Wamsley*

In 1969, Ralph Nader organized the Center for Study of Responsive Law to expose the unresponsiveness of federal government agencies. Within a year of its founding, however, the center was producing reports that demonstrated conclusively that federal agencies are not unresponsive at all. For example, one team of Nader's Raiders discovered that the pesticides division of the Agriculture Department sunk $10 million into a full-scale war on the fire ant despite scientific evidence that the war was doomed to failure or worse, all in response to pressures from Congressman Jamie Whitten, chairman of the House Agricultural Appropriations Subcommittee.[1] The National Air Pollution Control Agency found it far easier to resist the pressure of concerned environmentalists than that crunching in from industrialists and state and local governments to relax ambient air standards.[2] And the Food and Drug Administration responded to pressures from the food industry not to require retesting of such chemicals as monosodium glutamate and cyclamates before placing them on the grocery shelves, even though earlier tests had challenged their safety.[3]

Such studies suggest that the popular image of the bureaucrat as the unresponsive opponent of change, no matter what kind of change, may be seriously wrong. Federal bureaucrats may not exhibit unresponsiveness so much as what Donald Schon has called "dynamic conservatism," the willingness to change to remain the same, the tendency to fight to maintain an equilibrium in a changing world.[4] The real issue concerning bureaucratic responsiveness, therefore, may not be *whether* the bureaucracy is responsive, but *to whom,* and *under what circumstances.*

The answers to these questions are all the more important when we consider the tremendous growth in bureaucratic power over the course of American history. From the meager 2,120 individuals who comprised the federal establishment in 1801, the bureaucracy had grown to 1 million people by the time of the Second World War. Then, between 1940 and 1970 alone, the size of the federal civilian bureaucracy tripled—from 1 million to 3 million employees. Accompanying the growth in numbers, moreover, has been a growth in power and functions. Bureaucracy's growth strains the notion of separation of powers in American government, for it performs crucial legislative and judicial as well as administrative functions. Indeed, the bureaucracy has become, in a real sense, both the chief legislator and the chief adjudicator in the American system. The vast bulk of legislation considered by Congress originates in the bureaucracy, and it is the bureaucracy that makes the most potent contribution to the legislative process, thanks to its command of information. Moreover, the volume of statute law is overwhelmed by the volume of administrative law produced by the bureaucracy in the course of interpreting congressional intent through the formulation of regulations. Evidence for its predominate role in adjudication is seen in a statement by a former Commissioner of the Federal Communications Commission:

> While the Courts handle thousands of cases each year and Congress produces hundreds of laws each year, the administrative agencies handle hundreds of thousands of matters annually. The administrative agencies are engaged in the mass production of law, in contrast to the Courts, which are engaged in the handicraft production of law.[5]

In short, thanks to the growth of government activity resulting from the increased complexity and interdependence of modern life, the bureaucracy has emerged as the major locus of power in the federal government. Over the course of American history, the bureaucracy has been reformed, rationalized, reorganized, and reconstituted; but it has never grown weaker, only stronger, in relation to other governmental institutions. No matter which group of elites has won at various points in American history, the bureaucracy has never lost. Since bureaucracy is the great "doer" of the political system, to ask about the responsiveness of American national government is really to ask about the responsiveness of the federal bureaucracy.

As we proceed, it will become evident that we are less than pleased with patterns of bureaucratic responsiveness developing in the American political system and that we are holding it to some standard of democratic responsiveness. In all candor, we must admit this standard is not very well defined. It is easier to say what kinds of bureaucratic behavior we feel are not democratically responsive than it is to enunciate some positive but abstract statement. A responsiveness to only the most powerful, to the most articulate, to those with whom bureaucrats feel professional comraderie, or those always present to make a claim, falls short of our definition of democratic responsiveness. It also goes without saying that there are a number of bureaucratic organizations that find it difficult to be responsive to even the powerful and particularistic and that they also fall short of our ill-formed standard.

There are some who will insist that bureaucracies can *only* respond to the powerful and particularistic. Moreover, they would probably insist that if each agency so responds, the result will be a richly competitive bureaucratic pluralism. But stretching pluralist theory to cover the administrative part of the political process merely compounds the conceptual flaws of pluralism. For such an extension assumes a more perfect political competition than has been possible; it assumes some benign invisible hand which guides the political system to outcomes in a perfect public interest. Clearly, real life is not like that.

While it is defeatist to assume that agencies can only respond to the powerful, it would nevertheless be naive to assume that such is not their general proclivity. Power rests on political skills and resources, and large segments of the American public do not have enough of these commodities to make themselves felt in the agency-interest group-congressional committee milieu. Nor is there an agency which has a concern or interest for each segment of the public.

This essay is not a treatise on democratic theory, and space does not permit an extended exploration of the question of public interest and the democratic responsiveness of bureaucracies. Our real purpose is to shed some light on how to better analyze bureaucratic responsiveness and its determinants, and so our negative definition will suffice here.

To understand the pattern of bureaucratic responsiveness, however, it is necessary to understand the general determinants of bureaucratic behavior. Two sets of determinants particularly are crucial: the first arises from the bureaucracy's relations with other actors in the political system; the second from the bureaucracy's internal structures, procedures, and norms. If the former helps us to understand the kinds of forces to which the bureaucracy will respond, the latter helps us to understand the extent of this responsiveness. We will refer to these as the external and internal political economies of public organizations, and will examine each in turn.

## External Political Economy:
## The Search for Succor in the American System

Central to the whole pattern of bureaucratic responsiveness in America has been the generalized hostility traditionally endured by bureaucrats. Unlike Her Majesty's civil service in England, the bureaucrat has historically cut a sorry figure in the pantheon of American folk heroes. His very existence a challenge to deep-seated national norms of free enterprise, individualism, and local control, the federal bureaucrat has provided a convenient scapegoat for counter-elites from the time of Thomas Jefferson to that of George Wallace and Richard Nixon. Indeed, in the American lexicon, the term *bureaucratic* has become a synonym for lethargy, red tape, and ludicrousness.

The massive expansion in the size and powers of the federal bureaucracy has occurred in this atmosphere of intense distrust and the whole pattern of bureaucratic responsiveness in American government has been shaped by it. Lacking a basic and fundamental legitimacy, lacking succor in the body politic by right, agencies have had to work at developing it. In the process, a narrower organizationally-conditioned outlook has come to eclipse the broader publicly-conditioned outlook that might be desired in a professional administrator. As persons responsible for the organizational fortunes of the pesticide division of USDA, its leaders would probably point out in private that it would be suicidal to ignore the whims of an appropriations subcommittee chairman. But as professional individuals speaking in public, they would no doubt insist that the division should serve all agriculture, and, indeed, all the public.

The primary organizational need becomes survival, which requires vigorous pursuit of two precious commodities: legitimacy and resources. Those who command these commodities and so can insure agency survival or threaten it, thus have a first call on agency responsiveness; and the agency's behavior boils down to a concerted effort to define and carry out its task in a way that will stabilize and institutionalize supportive relationships with these "relevant others."

Since federal agencies formally draw their sustenance and authority from a Congress and a president elected by the people, a pollyana assumption might be that because these other branches of the government are responsible to the electorate, it would follow that bureaucracy is responsive to that same electorate.[6] But things do not work out with such charming simplicity. Not only is the bureaucracy too highly structured and cumbersome to respond flexibly to the popular will, if it were known (a point we will treat below), but also the "will of the people" is less than clear as it filters through the legislative and executive institutions. Some scholars have argued, or assumed, that the "institutional interests" of the presidency are as close an approximation as is possible of the "public interest,"[7] but sole reliance on the chief executive is a tactic used only by naive or adventure-loving agencies. Furthermore the Watergate scandals clearly show just how far the institutional interests of the presidency can diverge from any reasonable definition of "public interest." But regardless of how representative of the public interest the institutional interests of the president may be, the office is spread too thin to carry out and implement more than a fraction of those interests; and most assuredly the office cannot provide the kind of support agencies feel they need in the guerrilla war of bureaucratic politics.

To be sure, recent presidents have struggled valiantly to reorganize departments and to create staff agencies like the National Security Council, the Domestic Council, and the Office of Management and Budget in order to insure agency responsiveness to central presidential policy leadership. And these agencies have had some success, particularly in foreign policy. Nevertheless, it is debatable whether these new efforts have done more than barely keep up with the growth of bureaucratic power.[8] What is more, the efforts of such agencies to exercise control have often simply escalated bureaucracies' search for help from their allies to fend off unwelcome pressures from the president's staff. A look at the large number of anxiety-producing situations the typical agency endures will show that the number of occasions are painfully small when its executive cadre can feel justified in using up its reserve of political capital by turning to the president. Consequently, supplementary sources of support must be found.

One vital source is the legislature. But if the presidency offers a potential but inattentive force pushing agencies in the direction of responsiveness to a broader set of interests, the legislature has almost the opposite effect. Legislators have discovered that they can hold their own in the interinstitutional political donnybrook that is the American system only by processing their work load through specialized committees and effectively parcelling legislative power out to potentates of various subject-areas. In the absence of strong, centralized parties, the consequence is a pronounced particularistic, localistic, and parochial orientation in the legislature. Expression of the "popular will" in such circumstances is liable to have a peculiar slant. For the executive cadre of a public agency, the path of prudent behavior is clearly marked. Survival dictates a concerted effort to resonate with the peculiar characteristics of the key legislators in the substantive and appropriations committees and/or to develop allies among interest groups capable of influencing the same. This can be done by defining and performing agency tasks in a way that caters to the localistic and particularistic orientations of the key legislators (for example, fighting the fire ant for Congressman Whitten) or that can generate support among crucial nongovernmental actors with clout in the legislative arena.[9]

Thus, because of their defensiveness and security drives, and because of the peculiar dynamics of the legislative system, federal bureaucrats respond not to some broad public interest, but to the particularistic demands of key congressmen, to those nongovernment actors among the agency's clients, or to enemies who have the organization, efficacy, and intensity to influence legislative behavior. The bucolic picture diligently painted by pluralist theorists of multiple, competing groups interacting to produce results in the public interest scarcely portrays the post-partum life of the typical agency. Although broadly based coalitions are necessary to pass the legislation and establish the programs of a public agency, afterward it finds itself nose to nose with only a few intense, organized, and narrowly-focused interest groups and legislators. The more appropriate image of pluralism would, therefore, depict the agency desperately trying to work out a *modus vivendi* with the narrowly restricted group of "relevant others" who control its access to the legitimacy and resources required to occupy a permanent niche. Agencies must consequently work unceasingly to institutionalize a favorable environment. They establish advisory committees with representatives of powerful groups that must be accommodated or appeased; they formally include such groups in administrative structures; they aim propaganda at mass publics; they sometimes even venture forth to organize clientele groups if none exist, as the newly-created Department of Housing and Urban Development did in 1967 when it organized the Urban Alliance, a broadly based lobby for urban programs. The consequences are the development in each policy arena of a fairly well-defined policy subsystem linking the agency and its "relevant others" in a semi-stable, symbiotic state of equilibrium; but at the same time, a reduction of agency responsiveness to those outside the subsystem.[10]

One of the classic examples of how this process works can be found in Philip Selznick's study of the Tennessee Valley Authority. Confronted by harsh opposition to their central purpose of using the federal government to plan and develop a giant multi-state river basin and thus potentially alter community power relations, TVA administrators struck upon the perfect self-defense: they surrendered the initiative by adopting the doctrine of "grass-roots democracy," one that earned the agency an impressive degree of legitimacy, but at the expense of making it susceptible to cooptation by local rural elites. An agency that began as a force for environmental conservation and social change therefore became, over time, a major threat to the environment, an unquestioning exponent of industrial advance, closely allied with entrenched regional elites.

By contrast, consider the fate of the Farm Security Administration (FSA), a New Deal brain child designed to "put the bottom rail on top" in rural America. Where TVA stressed grass roots control and quickly found itself coopted by the local powers-that-be, FSA uncompromisingly hewed to the pristine road of promoting social change and as a result quickly found itself isolated and at bay. TVA discovered what it had to do to secure a niche and did it; FSA discovered what it would have to do and refused. Not until it was appropriately chastened and stripped of its early fervor did the FSA manage to revive, but only as the Farmers Home Administration (FHA), a vastly altered agency willing to work out a political exchange on terms dictated by the very rural elite its predecessors had fought.[11]

These contrasting strategies but similar fates of TVA and FSA underline the importance of the particular consensus-legitimacy pattern an agency establishes or fails to establish with external actors.[12] Since agencies differ markedly in power, purposes, and potential clientele, they naturally differ in the kinds of exchanges they can strike with "relevant others" and hence in the extent to which they will respond to external impingements. If we can specify some of the factors that shape the consensus-legitimacy pattern of particular agencies, therefore, we will have gone some distance toward explaining their degree and pattern of responsiveness.

A variety of factors affect the consensus-legitimacy pattern, the nature of the institutionalized niche, and thus responsiveness, but they can be grouped under four major headings.

*Characteristics of "Relevant Others."* As we have already indicated, agencies rely crucially upon the support they can muster among governmental and nongovernmental actors. While the bureaucracy as a whole potentially has the entire nation as clients, and any single agency may number clients in the millions, practically speaking an agency confronts a much more circumscribed set of key actors. To be effective in influencing agency behavior, a group must have clout and interest in the agency's activities. A numerically large but generally disinterested clientele is of little help to an agency confronted by a much smaller but deeply interested one, especially if the latter enjoys greater resources or influence at strategic points in the decision-making hierarchy. This has been the story of much of the consumer protection bureaucracy in the United States. Lacking active support from the masses of consumers whose interest tends to be diffuse and unfocused, such agencies as the Food and Drug Administration had to reach an accommodation with the handful of producers directly affected by their actions. Since the relevant legislators faced much the same pattern of interest, the result was a cozy triumvirate of legislators, industry, and agency—with the consumer conspicuously absent.[13]

By the same token, large Southern farmers and other agri-business tycoons, taking advantage of the seniority system, have firmly plugged-in to the most strategic legislative positions and have had few complaints about the responsiveness of the Department of Agriculture, an agency considered by those outside the agri-business community to be the epitome of bureaucratic obduracy. Responsiveness, in short, is not simply a matter of movement but of direction, and agencies will tend to move over time in the direction of those willing and able to devote economic resources, expertise, status, sense of efficacy, and connections, or any of the other components of political clout to influencing their operations.

Since different agencies face different constellations of "relevant others," however, they naturally vary in their patterns of responsiveness. For some agencies like the State Department or OEO, powerful attentive supporters are in embarrassingly short supply, rendering the agencies perpetually vulnerable to hazards like the budget-cutting knife. Others find themselves in the warm embrace of a single powerful client, an embrace that all too frequently becomes a virtual stranglehold. And still others enjoy the support of numerous, powerful clients whose competition allows the agency at least a modicum of independence.

Two features of an agency's "relevant others" are therefore crucial to its behavior: first, their strength, and second, their competitiveness. From the viewpoint of agency responsiveness, these two features cut in opposite directions, as the chart below suggests. By and large, the more powerful and competitive an agency's "relevant others," the more the agency can venture forth on its own, even if still within the parameters set by the basic consensus among the competing "relevant others."

Typology of Agencies According to the Characteristics of
Their "Relevant Others"

| Clout of "Relevant Others" | Conflict Among "Relevant Others" | |
|---|---|---|
| | Low Conflict | High Conflict |
| Weak | A Anomie (State, AID) | C Impotence (OEO) |
| Strong | B Captivity (FDA, FHA) | D Flexibility (ICC, Armed Services) |

Assignment of agencies to cells of this table is largely impressionistic and the purpose heuristic.

The case of the Interstate Commerce Commission suggests the utility of this basic typology. During many of its postpuberty years, the ICC found itself in a situation depicted in cell B on our chart —firmly under the thumb of a single client, the railroad industry.[14] However, with the emergence of the trucking industry and the rebirth of water transport as competitors in interstate transport and hence for the ICC's affections, many observers have noted a new flexibility and independence in the ICC's behavior. The ICC, in short, has moved from cell B to cell D on our chart. While this transformation in its client environment broadened agency perspectives, it hardly put the consumer in the driver's seat. Industry pressures, albeit in a more balanced cross-section, still run the show.

*Nature of the Task or Product.* Not only is agency responsiveness shaped by the characteristics of its "relevant others," however; it is also shaped by the nature of the task the agency must perform. In fact, these two variables are highly interrelated. An agency's task determines with whom it must deal. It thus importantly defines its "relevant others." But the nature of the task also does something else; it determines how the agency affects the "relevant others" and hence what kind of attitude they will take toward agency operations.

An agency with the task of regulating, for example, will inevitably encounter stiffer opposition than one dispensing subsidies, even though the subsidies generate considerable interest. The banking industry is thus a "relevant other" for both the Department of Housing and Urban Development and the Federal Reserve Board; but HUD tends to enjoy greater flexibility vis-a-vis the banks than does the Fed, if only because the Fed has the task of regulating the very guts of bank operations, while HUD's actions affect only some of the fringes. Since some agencies allocate positive values and others negative, some reward while others deprive, and some regulate while others subsidize, it is natural that agencies will differ in their relationships to those with whom they deal.

From the viewpoint of agency responsiveness, one of the most important characteristics of an agency's task is the extent to which it can be translated into ostensibly neutral technical terms. Agencies whose regulations or distribution formulae can be construed as arbitrary are defenseless before the guns of powerful clients. Not all tasks or products afford the agency the opportunity to shield itself behind the armor of pseudoscientific, so-called objective criteria. The antitrust division of the Justice Department, for example, is frequently hard put to make a neutral, technical defense of its choice of targets, with the result that more fish slip through the net than are caught. A similar dilemma confronts consumer agencies like the FDA: unable to document the effects that particular chemicals have on humans as opposed to animals, FDA has consistently buckled to industry pressures not to forbid their use. The Internal Revenue Service, however, offers a contrasting example. Despite implications that the Nixon administration sought to use it politically, despite seemingly infinite loopholes and questionable progressiveness of the income tax, it has developed a secure reputation for integrity and neutral, technical competence.

Given the importance of these agency task formulae and criteria, it is not surprising that they evoke some of the most savage backroom brawls in Washington. The predictable result is that agencies typically seek to winnow out anything in task formulae that is controversial. The FCC, for example, has timidly resisted introducing quality controls in its reviews of license renewals, fearful about the lack of objective standards in such a netherland.[15]

Another feature of task that helps give agencies breathing room is its dramaturgy or emotional potency. The National Aeronautics and Space Administration benefitted by the contractual largesse it could distribute. But beyond that, it was significantly aided by the high drama and vicarious adventure entailed in making sure the first footprints on the moon were American. AID, in contrast, awards a considerable number of contracts, but the lack of dramatic potency in its task has helped to keep it in a state of anomie.

The foregoing features of agency tasks or, more importantly, people's perceptions of those features, tasks, and products, can perhaps be used as a basis for categorizing policies and policy subsystems as distributive, regulative, and redistributive.[16] A distributive policy and policy subsystem deals with what is perceived to be a helpful, divisible, nonaggregable output on which there is general consensus on the value of providing it and the identity of who receives it. Moreover, everyone's chance of receiving the output is perceived to be about equal. Distributing the values does not raise the question Who gets the goody? so much as When does the goody get got? Examples of distributive policies and public organizations involved in them are: public roads and the Federal Highway Administration; public works and the Army Corps of Engineers.

A redistributive policy and subsystem is one in which the agency is seen as performing the task of taking values from one category of citizens and redistributing them to another. Broad categories of citizens are affected, status and economic standing of one group to another is perceived as being affected or potentially affected. Thus the struggle for legislative passage is usually intense and at a high level of abstraction involving parties and classes. Antagonisms developed at this stage usually carry over and become an environmental setting for administrative agencies that must implement the legislation, and the agencies may be the center of continuing debates over the correctness of the original policy. The main questions raised about the execution of the policy are Who is entitled? and Are they receiving only what they are entitled to? Examples of redistributive policies and arenas are rather few in the American political system and, in many instances, the federal bureaucracies merely oversee implementation of such policies by the states. Examples might include unemployment insurance and the state unemployment offices that administer the program, public housing and local housing authorities, welfare and state and local welfare agencies, and manpower development under the manpower administration of the U. S. Department of Labor.

Regulative tasks give rise to policies and policy subsystems originally established to control an industry or sector of society. Policies as originally expressed in statutes are perceived as specific in their impact, leaving little doubt who will benefit and who will be deprived unless policies are somehow altered in execution and adjudication. Regulation of air routes and rates by the Civil Aeronautics Board, radio and television franchises and frequency allocations by the FCC, or control of transport rates by the ICC are typical examples of regulatory arenas. The principal questions raised are: What are the mitigating circumstances that should affect the allocation of this reward or deprivation? and Is this way of allocating the value really fair? In other words, implementation is a constant rehash of the equity of the original statute.[17] Generally, the forces at work in such an arena push it toward self-regulation or capture of the process by the interests which were originally supposed to be regulated.[18]

An agency's tasks thus set the fundamental and inescapable pattern for its existence, and operate as a major variable in agency responsiveness.

*Agency Congruence with Political Culture.* A third ingredient shaping the environment of an agency and thus its responsiveness is the degree to which its goals and its means of achieving them are congruent with central societal values. Because of their insecure position, bureaucrats are especially vulnerable to what Peter Bachrach and Morton Baratz call "the other face of power," that is, the "mobilization of bias" which defines some governmental functions as appropriate and legitimate and others as not, and some things as problematic and negotiable and others as not.[19] But while all bureaucrats suffer from a heavy burden of derision and mistrust, some suffer more acutely than others because their activities can be construed as inherently illegitimate.

The Farm Security Administration in the 1930s and the Office of Economic Opportunity in the 1960s are prime examples of agencies that had to buck powerful cultural norms. Both sought to alter the distribution of power at the local level, the FSA by tampering with land tenure relationships and OEO by organizing the poor against unresponsive local governments. Both thus faced general negative attitudes toward welfare and ran afoul of powerful norms dictating federal noninterference with private property or with legally constituted local authority—norms that not accidentally served to sustain the power of local elites.

By contrast, the Federal Housing Administration, its operations geared centrally to the all-American goal of the free-standing, single-family home, won instant and easy acclaim. By the same token, the extension service of the USDA resonated so well with American political culture that the work of its county agents was enshrined in Norman Rockwell paintings as veritable symbols of Americana.

In short, congruence with political culture or lack of it plays a definite role in defining an agency's consensus-legitimacy pattern and, therefore, its responsiveness pattern. Only agencies blessed with chores solidly condoned by the prevailing culture can afford some flexibility vis-a-vis powerful clients, and even their flexibility has its limits because of the general hostility toward bureaucracy.

*Defensive and Manipulatory Skills of Agencies.* Public organizations do not merely react to stimuli; they can and do take steps to defend and insulate themselves and to manipulate "relevant others." The more defensive and manipulatory skills an agency has, the more it can either avoid being responsive or choose its responsiveness pattern —high, low, narrow, or broad.

An agency can do things like the following: identify with potent symbols and values; make its task seem technical and value free; strike a balance among contending groups seeking to influence its operations; and distribute its rewards, deprivations, and regulations in a way that neutralizes opponents and wins and keeps allies. The ability to follow such strategies, to shape the consensus-legitimacy pattern, and control responsiveness depends on the political skills of its leadership or the charisma of a leader.

Appointment of a respected individual can sometimes temporarily neutralize powerful opposition to an agency or avert takeover by a narrower set of "relevant others." However, prestige brought to a position must soon be followed by the exercise of political skill if the effect is to be sustained. William Ruckelshaus, President Nixon's appointee to head the Environmental Protection Agency, for example, came to the position with considerable status and managed to build a substantial popular following that helped him stand pat under pressure from the automobile industry for weaker air pollution standards. Even more striking, of course, was the towering preeminence that J. Edgar Hoover and General Lewis B. Hershey managed to attain, and which made their agencies virtually impervious to hostile pressures—even those emanating from the White House. Their attainments rested on consumate skills. Hoover identified the Federal Bureau of Investigation with law and order, kept it puritanically free of partisan political taint, capitalized on publicity gimmicks like the "Ten Most Wanted" list, and cemented relations with local governments and Congress by performing a variety of services to local police. Hershey carefully structured the Selective Service agency so that it could be identified with positive symbols, assiduously cultivated groups supporting national defense, and never missed a chance to display himself and the agency as the personification of down home America and patriotism.

Agencies can also distribute values so as to strengthen a base of support. The Soil Conservation Service switched from large projects aimed at development of river basins to smaller but more widely dispersed projects. This garnered them wider congressional support but also gave them broader, less intense, and more manageable "relevant others." Examples of selective distribution of values are a dime a dozen. The military wasted no time in locating a vast variety of military installations and defense contractors around Charleston, South Carolina, the hometown of long-time chairman of the House Armed Services Committee, Mendel Rivers, and in Georgia, the home state of Senate Armed Forces Committee chairman Richard Russell. The Department of Housing and Urban Development followed similar unabashed tactics in the distribution of hotly contested model cities grants. Of seven members of the House Appropriations Subcommittee in charge of HUD funds whose districts included cities that applied for model cities grants, no less than six received the grants, including such "major urban complexes" as Smithville, Tennessee, and Texarkana, Arkansas.[20] By contrast, only 63 out of 200 applicant cities nation-wide received grants.

*Funding Structure and Susceptibility to Scrutiny.* Another determinant of agency responsiveness is the extent to which the agency must rely on outsiders for sustenance and the extent to which its activities are open to scrutiny. Some segments of the federal bureaucracy operate on trust funds, users' fees, or other special funds that free them significantly from the influence of the president's budget, the principal vehicle for inducing agency responsiveness to broader public conerns. In the process, such special funds may force these agencies to be highly responsive to the special interests from whom the funds are drawn. Such interests tend to see special funds as their own funds for use of their own agency. For example the Highway Trust Fund generated by federal gasoline taxes amply nourishes the Federal Highway Administration and facilitates its resistance to political pressures bubbling up from city planners, conservationists, or poor people whose neighborhoods lie in the way of interstate routes.[21] In 1972, the administration and its "relevant others" waged a successful fight to prevent diversion of such funds to mass transit.

The comptroller of the currency operates on special fees paid by the banking industry, which consequently takes a rather proprietary view of the Comptroller's operations. And the Federal Reserve System earns several billion dollars each year from interest on government bonds that it holds in its portfolio. Not only does "the Fed" not have to appeal to Congress and the Office of Management and Budget (OMB) for funds, it is even immune to audit by the General Accounting Office. As a consequence, the agency can defy Congress and the president with virtual impunity, something it cannot do with regard to the banking community.

As important as the source of funds in determining agency responsiveness is the flow of information the agency generates about itself and its operations. Agencies like the CIA and the FBI enjoy considerable autonomy, if only because their operations are largely covert. Other agencies achieve much the same result because their operations are difficult to evelute precisely, either because the criteria of evaluation are too imperfect or the agency's impact on the citizen is too indirect. All these factors can thwart effective surveillance and thus narrow the range of impingements to which an agency must respond.

This brief analysis of the external factors determining the consensus-legitimacy patterns for federal agencies suggests an important paradox. Those agencies with the least tenuous, most secure niches are best able to respond to new demands and interests in the political system without threatening agency survival; yet, because of their security, they are least inclined to try. By contrast, those agencies most vulnerable to external political impingements and therefore potentially most responsive to broad public interests are under the most severe pressures to resist them and to reach an accommodation with some powerful ally and narrower interests that will give the agency some permanence. It is this central paradox that gives bureaucratic responsiveness its peculiar pattern.

### Factors of Internal Political Economy: Bureaucratization and Buffering the Task Core

But these external determinants constitute only half the equation that accounts for the paradoxical pattern of bureaucratic responsiveness. The other half consists of important *internal* political economy determinants. These include four things in particular: (1) agency "ethos," or norms, which define the agency's chore and its means of task accomplishment, (2) the agency's recruitment, socialization, and promotion/succession pattern, (3) the decision-making structure, and (4) the standard operating procedures.

Since it is through the shaping of its internal political economy that an agency adjusts to the demands of its powerful "relevant others," it is natural that the external and internal political economies of any agency will typically be closely interrelated. A large organization requires some modicum of stability and permanence in order to function. Stability and permanence, however, inevitably tend to limit an agency's ability to respond quickly even to powerful client demands. Taken to its logical extreme, the result can be what one sociologist has called "bureaucratic pathology," where agencies' traditions, structures, and operations subvert their stated missions and prevent any flexible accommodation to changing client demands.[22] A pathological agency is thus one that responds neither to powerful "relevant others" nor to some broader public, but rather operates chiefly in response to complex, rigidified, internal decision rules designed more to protect careers than to serve a public goal.

To determine the extent to which the federal bureaucracy has developed such pathological tendencies, it is necessary to look closely at the four major components of internal agency operations.

*Agency Ethos.* Of the four components of internal operations, agency ethos is probably the most important, for it influences all the others. An agency's ethos is the more or less explicit set of norms and beliefs that defines the agency's mission, both means and ends. The ethos thus gives agency cadre a sense of identity and guarantees some coherence in task accomplishment. Department of Commerce personnel tend, for example, to see themselves as promoters of American enterprise, aiding the growth of American industry. The Agriculture Department, by contrast, enshrines the American farmer as the keystone of its ethos, and shapes its policies to serve agricultural needs.

As a determinant of agency responsiveness, ethos can be important. For years, for example, advocates of greater food assistance to the hungry argued that the food assistance programs should be wrested from the control of the Department of Agriculture and placed in the Department of Health, Education, and Welfare on grounds that USDA's ethos led it to use the programs to serve the needs of the farmer (through the purchase of surplus commodities) rather than to serve the needs of the hungry (through the purchase of commodities needed for a decent diet). By the same token, the Bureau of Employment Security in the Department of Labor perceived as its mission serving the needs of potential employers rather than potential employees, with the result that the most chronically unemployed individuals were systematically overlooked by Employment Service personnel eager to improve their placement records.[23]

From the viewpoint of agency responsiveness, two dimensions of ethos are especially important. First, the ethos defines the agency's appropriate "relevant others" and hence the set of needs it strives to fulfill. It therefore settles some of the troubling background questions of agency raison d'etre (for example, should the Corps of Engineers be most concerned about protecting the environment or building dams?). Second, the ethos helps determine the extent to which particular client needs should be accommodated by setting the standards of professionalism for agency work. Thus the ethos of the Federal Housing Administration legitimizes efforts to help the home-building industry by stimulating new housing construction, but still requires detailed adherence to professionally-devised building standards, even though they may frustrate many homebuilders.

The rise of professionalism as a part of agency ethos has, in fact, constituted one of the most dramatic developments in the federal bureaucracy over the past half century. Not only has general management reached new levels of professionalization, but there has been a staggering increase in the number of professionals in functional specialties like science, engineering, cartography, etc.[24] But although the professionalization of the bureaucracy was premised on the fervent belief that it would protect agencies from the corrosive influences of partisan politics and private interest pressures, making them responsive to some broad public interest, things in practice have not often worked out that way. To the contrary, professionalism has proved capable of serving two other sets of interests instead of the broad public ones enshrined in the civil service reformer's dreams.

Far from equipping agencies to resist the pressures from "relevant others," professionalism has frequently made them more responsive to such pressures. Presumably objective, scientific, professional work routines and evaluation standards effectively shield agencies from outside scrutiny by the nonprofessional public, but simultaneously make them much more understanding of the "problems" of "relevant others" with whom they share the professional mystique and collegial empathy. Thus, for example, when consumer advocates dare to challenge the presumably objective, professional rulings of the Food and Drug Administration, they face a barrage of scientific obfuscation that sounds very much like what industry scientists would say. In fact and jargon aside, rulings are ultimately based on benefit vs. risk judgments for which no clear-cut scientific standards exist. Moreover, when all else fails, FDA spokesmen still fall back on their standard defense, which reflects a basic empathy for and confidence in the industry: that "industry is its own best policeman," and that the push and pull of free competition in the open market will remedy any regulatory slip-ups—a defense that conveniently disregards the vast and growing disparity between economic theory and market reality.[25]

In addition to serving the needs of "relevant others," however, professionalism also frequently subverts the reformer's dream by serving what are essentially career aggrandizement needs for agency cadre. This pattern is most common in agencies that serve weak, disinterested, or dispersed clients, and comes closest to the "bureaucratic pathology" depicted by Rogers. Thus, until recently, the Bureau of Indian Affairs' formal hiring standards stressed professional accomplishments so heavily that they virtually ruled out hiring Indians and their promotion to upper echelon positions. By the same token, professionalism in the welfare bureaucracy has served the needs of welfare professionals far more successfully than it has the needs of the recipients, for whom professionalism has meant insensitivity and endless red tape.[26]

The trend toward professionalism in the federal bureaucracy, in short, is tending paradoxically to reduce bureaucratic responsiveness to broad public interests rather than increasing it.[27] As the table below indicates, this professionalism does not always result in responsiveness to broad public needs.

Indeed, even those agencies like the Internal Revenue Service, which seem to have developed an ethos we call "public-serving professionalism" (to differentiate it from the "client-serving" and "cadre-serving" professionalism discussed above), fall short of serving the broader public in several important ways.

Technocratic pride has led to self-serving behavior on occasions.

Effects of Professionalization on Bureaucratic Responsiveness

| *Focal Point for Agency Responsiveness* | *Level of Professionalism* | |
|---|---|---|
| | *High* | *Low* |
| Powerful "Relevant Others" | "Client-serving Professionalism" FDA, FTC | "Corruption" Department of Interior in the Harding Administration |
| Career Needs of Agency Cadre | "Cadre-serving Professionalism" Bureau of Indian Affairs | "Extortion" Bureau of Customs 1800s |
| Broad, Public Needs | "Public-serving Professionalism" IRS, National Park Service | "Ineptitude" National Guard, pre-1917 Post Office Department |

The IRS has been loathe to accept adverse court rulings and has continued to try to enforce a rule in the face of them, thus forcing different clients to go to court on similar points. It has also been charged that it is slow to publicize rulings that benefit large numbers of private citizens or small businesses.

IRS's technocratic ethos ("Give us the law and we'll administer it as fairly and efficiently as possible") still leaves the agency neutral on crucial questions of tax law of central concern to the public at large. The ethos, in other words, conveniently places the IRS outside the realm of conflict. It allows the agency to avoid taking any position except that of consultant on the content of the law and to concern itself solely with efficient administration. In the process, however, it detracts from the IRS's democratic responsiveness, for if anyone is in a position to testify to the inequities of existing law from a position of public trust, it is IRS. Yet the agency's very technocratic professionalism that shields it from particularistic influences also aborts this value it could have to the broad public. It thus refuses to play the same active role on behalf of the broad public that other agencies play on behalf of narrow interests.

*Patterns of Socialization, Recruitment, and Leadership Succession.* Organizational ethos normally finds reflection in turn in an agency's recruitment, socialization, and leadership succession patterns. Public organizations do not merely draw their career men from a general civil service pool, or promote by applying merit standards to a limitless universe of qualified applicants.[28] Rather, the dominant cadre faction in effect asks the question, "What sort of men do we need to maintain our organization?" They then develop the procedures to find them in spite of, or by means of, civil service regulations.[29] They also develop definite processes for socialization and prescribe career patterns that shape and mold candidates for top positions.

Selective Service, for example, drew its cadre from national guardsmen and reservists and put them through a careful screening and socialization process.[30] The Forest Service draws from forestry schools and land grant colleges and carefully socializes[31]; the Foreign Service draws heavily on Ivy League liberal arts or political science majors and access to top career slots requires a well-defined career pattern.[32]

Such patterns keep the agencies' internal political economies aligned with their external political economies. Agencies' cadres are going to share general perceptions and outlooks with their most powerful "relevant others." The cadre of the U. S. Department of Agriculture at a general level shares fundamental perceptions with the leadership of the American Farm Bureau Federation. Both are products of the land grant colleges and tend to equate what is good for American agriculture with what is good for agri-business. No one who holds radically different perceptions is likely to rise to the top of USDA cadre.[33]

But having noted this general congruity between cadre and powerful "relevant others," it is important to point out that there is a line of demarcation between congruity with views of powerful clientele and the role demands of professionalism and task accomplishment. Cadre members cannot cross that line without drawing down the wrath and opprobium of their colleagues. A member of the Forest Service cadre can work hand in glove with the lumber industry in "harvesting" and "better utilizing" the government-owned forests. But his career pattern will suffer if he fails to conform to the elaborate criteria embodied in professional canons of resource management. It is this line of demarcation, this definition of professional role, that sometimes results in an agency being labeled as unresponsive by even those actors it serves best.

*Authority and Decision-Making Structure.* A third aspect of the bureaucracy's internal political economy that effects its responsiveness pattern is the character of its decision-making structures. To be sure, this relationship between authority structure and responsiveness has been ignored in much of the public administration literature, which focuses instead on the way authority structures affect efficiency. Nevertheless, the impact of decision-making structure on responsiveness is pronounced, for as Harold Seidman has recently noted, "organizational arrangements tend to give some interests, some perspectives more effective access to those with decision-making authority. . . ."[34]

One of the most crucial of these "organizational arrangements" is the degree of autonomy an agency enjoys within the larger administrative hierarchy. The executive branch is wracked by a constant struggle between the drive of agencies and powerful "relevant others" for autonomy and the drive of the president and his staff agencies for centralized policy coordination and control. Agency cadre usually prefer independence from higher level authorities in order to control as much of their own internal procedures, promotions, and resources as possible. Powerful nongovernmental groups interested in access and influence have often encouraged this drive for autonomy, hoping to insulate the agency from broader interests while making it more receptive to their narrower concerns. During the 1950s, for example, the savings and loan industry fought vigorously and successfully to help the office concerned with regulation of savings and loan institutions achieve its independence from the Housing and Home Finance Agency. The resulting Federal Home Loan Bank Board acquired the status of an independent regulatory body, which for all practical purposes left it independent of virtually everyone but the savings and loan industry.

Similar motivations were at work when the home-building industry and the Federal Housing Administration fought the latter's absorption into a proposed cabinet-level urban affairs department. The Department of Housing and Urban Development could not come into existence until plans were changed to accommodate the home building interests by guaranteeing continued autonomy and viability for FHA within the larger department. Consequently, much of the desired integrating function for HUD was undermined by organizational arrangements that tied the secretary's hands in dealing with FHA.

This undermining of central administrative coordination and control is not unique to HUD, however; it is a central characteristic of the whole federal bureaucracy and directly affects the pattern of bureaucratic responsiveness. Instead of an integrated set of functionally-unified departments, responsive to some general definition of public needs that might be provided by the president, the federal bureaucracy is really a bewildering smorgasbord of institutional types with varying degrees of autonomy and diversified decision-making structures.

Outside the twelve executive departments, there are roughly fifty-one agencies of astounding structural diversity. If one adds government corporations of mixed ownership, private corporations organized and financed by the government to furnish contractual services to federal agencies, and intergovernmental bodies, the number swells dramatically. Even within the executive departments, there is a welter of bureaus and offices with varying degrees of autonomy. An agency like HEW, for example, is a loose collection of warring fiefdoms only nominally subservient to a common sovereign.

To the extent that agencies inevitably yield to some of the centralizing pressures within the executive branch, or necessarily make their procedures and processes conform to such pressures, they are perceived by their powerful "relevant others" as unresponsive.

Occasionally agencies perceive the danger of so-called autonomy and reverse the pattern. For, if hard-pressed enough, an agency desires autonomy from nongovernmental as well as governmental "relevant others." The Grazing Service, for example, found that the suffocating embrace of the Stockmen's Association so flagrantly violated professionalism and put the agency under such pressure, that it sought, with the help of interests adversely affected by the arrangement, to be absorbed by the larger Bureau of Land Management.[35] This gave them some breathing room by throwing the Association into competition with other powerful interests surrounding the Bureau. Unfortunately, such examples tend to be the exception rather than the rule.

In general, the forces for autonomy have won out over the forces for centralization despite herculean efforts by virtually every president in modern times. Agencies, egged on by their powerful "relevant others" and their own perceptions of professionalism, have sought to maximize their individual discretion vis-a-vis the presidency and his staff agencies, thus diminishing bureaucracy's overall responsiveness and frustrating unified approaches to basic societal problems.

The same tensions between centralization and decentralization that are at work in the executive branch as a whole are present within an agency and affect responsiveness. The demands of internal political economy lead an agency to divide responsibility and authority and parcel it out for specialization and effective task accomplishment. But this specialization and division leads to parochialism of perceptions within the agency cadre and increases the problem of cadre control over an agency's internal political economy. In the case of this internal tension, it is more difficult to generalize about the desires of powerful "relevant others." If any generalization is possible, it may be that they prefer to see decision-making authority lie where they are best equipped to influence it. Some interests are well-organized and powerful at a local level and would thus prefer a tendency toward decentralization and discretion being exercised by field agents. Others feel they can be most effective at top levels, and therefore look more benignly upon centralization of authority and decision-making in an agency. Those that feel the centralization-decentralization issue is not distinctly tipped in their favor will feel an agency is unresponsive. Needless to say, no matter how much an agency may overtly or inadvertently serve them, few powerful "relevant others" are satisfied.

*Procedures of Task Accomplishment.* The fourth aspect of agencies' internal political economies affecting their responsiveness is the routinization and procedures surrounding task accomplishment. Indeed, control over procedures is one of the major reasons that an agency's cadre struggles to establish and maintain a certain authority pattern and a certain position within its larger hierarchical setting. Routines and standard operating procedures (SOPs) are after all the heart of an agency's existence and its collective behavior. Every public organization must divide its work and responsibility to gain efficiency and the effectiveness of specialization. In order for large groups of humans to coordinate specialized efforts in accomplishing complex work, it is necessary to establish routines and SOPs. The positive aspect of this is that bureaucratic organizations can handle large amounts of complicated but routine work in a relatively expeditious fashion. But this aspect is generally overlooked, especially by those who are greatly concerned with a particular agency's output or operations and stand to lose or gain by them or by the length of time taken to produce them. Rather than being impressed by the vast amount of routine work handled expeditiously, they are more likely to be negatively impressed by some failure to give special handling or expeditious treatment to a matter that concerns them. Thus the very procedures that enable agencies to perform with general effec-

tiveness by universalistic criteria can make them appear unresponsive to those who wish special treatment on particularistic grounds.
It is true that agency procedures can be dysfunctional, time consum-
ing and tied up in red tape. But more often they are so perceived
by those seeking special treatment rather than actually being that
way as measured by sound objective criteria.

There is another aspect of SOPs that contributes to perceptions
of nonresponsiveness; that is the inability of agencies to respond to
new situations. As Graham Allison points out, SOPs make up scenarios or set organizational responses to differing circumstances.[36]
Each agency has a limited repetoire of scenarios at hand to cope with
a seemingly endless variety of changing circumstances, many of
which are foisted upon it by "relevant others." But patterned and
coordinated human behavior is hard to achieve and maintain. The
number of scenarios can never be very large nor can they be infinitely
flexible. Agencies are thus often unable to cope with new circumstances or have trouble adjusting to a scenario and its procedures
to such circumstances. The more highly structured and interdependent the SOPs, the greater the foul-up factor and the greater the
appearance of nonresponsiveness.

Scenarios and SOPs also tend toward rigidity and nonresponsiveness if they are more closely tied to an organization's ethos.
While all SOPs in the long-run are consistent with ethos, some are
more closely tied to it than others. For Selective Service, the procedure of keeping members on local boards until they wished to retire
was consistent with its grass-roots and volunteer ethos, but it was
not so closely linked that it could not be abandoned quickly under
pressure from the House Armed Services Committee. But the procedure of taking all cases before the local board for a decision, even
though they could give only a cursory treatment to the great bulk
of them (and apply very poor knowledge to most of those), was such
a vital reflection of ethos that it remained unchanged despite challenges from a host of powerful "relevant others." SOPs especially
tend toward rigidity if they are based upon some form of "professional" performance standards. Though professionalization has been
hailed for its contribution to efficiency and the fact that it occasionally wards off political venality in situations like the efforts to cover
up Watergate, it also paradoxically dilutes responsiveness. By sanc-

tifying their procedures through identification with presumably neutral professional standards, agency cadre and their nongovernmental professional colleagues seek to insulate the bureaucracy from external attack, buffer the technical and task-accomplishing core from disruption, and finally, to rationalize procedures with which they are comfortable. The Bureau of Public Roads, for example, has worked closely with the Association of State Highway Officials to develop a potent road locator procedure that until recently insulated highway planners from the troublesome complaints of environmentalists and residents along proposed interstate routes by making the destruction of parkland, open space, and central city neighborhoods appear to be the inevitable consequence of Divine Writ, which deemed "cheapest right of way" the principal criterion.[37] The military have been equally successful in fending off inputs from civilians by wrapping their major weapon purchase decisions in the sanctified garb of technical pseudoprofessional norms. In short, despite the hopes of civil service reformers, the emergence of professionalism in the bureaucracy has been less successful in enhancing responsiveness than in rigidifying and sanctifying established procedures.

*A Case Study.* The relationship of mission and procedures to responsiveness may be seen more clearly if we examine a case of an attempted change of these aspects of a public organization. Drastic alterations of mission and procedure are conspicuous by their rarity. Nevertheless, they do occur. One of the most striking recent cases is the Federal Housing Administration (FHA).

Created by the National Housing Act of 1934, the Federal Housing Administration was charged with arresting the decline in urban housing conditions produced by a generation of urban neglect and a half decade of serious economic depression. To carry out this mission, FHA was authorized to guarantee long-term, low interest loans by private lenders to potential homebuyers who were in need of housing but too poor to afford the prevailing high down payment and high cost mortgages.

FHA very quickly learned that its two most powerful clients were the homebuilders and bankers. Indeed, it scarcely accomplished anything without their cooperation, and in the long run, survival depended upon their support. Therefore, FHA early adopted an organizational ethos befitting a conservative small-town bank. This ethos, whatever its merits, failed to arrest the decline in inner-city housing. Agency cadre were recruited primarily from the real estate and banking communities and established "economic soundness" as the keystone of their procedures. Loan applications were approved only if the applicant could demonstrate an ability to make the payments, and even then only if the house gave promise of lasting the life of the mortgage. In practice, however, FHA cadre interpreted this to mean that agency programs were restricted to the white middle class and to new construction outside central cities, particularly during the post–Second World War period when the scope of FHA programs expanded dramatically. Between 1946 and 1967, for example, FHA-insured mortgages accounted for 4.4 million new units of housing, but only 11 percent of FHA mortgages went to the 40 percent of the population whose housing needs were greatest. Eager to avoid risk and anxious to please the production conscious homebuilders, FHA turned its back on the city and subsidized the dramatic postwar white middle class exodus to the suburbs. To the FHA, the poor and the cities were somebody else's responsibility. Central city areas were therefore "redlined," that is, declared unsuitable for mortgage guarantees, because they were "risky." Success tended to be measured in low default rates. In addition, FHA enthusiastically adopted the real estate and banking communities' view on residential segregation, stipulating in its procedures that loans would be guaranteed only in "homogeneous" (racially segregated) neighborhoods.[38]

The complexity of what is meant by responsiveness is seen in the FHA case. Clearly it was responsive to a narrow range of powerful "relevant others." At the same time, those interests to which it was so responsive would have been quick to label it unresponsive because of its bureaucratization and professionalization of its task core. Builders often railed against its detailed specifications for guaranteeing the durability of new homes. Nonetheless, FHA clearly had established an intimate and supportive clientele relationship with the homebuilding industry through its stress on new construction.

FHA did succeed in appearing broadly responsive. It generated considerable popular support by promoting the central societal norm of private homeownership and by facilitating the escape from the city of countless whites. But that appearance of broad responsiveness masked a far more salient responsiveness to a narrow set of real estate and mortgage interests. Additionally, broad responsiveness, whether real or feigned, stopped short of including millions of inner city dwellers who needed decent housing, particularly people of racial minorities.

What might urban development look like today if FHA had helped provide a viable alternative to the flight to suburbia? Whatever the answer, it is clear that it contributed significantly to the crisis of the city by hastening the middle class exodus while denying assistance to slum areas or the "gray areas" on the cities' fringes and effectively foreclosing suburbanization for blacks. An agency established to ease the housing crisis and improve the cities had, in a real sense, done the opposite because of its primary responsiveness to a narrow range of powerful interests.

Some measure of the difficulty in changing an agency's responsiveness pattern can be seen in what it took to alter FHA's: approximately a hundred urban riots that turned the cores of American cities into flaming combat zones and recommendations from three presidential commissions or task forces. The riots dramatically focused public and official attention on the failures of federal housing and urban development programs. With the press, the urban poor, and even some segments of the academic and business communities clamoring for a re-orientation of priorities, the president and Congress began to move. President Johnson convened a series of task forces to generate new urban-oriented programs designed for the inner-city poor. In the wake of the riots, Congress finally acceded to the formation of a cabinet-level urban affairs department, much to the regret of the FHA and its clients, who feared a loss of autonomy. At the same time, Congress, under presidential prodding, began to whittle away at the "economic soundness" doctrine that was the heart of FHA's ethos. In the Demonstration Cities and Metropolitan Development Act of 1966, Congress eliminated "economic soundness" as a prerequisite for mortgage insurance in riot or riot-threatened areas, and substituted for it the more liberal doctrine of "acceptable risk."

Thus, in 1967, FHA at last made a dramatic effort at reversing its mode of operation and responding to a different set of impinge-

ments. The conclusion had become clear, even to FHA, that it had
to take part in saving cities' cores. At an important FHA directors'
conference in October 1967, FHA Commissioner Philip N. Brownstein sought to alter completely the agency's ethos, mission and
procedures. "Every government organization must change as the
needs of the country change," Brownstein cautioned the FHA top
brass. Since low-income housing was the crucial housing need of the
nation, FHA had to "regain the organizational drive, dedication,
sense of urgency, and speed of action" of its youth and launch a "new
crusade—to see that our programs are used to the fullest extent
possible to improve housing conditions for low- and moderate-
income families and to revive the inner city." Brownstein declared:

> We have got to recognize that stimulating a flow of mortgage funds
> into the inner city, yes even into the slums, for the transfer of houses,
> for rehabilitation, and for new construction, is an F.H.A. *mission of
> the highest priority.* No longer can we afford to wait until an applicant
> comes in and bludgeons us into this kind of activity.
>
> I want you to go out looking for applications . . . I want you to
> be prudent as well as urgent, but I want you to be prepared to *take
> the risks necessary* to accomplish the job and to know that you will
> be fully supported in the decisions you make.[39] (stress added.)

For FHA, therefore, the handwriting was on the wall in bold
clear letters. With the nation's housing programs under intense public scrutiny, the agency primarily responsible for those programs
could hardly avoid feeling the heat. "Responsiveness," therefore,
could be justifiably defended as a prerequisite of survival, the ultimate bureaucratic rationale. Thus, in beckoning the FHA directors
to a "new crusade," New Frontier–appointee Brownstein sought to
reach his agency's cadre where they lived. "Just as sure as you are
sitting here today," he warned in the closing portion of his 1967
speech,

> if F.H.A. fails to respond effectively and affirmatively to this challenge,
> if F.H.A. fails to produce the results needed, then no longer will
> F.H.A. be looked at as our nation's housing agency and the need and
> justification for its continuation may very well be the central theme.
> Undoubtedly, alternative organizations will be developed because the
> need is too great and too critical to leave a void.

I have given a number of reasons why I believe F.H.A. must mount a major effort to accelerate and expand use of those of our programs which can serve families of low- and moderate-income and revive and rebuild the inner city. Let me give you one more reason. *You should work at this task as though your job depended on it— because it may.*[40]

The fact that the total volume of FHA business had been declining over the previous decade added sharpness to these comments. Private financial intermediaries had moved more actively into the middle income real estate financing field and it was clear that FHA had no real alternative.

By the mid-1960s, therefore, FHA presented what looked like the ideal conditions for a change in responsiveness pattern. Indeed, it faced a threat to its very survival unless it responded to newly recognized social needs, needs its procedures had earlier prevented it from addressing. What is more, its director, claiming clear presidential backing, laid out the new course with extraordinary clarity, linked to the ultimate sanction of organizational rewards and penalties. Under the circumstances, a change in responsiveness should have been a foregone conclusion.

The nature of the change in responsiveness that resulted, however, is enough to give pause to those who would seek to make such changes. The upshot of it all has been one of the most serious housing scandals in the history of the nation. Challenged at their tenderest point—their professionally-inspired ethos and procedures—FHA local officials responded incompetently with bureaucratic over-kill. Indeed, the bumbling incompetency seemed almost vengeful, as though FHA's cadre were saying spitefully, "If you're going to press me to change, you'll have to suffer the consequences."

Aided by the 1968 Housing Act's creation of a special risk fund to back up mortgages in formerly red-lined areas, FHA officials threw caution to the winds and opened the flood-gates to financial predators for one of the greatest gold rushes in real estate speculation history. Under the new dispensation, real estate speculators—backed by mortgage lenders, savings associations, and banks—purchased run-down central city dwellings for a song (often using block-busting tactics), made cosmetic repairs, secured grossly inflated appraisals from FHA appraisers, and then "sold" the dwellings at vastly over-

stated prices to the inner-city poor on mortgages guaranteed by
FHA. Once the transaction was completed and the speculator had
pocketed his money, the poor family found itself with a dwelling
seriously needing basic repairs, despite the FHA okay. Unable to
afford the upkeep, let alone the more fundamental improvements,
the only alternative was to milk the dwelling for all it was worth and
then abandon it.

The result has been an epidemic of foreclosures. In Detroit and
Philadelphia, for example, the Department of Housing and Urban
Development has become the major owner of single-family residential housing because of defaults. With "you asked for it" replacing
"economic soundness" as its basic ethos and without the clear guidelines and procedures provided by the "soundness" approach, the
FHA has become a major force encouraging central city block bust-
ing and wide-spread abandonment. Unwilling and unable to adjust
their programs to the special needs of the poor, FHA personnel,
probably unwittingly, designed procedures perfectly suited instead
to the needs of real estate speculators and financiers feeding on the
poor. In short, what was supposed to result in a different and broader
responsiveness ended up being a new rip-off.[41]

The case of FHA is likely to lead to pessimism about changing
the responsiveness patterns, perhaps improperly, for such patterns
can be changed. It is merely that it is not easily done. The FTC
shifted somewhat in recent years from a stance of cronyism with
business to more of a consumer advocate role. In so doing, it shifted
from an extreme responsiveness to business to a more broadly based
one resting on the president and the new consumer-advocate
groups.[42] Whether or not it can hold the new pattern remains in
doubt, but change does occur. For example, the Office of Education
within HEW underwent drastic change from a pathological state of
entropy to one of broad responsiveness as a result of the Elementary
and Secondary Education Act of 1965 and a series of ensuing basic
reforms and reorganizations.[43] Change depends, however, on certain
preconditions we shall return to later.

### Can Responsiveness Patterns Be Classified?

In the foregoing pages we have identified (1) those variables
determining to whom an agency is responsive, and (2) those variables

determining the limits of that responsiveness. Is there sufficient knowledge at hand to categorize or classify the responsiveness patterns that are fashioned by these two sets of variables? Perhaps.

We would like to suggest some possible relationships between responsiveness patterns and task characteristics that might provide a basis for classification. The heart of such a classification would seem to rest upon (1) the perceptions an agency's "relevant others" have concerning the implications of its task for them; and (2) its ethos, the normative order influencing the choice of strategy for task accomplishment and helping shape the responsiveness pattern. We recognize that such a classification system has its problems. Because it is based on perceptions held by others, it does not rest on easily established fact. In addition, it is complicated by the fact that many agencies perform a variety of tasks. Nonetheless, we think the perceptions of an agency's "relevant others" are discernable and its task characterizable, sufficiently so to suggest a classification scheme.

One identifiable set of responsiveness patterns are those of high intensity and narrow breadth. These seem to be most frequently related to agencies with regulative tasks. Such agencies face an environment filled with powerful, intensely interested "relevant others" outside government that can significantly hurt it or even threaten its survival. We have previously noted that this narrow breadth of responsiveness can range from a single interest that has made an agency its captive to several which compete for its attention. The exact pattern depends on the weight of variables discussed earlier, but the "high-narrow" pattern of regulative agencies holds.

We hypothesize that such agencies tend to follow a strategy of task accomplishment resting heavily on legalism and proceduralism. In other words, they seem to emphasize procedural due process and project a concern for improving it in an effort to alleviate the powerful pressures upon the agencies. Indeed, many of the pressures by the affected interests are framed as matters of due process, which may or may not be the real point at issue. (Examples: advance notice of rule changes, elaborate predecision consultation and hearings, formation of advisory committees, formal adjudicative process, etc.) All of this is directed at providing an acceptable answer to the questions whether or not there are mitigating circumstances to be considered in allocating the values in question and whether or not the way the values are allocated is really fair.

Another identifiable group of responsiveness patterns seems to be those of high intensity and wide breadth and are associated with agencies involved in redistributive tasks. Redistributive policies may generate intense struggle during their legislative stage of development, but the fight is at a philosophical level and between broad categories of citizens. Once policy enters an administrative stage, the antagonisms and intensity of feeling of the earlier stage carry over as a background variable for the agency and policy. This happens because conflict over legislating the policy was broad, and material or symbolic values are taken from one broad category of citizens and redistributed to another. Though there are few if any specific, powerful interest groups leaning on the agency, nonetheless previous antagonisms, continued friction over values of political culture affected by the policy, and occasional harrassment by individual congressmen in positions of power make the cadre of such agencies apprehensive. The responsiveness pattern is one of high intensity (frequency and fervor of interaction with environment), but it is broad, diffuse, and with few exceptions, unfocused. It does not emanate from sources that are always powerful and clearly distinguishable.

Redistributive agencies thus may tend to develop a mode of task accomplishment best described as bureaucratized. This style is careful, precise, efficient, "by the rules," and aimed at seeing that those receiving the "goody" are correctly entitled to it. Not surprisingly, the resulting responsiveness pattern is one in which the agency tends to be far more attentive to broad, negative norms and attitudes than it is to those inefficacious and weak recipients of the redistributed value. The latter tend to be treated formally, suspiciously, and efficiently by the agency.

If a redistributive agency is successful in its task accomplishment strategy, it can keep hostility diffuse and avoid the coalescing of antagonism into groups that can threaten its survival. If it fails, as did the OEO or FSA, it can inadvertently mobilize and aggregate specific powerful and hostile groups (in their cases governmental members or local power elites) that can threaten its destruction, drastic alteration, or at least unsettling harrassment. Such agencies, like all public organizations, are attentive to their subject-matter and appropriations committees in Congress, but beyond that a diffuse and broad pattern of responsiveness holds.

Finally, there may be a responsiveness pattern that falls into a mixed category. In this mixed pattern, an agency may interact with high intensity and a narrow range of powerful "relevant others," but at the same time, the interaction is somewhat offset by a responsiveness of low intensity and considerable breadth to a large number of specific groups of limited power. The high and narrow responsiveness discussed earlier generally encompasses attentiveness to congressional committees, of course, but in the mixed category there is a special responsiveness to committees that goes further. This is because both the committees of authorization and appropriations take a direct hand in deciding specifically "When who gets the goody" and its exact size—deciding immediate cases of how the pork shall be sliced, not cases in the abstract, distant future, or in general categories. Additionally, the mixed pattern includes on its high and narrow side specific middle men, the translators of dollars into concrete, asphalt, or some other form of output, groups like the American Association of State Highway Officials and the American Road Builders Association, to which the Federal Highway Administration must be particularly attentive.

In the low intensity and broadly dispersed part of the distributive agencies' mixed responsiveness pattern fall a seemingly infinite number of local groups that stand to gain or lose by the distribution and its timing. While these groups can make themselves troublesome by working through a congressman if he is strategically placed, few are able to aggregate or mobilize enough power resources to seriously threaten the legitimacy or resource base of a distributive agency.

Such agencies adopt a style of task accomplishment that is technicized and maximizes the mere appearance of broad responsiveness. They use the stance of technical expertise to buffer the task-accomplishing core and ease pressure from the high and narrow range of their pattern while maintaining quiesence in the low and broad range. Elaborate technical formulae, complex feasibility studies, and incomprehensible cost-benefit studies are their stock in trade. These things sanctify the agencies' authority and provide a placating answer to the question "When does the goody get got?" In other words, this strategy of task accomplishment lines up the recipients and gets them to accept their place in line with minimum complaint. For example, it is not unusual for the Corps of Engineers to do one feasibility study after another over a twenty-year period. In the end, Lake Charles, Louisiana, gets its ship channel, but the reasons for its being "more feasible" after twenty years study remain a technical mystery. To be sure, the powerful interests in the high and narrow part of the pattern are generally served first, but at times a distributive agency may be able to change this by combining the stance of technical expert with the tactic of playing the powerful few against the weaker many.

The technical stance serves the distributive agency well in both ranges of its reponsiveness pattern: the high and narrow and the broad and low. The charts below attempt to summarize the foregoing discussion.

Classification of Responsiveness Patterns

| *Nature of Responsiveness* | *Nature of Agency Task* | | |
|---|---|---|---|
|  | *Regulative* | *Distributive* | *Redistributive* |
| *Narrow* | | | |
| High Intensity | X | X | |
| Low Intensity | | | |
| *Broad* | | | |
| High Intensity | | | X |
| Low Intensity | | X | |

Classification of Strategy for Task Accomplishment

| *Strategies of Task Accomplishment* | *Nature of Agency Task* | | |
|---|---|---|---|
|  | *Regulative* | *Distributive* | *Redistributive* |
| Bureaucratic | | | X |
| Technocratic | | X | |
| Legalistic | X | | |

## Conclusion

What emerges from all of this is that the stereotype of bureaucracy as unresponsive is like all stereotypes, inaccurate. Bureaucracy is indeed responsive. The problem, it seems, is that it is not democratically responsive to some broad mass of citizenry. Since American political culture is unreconciled to bureaucracy and the towering eminence it has achieved among governmental institutions, our desire for it to be "democratically responsive" is particularly acute. Accordingly, we expect a responsiveness that is not only unrealistic, but which is scarcely expected of other major institutions.

Public bureaucracy will, because of inherent features, be responsive to those "relevant others" that have power resources and the will to use them. That characteristic by itself need not determine whether responsiveness is broad or narrow; but, unfortunately for our culturally-shaped ideals, the distribution of power in the American system works to narrow responsiveness. The chief executive could force a broader responsiveness, but his efforts have been largely ineffective and sporadic. The Congress, as noted, tends to narrow responsiveness with its localistic and particularistic biases. Interest groups hold the greatest amount of power among all the participants in the American political struggle. They are always at hand and their pressures are insistent and narrowing. Finally, there is that cluster of variables we have referred to as the internal political economy of public organizations, or the bureaucratization of the task core. Unfortunately, it is also a powerful force for narrowing responsiveness, one that can even frustrate the powerful allies of an agency because of its sometimes pathological aspects.

Is there some way to offset these pressures that narrow the responsiveness of bureaucracy? Unfortunately, there is no easy cure. There are things that can be pointed to. Despite the stain of Watergate, enhancing the president's ability to formulate policy and monitor its implementation, especially through the planning and budget processes, and reforming Congress, particularly the committee and seniority systems, might help to some degree. It would also help to restructure agencies and alter key processes like recruitment, or to educate administrators to be more sensitive to broad public interests, to the forces that narrow responsiveness, and to ways that they can move organizations toward the broader interest, as by broadening participation in decision-making processes. Finally, citizen awareness and participation may be heightened and issue-entrepreneurs like Ralph Nader nurtured.

If bureaucracy is to be made more responsive, the problem must be attacked on all of the fronts mentioned above. However, we feel students of American government and politics bear a special responsibility for the development of a better understanding of the political economy variables of public organizations and how they interrelate to shape responsiveness patterns. We must know what shapes a particular pattern in order to change it. This is the essential prerequisite to change. With better understanding, there is hope. As Harold Seidman, who has led the way in this area, puts it, "The behavior of adult institutions *can* be changed."[44]

A heavy responsibility thus rests upon students of politics and government. But, even if understanding increases dramatically and changes are pressed for vigorously, American democracy will have only begun to solve the problem of bureaucratic responsiveness. The growth of bureaucratic power and importance, and its tendency toward narrow responsiveness, will remain one of the serious, unsolved dilemmas of the American political system for some time to come.

# The Political Responsiveness
## of the American States
## and Their Local Governments

*Ronald E. Weber*

The enactment of the Federal Revenue Sharing Act of 1972, the first step in Richard Nixon's "New Federalism" program, rested upon the argument that the states and their localities know and understand their problems better than does the Congress and the federal bureaucracy and, therefore, decisions on how to use federal aid should be made at the state and local level. In urging the passage of revenue sharing by the 92nd Congress, President Nixon argued:

> If we have faith in the American people—and I for one do—then we must recognize that in thousands of communities, each with its own problems and priorities, there live people quite capable of determining and meeting their own needs and in all probability doing a better job of it than the Washington bureaucracy. Quite simply, today's local needs are likely to be met best by local solutions.[1]

Despite the president's optimism, reformers, academics, and average citizens alike have been critical of the role that state governments and their localities have played in the American federal system. A major concern is: Are the states and their localities able to respond to the needs and wishes of their people responsibly? Furthermore: What kind of record have states and local governments established in responding to the problems of their citizens? Many a skeptic believes that the answer to these questions would probably suggest that the states and their localities are severely wanting in their capability to respond to the problems of the 1970s and that their past record of responsiveness is unencouraging. But before one can really answer accurately these questions and assess the possible consequences of the federal decision to return "no strings attached" federal aid to state and local governments, the empirical evidence on how the states and their localities have previously responded must be examined. That is the broad purpose of this essay.

In this time of seemingly unprecedented lack of confidence in the public and private institutions in this country, state and local governments like the federal government inspire the confidence of only a minority of the citizenry in attempting to deal with their problems. The Harris poll, commissioned under Senator Edmund Muskie (D., Me.) by the Subcommittee on Intergovernmental Relations in late 1973 reveals that only 24 percent of the public has a great deal of confidence in the people who run state government and reports a slightly higher 28 percent who express a comparable degree of confidence in the people who run local government in this country (see table 1). Of major institutions of government, only the executive branch of the federal government and the White House were held in lower confidence than state and local governments by the public.

State and local leaders, who were sampled at the same time on the same questions, however, were much more confident than the public in the leadership of local government (50 percent expressing a great deal of confidence), while being about equally as confident as the public in state government (27 percent). When asked to compare their present confidence in state, local, and federal government with that of five years ago, the respondents from the public sample tended to be less confident in all three levels of government. The leaders, on the other hand, were inclined to express more present confidence in state and local governments and much less confidence in the federal government.[2]

The data from the Harris public survey indicate clearly that citizen confidence in the institutions of state and local government is low today and lower than it was as recently as five years ago. A comparison of the data from the leader survey suggests that state and local leaders are somewhat more confident than the public on how they are running their institutions and that perhaps they misunderstand the extent to which the public is disillusioned with state and local government and their leadership.

**Table 1**

Public and State-Local Officials' Level of Confidence in the People Running Various Institutions in the United States, 1973

| | Public | | | | Leaders | | | |
|---|---|---|---|---|---|---|---|---|
| *Institution* | *Great Deal* | *Only Some* | *Hardly Any* | *Not Sure* | *Great Deal* | *Only Some* | *Hardly Any* | *Not Sure* |
| U. S. Supreme Court | 33% | 40% | 21% | 7% | 44% | 39% | 17% | 0% |
| U. S. Senate | 30 | 48 | 18 | 4 | 31 | 56 | 11 | 2 |
| U. S. House of Representatives | 29 | 49 | 15 | 7 | 26 | 59 | 14 | 2 |
| Local Government | 28 | 49 | 19 | 4 | 50 | 44 | 6 | 0 |
| State Government | 24 | 55 | 17 | 5 | 27 | 59 | 13 | 0 |
| Executive Branch of Federal Government | 19 | 39 | 34 | 7 | 17 | 52 | 28 | 2 |
| White House | 18 | 36 | 41 | 5 | 21 | 43 | 35 | 1 |

*Source:* United States Senate Committee on Government Operations, Subcommittee on Intergovernmental Relations, *Confidence and Concern: Citizens View American Government* (Washington; United States Government Printing Office, 1973), 2:77–84; and 3:40–47.

The states have become more and more the whipping boy for failing to offer adequate solutions to major domestic problems stemming from rapid social and economic change. Malapportioned state legislatures were slow in assisting the feeble efforts of local government to cope with the myriad of problems comprising the urban crisis in this country. Inelastic forms of state taxation—those taxes unresponsive to growth in the economy—have hampered states and their local governments in raising adequate sums to meet the educational and health needs of growing populations. The unwillingness and the inability of the states to respond with solutions for major domestic problems has led to a call for drastic solutions. If the states are unwilling or unable to solve domestic problems, why not abolish the state as a unit of government? If the national government must assume more and more responsibility for domestic governmental functions because the states and their local governments do not perform them effectively, why keep the states as units of government? Theodore Lowi, in his thorough-going critique of American interest group liberalism, argues that the states should be replaced by regional governments.[3]

The abolition of state governments and the establishment of regional governments would require drastic surgery upon the structure of the American federal system. Such a radical solution assumes that state governments are in fact unresponsive to the wishes and needs of their citizens and therefore are unneeded in the federal system. The conventional wisdom that state governments are unresponsive has become so ingrained among our perceptions about American politics that people rarely question the validity of the statement. Consequently, people tend to look to Washington or to their local city hall for the solutions to their most pressing problems. Since state governments are not perceived as responsive problem solvers, they do not get asked to solve the problems. Thus, the conventional wisdom about the unresponsiveness of the states has started a vicious circle from which state governments are hampered in attempting to escape and become more responsive.

The goal of this essay is to break the vicious circle and to examine evidence about the responsiveness of state governments in the American federal system. In addition, I will discuss and evaluate both the alleged barriers to state governmental responsiveness and the reform proposals suggested to eliminate them. Finally, on the basis of my evaluations and analyses, I will indicate some useful prescriptions for reform and speculate upon several alternative futures for American state governments.

### Responsiveness to Whom?

The fact that the states and their local governments spent approximately 170 billion dollars in fiscal year 1971 indicates that they are indeed at least partially responsive to the demands of some individuals and groups. Whether these dollars are spent in the pursuance of the public interest, whether the individuals and groups who receive the benefits are narrowly or widely based, and whether these expenditures are really responses to public demands are empirical questions of utmost importance. I cannot hope to attempt to answer them in this essay, for academic researchers have only begun to scratch the surface in dealing with these kinds of questions. Instead, I will examine areas of nonfiscal state policy making to reach some tentative conclusions about the degree of political responsiveness which exists in the states.

Before examining political responsiveness in the states, a definition of political responsiveness is in order. I take political responsiveness to be a condition in which the wants and needs of individuals and groups within a political jurisdiction are substantially embodied in the form of action by individuals and institutions possessing the legal powers to act on behalf of these individuals and groups.[4] Much like beauty, responsiveness exists in the eye of the beholder.

This definition sees responsiveness occurring when policy makers take some form of action consistent with the demands for action by individuals and groups. Simply listening carefully to the demands of citizens or groups without taking some action does not constitute responsiveness. I prefer this definition of the term for it permits me to attempt a broad answer to the question of to whom the states are being politically responsive. In addition, this definition recognizes that political responsiveness may be a state of mind from which certain behavior may flow. Thus, my definition is very much like that of "substantive representation," which emphasizes that representation of interests occurs only when the substantive demands of the interests are indeed embodied in policy.

The conventional answer to the question of to whom state governments most often respond is special interests. The notion is that groups of people who are intensely concerned with a policy issue and who can mobilize large numbers of people and ample financial resources to support a policy position almost always get their way in state politics. As Artie Samish, the once notorious California lobbyist, suggests: "First, organize the interest group and convince the members to contribute funds for their own interests. Then, spend the money wisely to elect those who would be friendly to those interests."[5] A well-established axiom in practical politics is that organization of individuals with common policy interests into pressure groups is necessary to get those interests embodied in public policy.

In the states the whole notion of pressure groups and their effectiveness is bound up with a view that most lobbying involves some form of unethical or corrupt practices to influence policy makers. The view of the Illinois legislature espoused by Mike Royko in *Boss*—the critical study of Chicago's Mayor Richard J. Daley—is all too common:

> Money was there for those who wanted it, and many did. Lobbyists expected to pay for votes. Their generosity was matched by the legislators' greed. If a day passed without profit, some legislators would dream up a "fetcher" bill. A "fetcher" bill would, say, require that all railroad tracks in the state be relaid six inches farther apart. It would "fetch" a visit from a lobbyist, bearing a gift.
>
> For the squeamish, there was the lobbyists' card game. The limit varied, but some nights a legislator was guaranteed winnings up to one thousand dollars. After that, he was on his own, but the thousand dollars was a cinch. He did not have to tell his wife he was a grafter, just a lucky poker player.[6]

The average state legislator is seen as an unprincipled boob who is willing to sacrifice the interests of the public, the state, and his constituency in pursuit of personal gain. Although many people might wish that this opinion of state legislators were less widely held, the recent widely publicized racetrack scandals in Illinois and real estate scandals in Texas suggest that there is still evidence to support this lowly conception of state legislators and their interactions with lobbyists. If state legislators are only interested in personal gain and if lobbyists offer them personal rewards in exchange for favorable votes on policies, the obvious conclusion is that the special interests will win out in any contest with public or constituency interests.

A more common explanation than the "corrupt legislator" for the extensive influence of special interests on state policy making is that individual legislators themselves are often members of special interest groups, and when acting upon measures affecting the interests of any group to which they belong, they will act to uphold the group's favored policies. For most, being state legislators is not their only occupation; many are lawyers, small businessmen, insurance or real estate agents, farmers, labor union leaders, and teachers as well. When matters affecting their occupational interests are considered, either in committee or on the floor, the most natural thing to do is to argue and vote according to their trade. Thus, a legislature composed primarily of small businessmen and farmers should be most hospitable to the positions of employer associations and the American Farm Bureau Federation on various policy matters. Legislators find themselves in the rather enviable position of being able to enact policies which are personally beneficial as well as advantageous to special interests financially able to aid them in reelection bids.

Although the conventional wisdom about the success of the special interests in the states is largely true, no one has ever been able to establish that state governments are more responsive to pressure groups than to the public in general. While the answer to this question is beyond the scope of this essay, no evidence exists that pressure group interests are inevitably in conflict with the interests of the mass public. To establish that, I would have to accept the notion that the two sets of interests—special and public—are usually in conflict. But some of my own studies of state policy making suggest that the interests of interest groups and the public are sometimes in concert. For example, the labor movement and the mass public both want to see the passage of state legislation permitting public employees to organize unions.[7] The more inclusive the membership base of an interest group, the greater the likelihood that the desires of the interest group and the mass public will coincide. Any matter of policy under discussion also is likely to have various interest groups arrayed on all sides of the issue, with some agreeing and some disagreeing with mass public opinion. In such situations some of the interest groups will be successful in achieving what they want, and unfortunately, little is known about whether the groups who generally win are those which agree with the public's position or those which seek a goal inconsistent with public opinion.

Despite the conventional wisdom about the success of interest groups in promoting their special interests, state governments appear to be rather highly responsive to mass public opinion when acting upon nonfiscal policies like capital punishment laws, parochial school aid legislation, teacher and police unionization laws, and right-to-work laws. Only in the area of firearms control do I find

much lower levels of responsiveness to public opinion. On the basis
of a continuum running from 0.00 (complete nonresponsiveness to
mass public opinion) to 1.00 (perfect responsiveness to majority
public opinion), I have measured how well the states are doing in
responding to the will of the majority of their citizens.[8] Table 2
presents the average responsiveness scores for all fifty states for
several policy areas at two points during the 1960s.

**Table 2**
Average Responsiveness Scores for Selected
Policy Areas in the Fifty States

| *Policy Area* | *1962* | *1967–69* |
|---|---|---|
| Capital Punishment Laws | .966 | .939 |
| Teacher Unionization Laws | .952 | .767 |
| Police Unionization Laws | .944 | .899 |
| Right-to-Work Laws | .843 | .918 |
| Parochial School Aid Laws | .806 | .900 |
| Firearms Control Laws | .606 | .643 |

The findings in table 2 suggest that the states on the average
are quite responsive in nonfiscal policy making. Where the mass
public wants capital punishment laws, the states have enacted them;
in those states where the mass public does not desire capital punishment as a penalty for murder, such a law is unlikely to exist. On the
other hand, the much lower average scores for firearms control
indicates that the states are not giving the mass public what it wants.
The mass public wants rather strict regulation of hand guns (for
example, the requirement of a police permit in order to purchase a
pistol), but the state legislatures have been very slow in passing such
laws. Part of the explanation undoubtedly is that a special interest
group with a large membership base—the National Rifle Association
(NRA)—opposes stricter regulation of firearms.

In looking at the results in table 2 across time, the states are
falling further out of step with their mass publics in teacher and
police unionization policy. During the 1960s the state mass publics
came more and more to support legislation to permit teachers and
police to unionize. But the state legislatures have not responded as
quickly to this increased public support and, thus, the states on the

average were less responsive in the late 1960s than they were in the early part of the decade. In other policy areas, however, like right-to-work, parochial school aid, and firearms control law, the trend is for responsiveness to increase. These results should caution those who argue that state governments are becoming increasingly less responsive to public opinion.

Although the six policy areas discussed here are only a limited, nonrandom sample of cases from a large universe of policy areas, the data suggest clearly that the states are much more responsive to public opinion than might have been thought. In addition, any idea that the states are becoming less responsive as time passes is called into question.

## Barriers to State Governmental Responsiveness

Even though I have indicated that state governments on the average are quite responsive to their mass publics, state governments would probably be even more responsive except for a number of barriers to responsiveness. These barriers constrain the states and their local governments from doing all they should be doing to fulfill the needs and wishes of their citizens. Reform efforts are often directed at removing these barriers, so that the states and their local governments can be even more responsive to their citizens.

The major barriers to state governmental responsiveness to be discussed in this section are generally structural, and include antiquated state constitutions, state statutory control over the affairs of local government, malapportioned schemes of representation, nonprofessionalized legislatures and bureaucracies, inelastic fiscal systems, and overly complex electoral systems for choosing state and local officials. I will examine these barriers to responsiveness, assess their relative importance, and evaluate the proposed reforms.

*Constitutionalism.* As every textbook on state and local government quickly points out, the fifty American states occupy a generally favored place in the American federal system because they are given all powers not expressly taken or forbidden by the United States Constitution. Consequently, almost all of the power over what you or I do every day is vested in the states. The states potentially can require their citizens to do anything or prohibit people from doing anything as long as their actions are not arbitrary, capricious, or discriminatory. Limitations on what state governments can do are included in the United States Constitution and in each state constitution.

State constitutions, historically, have been limiting or constraining documents. A fear of government power led the people of the colonies and territories to proscribe severely what state governments could do. Like the United States Constitution, most of the constitutions of the early states made the governor a figurehead and placed most of the states' powers in the hands of state legislatures. Because state legislatures became dominated by the strongest interests of the time, Jacksonian democracy, in rewriting existing constitutions and in formulating constitutions for new states, started to restrict the powers of state legislatures, prohibiting them from legislating on certain matters. Favorite subjects for prohibition were state lotteries and the use of money in public school funds for purposes other than public education. In so doing, the state constitutional conventions were undoubtedly being responsive to the wishes of the public at that time, for the usual procedure was for a state's electorate to ratify the actions of a constitutional convention before the new document would take effect.

Once embodied in a state constitution, any particular provision is hard to change or remove. Procedures for amending or revising state constitutions are generally more cumbersome than the procedures for changing statutory law. For example, in more than half of the states, the constitutional amendment procedure requires proposal of the amendment by more than a simple majority of the legislature, often in two consecutive sessions, and then ratification by the electorate. This procedure is not only time-consuming but also laden with many crucial opportunities for any particular opponents of change to shoot down the proposed amendment. Not surprisingly the most noncontroversial matters can be easily changed, while matters attracting almost any organized opposition are not likely to survive.

The essential problem with state constitutions and their impact upon governmental responsiveness is that public opinion on various policy matters may change much faster than state constitutions. In the 1830s and the 1840s the dominant opinion may have favored prohibiting state lotteries. But today, when public opinion is probably the opposite in many states, the state constitutions may still contain those old provisions. In order for the states to respond to the wishes of the present-day public in such areas, constitutional amendments have to be proposed and ratified. The plain and simple truth is that once a matter of policy is embodied in a state constitution, revising that policy to bring it into conformity with changing public wishes becomes much more difficult.

During the past three decades (1940–70) reformers in state after state have recognized that state constitutions have been a strong barrier to governmental responsiveness. Constitutional conventions have been held in some seventeen states. But only Georgia, Missouri, New Jersey, Michigan, Connecticut, Florida, Illinois, North Carolina, Virginia, and Montana have actually adopted new documents. The pace of change has been quickening, however, with the last five states having enacted new constitutions within the past five years. These newer constitutions tend to be sleeker documents with fewer words than their predecessors (see table 3). They also are characterized by streamlined provisions governing the three branches of state government and providing meaningful home rule for local governments. Illinois' 1971 constitution allows the governor to reorganize the agenices under him by executive order and institutes a broad system of home rule for local governments. The new Montana constitution lifted the previous limits on the state property

**Table 3**

States Enacting New Constitutions since 1969

| State | Date of Const. | No. of Words in New Document | No. of Words in Old Document |
|---|---|---|---|
| Florida | 1969 | 21,286 | 36,230 |
| Illinois | 1971 | 17,500 | 21,580 |
| North Carolina | 1971 | 17,000 | 17,000 |
| Virginia | 1971 | 8,000 | 34,250 |
| Montana | 1973 | 12,000 | 28,000 |

*Source:* Council of State Governments, *The Book of the States,* Vols. 17, 18, and 19; and *State Government News,* Vol. 15 (July 1972).

tax, strengthened legislative powers, and gave voters the power to choose their own forms of local government. Generally, these newer constitutions are more flexible than their predecessors, thus permitting state and local officials wider latitude to meet the needs and wishes of their constituents.

Reformers who wish to make state governments more responsive have also pursued a more piecemeal approach to constitutional change, particularly in those states where sweeping change has not been possible to achieve by means of a constitutional convention. In some states, the strategy of reformers has been to attempt to modify their whole constitution section by section over an extended period of time. This approach has been adopted to achieve some meaningful reform in those states where the possibility of wholesale constitutional reform may be chancy. The defeat of new convention-written constitutions within the past decade in New York, Maryland, Rhode Island, Arkansas, New Mexico, and North Dakota suggests that wholesale reform efforts are risky and that perhaps the more time-consuming piecemeal approach may prove more practical. Pennsylvania, for example, during the 1950s and 1960s modernized its basic document using this approach, with constitutional study commissions developing the proposed reforms. Rhode Island, having learned from past experience the risk of attempting wholesale constitutional revision, in 1973 called a limited convention and successfully proposed several major amendments which were ratified by its voters. Most constitutional change still comes as the result of the piecemeal approach, despite the increasing popularity of constitutional conventions in recent years. In 1972 only 4 of the 326 constitutional proposals successfully adopted originated in constitutional conventions. The other 322 were piecemeal approach amendments.

The evidence then is that the states have been making significant progress on constitutional reform. Today more state constitutions than ever before are modern, flexible documents, giving state and local officials the power and the ability to govern effectively. More constitutional change will certainly come in the 1970s (New Hampshire, Louisiana, and Texas have already called constitutional conventions) through both the convention and piecemeal approaches. Nevertheless, a large number of states still have documents which severely hamper their ability to act responsively in policy making.

*State Control of Local Government.* Constitutionally, in a strict legal sense, all units of local government in the American political system are creatures of the states and therefore subordinate to state governments. This is a well-established principle affecting particularly municipal corporations and county governments. To the extent that local governments are autonomous and self-governing today, they have been granted these powers by their respective state governments. What the state government has granted at one time, it can take away at another. Local governments, therefore, are at the mercy of state governments in developing a capability to respond to the wishes and needs of their citizens.

Broad home-rule powers are what local governments have been seeking and what state governments have been opposing. Over time the localities have been slowly winning this struggle. Approximately forty of the fifty states permit some form of municipal home rule. The states, however, have not moved as far to facilitate county home rule, with only about fifteen states allowing some type of home rule for counties. And municipal or county home rule in many states may not be home rule in reality. Local governments may be empowered only to make decisions on matters which the state government has delegated to them. For example, certain functions like planning and environmental control cannot be performed by local governments unless the state government enacts permissive legislation.

The broad home rule powers advocated by interest groups representing local governments and by the Federal Advisory Commission on Intergovernmental Relations (ACIR) involves a mixture of the following ingredients: (1) Localities should be empowered to select, by popular referendum, the type of structure for the local government. Presently, state constitutions often prescribe the internal structure for local governments, particularly counties. State legislatures tend to classify municipalities and counties on the basis of population and the property tax base, thus, limiting local governments to whatever structures have been deemed most appropriate for localities of their population and property tax base size.

(2) Local governments should be granted, subject to popular referendum, the power to perform all functions and to exercise any financing powers not expressly reserved, preempted, or restricted by

state legislatures. This reform would leave the localities free to decide whether to perform a governmental function and what forms of taxation to impose on their citizenry, without legislative permission. The state legislature still could reserve certain functions and tax sources for the state government, but in the absence of state action the localities would be free to go ahead as they wish.

(3) State constitutional and statutory restrictions on local government debt should be removed and the localities empowered to issue bonds, subject to popular referendum. Presently, local government debt limits are generally based on the size of the property tax base. In a typical state, local government debt cannot exceed more than a designated percentage of the total assessed value of real and personal property in the local jurisdiction. In a number of states the designated percentage is very low—Indiana (2%), Rhode Island (3%), Arizona (4%), Montana (5%), North Dakota (5%), Oklahoma (5%), West Virginia (5%), and Wisconsin (5%).[9] Such debt limitations have hampered severely many large cities from undertaking needed capital improvements. Such cities are not only bonded up to their limits but also find their property tax bases shrinking, thus reducing their overall debt limitation figure in actual dollars. As long as debt limitation provisions are tied to the property tax base, any local government whose tax base is shrinking will be less able to bond for needed improvements.

(4) Local governments should be given the flexibility to transfer functions between municipal and county governments whenever desired, to contract with other governments for the performance of functions, and to cooperate with other local governments in providing services when it is the desire of localities to do so. All states have authorized interlocal agreements and contracts for certain purposes. In most cases, however, the authorizations are usually limited to specific functions or certain classes of local governments. And oftentimes, the local governments who wish to execute an interlocal agreement or contract first must get specific authorizing legislation from the state legislature.

Over the past decade or so, the states have been making progress in granting meaningful home rule to general purpose local governments. Colorado, Hawaii, Idaho, Illinois, Massachusetts, Missouri, New Hampshire, New York, Vermont, and Washington now provide for more local option in the internal structure of municipalities and other types of local governments.[10] About half of the states authorize county governments to adopt county executive or county manager forms, which usually give a greater measure of home rule. And state governments, slowly but surely, are relaxing restrictions on local governmental taxing and bonding powers. To stem rising property taxes, the states have been giving local governments authority to levy local option taxes—usually some form of a sales or an earnings tax. More states are either completely removing local government debt limits or granting widespread exemptions to the general limits, subject to the vote of the local citizenry.

The overall picture is still one of widespread state government control of local governments, but the trend is toward permitting more meaningful home rule for general purpose local governments. However, many local governments have not jumped at the opportunities. In a number of states where counties are free to frame home rule charters, they have not seized upon this option. Consequently, the National Association of Counties (NACO) not only must lobby state legislatures to permit county home rule but also must wage a constant educational campaign to get county governments to adopt county home rule charters. County government officials and taxpayers who feel overburdened often prefer the status quo. Thus, state control of local governments is not the only barrier to local government responsiveness. The local governments themselves may be as potent a barrier to responsiveness as any state controls. And I suspect the key to getting local governments onto the track of seeking home rule depends upon the ability of the local citizenry to arouse concern with the subject.

*Malapportionment of State Legislatures.* Until the middle 1960s, the state legislatures of fifty states for the most part were composed of representatives elected from malapportioned districts. No matter which measure was used, the general conclusion was that the legislatures in all but a few states were inequitably apportioned.[11] Malapportionment was attacked by reformers not only because it devalued some citizens' votes vis-a-vis others but also because it led to certain undesirable political and policy consequences. According to Malcolm Jewell,

A legislature dominated by members from the farms, towns, and small cities is not likely to be sympathetic to the needs of the larger cities. Home rule legislation and laws to deal with the specific problems of the larger cities—slum clearance, metropolitan transit, annexation, for example—often fail because of the ignorance and indifference of rural legislators. Urban underrepresentation affects the outcome of votes on labor and welfare legislation and in the South on segregation questions. Cities are often seriously handicapped by the state legislature in the type of taxes they can levy and the size of the tax rates permitted. Perhaps the most direct evidence of discrimination against urban areas lies in the formulas established by state legislatures for the distribution of state aid or of certain proportions of state collected taxes.[12]

Thus, the argument of the reformers was that many of the policies desired and needed by city residents were not being enacted. In effect, malapportionment was preventing state legislatures from responding to wishes of certain constituents and causing them to be overresponsive to others.

Several systematic studies by political scientists suggest that the reformers overstated the policy consequences of malapportionment. Generally, this research revealed that whether a state was malapportioned or well-apportioned, its policy choices were not very different when other factors were also taken into account. In essence, policy differences were more a result of socio-economic differences between states than of differences in apportionment schemes.[13] In my own studies, I have also found that differences in apportionment schemes failed to explain differences in responsiveness.[14] All in all, these studies tend to throw cold water on the arguments of those who called for reapportionment hoping to improve prospects for their favored policies.

Reapportionment of state legislatures came, however, as the result of 1962 and 1964 U. S. Supreme Court decisions,[15] which led almost every state to reapportion its legislature on the basis of one-man, one-vote, usually under the compulsion of a court order. Reallocation of the legislative seats did not always occur easily; protracted struggles often took place with legislatures enacting reapportionment plans which violated judicial guidelines. The courts would then impose their own plan. In Illinois, for example, the federal district court ordered the legislature to reapportion its legislative districts by a certain date or face a judicially-ordered at-large election for legislative seats. When the legislature failed to meet the court's deadline, the federal court judge brought representatives of both political parties in the legislature together and worked out a plan to which they agreed. Some states like Florida, Indiana, Mississippi, New Jersey, New Mexico, and New York enacted several reapportionment plans before they found one that the courts would accept.[16] By 1967, the legislative districting schemes of almost all the states were in substantial conformity with the U. S. Supreme Court's one-man, one-vote norm. The degree of change which took place in five years can be seen in table 4. Where most legislative chambers were malapportioned in 1962, the apportionment situation was the opposite by 1967. In essence, the reformers who called for equitable apportionment schemes had achieved their goal.

**Table 4**

State Legislative Apportionment in 1962 and 1967
by Degree of Malapportionment

|  | *1962* | *1967* |
|---|---|---|
| Number of States with Malapportioned Legislatures | 49 | 6 |
| Number of States with Well-Apportioned Legislatures | 1 | 44 |

*Source:* William J. D. Boyd (ed.), *Apportionment in the Nineteen Sixties* (New York: National Municipal League, 1967). A state legislature is categorized as malapportioned if less than 45 percent of state's population can elect a majority in either chamber of the legislature.

Following the 1970 census, the states again reapportioned their state legislative seats. As in the previous decade, the courts were involved in the process. Time and again when the legislature or a reapportionment commission enacted a districting scheme, the losers in the earlier struggle would petition the courts for relief. And until early 1973 the courts usually required the enactment of a redistricting scheme in close adherence to the one-man, one-vote norm.[17] The reformers, however, suffered a major setback on legislative apportionment on February 21, 1973, when the U. S. Supreme Court relaxed the one-man, one-vote rule to permit Virginia to follow county lines in apportioning its legislative districts. The court decision produced districts in Virginia's lower house varying in population approximately 16 percent from the largest to the smallest.[18] At a time when the legislative apportionment issue seemed resolved in most states, this new decision may completely reopen the issue and possibly force the U. S. Supreme Court to review the one-man, one-vote apportionment schemes already enacted.

With all of the attention and conflict, one might expect a generally large impact from the changes in apportionment. In the legislatures themselves, the impact has been profound. Rural seats have generally been shifted to suburban areas. In a few states, even some central city seats have been reallocated to suburban areas. As a result, the legislators tend to be younger and more cosmopolitan in outlook. Reapportionment has also tended to increase the level of interparty competition for the legislative bodies and to produce legislatures more willing to enact measures to facilitate legislative professionalism.

At the policy level, the great benefits expected from reapportionment have tended not to materialize. Rural legislators, hostile to the demands of central city residents, were often replaced by suburbanites equally hostile to city interests. By the time reapportionment came about, the nation's large cities were either not growing or actually declining in population. Several studies of the relationship between reapportionment and policy change within states suggest that reapportionment has had little impact upon policy.[19] And I have found no relationship between apportionment change in the 1960s and changes in state policy responsiveness.[20] One should be cautious, however, in discounting the impact of reapportionment upon state policies until more and better studies of the problem have been undertaken.[21]

Malapportionment no longer exists, in its most odious form, as a barrier to state responsiveness. Apportionment schemes, however, may still distort the interests being represented through the use of the gerrymander and multimember districts. And the *Mahan* v. *Howell* decision reopens the possibility that the states will be permitted to return to some degree of malapportionment. Thus, although no state's legislature is as badly malapportioned as it was before the court decisions, the reformer's task is still not completed.

*Nonprofessionalized Legislatures and Bureaucracies.* At a time when the national administration is extolling the ability of the states and their local governments to respond to their problems, a large question still remains as to whether state legislatures and state bureaucracies are able to respond effectively to the many problems of the day. When compared to their counterparts at the federal level, state legislatures and state bureaucracies have not attracted as many of the "best and the brightest" personnel as have the Congress and the federal bureaucracy. The best people tended to gravitate to Washington as the national government increased its power in both domestic and foreign affairs. People who wished to be involved in solving the many domestic problems of this country found that Washington was where the action was. In effect, the national government has held a competitive advantage over state governments for several decades in the competition to recruit the best people for government service.

While the national government has strived to make public service as attractive as possible, state governments have done very little until recently to make service at the state level appealing. The norm at the state level all too often has been the amateur legislature and the patronage-based bureaucracy. Consequently, the states often were governed by legislators and bureaucrats who would serve for only short periods, taking time off from their regular professions. The goal of the reformers has been to professionalize both the legislatures and the bureaucracies of the states, thus equipping them to be effective institutions for policy making.

Professionalization of the state public service is expected to lead to recruitment of people who wish to pursue long-term careers in the bureaucracy or desire to serve full-time in the legislature. Their first loyalty then would be to the public service and their institutions. The bureaucrat's career will be determined by activities in the executive arena, not by loyalty to any political party or governor. The legislators will be able to devote all of their time to the legislative arena; if compensated adequately, they should not need to sustain another profession back home or to yield to corruption by special interests. And the bureaucrat and the legislator should begin to think of themselves as professionals who have the intelligence, expertise, and ability to work in a professional manner to solve state problems.

Professionalization has occurred more rapidly in state bureaucracies than in state legislatures. The civil service reform movement of the late nineteenth and early twentieth centuries began the process of professionalization of state bureaucracies. Innovative states like New York (1883), Massachusetts (1884), Wisconsin and Illinois (1905), Colorado (1907), New Jersey (1908), Ohio (1912), California and Connecticut (1913), and Maryland 1920) were the first to enact some form of merit system for state employees.[22] The federal government in the late 1930s gave strong impetus to the development of comprehensive state merit systems by mandating such systems for state and local employees paid from certain federal aid funds. By the end of the 1960s, some thirty-three states had comprehensive state merit systems in operation, with the remaining seventeen providing merit coverage to federal grant-in-aid employees.[23] Many of the same states that were among the first to adopt merit systems are trying presently to make careers in state bureaucracies desirable by offering competitive salaries and fringe benefits to their employees.[24] New York, California, Ohio, Illinois, and Connecticut all pay higher salaries to their employees than most other states. Although the exact levels of professionalism in state bureaus are difficult to measure, the existence of comprehensive merit systems and the levels of compensation paid to state employees suggest that a large number of states have developed fairly professionalized bureaucracies.

In many of these states, the reformers have shifted their efforts from merit system reform to other methods to advance professionalism. The emphasis now is on the development of comprehensive personnel systems, employee training programs, and nationwide recruitment of personnel. In the states where executive branch reorganizations have occurred, the functions of civil service commissions have been transferred usually to personnel departments which report directly to the governor. These reforms aim to make merit systems work more effectively as well as to strengthen the power of the governor in personnel matters. Comprehensive personnel systems allow state employees greater job mobility and thus greater opportunities for meaningful careers in the public service. At the same time, governors can control department heads who formerly were unresponsive because of their civil service status.

While state bureaucracies have been involved in the process of professionalization for a number of years, the efforts to professionalize state legislatures are more recent. As recently as 1960, none of the states paid the kind of salary or provided the level of staff services necessary to attract a full-time, professional legislator. Most states until very recently have chosen to treat state legislatures as second class institutions by limiting severely the length of legislative sessions and by holding down legislative compensation. Often session length and compensation limitations were embodied in state constitutions and were not easy to change. And many legislators themselves were very satisfied with their part-time institutions and would vote down various legislative reform proposals. Many did so because they knew their constituents were opposed to legislative professionalism because it costs money, and some legislators undoubtedly did so because they recognized there would be no place left for them in a professionalized legislature.

Reformers advocating legislative professionalism have been pushing a number of specific reforms.[25] Some of the most important are: (1) legislatures should be permitted to meet in annual sessions of unlimited length, (2) a state legislator's salary should be at least $10,000 annually and range from $20,000 to $30,000 a year in the larger states, (3) legislators should be provided with private office space for themselves and their assistants, (4) staff support for both committees and individual members should be strengthened, and (5) legislatures should adopt conflict of interest laws specifically applying to legislators. Although many other reforms have been suggested by the Citizens Conference on State Legislatures and other reform groups such as the National Legislative Conference and Common Cause, these five would adequately distinguish professional from nonprofessional legislatures.

As of early 1974, only California and perhaps New York can be labelled as having professional legislatures on the basis of the five criteria. A total of thirteen others meet the salary criterion, but fail on one or more of the others. Only thirteen states meet the unlimited annual session criterion. And even fewer states meet any of the other three criteria. According to the Citizens Conference on State Legislatures, California and New York rank clearly on the top as having the most professionalized legislatures (see table 5 for the CCSL rankings of all fifty state legislatures). Five other states (Illinois, Florida, Wisconsin, Iowa, and Hawaii), which rank behind California and New York, cluster together as a group possessing many of the aspects of professionalized legislatures.[26] The other forty-three states definitely lag behind these seven in developing legislatures with the capacity to make policy effectively.

What kind of impact does this wide variation in legislative professionalism have on state policy making and political responsiveness? The Citizens Conference on State Legislatures reports that "highly capable legislatures tend to be generally innovative in many different areas of public policy, generous in welfare and education spending and services, and 'interventionist' in the sense of having powers and responsibilities of broad scope."[27] A more recent and systematic study, however, suggests that legislative professionalism

**Table 5**

Citizens Conference on State Legislatures Rank Order
of the Fifty State Legislatures

| Overall Rank | State | Overall Rank | State | Overall Rank | State |
|---|---|---|---|---|---|
| 1 | California | 18 | Idaho | 35 | Missouri |
| 2 | New York | 19 | Washington | 36 | Rhode Island |
| 3 | Illinois | 20 | Maryland | 37 | Vermont |
| 4 | Florida | 21 | Pennsylvania | 38 | Texas |
| 5 | Wisconsin | 22 | North Dakota | 39 | New Hampshire |
| 6 | Iowa | 23 | Kansas | 40 | Indiana |
| 7 | Hawaii | 24 | Connecticut | 41 | Montana |
| 8 | Michigan | 25 | West Virginia | 42 | Mississippi |
| 9 | Nebraska | 26 | Tennessee | 43 | Arizona |
| 10 | Minnesota | 27 | Oregon | 44 | South Carolina |
| 11 | New Mexico | 28 | Colorado | 45 | Georgia |
| 12 | Alaska | 29 | Massachusetts | 46 | Arkansas |
| 13 | Nevada | 30 | Maine | 47 | North Carolina |
| 14 | Oklahoma | 31 | Kentucky | 48 | Delaware |
| 15 | Utah | 32 | New Jersey | 49 | Wyoming |
| 16 | Ohio | 33 | Louisiana | 50 | Alabama |
| 17 | South Dakota | 34 | Virginia | | |

*Source:* John Burns, *The Sometime Governments* (New York: Bantam Books, 1971), 49.

makes little difference in policy making, with differences in levels of income in the states explaining the most variation in policy outputs.[28] My own research suggests that the impact of professionalism on responsiveness is not consistent. Professionalism is related weakly to most measures of responsiveness, and even when there is a strong relationship, it may be positive or negative. I find that professionalism is sometimes associated with increased responsiveness as the reformers would hope, while at other times I find strong negative correlations.[29] In those policy areas, the hunch of some observers that amateur legislatures might be more responsive than professional legislatures appears confirmed. All of this research suggests that nonprofessionalism should be regarded as a potential rather than a real barrier to responsiveness.

Although the states have been making much progress in developing professionalized bureaucracies and legislatures, much remains to be done to remove nonprofessionalism as a potential barrier to responsiveness. The greatest amount of effort still remains for the reformer of the state legislature. As state legislatures become increasingly professionalized, significant improvements should also occur in professionalizing the bureaucracies. Once a legislature is sold upon professionalizing itself, it should be generally receptive to measures which attempt to improve the level of professionalism in state bureaucracies.

*Inelastic Fiscal Systems.* Since so much of what government does involves the expenditure of money, elastic fiscal systems are needed to be responsive to the needs and wishes of their citizens. Governments, whose revenue raising powers are constricted, find themselves in the unenviable position of having to dissatisfy some constituents because they do not have enough resources to go around. In the American federal system, the national government has been blessed with the most elastic fiscal system, while the states and their localities have chosen for themselves the least elastic forms of raising revenue. One of the strongest arguments made for general federal revenue sharing was that it would open up to the states and local governments an elastic source of revenue—the graduated income tax—which many of them had not been using.

An elastic tax system is one which will be responsive to changes in taxpayers' income over time.[30] Income taxes, particularly those with graduated rates, are the most elastic forms of taxation state governments employ. Property taxes and sales taxes rank next.[31] Excise taxes are the most inelastic forms of taxation. Thus states which derive the largest proportions of revenue from income taxes will have the most elastic tax systems and have the greatest ability to satisfy citizen and group demands without having to change tax rates.

As of 1970, only three states (Massachusetts, New York, and Oregon) derived more than 50 percent of their revenue from individual and corporate income taxes; three others (Nevada, Washington, and Wyoming) impose neither tax. Some states have placed excessive reliance on the less elastic types of taxes. New Hampshire raises two-thirds of its revenues from excise taxes, while Nevada garners almost half of its taxes from that source. Florida, Hawaii, Mississippi, Washington, and West Virginia raise about half of their state revenue from the sales tax. The property tax yields very little revenue for operating state government programs because the states generally have reserved its use for local governments.[32]

Another facet of state government finance which limits the ability of the states to respond to citizen and group demands is the extent to which the tax revenues of the state are earmarked for specific purposes. A state which earmarks most of its revenue has little flexibility to shift funds in response to new demands. In such situations state legislatures are faced with the unavoidable dilemma of either raising taxes to satisfy the new demands for services or telling those who desire the new services that they cannot be performed because no revenue is available to support them. Either way the legislature is bound to make somebody unhappy. Revenue earmarking has been very popular in many states and often has been advocated by interest groups who wish to get certain services financed and then protected from later possible underfinancing because of revenue diversions. Thus, highway programs are often financed by motor vehicle and motor fuel taxes, conservation programs are supported by the proceeds from fish and game licenses, and mental health services may be funded by "sin" taxes on alcohol and tobacco products. All states earmark some of their revenue. Minnesota, Tennessee, Louisiana, and Alabama have tended to earmark the largest proportions of their revenue (over 70 percent), while states like New Jersey, Delaware, Rhode Island, Alaska, Hawaii, and New York have earmarked very little income (less than 10 percent).[33] As more and more states attempt property tax reform or replacement, the trend is to earmark the replacement revenues for property tax relief only. The feeling is that if the replacement revenue is not earmarked, within a few years it will be diverted for other purposes and property taxes will again increase.

State governments are also sometimes proscribed from using certain taxes to raise revenue. One of the most popular prohibitions has been forbidding use of the income tax. The Illinois legislature for years wanted to enact an income tax, but needed a constitutional amendment to do it; finally, after the voters approved an amendment authorizing the tax, the legislature adopted one in 1969. Michigan with one of the most modern state constitutions still has a provision prohibiting graduated rates for an income tax. State constitutions may also restrict the legislature's ability to reform property taxes. Quite commonly, property taxes must be levied at the same rate for residential, commercial, and agricultural property. Legislatures that wish to classify property in such a way to permit the levying of various rates are often frustrated by having first to amend the constitution. To the extent that state constitutions contain provisions on taxation, the legislatures are denied flexibility in raising revenue to respond to demands.

All these factors work to limit the tax capacity of the states and their local governments. Those states which rely most heavily upon the least elastic forms of taxation tend to have the lowest tax capacities on a per capita basis. And reliance on inelastic types of taxes means that a state's tax capacity will not increase very rapidly over time. Actual measurement of tax capacity is very difficult but is necessary to discover what kind of effort a state is making to utilize its tax capacity. Furthermore, much of the impetus for the adoption of the general federal revenue sharing program came from state and local governments which argued that they were already taxing beyond their capacities and thus needed more federal aid to fund their programs. Most proponents of revenue sharing maintained that their tax effort was already equal to or exceeding their tax capacity. Although most of these revenue sharing proponents undoubtedly perceived correctly that their constituents feel that they are already overtaxed, the data from two recent studies suggest the opposite.

The Advisory Commission on Intergovernmental Relations, in the most comprehensive study of state and local fiscal capacity and effort ever completed, reports that thirty out of the fifty states were exceeding their tax capacities in the late 1960s. The variation across the states was incredible, with Hawaii taxing at 208 percent of its capacity and Washington at 150 percent, while the states of Nebraska, New Hampshire, Nevada, New Jersey, Ohio, Texas, Wyoming, and Illinois were taxing at less than 75 percent of their capacities. Local governments in only twenty states were taxing beyond their capacities, and the variations here were less dramatic, ranging from a high of 143 percent in New York to a low of 40 percent in Delaware.[34]

Another study using more recent fiscal data reaches about the same conclusion. In 1970 only thirteen of the states were overutilizing the capacities of their state-local tax bases. New York was making the most tax effort (125 percent), followed by Wisconsin (124), Vermont (118), Hawaii (117), and California (112). Thirty-seven states, however, were underutilizing their state-local tax capacities. Seven of these (Alaska, Texas, Arkansas, Ohio, Delaware, Alabama, and Oklahoma) were operating at less than 80 percent of tax capacity.[35] A comparison of the two studies of tax effort suggests that the number of states overutilizing their tax capacities has been declining in recent years. The bleak state-local fiscal picture often painted by some proponents of federal revenue sharing just is not true. A large number of states have unused slack fiscal capacity. Pennsylvania, for example, could have raised $663 million more in state-local taxes in 1970 if it had been operating at full capacity. Likewise, Indiana which prides itself on starving public services, could have raised $320 million more for the state and local governments by taxing at full capacity.[36] Another indication coming from a comparison of the two studies is that the range in tax effort from the highest to the lowest states is decreasing over time. The states which in the earlier period were really underutilizing their tax capacities have been increasing their tax effort in recent years. In essence, more states are reaching the point where they are employing their tax capacities most efficiently, neither under- or overutilizing them to any great extent.

On the basis of these two studies of tax effort, I can only conclude that the president and the Congress were oversold on the revenue needs of state governments when they considered and acted upon the general federal revenue sharing program. One only needs to look at the current revenue situations in most of the states to realize that the states are no more strapped for revenue than Howard Hughes. A Council of State Governments survey in late 1973 indicated that a large number of states were running rather large revenue surpluses. California, for example, reported a surplus of around $850 million. Very few states indicated that any kind of tax increase was in the offing. This rosy financial picture for most state governments was attributed to tax collections that exceeded estimates because of a then growing national economy and the receipt of federal revenue sharing funds.[37] Although most plans for use of these funds were incomplete at the time of this writing, some governors are already on record about how they plan to use the surplus. William Milliken of Michigan proposed to his legislature a large program of property tax cuts, and California's Ronald Reagan suggested that the surplus there be used for tax cuts. How ironic it is for the states in one year to beg the Congress for a general federal revenue sharing program and in the next year to consider using some of that additional revenue for state tax cuts.

The current revenue situation of California and Michigan demonstrates the virtue of having elastic tax systems. As the slight recession of 1969–70 ended and a period of economic growth returned, states like California and Michigan with elastic tax systems found their tax revenues growing faster than personal income and the gross national product. As I argued earlier, elastic tax bases yield the greatest amount of flexibility for the states to respond to citizen and group demands. And when public pressure is for tax relief rather than more services, those states are best able to deliver tax cuts.

My conclusion then is that some states have tax systems which give them the capacity to respond more effectively to demands than other states can. The earmarking of revenue sources for specific services and constitutional limitations upon the use of revenue sources also hamper the states in responding flexibly to demands. The states and their localities, however, are generally not overtaxing their citizens. If anything, more states are undertaxing. And to the extent that the general federal revenue sharing program discourages states from taxing their own people, the program is a misdirected use of federal tax resources.

*Diffusion of State Executive Power.* State constitutions usually say explicitly that the executive power of the state is vested in the office of the governor. Yet the same constitutions have created a number of other directly elected executive offices with power over certain governmental functions. Quite commonly, the state will also have a popularly elected secretary of state, an attorney general, a treasurer, and an auditor. These executives are responsible to no one but the people who have elected them. In such circumstances, a governor may have difficulty getting them to work with him in achieving certain policy goals or in the administration of programs. Inevitably, jurisdictional disputes occur with two or more executives maintaining that each has the sole responsibility for performing a certain function. A typical dispute occurs when a state attorney general and a department head appointed by the governor argue over who should hire and supervise legal help. The attorney general usually maintains that his office should control all of the state's legal work, while the department head wants his own lawyers so that he can directly supervise and control the legal matters in his department. The essential problem in almost all of the states is that executive power tends to be diffused, making it hard to determine who should be held accountable for the many actions of the executive branch.

This is a very frustrating situation for many governors, for they are really caught in the middle. On the one hand, they can try persuasion to get other executives to cooperate, but they also know that too much persuasion may backfire and cause the other executives to balk. On the other hand, the governor may decide to tend to his own office and not bother to get the cooperation of the other executives. This may be a dangerous course of action because electorates usually hold governors responsible for the failures of state government while continuing to reelect incumbent secretaries of state, attorneys general, treasurers, and auditors term after term. The governor, being the most visible state executive officer, ends up taking blame for not only his own mistakes but also for many of the errors of the other elected executives. Responsive state government is bound to be more difficult to achieve under such circumstances.

So far I have only been discussing the diffusion of executive power among the major state executive offices which are elective in all but five of the states. A large number of states, however, have gone beyond these major offices and made a number of other offices electable by the people. Depending upon the state, a superintendent of public instruction, an agriculture commissioner, a labor commissioner, an insurance commissioner, an inspector of mines, a land commissioner, and public utility commissioners may be elected directly by the people. In a number of states, even university regents and state boards of education are elected. At the one extreme, both Louisiana and Oklahoma elect the executives for thirteen agencies. Louisiana even elects a Custodian of Voting Machines. The streamlined executive system is used only in Alaska and New Jersey. Alaska elects a governor and lieutenant governor, while New Jersey elects only the governor.[38]

Even though reformers have urged that the executive branches of state government should be restructured to make the governor and perhaps a jointly-elected lieutenant governor the only elected executive officials, little success has been achieved in affecting this reform.[39] Between 1966 and 1972, only four of the states which approved new or revised constitutions actually reduced the number of elective executive officers. Delaware's new constitution makes the offices of treasurer and insurance commissioner appointive rather than elective, and Illinois abolished the office of Superintendent of Public Instruction and authorized the legislature instead of the people to select the Auditor. Montana and Pennsylvania reduced the number of elective offices by one, with Montana making the Treasurer an appointive office and Pennsylvania abolishing the Secretary of Internal Affairs. Florida, however, in its new constitution retained all of its elected offices and actually added one—a lieutenant governor—to bring its total to nine elected offices. Clearly, the trend in recent years has not been to abolish the plural executive system.

Election of plural executives has not been the only reason for the diffusion of executive power. Oftentimes, governors face a myriad of structural problems in attempting to control state bureaucracies.

In some states, such as Arizona, Oklahoma, and South Carolina, major department heads are appointed by independent boards or commissions, over which the governors have very little control. In other states, such as Minnesota, New Hampshire, and Wisconsin, the governor has the power to appoint major department heads, but only for fixed terms of office which usually overlap gubernatorial terms. Thus, a new governor will come to office faced with department heads appointed by his predecessor, and he must wait until their terms expire before he can appoint his own. In only a few states, such as Tennessee, New York, and Indiana, does the governor really have a free hand in appointing the people who will be serving him as department heads.

In addition to the problems growing out of restricted appointment powers, governors usually find it difficult to make changes in the administrative structure of state governments. Specific organizational schemes may be prescribed by the state constitution or by an elaborate statutory framework. Changes can be made in these situations only by constitutional amendment or by persuading the legislature to rewrite the relevant statutes. Since both of these routes have proven to be time-consuming, governors have been seeking the power to reorganize state agencies by executive order subject to legislative veto.[40] The governors in some fourteen states now have this power, but only a few governors have actually used it to affect major reorganizations. A most notable example of this power in use occurred in 1968 when Governor Reagan of California consolidated a number of agencies into four super agencies.[41] The trend has been for the states to reduce the problem of weak gubernatorial control of state bureaucracies by either having the legislature enact an administrative reorganization plan or giving the governor the power to reorganize by executive order.

Despite all the structural changes in state executive branches in the past decade or so, executive power is still largely diffused in most states. Only Alaska, Hawaii, and New Jersey really have the type of executive branch organizations favored by reformers. This diffusion of executive power as it varies across the states frustrates governors as they attempt to make and implement policy. Undoubtedly, state governments could be more efficient and, perhaps, responsive if executive power were less diffused than it is today.

## The Barriers Compared

Now that I have discussed and assessed individually the alleged barriers to responsiveness in state policy making, I am faced with the difficult task of comparing the relative importance of the alleged barriers in hampering state government responsiveness. I am inclined to attach much more importance to the inelastic fiscal systems and state control of local governments than to the other structural barriers. Because so many policies which the states and their localities pursue involve the expenditure of money, an elastic fiscal system would seem to be a crucial condition for government responsiveness. The financing of too many services still is borne by the property tax base, which is just not as elastic as income and sales taxes in times of economic growth accompanied by high rates of inflation. Local governments today find their costs for fuel skyrocketing. Schools and hospitals are going broke trying to keep up with the rising costs of food for their students and patients. Public service unions are demanding large salary increases for their members from state and local governments so that the workers can at least stay even with inflation. While all of these costs are rising, the yield from local tax bases is not keeping up, and more and more local governments are having to cut services to balance their budgets. This current experience should convince state policy makers to consider seriously reform of their tax structures to ensure sufficient elasticity to cope with inflation.

Local governments can only be hampered also by state control of so many of their affairs. Because local governments must often wait upon state legislatures to give them the power to act in many policy areas, local governments are sometimes powerless to deal with new and emerging problems. Several years ago when protection of the environment became an issue of public concern, many localities were unable to do anything in response to citizen demands because the states had not yet delegated the responsibility for regulating emissions into the air and water to local governments. The states had the authority to act to protect the environment by virtue of their broad police powers. When the legislatures acted, most of them did not give the localities broad authority to act in this policy area;

instead they reserved many powers to the state alone, meaning that citizens would have to turn to the state for action in a policy area where the localities could have been a major force in policy making. The pattern of state response to the problem of protecting the environment is all too typical of what has happened in the past when new problems emerged, and is likely to be the pattern in the near future. However, given the incredible diversity of local needs, the states by all rights should be decreasing the control they exercise over local governments.

Of the four other alleged barriers to responsiveness, I would single out state constitutionalism as the next most important, because many of the structural barriers are embodied in the constitutions. Fiscal systems may use inelastic tax sources because the constitution mandates them; local governments may not have real home rule because the constitution gives all powers to regulate municipalities to the state legislature. State legislative districts were often malapportioned because the state constitution required it; state legislatures could meet only once every two years for menial compensation because the state constitution prescribed the meeting times and the salaries.

I am least inclined to view legislative malapportionment, an absence of legislative and administrative professionalism, and diffusion of executive power as important barriers to responsiveness. All of these barriers have been the subject of some empirical study, and the conclusions have generally suggested that none of the three account for much of the differences in policy making which exist across the states.

## Alternative Futures in State Government Responsiveness

As the United States is about to enter its third century of independence, the capacity of state governments to respond effectively to the problems of the late twentieth century is still open to question. Dramatic gains have occurred since 1945, resulting in fewer meaningful barriers to state governmental responsiveness. But while state governments have been increasing their abilities to handle many problems, the enormity of the problems themselves seem to have increased even faster. The population migrations of the rural poor,

oftentimes black, to the central city and the movement of the affluent, usually white, from the central city to the suburbs have exacerbated problems which were insignificant at the end of the Second
World War. The "welfare mess," decaying central cities, inadequate
and underfinanced school systems, and a polluted environment—to
name just a few contemporary problems—call for solutions that no
level of government seems able to offer. Malapportionment of state
legislatures may be past history, legislatures may be professionalizing
themselves, and local home rule for cities and counties may be on
the increase, but the persistent problems of the states and their
localities seem to be worse than ever. Even a massive infusion of
money in some states seems to have produced little progress on the
problems. No wonder that a majority of the nation's public in 1972
regarded our total governmental system as only fair or poor in
efficiency, responsiveness, honesty, fairness, and justice.[42]

The Nixon administration took a rose-colored view of the future
of state governmental responsiveness. Its view of the states and their
localities caused it to bet some of the federal government's revenue
on that future. Already five installments of federal general revenue
sharing money totaling about $14.3 billion have been distributed to
the states and their localities, with another $16 billion due for distri-
bution over the next two and one-half years. In addition, President
Nixon proposed replacing some seventy existing categorical federal
aid programs with four broad purpose special revenue sharing programs for education, law enforcement and criminal justice, manpower training, and urban community development. The president's
goal, clearly, was to shift the power of decision making on many
programs away from Washington to the nation's state capitols, city
halls, and county courthouses. He believed that the states and their
localities often could not meet the needs of their citizens because
federal programs removed decision-making power from them and
because of revenue deficiencies. His general and special revenue sharing programs were directed toward remedying those two problems.
He firmly believed that if the states and their localities have decision-
making power and additional revenues they would be able to solve
their problems without undue federal interference. In essence, he
expected the states and their localities to become increasingly responsive as a result of his revenue sharing programs. The Congress,

however, took a skeptical approach to Nixon's special revenue sharing proposals and turned thumbs down on all of them.

Since the revenue sharing program is just beginning, it is really too early to assess how the program effects state government responsiveness. Some potential trouble spots, however, can be identified. The general revenue sharing money cannot be used to finance local schools, one of the most important and expensive functions of government. Education was conspicuously omitted from the list of priority expenditures for which revenue sharing money could be used, and, under the terms of the law, revenue sharing money can only go to general local governments like counties, cities, and towns. In effect, most local school districts were excluded from receiving any revenue sharing money. Since the financing of local schools is heavily dependent on the property tax, which is the focus of a taxpayer revolt in many parts of the country, the likelihood is that very little new revenue for local schools can be generated in the near future without additional efforts by the states or the federal government. General revenue sharing has little potential for aiding the plight of local school districts. And the special revenue sharing program for education will do nothing more than replace some existing federal aid to education programs; it will generate no new federal revenue for local education. In fact, some states and cities which have benefited from the compensatory education formulas of the present Elementary and Secondary Education Act would get less money under the special revenue sharing program for education.

Another potential problem with the general revenue sharing program revolves around the formula for fund distribution. In contrast to many existing federal grant-in-aid programs, the general revenue sharing formula distributes the money primarily on a population basis. The largest states and localities get the most money. It does not take differences in state income into much account. The poorer states and localities do not do as well under general revenue sharing as they do under other existing federal programs. To the extent that the president plans to replace existing federal aid programs with special revenue sharing programs which distribute monies on the basis of formulae like that of the general revenue sharing program, the poorer states and localities will suffer. The Congress and previous executives have long recognized that the poorer states and localities often have had greater needs for certain programs and revenue and took this into account when enacting many federal aid programs. The formulae of the revenue sharing programs threaten to undo all the efforts of previous administrations to redistribute income from wealthy states to poor states.

A third potential problem, which can be identified on the basis of cursory evidence only, is that particular states and localities do not have any high priority expenditure needs and are thus spending the money frivolously or using it to reduce taxes. Lou Cannon and David S. Broder, in a survey of the impact of Nixon's New Federalism program upon state and local governments, report that some localities' revenue sharing money is being spent on low priority programs. "Corpus Christie, Texas, spent $100,000 on tennis courts and $100,000 for landscaping the golf course. Burlington, Vermont, spent $160,000 on an ice rink and bathhouse and $300,000 on uniforms for the municipal band. Pasadena, California, spent $498,000 for resurfacing and lighting tennis courts and Los Angeles spent $474,000 for a helicopter capable of transporting 15 firemen. Aurora, Colorado, spent $536,000 on a golf course."[43] In Bloomington, Indiana, my own locality, a large chunk of revenue sharing money is being used by the townships to equip volunteer fire departments with the finest fire engines available and elaborate fire stations. At a time when other states and localities, particularly central cities and school districts, need all the revenue they can find, it is absolutely ludicrous for jurisdictions which have no need for it to get money. The Nixon program, by channeling money for unneeded state and local purposes possibly may distort the public priorities of this nation seriously.

The alternate future that I see for state government responsiveness is not as rosy as that envisioned by the former administration. As I have argued earlier, this nation has a number of pressing domestic problems which remain unsolved, and the states and their localities are destined to play a large role in their resolution. The philosophy of the present administration is that the states and their localities should play an even larger role in resolving them. To the extent that some of the barriers to responsiveness discussed above exist, the state and local governments will be hampered in resolving these domestic problems in a way that satisfies the public and major interest groups.

In essence, efforts must continue to remove the present barriers to responsiveness.

Of them all, the one which cries out most for reform is the tax system. Whether liberals and academics like it or not, Governor George C. Wallace of Alabama tapped the pulse of the public on the issue of tax reform in his short-lived 1972 presidential campaign. The public clearly perceives that the existing tax system in this nation is unfair in its treatment of the average citizen. The recent revelation that Richard Nixon paid very little federal income tax and no state income tax while president can only reinforce public dislike for the unfair tax system. State and local taxes, particularly the property tax, as well as the federal tax system, need to be reformed. In the process of tax reform, the states need to keep in mind a number of guidelines which can be developed out of their past experience. (1) The new system should be more elastic than the former one. (2) The earmarking of tax revenue for particular functions should be ended. (3) The states should give the localities, particularly counties, greater freedom to choose the taxes they want to impose. (4) The total tax system should be fair in its imposition of burdens on all taxpayers. For example, income taxes on individuals and corporations should be graduated and be generally free of loopholes. Sales taxes should exempt food, drugs, and other necessities, and provide for systems of tax credits to low income people. The important factor is that the tax reform should take place in such a way to ensure that the public knows and believes that they are getting a fair shake. The tax reform should be fair to all and not be an occasion for fashioning even more loopholes for the well-heeled and business interests.

Another structural reform which might prove quite useful to both state and local governments would involve the establishment of ombudsmen offices or complaint bureaus. Many citizens' gripes about government relate to the performance of particular services. Their garbage has not been collected, or the title to their motor vehicle has never arrived. And they become frustrated with government as they get the bureaucratic runaround. State and local governments could alleviate much of this frustration by establishing some agency to handle the complaints and empowering it to call on the carpet those bureaucrats or employees who have been failing at their jobs. The telephone numbers of these agencies should be prominently publicized, and the state agency should have a toll-free number for use from long distance. These state and local agencies could, by successful handling of complaints, reduce the level of citizen alienation to government.

A further reform which might enable state and local governments to be more responsive would be the establishment of needs assessment programs. State legislators and city councilmen can often be misinformed as to public and elite opinions because very few states or localities have systematic methods for gauging opinion. The states should develop systematic and full-scale needs assessment programs to determine what the public and elites believe should be done by state governments. Part of the needs assessment program could be devoted to local problems and that information could be made available to local decision makers. Such a needs assessment program should be systematic and might involve the polling of the public and in-depth interviews with elites. Most state universities have the expertise to implement such programs for state governments. The outgrowth of such a needs assessment program would be to provide accurate information on needs to the decision makers who are called upon to enact new programs and to allocate funds among existing programs. More informed policy making might well lead to more responsive policy making.

In summary, many challenges face state and local governments in the last three decades of the twentieth century. The capacity of these governments to handle problems in a responsive manner is somewhat greater than it was at the end of the Second World War. Much more needs to be done by the states and their localities in generating a responsive capacity if they are to fulfill the vision promoted by the Nixon administration, or even my vision of what they should be doing. As the arena of domestic policy making shifts more and more to the state and local levels, we can all be assured that observers of state and local government will continue to have much to comment about as the governments struggle to cope with the many public problems.

# Accountability and Responsiveness of the Military Establishment

*Edward F. Sherman*

Control of the military is one of the central issues in American society today. When the United States failed to revert to a peacetime economy after the Second World War, the defense establishment became the single most powerful force in Washington. Its "total influence," as President Eisenhower observed in his farewell address in 1961, "—economic, political, even spiritual—is felt in every city, every State house, every office of the Federal government."[1] The Cold War attitude of uncritical support for the military began to dispel by the 1960s as the so-called military-industrial establishment became a popular target of critics and new social movements gave rise to an active and virulent anti-militarism, but its power was little affected. The size of the armed forces, fed by the draft, continued at high levels in order to meet American treaty commitments abroad, and defense continued to command a lion's share of the national budget.

With the expansion of the Vietnam War in the middle 1960s, the military enjoyed the inevitable wartime inflation of its budget and manpower and, as much by the default of other agencies as by design, assumed broad new powers over war strategy, intelligence, internal security, foreign aid, and foreign policy. The military took its knocks in the Vietnam War, battered as it was by internal dissent, low morale, drug abuse, graft, and war atrocities, and perhaps unfairly blamed for the unsatisfactory conduct of an unpopular war. Nevertheless it emerged from the nightmare of Vietnam with its economic and political power relatively undiminished. As demonstrated by the budget battles of 1973 and 1974 which resulted in the slashing of many domestic programs while the military received a healthy increase, the defense establishment still holds a preeminent position in the list of governmental priorities.

The power of the military in American society, although perhaps exaggerated by its critics, is a matter of legitimate concern. Its influence on the national economy through defense spending and on social and political policies by virtue of its size in the federal government represent a significant centralization of power that is especially troubling because of the nature of the military. It is a particularly single-minded bureaucracy which, because of its traditionalism, rigid career-patterns, respect for order and regimentation, and dedication to martial values, is sometimes at odds with the ethos of our civilian democratic society. The military structure is well-equipped to capitalize on its power and influence. As General David M. Shoup, former commandant of the U. S. Marine Corps, observed in 1969, "military planners have their doctrinal beliefs, their loyalties, their discipline—and their typical desire to compete and win" and "the civilians in government can scarcely play the same policy-planning game."[2] Military policy makers are not subject to the electoral process, and because of their tight rank structure and similarity of career patterns, they are often insulated from the public concerns and pressures which influence the thoughts and policies of civilian politicians. The tendency of the military to favor authoritarian, antidemocratic policies at home and militaristic policies abroad poses a problem in any democratic society.

Gaining adequate control over government bureaucracies and insuring their accountability is never easy, but the military is an especially difficult case. First, the military occupies a special place in society because the protection and very survival of the nation is ultimately in its hands. Even the traditional American distrust of the military has frequently been overcome in the face of real or perceived military threats from abroad. The phrase *national security* has often been invoked to justify increases in military appropriations, subordination of individual rights, and disregard of normal constitutional processes. Thus, the usual administrative and legal mechanisms have not always been effective in controlling the military because of exceptions made in the belief that it might otherwise be hindered in its vital mission of defense.

Second, the military, on account of its tradition, structure, and function, has always been set apart from civilian society and allowed considerable autonomy over its own internal operations. Unlike other governmental agencies, it has its own legal standards of conduct and system of criminal justice for its personnel. The courts have recognized its autonomy in many areas, being generally unwilling to interfere with the way it trains and disciplines its men and conducts its operations.

Finally, control over the military has been especially difficult in the period since the Second World War because of its influence in other branches of government. The military has had important allies in both the executive and legislative branches who, because of similar ideological, political, and economic interests, have taken the cause of the military as their own. Thus, the control system intended by the framers of the Constitution has sometimes failed to insure critical evaluation by Congress of military budgets and adequate supervision of the military by civilian officials in the executive branch. Further, the fact that weapons systems and military hardware are enormously complicated, that military matters are often screened by secrecy from the public, and that responsibility for overseeing the military is diffused among many offices and officials has contributed to the extraordinary degree of freedom accorded the military.

If the military has been especially successful since the Second World War in acquiring power and influence and in avoiding external restraints, there nevertheless appears to be little consensus in the nation as to what, if anything, should be done about it. The economic power of the military-industrial complex is accepted by many as a danger in the abstract, but any attempt to reduce its power runs head on into fears of finding ourselves weaker than our enemies, and, in the areas economically dependent on the military or defense contracts, into fears of loss of jobs and recession. There is a general feeling that the Vietnam war was a mistake, but less consensus on the desirability of new procedures to govern the application and use of military power. There were highly publicized breakdowns of supervision over the actions of commanders and men in the Vietnam War, but there have been no significant changes in military structure or procedures. Problems of dissent and low morale in the military brought to public consciousness harsh and authoritarian methods of training and discipline and the denial of many basic constitutional rights to servicemen. Except for a few changes especially intended to attract volunteers for the new volunteer army, however, few steps have been taken towards developing a military which places greater value on individual rights and democractic ideals. These contradictions reflect an ambivalence toward the military that is perhaps inherent in a democracy like ours. On the one hand, there is a desire for a limited, civilian-controlled military which respects human dignity and democratic ideals; and on the other, there is a feeling that the national security requires a well-oiled military machine on the Prussian model, which can be called upon to apply lethal force whenever or wherever desired. These contradictory ideals account for the special difficulty of obtaining accountability and responsiveness from the military.

Accountability refers to the lines of authority and responsibility which determine where an institution gets its powers and from whom it gets its orders, instructions, or guidelines—in short, to whom it is answerable. The formal lines of accountability for the military establishment can be found in the Constitution and federal laws; they include the president, civilian secretaries, Congress, congressional committees, and courts, but they really tell us very little about where the actual power lies. When the Constitution was drafted, the military was no more than an army and navy, composed of only 840 men, whose principal function was to conduct the limited and formalistic warfare of the eighteenth century. Today the military is infinitely more complex. It is not one institution, but an amalgam of institutions, embracing the uniformed services, the civilian defense bureaucracy, and the industrial defense axis, and collaterally related to such varied institutions as government agencies like the intelligence and security network, veterans' groups, labor union and trade organizations, and universities. Thus, military accountability involves management, regulation, and manipulation from a variety of diverse sources many of which cannot be found in the legal constructs of formal responsibility.

Responsiveness is an even more difficult concept to apply to the military establishment. It refers to the degree to which an institution fulfills its objectives and responds to the legitimate expectations of society. As the principal institution vested with the management of violence for society, the military might be judged solely by its success on the battlefield and in deterring aggression through its defense readiness. But these functions are not easily susceptible to ordinary standards of evaluation—as is shown by the popular saying, "You can't put a price tag on defense." Furthermore, the contemporary military establishment performs many functions in our society which go beyond preparation for and conduct of hostilities, and its impact far exceeds that of traditional armed forces. We find in American society today considerable disagreement as to what we can and should expect from the military establishment. Thus evaluation of military responsiveness involves the application of necessarily subjective criteria which derive from a concept of the proper function and role of the military in a democratic society.

### Constitutional Limitations on the Military

The principal source for control of the military in our society is the Constitution. Concern over the power of the military and its impact upon the lives of Americans was one of the principal causes of the American revolution. The British army of King George III, made up largely of career soldiers, was seen by the American colonists as unresponsive to their interests and a threat to their liberties. Thus, despite recognition of the need for military protection in the new American nation, the drafters of the Constitution placed distinct limitations upon the military, aimed not only at curbing individual abuses like the quartering of troops in homes but also at preserving the democratic nature of the American government. Control over the military was to be divided among the various branches of the government, an arrangement that is one of the significant accomplishments of the American Constitution. "The doctrine of separation of powers," Justice Brandeis wrote in 1926, "was adopted by the Convention of 1787, not to promote efficiency but to preclude the exercise of arbitrary power."[3]

A major objective of the Constitution was to curtail the power of the executive over the military, as described some seventy-five years later by Abraham Lincoln:

> Kings had always been involving and impoverishing their people in wars, pretending generally, if not always, that the good of the people was the object. This our Convention understood to be the most oppressive of all kingly oppressions; and they resolved to so frame the Constitution that no one man would hold the power of bringing this oppression upon us.[4]

Thus, although the president, like the British king, was made commander in chief of the armed forces, Congress was given the power to declare war, raise and maintain the armed forces, make the rules for their governance, and appropriate money for their support.[5] The president was expected to exercise effective control over tactics and field operations, but Congress, through its overriding powers, was to have ultimate control over the military. There was no provision for direct control of military conduct; it was felt that the military could not get out of hand while subject to the control of the people's elected representatives whose power, in turn, was checked by the executive branch. The third branch of the federal government, the judiciary, was not directly involved with the military, but through the doctrine of judicial review, established in Justice Marshall's 1803 opinion in *Marbury* v. *Madison,*[6] it was empowered to apply and interpret the Constitution, and thus the Supreme Court and the subordinate federal courts would ultimately play a significant role in controlling the military.

*Manpower Recruitment and Draft.* One of the principal, but least successful, ways that the founding fathers attempted in the Constitution to keep the military in check was by forbidding the establishment of a standing federal army. The states were expected to maintain militia for necessary defense, thus presumably making a permanent federal army unnecessary. Congress could call forth the militia for only three purposes—to execute the laws of the Union, to suppress insurrections, and to repel invasions.[7] Congress was given the power to organize, arm, and discipline the militia and to govern those militia employed in the service of the United States, but the states were given the power to appoint the officers and train the militia.[8] Since the militia were creatures of the states, there was no apparent power in the federal government to draft men into a federal army.

These constitutional limitations on the power of the federal government were sorely tested by historical developments in the nineteenth and twentieth centuries. Shortly after the ratification of the Constitution, Napoleon introduced the first nationwide system of conscription in Europe, forever changing the nature of modern warfare. With Napoleon's "democratization" of war, as historian Walter Millis has called it,[9] came a nationalistic fervor which resulted in the replacement of the limited professional armies of the eighteenth century with huge armies of low-paid conscripted soldiers. Conscription quickly swept Europe. Not until the Civil War did the United States institute its first national draft, which prompted opposition and rioting in some parts of the country but which prevailed despite the absence of a Supreme Court determination as to its constitutionality.[10] A national draft was imposed again in the First and Second World Wars and was upheld by the Supreme Court as constitutional during war time.[11] The draft remained a fixture of the Cold War, becoming the subject of much opposition and litigation in the Vietnam war period. Thousands of young men refused induction into the military, many defending their actions on the grounds that a peacetime draft is unconstitutional. However, the lower federal courts unanimously ruled against them, and the Supreme Court steadfastly refused to hear the cases.[12]

The unpopularity of the draft—often attacked for its role in compelling unwilling draftees to fight in a war they oppose, for its social and economic inequities, and for its failure to provide the kind of manpower the military wants—led to a volunteer army in 1973. The Selective Service system remains in waiting, however, and so the volunteer army has not meant a return to the original constitutional policy disfavoring a standing army and compulsory military service. Although the Constitution provided a focus for political opposition to the Vietnam War, the unwillingness of the courts to find in the Constitution prohibitions on the federal government's power to conscript indicated that any future limitations on that power will probably have to come through the political process.

*Power to Declare and Make War.* The power to declare and make war determines who will decide when and how the military will be used in our society. Although the Constitution gives Congress the power "to declare war" and the Supreme Court has stated that nothing in the "Constitution is plainer than that the declaration of war is entrusted only to Congress,"[13] the clause has become one of the most disputed in the Constitution. Recognizing that situations might arise where the president would not have time to obtain a declaration of war from Congress, the Constitutional Convention used the word *declare* rather than *make* war in order to leave to the executive the power to repel sudden attacks.[14] Recent advocates of broad executive war-making powers have argued that the word *declare* only meant "a kind of formal acknowledgement of the fact that a state of war exists" and that the power to bring the country into war was left with the president.[15] However, the debates at the Constitutional Convention do not support that interpretation, and every major war before the Korean War was explicitly declared by Congress (the War of 1812, Mexican War, Civil War, Spanish American War, the First World War, and the Second World War).[16] Early presidents were especially careful in deferring to Congress before committing troops to even minor hostilities. John Adams asked Congress for authority to protect American ships from French attacks in the Atlantic.[17] Jefferson sent a naval squadron to the Mediterranean to protect American commerce against the Barbary pirates, but ordered it not to engage in offensive action against the pirates until authorized by Congress.[18] Secretary of State John Quincy Adams replied to an inquiry from another nation in 1824 as to what response the U. S. might take under the Monroe Doctrine if there were European intervention in Latin America by saying, "you understand that by the Constitution of the United States, the ultimate decision of this question belongs to the Legislative Department of the Government."[19]

There were, however, many instances of presidents acting without a congressional declaration to send armed forces into situations in which hostilities ultimately resulted. There were undeclared hostilities with France, Tripoli, and Algiers early in the nation's history. As American power increased in the nineteenth and twentieth centuries and notions of manifest destiny took hold, presidents frequently ordered troops abroad to protect American lives and property or to provide for defense pursuant to treaty commitments. The constitutional justification was based not only on the president's powers as commander-in-chief, but also upon his special responsibility to conduct foreign affairs and to execute and enforce the laws. In 1950 in the Korean War, and again in 1965 in the Vietnam War, presidents committed sizable numbers of troops to hostilities which developed into major, long-term wars without a declaration of war or express authorization by Congress. Supporters of the president argued that declarations of war were obsolete in a day when there was often no clear-cut initiation of hostilities as in guerrilla-type wars and when it was often diplomatically disadvantageous to declare war despite the need to participate in hostilities.

Challenges by citizens in the courts to executive war-making in Vietnam were generally unsuccessful. Justic Douglas, in a dissent from the Supreme Court's refusal in 1966 to review the dismissal of a suit by three servicemen who claimed their orders to Vietnam were illegal because the war had not been declared by Congress, stated the issue in these words: "Does the President's authority to repel invasions and quiet insurrections, his powers in foreign relations and his duty to execute faithfully the laws of the United States, including its treaties, justify what has been threatened of petitioners?"[20] The Supreme Court steadfastly refused to answer that question throughout the Vietnam War as two presidents escalated, deescalated, and modified the war effort without express congressional authorization and often without consultation with Congress. A number of lower federal courts ruled by the early 1970s that the legality of the war was "justiciable," that is, that the courts would consider it, but their standards of review were narrow and they generally found that Congress had authorized the war through appropriations, the draft, and other legislation.[21] After direct American participation in Vietnam ended, one lower federal court ruled that the continuation of the air war in Cambodia was unconstitutional, but the decision was reversed by the appellate court and review was refused by the Supreme Court.[22]

Late in the war Congress began to assert its constitutional powers over war-making. Bills aimed at cutting off support for the war found increasing support, but not until combat in Vietnam had ended was a cut-off bill passed by both houses, stopping appropriations for bombing in Cambodia on August 15, 1973.[23] Three months later, Congress overrode a presidential veto of the first legislation in history which has attempted to define the respective war powers of the two branches. This "war powers" act provided that when the president commits American troops to hostilities abroad or substantially increases the number of troops equipped for combat in a foreign country, he must report to Congress within forty-eight hours the circumstances, authority for, and scope of the action.[24] He must stop the operation unless Congress approves it within sixty days, except that he may continue it for thirty days more if necessary to protect the American forces. Congress may order the operation stopped within that period by passing a concurrent resolution that would not be subject to presidential veto. President Nixon charged that the act "seriously undermines this nation's ability to act decisively and convincingly at times of international crisis"[25] and continued to maintain that the president has inherent powers to commit troops abroad without congressional authorization. Thus, although the act indicates firm congressional resolve to retain a role in war-making, without a definitive court test the war powers controversy remains unresolved.

The war powers controversy, although principally a struggle between the executive and legislative branches, bears directly on the question of control of the military. The concept of civilian control of the military envisions that the military should only execute orders to engage in hostilities, that it should neither decide when or how force will be used nor question an order from the appropriate civilian authority to use force. However, the military's role in such decisions is generally far from passive. War is the military's specialty and business, and decisions about going to war and how to conduct it necessarily involve military advice in advance and implementation afterwards. The resources which the military commands—a virtual monopoly over information about the combat readiness of the armed forces, expertise in predicting the effectiveness of military operations, and considerable control over intelligence relevant to the conduct of military operations abroad—make its participation essential to any war-making decision.[26]

It is appropriate that the military should obey the orders of the commander in chief concerning use of military force. The military is not in a position to judge that a president has overstepped his constitutional powers and therefore to refuse to implement his combat orders; such a response would place the military in the dangerous role of choosing which branch of the government to support. However, indications are that the military did more than merely execute executive orders in the Vietnam War; rather, it seems to have been a willing and active partner in executive war-making there. This is not surprising as military men are accustomed to seeking military solutions to problems, and the military as an institution has a certain self-interest in a war. The military can benefit from a war in everything from expanded budget and manpower and political influence, to practical opportunities to test new weaponry and gain combat experience for its men and promotions for its career officers. This does not mean that the military always sees its interests as served by war or that military men cannot and do not subordinate institutional self-interest to national interests. Samuel Huntington has criticized "the traditional liberal identification of the military with war and violence" and calls erroneous the "view that the military have a greater preference for war than do civilians."[27] However, although some of the strongest hawks in the early Vietnam War were civilian advisors, there is little in the history of that conflict to indicate counselling of restraint on the part of military advisors. Military intelligence, contingency planning, and recommendations were relied on heavily by the executive branch in escalating American involvement in Vietnam, and the Pentagon Papers and other inside sources indicate that military advisors and the Joint Chiefs of Staff consistently urged expanded use of force.[28]

The military is also especially well-suited to serve as a partner in executive war-making because of its resources and capacity for maintaining secrecy. A key ingredient of executive war-making in Vietnam was secrecy from both the public and Congress; the executive branch justified the secrecy and the deceptions used to maintain it as necessary because of the type of war and the delicacy of negotiations. The discipline, sense of loyalty, relative lack of legal and moral questioning, and general ideological uniformity of military men made them ideal agents for carrying out the executive wishes. Not infrequently, the military was called upon to do the dirty work— such as making the kind of reports regarding incidents in the Gulf of Tonkin in 1964 which could justify armed reprisal, and falsifying the reports of secret bombing of Cambodia and Laos in 1969, 1970, and 1971. However, there is little indication that the military felt at all squeamish in carrying out these tasks and countless other secret and questionable operations in support of the war, matters like military surveillance of civilians and civilian groups, development of bacteriological warfare agents, and widespread use of chemical defoliants and gases contrary to the majority position in international law.[29] Such things seem to have been performed by the military as much through its own initiative as through obedience to the orders of the commander in chief.

The military in any society is likely to pose a danger if it is in too important a position concerning war-making decisions, and that danger is especially acute in wars carried on without express congressional authorization and where many of the true facts are shielded from public disclosure and debate. Once a foreign crisis slips over into actual armed conflict, the military is at a decided advantage. It becomes increasingly in control of information concerning the conflict and of the options available to the executive. That was illustrated by the frustrations of congressmen and even civilian policymakers in trying to get an objective picture of what was going on in Vietnam, when reports and statistics were intentionally falsified and even visits to the front were often carefully managed and staged by the military.[30] Despite the special expertise of the military in military matters, it is doubtful whether it should be allowed to become the principal source of information and advice concerning wartime decision-making. As Sidney Hyman has observed, "Human rivalry in all its forms is so subtle, unmeasurable, irrational, and haphazard, that it makes little sense to entrust its resolution to a single hypothesis promulgated by a single group of experts, with all their vulnerability to the virus of self-centered advocacy."[31]

The war powers controversy has highlighted both the danger of insulating executive warmaking from public and congressional scrutiny and the special difficulty of obtaining accountability from the military in its role in making and implementing war policy. Congressional attempts to reassert its war-making authority and its right to know all facts relevant to such decisions are a step in the right direction. Changes in both structure and policy should also be considered to insure that the executive obtains the advice of as many different sources as possible and keeps close counsel with Congress. Along these lines, Senator Jacob Javits (R., N. Y.) proposed in May 1974 seven measures to reestablish Congress as a "truly coordinate branch" of government.[32] These included requirements that the president report annually to Congress on steps taken to implement laws and resolutions passed in the previous session, that every congressional committee establish a liaison office with the executive department it oversees to provide guidance in carrying legislation into action, and that Congress clarify the term *national security* to encourage greater disclosure and dissemination of information concerning government activities. Former Eisenhower speechwriter and historian Emmet John Hughes has proposed other institutional changes to redress the balance of powers, including congressional control of selective service, formal liaison between the White House and congressional leaders during significant foreign-policy deliberations, and submission to Congress of any executive agreement of a military nature with a foreign country.[33] Such changes would undoubtedly require expansion of the resources and capacities of Congress to process larger quantities of information and provide more efficient advice and consultation to the executive branch.

Some conscious limitation of the military role in executive decision-making also seems desirable. There has been a gradual infiltration of civilian offices and agencies with military personnel. The Pentagon reported in September 1973, in response to a congressional inquiry, that 515 active duty military officers were assigned fulltime to government agencies outside the Department of Defense, 39 of them assigned to the president or White House, five to the vice-president, and substantial numbers to the Selective Service Commission, National Aeronautics and Space Administration, Department of Transportation, and Atomic Energy Commission.[34] Some ten generals and admirals now serve as deputy assistant secretaries of defense, holding key positions in such offices as manpower (which accounts for 56 percent of the defense budget), research and engineering, intelligence, and telecommunications.[35] Upon his appointment as White House chief of staff in 1973, General Alexander M. Haig brought with him at least three active duty and retired military staff assistants.[36] The practice of having top executive aides be career officers encourages a palace-guard type of military manipulation and intrigue which can be inimical to democratic government. Limitations on the assignment of active duty officers and on the hiring of retired officers within a certain period after retirement are needed in order to restrict military influence over civilian departments and agencies. The ability of civilian agencies to provide policy advice, intelligence, and contingency planning which are now largely the monopoly of the military should be expanded, and procedures requiring recourse to such agencies by executive policy planners should be established. Finally, structures and procedures are needed to provide continual congressional contact with military policy decision making to prevent the military-executive alliance from freezing out Congress in its proper constitutional role as authorizer and monitor.

*Operations of the Military.* Congress, through its constitutional power "to make rules for the government and regulation of the land and naval forces," has the authority to establish the standards for the operation of the military. It has done this through legislation passed over the years dealing with the operations of military and the defense establishment—setting forth the organization of the armed forces, personnel, training, supply, and procurement. However, much of the legislation is general in nature and the details must be filled in by executive and service regulations issued by the president, secretary of defense, secretaries of the services, and military commands under them. There is some uncertainty about the exact authority for such regulations; Congress often expressly provides that the executive shall have the power to issue regulations for the proper administration of its legislation, but the president (and, through him, the secretaries and subordinate military commanders) may also have the power to issue regulations to carry out his responsibilities as commander in chief. Regulations are considerably more detailed than most of the legislation and provide comprehensive guidelines for all aspects of the operation of the military. Even the regulations, however, cannot be detailed enough to cover all eventualities, and so considerable discretion in day-to-day matters is left in the commanders and officials who will administer them.

Legislation governing the defense establishment passes through the Armed Services Committees and often reflects particular concerns of the committees or the Congress at the time. Since Congress has the ultimate power to legislate on all matters affecting the military, it can often influence the military to take certain actions even without legislation. Thus, Congressman Mendel Rivers, the powerful chairman of the House Armed Services Committee in the 1960s, indicated his displeasure at an army directive in 1969 which liberalized the military position on political dissent by servicemen and was instrumental in getting the Department of Defense to adopt a directive with tougher language.[37] Senator Richard B. Russell, chairman of the Senate Armed Services Committee, is said to have persuaded the navy to take the World War II battleship, the New Jersey, out of mothballs and spend $27 million to refurbish it and send it to Vietnam.[38] But although Congress has the ultimate power to control the military, its lack of manpower to develop and administer the precise rules needed has forced it to leave the effective operation of the military to the executive branch.

The secretary of defense is directly under the president and has control over the entire defense establishment. The Department of Defense was created in 1948 as a sort of umbrella to cover the secretaries of each service. Within a short time it was reorganized to make the secretary of defense the principal defense officer under the president with plenary power over all the services. However, each of the services is a huge bureaucracy in itself, and even the most ambitious secretaries of defense have failed to make much headway in effectively controlling the military. Each service, headed by a civilian secretary, is an amalgam of civilian and military personnel. The secretary normally has high-ranking military men as his aides and in key positions throughout the department. This has sometimes caused difficulties because of the loyalties of career officers to their service. Tristram Coffin has written, "A Navy secretary imported by President Truman to ride herd on rebel admirals told me he had no one in his office he could trust except the secretary he brought with him, that his mail was opened and read, and his telephone probably tapped."[39] Disclosures in 1974 that the Pentagon had a spy on Henry Kissinger's staff who passed it top secret information during Kissinger's secret negotiations to end the Vietnamese War in 1971[40] provides another example of the clash of loyalties sometimes present in military-civilian relationships. However, the split is not always a military-civilian one, and close working relationships are frequently established between the civilian and military staffs. The Joint Chiefs of Staff was created in 1947 to serve as the principal military advisors for the president and secretary of defense. It is composed of the chief of staff of each service and has a staff of four hundred officers. Although not directly in the chain of command from the president to the secretaries to the military commanders, the joint chiefs exercise considerable control over military policies and, by virtue of the membership of the highest commander of each service, is effectively able to influence decisions.

Although the president is the commander in chief, presidents have often had difficulty in asserting their authority over the military. "None of our Presidents," writes Morton H. Halperin, deputy assistant secretary of defense from 1967 to 1969, "has been content with his relations with the military."[41] President Truman faced direct opposition to his policies from his field commander, General MacArthur, but had the unanimous support of the Joint Chiefs of Staff. President Kennedy had to deal with incipient revolt within the Pentagon over certain programs of Secretary of Defense McNamara. Secretary of Defense Laird is said to have mollified the military by increasing the influence of the Joint Chiefs of Staff, especially over war policy and budget matters, weakening the structures introduced by McNamara to impose civilian management and control over the military from the top.[42]

The relationship between the executive branch and the military is a complex matter, often more like that between two branches of government than a straight-line chain-of-command. Each uses its own power bases with Congress, pursues its own interests in the political arena, and jockeys with the other for advantage or accommodation. The military is at best in a difficult position, subject both to the criticism of being too subservient to the executive branch, especially in politically sensitive matters, and of being too independent and concerned with its own interests. There is no easy formula for determining what the relationship should be, but the equilibrium reached in recent years, especially in the Vietnam War era, seems to have resulted in the worst of both alternatives. On the one hand, civilian controls over the military and supervision of its internal operations and budget have been inadequate, while, on the other hand, the military has often been so closely identified with executive war policies that it has been unable to provide a professional and independent point-of-view for balance in the decision-making process. New structures seem to be needed, perhaps new agencies both within and without the Department of Defense to provide a more independent mechanism for monitoring the military and to provide more countervailing forces to the sometimes overly easy alliance in policy matters between the executive branch and the military.

*The Lavelle Affair—A Case-Study in Operational Control of the Military.* The Lavelle affair concerning unauthorized bombing in North Vietnam in 1971 and 1972 provides an interesting example of the ineffectiveness of formal lines of authority for insuring operational control over the military. The affair first came to light when Sgt. Lonnie Franks, assigned to Udorn Air Base in Thailand, wrote his senator, Harold Hughes (D., Iowa), in 1972 that he and others had been ordered to falsify reports that "our planes have received hostile reactions . . . whether they have or not. . . . The President probably does not even know about the situation."[43] Hughes' inquiries led to an Air Force investigation which found that General John D. Lavelle, Commander of the 7th Air Force in Vietnam, had ordered bombing attacks over a four-month period in 1971–72 on targets in North Vietnam which he considered to be dangerous. There had been no provocation as required by presidential rules of engagement in force at the time, and reports had been falsified, to indicate that the raids were "protective reaction" strikes. General Tyan, air force chief of staff, consulted with Secretary of Defense Laird and Secretary of the Air Force Seamans, and they determined that the incidents should be kept secret, even from the Armed Services Committees in Congress. Lavelle was offered another command with a two-grade reduction in rank, but he refused it and was retired at the three-star rank of lieutenant general, one rank below his present rank.

The matter would probably have been left there but for Representative Otis G. Pike (D., N. Y.), a former marine pilot, who got wind of the story. His inquiries to the Pentagon and a speech on the floor of the House on May 15, 1972, raising questions about the matter, resulted only in noncommittal responses from military authorities. He was finally told, first by General Tyan and then by Secretary Laird, that he could be given the true facts only if he kept them to himself. That he refused to do. The House Armed Services Committee held hearings on the matter in June 1972. Despite Lavelle's testimony of direct violation of the rules and falsified reports, the leadership of the committee indicated satisfaction with the military's handling of the case. However, public interest continued, much of it, in an election year, generated by critics of the military and the administration. Senator William Proxmire (D., Wis.) called upon the Air Force to bring court-martial charges against Lavelle, and an air force lieutenant and Air Force Academy graduate, Delbert R. Terrill, Jr., filed court-martial charges against Lavelle for violation of a lawful order "because my superiors and fellow officers have failed to come forward."[44] Senator Stennis, chairman of the Senate Armed Services Committee, announced that the committee would hold hearings in September.

General Lavelle's testimony before the Senate committee contained some surprises. He testified, contrary to his previous testimony, that he had received permission from Admiral Thomas H. Moorer, chairman of the Joint Chiefs of Staff, and General Creighton W. Abrams, commander of the U. S. forces in Vietnam, before he ordered attacks on North Vietnam in late 1971. Civilian control over the military had now become a critical issue in the case. The potential seriousness of Lavelle's actions is shown by the fact that at the time the Nixon administration was engaged in delicate peace talks with the North Vietnamese and was claiming, in frequent responses to North Vietnamese allegations, that it was respecting the bombing ban instituted by President Johnson in 1968. The first of Lavelle's unauthorized missions was on November 8, 1971, while Henry A. Kissinger, the president's national security advisor, was carrying out secret peace talks with Le Duc Tho, the senior North Vietnamese negotiator. An editorial in the *Louisville Courier-Journal* expressed the concern that the affair indicated a military out of control:

> A lone general defying the Commander-in-Chief is relatively simple to deal with. He can be busted a notch, dismissed from the service with a handsome pension, even be falsely classified as partially disabled, so that much of his pension will be tax-free—all of which was done for and to General Lavelle. If the buck stops there, all will be forgotten soon. But if old-fashioned ideas of duty and honor have since begun bothering General Lavelle, making his scapegoat role uncomfortable, and he's now revealing that some of the nation's highest military commanders conspired to disobey the orders of the President—thereby taking the nation's war policy into their own hands—then the nation and its military establishment are about to be thrown into a severe crisis. Such a revelation would indicate that the military no longer feels obligated to function within the limits set upon it by the Constitution, which specifies that the civilian President is the supreme commander and is to be obeyed.[45]

The new testimony raised doubts about the pending nomination by the president of General Abrams as army chief of staff, and Senator Stennis announced that the nomination would be held up until the committee heard further testimony. In hearings behind closed doors, Admiral Moorer and General Abrams reportedly testified that although they knew of the raids, they did not know that they were being conducted outside the rules of engagement. Admiral Moorer also denied that the navy had conducted unauthorized raids during the same period, disputing testimony of naval pilots, some of it conflicting, that the navy had also engaged in non–"protective reaction" bombing. On October 6, 1972, the Senate Armed Services Committee voted to confirm General Abrams as army chief of staff and to retire General Lavelle as a two-star major general. The committee professed to be satisfied that only General Lavelle had violated the president's rules and made no comprehensive report nor recommendations for preventing such episodes in the future.

If the Congress lacked interest in getting to the bottom of the Lavelle affair, the executive, whose orders had presumably been violated, was even less inclined to do so. In an election year in which its renewed bombing of North·Vietnam a few months after Lavelle's unauthorized bombing was an issue, the administration seemed to want nothing more than to have the matter put to rest. At a news conference with Admiral Moorer after the Senate committee's hearings were completed, Secretary Laird stated that civilian control is exercised effectively over the military. "I am completely satisfied with the system we have," he stated. "I think it would be a very grave error to make basic changes."[46] He specifically rejected proposals that a civilian official be posted in each major command reporting directly to him. The court-martial charges against Lavelle were dropped shortly afterward by the air force.

New dimensions were added to the affair by revelations in 1973 that the military had secretly engaged in bombing in Cambodia and Laos from 1969 to 1971 and had falsified reports, even to Congress, while the adminstration was claiming that it was respecting the neutrality of those nations. The president admitted ordering the bombing in 1969 and early 1970. The White House gave its approval the day before each of the 3,875 raids, the orders going directly from the secretary of defense to the military commanders, breaking the chain of command by excluding the civilian secretary of the air force.[47] The secrecy was said to have been necessary to obtain the acquiescence of Prince Sihanouk, then ruler of Cambodia, an allegation denied by Sihanouk from his exile in China. The bombing in late 1970 and 1971, involving 3,634 tactical air strikes in support of Cambodian government ground forces, was ordered by American field commanders without prior Pentagon or White House approval, but apparently in keeping with official policies. A Pentagon White Paper defended the use of the dual reporting system used to conceal the location and nature of the raids as consistent with the official policy of providing security information only to those with a "need to know."[48]

These revelations raised the question as to whether the bombing by Lavelle had also been ordered by the administration and Lavelle made the scapegoat. Thus, the Lavelle affair may not have been a case of a military commander substituting his own judgment for that of the commander in chief, but rather a case of the military carrying out executive orders including deception of Congress. In either case, it continues to raise troubling questions about operational control of the military in our society, questions which neither the executive nor legislative branches were willing to deal with. If Lavelle was acting on his own or only with approval from his military superiors with presidential authorization, the military would seem to be in a dangerously powerful position to escalate a war in spite of administration attempts to limit it. If Lavelle was acting on orders from the president, then the military was a partner in deception of the public and the Congress. Senator Stuart Symington (D., Mo.), in reference to the secret Cambodia bombing, raised the important question of whether military appropriations and other legislation were obtained from Congress "under false pretenses."[49] The Lavelle affair stands as a troubling and still unexplained episode indicating the complexity of the military role in war making and the unsatisfactory nature of present structures for exercising accountability and control.

*Military Appropriations.* Recognizing the power of the purse, the framers of the Constitution sought to limit the commander-in-chief's control over the military by giving Congress the exclusive power to appropriate funds for the support of the armed forces. They also feared abuse of this power by Congress, adding a provision originally instituted in England after the Glorious Revolution of 1688 that appropriations of money for the support of the army be limited to two years.[50] However, this limitation has proved to be hollow, for no modern military organization, dependent upon ongoing weapons research and technology, could function with only one-year budget commitments. The restriction has been avoided by simply going through the motions of a yearly budget process which in fact permits long-term outlays for the military. Congress' power over appropriations has also failed to provide much check upon military budgetary autonomy. The military, especially since the Second World War, has developed its own power base within Congress, and, with some notable exceptions, has been able to obtain appropriations from Congress without concomitant limitations and controls.

The military's budgetary success with Congress is due in part to the nature of the congressional committee and seniority system. The House and Senate committees which control military authorizations and appropriations have generally been controlled by a small number of senior senators and congressmen whose power derives from their seniority and patronage privileges, their close relationship with the military bureaucracy, and their own ability to manipulate and handle power. The military has also carefully courted key senators and congressmen with offers of military spending in their districts. Mendel Rivers, chairman of the House Armed Services Committee during the 1960s, was one of the best rewarded congressmen; his district in Charleston had nearly a dozen important defense installations, and when he visited military installations he was treated with the deference due an emperor. A battleship was even named for him while he was still alive. The civilian side of the military-industrial establishment also provided its share; in the first four years of Rivers' chairmanship, corporations like Lockheed, McDonald-Douglas, J. P. Stevens, Avco, and General Electric built plants in his district, defense-related activities accounting for 55 percent of the payrolls in the district.[51]

The Armed Services Committees were formed in 1946 through consolidation of the old Military Affairs and Naval Affairs Committees. They originally dealt with policy matters like military organization and personnel and were involved in only those budgetary matters related to manpower recruitment. In the late 1950s and 1960s they gradually expanded their powers so that today about one-third of the defense budget—including appropriations for research, development, testing and evaluation of weapons systems, vehicles, aircraft, missiles, and ships, and for the salaries of active forces and reserves—must be authorized in the Armed Services Committees' annual military procurement authorization bill. The authorization bill must be passed by both houses and signed by the president *before* an appropriation bill can be passed by the House or Senate. Because of the complexity of the authorization bill, the approval of the Armed Services Committees has usually been tantamount to passage by Congress.[52]

The Senate Armed Services chairman during the 1950s and 1960s was Senator Richard B. Russell (D., Ga.), a courtly bachelor who spent most of his adult life in the Senate. Russell was a strong supporter of the military and wielded considerable power to insure that the services received what he felt they needed. When Russell became chairman of the Senate Appropriations Committee in 1969, he was succeeded by Senator John Stennis (D., Miss.), who carried on the tradition.

The House Armed Services Committee has had only three chairmen over the last nineteen years, all of them southerners with close ties to the military—Carl Vinson of Georgia, L. Mendel Rivers of South Carolina, and F. Edward Hébert of Louisiana. The committee has forty members, and appointment to it is much sought after, giving enormous personal power to the chairman. Vinson, Rivers, and Hébert all saw their role as insuring that the military obtained the budgets and other legislation they needed. Rivers once said of the military that "the only lobby they have is the Committee on Armed Services"[53]—something of an exaggeration since the Pentagon has 339 full-time lobbyists with a budget in excess of $4 million, the largest lobbying operation in Washington.[54]

The actual responsibility for reporting out appropriations bills for the military rests with the defense subcommittees of the Senate and House Appropriations Committees. Since the Armed Services Committees must give previous authorization for about one-third of the military budget (primarily involving research and development of weapons systems and material), funds cannot be appropriated in excess of those limits. The Defense subcommittees can reduce the budget levels authorized by the Armed Services Committees for that third of the budget, but cannot increase them. The other two-thirds of the defense budget does not require authorization before appropriation, but most of those items are relatively fixed expenses for the operation and maintenance of the armed forces and retirement benefits (salary levels are established by the Armed Services Committees, but the annual appropriations requests for salaries go directly to the defense subcommittees). The Congressional Budget and Impoundment Control Act of 1974 may affect the power of these committees by creating new budget committees, aided by a Congressional Budget Office, which, beginning on October 1, 1976, will analyze executive budget requests and issue concurrent resolutions setting spending levels for each category including defense.[55]

Like the Armed Services Committees, the Defense Subcommittees have had extremely powerful chairmen during most of the period since the Second World War who have generally supported the military in their budget requests. The present chairmen of both subcommittees are also chairmen of the full Appropriations Committee. Senator Richard B. Russell (D., Ga.) was chairman of the

Defense Subcommittee in the Senate at the same time that he was chairman of the Armed Services Committee, finally resigning the Armed Services Committee position in 1969 when he also became chairman of the full Appropriations Committee. Senator Allan J. Ellender (D., La.) took over as subcommittee chairman upon Russell's death in 1971. Ellender has not been as supportive of the military as Russell was, reflecting somewhat the growing dissatisfaction in Congress in the 1970s with the spiraling cost of the arms race and defense spending. The chairman of the Defense Subcommittee in the House since it was created in 1947 is George Mahon (D., Tex.). He has not lost a floor fight on a defense appropriations bill since 1958. Mahon is an advocate of a strong defense posture but has also established a reputation as a budget trimmer (although critics have charged that he is more willing to cut social programs than defense requests). A frequent critic of defense spending, House Appropriations Committee member Donald W. Riegle (D., Mich.), observed: "There's a long term tendency to put the more progressive and liberal members on the authorizing committee where they can sort of vent their fury, but then to maintain an armlock on the final expenditure of money by putting the more conservative members on the Appropriations Committee."[56]

The devotion of the Armed Services and Appropriations Committee chairmen in recent years to the military seems to be more a product of ideology than of obeisance. "Yes, I'm a friend of the military," commented Chairman Hébert, "but I'll take them to the woodshed and spank them any time."[57] Chairman Rivers was hardly a lackey of the military; he was known to have summoned generals, admirals, and even secretaries of the service and dressed them down like schoolboys.[58] However, despite the personal power which chairmen can exercise, the Armed Services and Appropriations Committees have not provided a very effective check over the past twenty years on the size of military budgets or the military's appetite for expensive weapons systems. Again and again, the committees have been sold on elaborate new weapons systems, sometimes duplicating systems already possessed by other services. There have been some enormously costly failures, such as the $1.5 billion B-70 bomber program, which resulted in only two prototypes—one crashed in 1966 and the other was put in an Air Force museum; the $1.3 billion

Sheridan light tank, which proved to be so sophisticated that it was unusable in most combat situations (those sent to Vietnam malfunctioned and were finally put into storage); and the $23 billion spent on different kinds of missile systems for each of the services, many of them duplicating others and obsolete even before they were completed.[59]

The committees and Congress have been reluctant to second-guess the military as to what is needed to keep the U. S. abreast of the Russians in armaments. Congressman Les Aspin (D., Wis.), a critical member of the Armed Services Committee, explains: "The weapon systems are complicated, people don't like to vote against defense measures, and there's always that lurking fear that there's some secret classified document which shows that this thing is really necessary and not just the pet project of some general. . . . You can't pick up a newspaper without reading that some admiral said that the Soviet Navy is threatening us in some way."[60] "I'll tell you why they [Congress] support us," says Chairman Hébert, "We're about at parity with the Russians now. If we stop now where we are, we will lose parity and become inferior."[61]

When the executive branch has weakened in its resolve to pursue the arms race, the military has often gone over its head to the congressional committees to get the appropriation. In 1960, Congress approved a $400 million appropriation for the army to begin building the Nike-Zeus AMB (ultimately to cost $13–14 billion) which had been rejected by Secretary of Defense McElroy; he refused to spend the money, an earlier example of executive impoundment of appropriated funds which became so controversial in the second term of the Nixon administration. In 1962, Chairman Vinson threatened to put a mandatory spending clause in an appropriation bill for $500 million for the controversial RS-70 reconnaissance bomber which the administration did not want and he agreed not to do so only after a compromise worked out with President Kennedy.[62]

By the late 1960s, the mood of Congress had changed somewhat, although the Armed Services and Appropriations Committees were still generally favorable to military hardware appropriations. The defeat of the administration-supported ABM bill in 1969 was the first time that a major military appropriation bill had been defeated on the floor of the Senate.[63]

One reason that the military has done so well with the Congressional appropriations is its liaison with defense manufacturers in lobbying. Adam Yarmolinsky, deputy assistant secretary of defense under President Kennedy, has written:

One high Nixon administration official with experience in lobbying for the Pentagon said that most defense lobbying was done as a joint Pentagon-industry venture after the Pentagon had approved a weapons system and wanted to sell it to Congress. He said the Pentagon had Congress organized like a "Marine Corps landing," with generals, admirals, and top civilians "always ready to run up to the Hill whenever a problem develops." The visible part of the Pentagon's lobby force is its "legislative liaison" office, which in 1967 was appropriated a total of $3,810,458—more than ten times the $277,524 in lobby expenses reported by the United Federation of Postal Clerks, the biggest spender that year among private groups required to report their spending under the federal Regulation of Lobbying Act.[64]

The fact is that the military has such superior resources that congressional committees, even if they wanted to, cannot be very effective watchdogs. The limited staffs of the committees cannot on their own conduct comprehensive studies of the military budget or check the claims of the military concerning weapons systems. A 1969 speech by J. William Fulbright, chairman of the Senate Foreign Relations Committee, indicates the impotence felt by a vigorous critic of the military in dealing with budgetary matters:

I must confess that I have not really exerted myself as much as I might have in an effort to control the military. Actually I have been under the feeling that it was useless and utterly futile, that nothing could be done, for example, to cut an appropriation for the Defense Department no matter what I did. This is something that started with World War II. The Congress does not review or investigate or exercise control over Defense spending. They vote these bills through with hardly any debate. You get five minutes to ask questions in the hearings and nobody really wants to ask questions. The majority of Senators doesn't want to take responsibility for second guessing the military.[65]

The power of the military and its industrial suppliers has been the subject of an enormous number of books, and studies on the question "how to control the military" has become a popular theme in recent years. Ralph Lapp,[66] John Kenneth Galbraith,[67] Fred J. Cook,[68] and Seymour Melman[69] among others, have inveighed against the concentration of power in the military–industrial establishment. Admiral Hyman G. Rickover, in testimony before a congressional committee in 1968, described the partnership of the Defense Department and private industries as the "fourth branch of government" and warned that the federal bureaucrats and corporation officials were "men exerting power without financial responsibility."[70]

Realistic solutions are not easily come by because of the sheer size of the defense establishment and the diffuse lines of control. Structural changes could help. Better audit and monitoring procedures are needed in the Department of Defense, although attempts such as Secretary McNamara's cost-effectiveness programs met resistance within the defense bureaucracy and produced their own failures, such as the costly misconception of the TFX (F-111 fighter) project.[71] Internal controls on defense purchasing are clearly inadequate; only 12 percent of defense contracts are let after competitive bidding.[72] A 1973 staff study of the Joint Subcommittee on Priorities and Economy in Government found that the average price reduction on government contracts was 51.9 percent when competitive bidding rather than sole-source procurement was used.[73] It expressed doubts about the "willingness of the Pentagon and the defense industry to cut costs" and urged mandatory competitive bidding in many more areas. Stricter statutes and regulations, and stricter enforcement of them, are also needed to prevent ex-military officers and ex-defense department employees from using their contacts and influence on behalf of defense contractors, which hired 1,101 high-ranking Pentagon civilian officials and retired military officers in 1972.[74]

Cost overruns on government contracts are inevitable in an inflationary economy, but the number of unjustified overruns could be reduced if stricter standards governed estimated costs, monitoring, and compliance. The defense department absorbed enormous cost overruns of questionable justification during the Vietnam War, like the $2 billion bailout of Lockheed on the C-5A project and the concessions made to Sperry Rand, Litton Industries, and Grumman.[75] The actions of Roy L. Ash, president of Litton Industries and later director of the Office of Management and Budget, who threatened to go over the heads of navy officials in a contract dispute,[76] is not untypical of the kind of political influence used by defense contractors today. There is a serious need for both congressmen and members of the executive to scrutinize their use of pressure on behalf of private contractors and for precise guidelines to be developed.

The need for government employees to be protected against retaliation for doing their job honestly and resisting pressures can be seen in the case of A. Ernest Fitzgerald, whose position as a high level analyst for the air force was abolished in 1969 after he disclosed the Lockheed cost overrun in testimony before a congressional committee.[77] He was ordered reinstated in an equivalent position by the Civil Service Commission, but the fact that the order came four years later indicates the uncertainty, slowness, and expense presently involved in obtaining redress. In a similar case, Gordon Rule was transferred from his position as director of procurement for the Navy Material Command in 1972 after he told a congressional committee of pressures being applied by Ash in the Litton contract dispute. After serving in a lower position, he was ultimately reinstated.[78]

Statutes and regulations which expand public disclosure concerning awarding and administration of defense contracts could have some deterrent effect upon influence peddling. However, it is unlikely that untoward influence and pressure can be significantly reduced without effective mechanisms for investigating and imposing penalties for improper conduct. An independent agency functioning as an ombudsman with authority to investigate, initiate legal or criminal actions, and publicize misconduct and abuses is badly needed to provide a check on the defense contracting process.

Basic internal changes are also needed in Congress to alter the traditional sweetheart relationship between the military and the hierarchy of the Armed Services and Appropriations Committees. Pentagon power over defense appropriations might be reduced by several means—abolition or curtailment of seniority rights for committee chairmanships and appointments, limitations on the powers of committee chairmen with remedies against abuses, larger investigatory and research staffs for congressional committees, cutbacks on pentagon funds for lobbying and public relations,[79] and greater openness in committee deliberations (the Senate Armed Services Committee, for example, met behind closed doors 79 percent of the time in

1971).[80] Application of conflict of interest rules to congressmen, such as forbidding their voting, in committee or on the floor, for bills benefitting corporations in which they own stock, and campaign financing reform could reduce the influence of the corporate side of the military–industrial complex. Finally, there should be rules to restrict direct military wooing of congressmen—such as free use of military planes, military-paid junkets to defense establishments (often overseas), and affairs like the "appreciation dinner" given Senator Stennis in 1969 when the military flew top defense personnel, senators, and friends to Jackson, Mississippi, for an extravaganza complete with music by a navy choir, an army WAC band, and the air force "Strolling Strings."[81] One of the most questionable practices—giving members of Congress high ranking commissions in the reserves—was ruled unconstitutional by a federal district court in 1971. This decision was reversed in 1974 by the Supreme Court, which held that citizens and taxpayers had no standing to challenge the practice in the courts.[82]

These kinds of reforms, if carried out, would contribute to a more responsible military budget process. But it is obvious that military spending will not be adequately controlled by these or any other means without fundamental changes in the priorities of the public. An arms race mentality and nationally held militaristic values have given the military extraordinary influence over the federal budget and allowed it to dominate the ordering of national priorities. The new budget procedures adopted by the Congressional Budget and Impoundment Control Act of 1974 should improve Congress' ability to make an orderly and comprehensive review of the budget and to examine military appropriations in light of other needs. The ultimate battleground is Congress, which will either continue to respond to the claims of the defense establishment or to a new sense of priorities communicated to it by the public.

*Discipline and Punishment of Military Personnel.* Throughout most of our history it has been taken for granted that military life is so different from civilian life that the military has to have a separate and distinct legal system and that civilian courts have no business interfering with the way the military disciplines and punishes its men. General William T. Sherman expressed this philosophy in testifying before a congressional committee in 1879: "An army is a collection of armed men obliged to obey one man [and] all the traditions of civil lawyers are antagonistic to this vital principle."[83]

Congress, in the exercise of its constitutional power "to make rules for the government and regulation of the land and naval forces," has passed legislation governing the conduct of military trials but has preserved the typically military structure of the court-martial. Thus, when the present Uniform Code of Military Justice (UCMJ)[84] was passed in 1950, Congress acceded to military demands that commanders be left in control of court-martial machinery and appointments and that appeals be provided only within the military justice system. The UCMJ guarantees broad due process rights in courts-martial (such as the right to warnings before interrogation and to appointed military counsel), but critics argue that such rights can be meaningless in the face of command control, packed courts, and inadequate appeals.[85]

One area in which the civilian courts have long been willing to intervene in military law matters concerns court-martial jurisdiction. In the famous 1866 case of *Ex parte Milligan,*[86] the Supreme Court ruled that a civilian could not be tried by a military court and ordered the release of a southern sympathizer who had been condemned to death for treason by a Union court-martial. The UCMJ in 1950 purported to establish a total criminal law system which covered all offenses committed by servicemen while on active duty, as well as offenses by certain civilians. But because a court-martial does not provide all the constitutional safeguards found in a civilian court (for example, the right to indictment by grand jury and trial by peers chosen at random),[87] the Supreme Court ruled in 1955 that court-martial jurisdiction must be limited to the "narrowest jurisdiction deemed absolutely essential to maintaining discipline."[88] It struck down court-martial jurisdiction over discharged servicemen for offenses committed while on active duty and over civilian employees and dependents of the military for crimes committed overseas during peacetime.[89] In 1969, in the landmark decision of *O'Callahan* v. *Parker,*[90] it further held that courts-martial cannot exercise jurisdiction over servicemen's offenses which are not service-connected, reversing the court-martial of a sergeant for rape committed while off-duty and off-post. As a result, servicemen today are entitled to a civilian court trial for many offenses not committed on military premises, although exactly what are service-connected offenses is still being litigated.[91]

Even though civilian courts would traditionally hear cases challenging court-martial jurisdiction, they would not consider claims that the court-martial proceedings were unconstitutional in other ways. However in 1953, in the case of *Burns* v. *Wilson*,[92] two servicemen who had been sentenced to death by a court-martial for murder and rape sought a writ of habeas corpus claiming that, although court-martial jurisdiction of them was proper, they had been deprived of their constitutional rights by being held incommunicado by military authorities and interrogated for five days until they confessed. The Supreme Court decided that a federal court could go beyond the jurisdictional issue and consider whether there had been a denial of constitutional rights the military had failed to consider.

Since the *Burns* case, there has been disagreement among federal courts as to how broad the Supreme Court intended habeas corpus review of courts-martial to be, and the Supreme Court has not again spoken directly on the issue. Some circuit courts have held that if a court finds that the court-martial and military appeal courts gave "full and fair consideration" to the serviceman's claims that his constitutional rights had been denied, it must deny the writ even if it believes that he was in fact deprived of a constitutional right.[93] Other courts, which seem to be gaining among the circuits, have held that a federal court should review all claims of denial of constitutional rights in a court-martial and reverse the conviction if it finds such a denial.[94] Following this standard, federal courts have reversed court-martial convictions on such grounds as that the defendants were not provided adequate counsel or were convicted on the basis of evidence obtained through an illegal search or a confession illegally obtained.[95]

The Vietnam War brought a rash of new legal challenges to court-martial practices. The military appeal courts are the principal remedy for servicemen who feel their constitutional rights were violated in a court-martial,[96] and the Court of Military Appeals, although it has generally had conservative members highly conscious of its special relationship with the military, has a good record for keeping military due process rights abreast of expanding civilian constitutional doctrine.[97] However, the possibility of ultimate review by federal courts on habeas corpus provides a certain check on the military courts, and federal court challenges to court-martial procedures, although often unsuccessful, have had an impact. After a federal court held that summary courts-martial violated servicemen's constitutional rights to due process and counsel,[98] the army and air force changed their procedures to require lawyer defense counsel in summary courts.[99] There has been a split in the federal circuit courts on this issue in cases challenging the continued refusal of the navy and marine corps to provide counsel,[100] although the Court of Military Appeals has ruled that it is improper to admit as evidence of prior convictions any prior summary court-martial conviction where the defendant was sentenced to confinement without being represented by a qualified defense counsel.[101]

One of the most concerted challenges to fundamental court-martial practices arose out of the convictions of Vietnam War dissenters under the "general articles" of the UCMJ which forbid "conduct unbecoming an officer and a gentleman"[102] and "disorders and neglects to the prejudice of good order and discipline" and "conduct of a nature to bring discredit upon the armed forces."[103] Two federal circuit courts found one or both of the articles unconstitutionally vague and overbroad, reversing the convictions of an enlisted man who had handed out a leaflet attacking the war[104] and of Captain Howard Levy who had criticized the war to other servicemen and stated that he would refuse to go to Vietnam if ordered to do so.[105] The Supreme Court reversed both circuits.[106] Justice Rehnquist, writing for a 5–3 majority in *Levy,* found that there was sufficient elaboration in the *Manual for Courts-Martial,* military cases, and military custom to give a serviceman notice of what was criminal and that, given the need of the military to impose limitations on conduct different from those applicable in civilian life, a presumptive validity should be given to Congress' use in the general articles of imprecise language which sweeps more broadly than is permissible in civilian statutes. Justice Stewart argued in dissent that the "uncertain regime" of the general articles, which were both unduly vague and overbroad in the area of First Amendment rights, was not justified in the "vastly altered historic environment" of the contemporary military where members are no longer part of a small, professional, and voluntary cadre isolated from the mainstream of civilian life.[107]

Justice Rehnquist's majority opinion in the *Levy* case conceded that there might be marginal applications where the general articles would infringe on First Amendment rights of servicemen but found that Captain Levy's urging of enlisted men to refuse to obey orders to combat was not protected free speech. Thus, it is possible that the general articles could still be found unconstitutional in a case in which the speech is found to be protected by the First Amendment. A 1972 decision by the D. C. district court, which was not appealed by the military, would seem to be such a case; the court reversed the court-martial convictions of two servicemen who had passed out a mildly critical antiwar leaflet on a military post, holding that the specification under the general article for which they were convicted—making "disloyal statements"—was unconstitutionally vague and overbroad.[108] The court stated that soldiers "in their off-duty hours, in barracks 'bull sessions,' and even in leaflets . . . can express their views on political issues, so long as they do not directly prejudice good order and discipline. While soldiers can be compelled to obey orders, they cannot be compelled to an ideological orthodoxy prescribed by their superior officers."[109]

In light of the the decisions which have struck down or undermined a number of provisions of the UCMJ, and of the continued feeling by many servicemen that courts-martial procedures are unfair,[110] there is now clearly a need for Congress to consider changes in military justice. However, military justice reform has to get past the critical scrutiny of the services, which have opposed most of the major reforms of this century, and Congress has been slow to act. The last reform legislation, the Military Justice Act of 1968, was tied up in Congress over ten years, and the final act contained only a fraction of the reforms sought.[111] A number of current bills which would make major changes in military justice have been pending since the late 1960s. Bills introduced by Senators Bayh (D., Ind.) and Hatfield (R., Ore.), and Congressman Bennett (R., Fla.) would establish an independent court-martial command to exercise most of the appointive and administrative court-martial functions presently performed by the commander or his subordinates.[112] They would also provide for random selection of court-martial members from a jury pool including most enlisted men, adopt civilian court procedures for pretrial release from confinement and preparation for trial, create a right to appeal directly to the Supreme Court, reduce court-martial jurisdiction over civilian offenses committed in the U. S., and remove a number of vague offenses. The services, conscious of the criticisms and anxious to head off major congressional tampering with military justice, have adopted some administrative changes to establish more independent court-martial commands and reduce the role of the commander,[113] but the major structural deficiencies in the system still remain.

The amount of change which is desirable in the court-martial system depends a great deal upon one's view of the function of military justice. The generally expressed military position is that a civilianized system of justice is unsuitable because of the unique demands of obedience and discipline in military life.[114] Although the military maintains that a serviceman receives as fair and judicial a trial as in a civilian court, it considers the distinctive features of the court-martial (such as the role played by the commander and the specially selected "jury" of officers with, at most, one-third enlisted men) as essential to its disciplinary function. Critics maintain that as long as the court-martial, in the words of the Supreme Court in the *O'Callahan* decision, "remains to a significant degree a specialized part of the over-all mechanism by which military discipline is preserved,"[115] it cannot provide a fair and impartial trial. They argue that military life is no longer so very different from civilian, as there has been a gradual convergence of the two social structures, and that the military possesses sufficient nonjudicial powers to maintain discipline without undermining the fairness of the court-martial which is a criminal trial with serious consequences for the serviceman.

Even if pending reform bills were passed, some persons doubt that a separate court-martial system administered entirely by military men is any longer necessary or desirable in a democracy. The principle of separation of powers present in a civilian trial by which different functions are performed by diverse and independent individuals (a grand jury of citizens, a private defense attorney, a jury chosen at random from the community, and separate trial and appellate judges with tenure) is notably lacking in a court-martial. Even if the officers who serve as judge, counsel, and jury are independent of the commander who has brought the court-martial charges, they are still part of a small, tight-knit class within the military command structure, and their promotions, assignments, and careers are very much associated with military interests and policies. The absence of tenure and job security as to assignment make military defense counsel and judges even more susceptible to pressures from within the military establishment.

After the Second World War many western nations experienced popular dissatisfaction with their military justice systems. Great Britain altered the all-military character of the court-martial by making judges and counsel in military trials civilians. West Germany, Sweden, Austria, and Denmark abolished the court-martial, providing for trial of servicemen in civilian courts with limited disciplinary powers in commanders.[116] These actions were taken in the belief that a separate system of justice administered by military men encouraged militaristic tendencies in the armed forces and detracted from the fairness of trials. Although the American court-martial does not have the same kind of history of subordination of justice to political ends as in Germany and Austria, it has still sometimes displayed disturbing tendencies towards abuse of power and arbitrariness. The court-martial was one of the principal means of curbing dissent in the military during the Vietnam War. Acquittals of dissenters were rare, and extremely high sentences were common, a result especially troubling in light of the number of convictions which were overturned by military and civilian courts long after the chilling of free speech protected by the First Amendment had its effect. As a federal judge observed in a 1973 case striking down regulations giving commanders broad powers to exclude newspapers and other written materials from posts, "Military authority is not trained or attuned to the sensitivity involved in questions relating to First Amendment rights."[117]

Persons in positions of authority in other institutions—such as police, prison wardens, and school administrators—also sometimes show similar insensitivity towards individual rights. However, they lack the power to charge subordinates with criminal misconduct in a judicial system entirely administered by members of their authority group. The monopoly over court-martial functions by the officer class contains a potential for abuse which, even given a basic sense of fairness in most officers, is undesirable in a legal system.

There now appear to be strong reasons for Congress to consider civilianizing certain court-martial functions as in Great Britain or abolishing courts-martial as in West Germany and Sweden. The Congressional Black Caucus and the American Civil Liberties Union have recommended abolition.[118] There would be no constitutional bar to trial of servicemen in federal courts, even at American bases abroad where divisions of federal courts could be established. As in West Germany and Sweden, trials by courts-martial could be permitted during time of war. Administrative problems in converting to trial of servicemen by civilian courts do not appear insurmountable. Most important, the British, German, and Swedish experiences do not indicate any adverse effect upon military efficiency and discipline resulting from civilianization or abolition of courts-martial, and, in fact, indicate a generally favorable impact upon the quality of military justice.

*Training and Disposition of Military Personnel.* The military has traditionally been allowed a free hand in the training and disposition of its personnel. The services have their own procedures for dealing with servicemen's complaints, which do not provide for appeal outside the chain of command. Complaints made to members of Congress or to service secretaries are routinely forwarded to the appropriate military command for reply. They sometimes result in relief, but this is a haphazard kind of remedy which generally only helps the individual involved and does not alter practices.

The Vietnam War resulted in a flood of suits in federal courts seeking judicial relief from military actions claimed to be illegal, unconstitutional, arbitrary, or unjust. They challenged inductions and activations, orders to Vietnam and transfers to other posts, refusals to discharge for medical or other reasons, pending courts-martial and less-than-honorable discharges, methods of training and discipline, and refusals to permit meetings, distribution of literature, and other exercises of free speech. Early in the war, the courts generally dismissed such suits, quoting from a 1953 Supreme Court decision which denied review of the army's refusal to assign medical duties to a doctor who would not answer questions concerning his previous Communist affiliations:

Judges are not given the task of running the army. . . . The military constitutes a specialized community governed by a separate discipline from that of the civilian. Orderly government requires that the judiciary be as scrupulous not to interfere with legitimate army matters as the army must be scrupulous not to interfere in judicial matters.[119]

The first substantial break in this nonreviewability doctrine occurred in suits by ex-servicemen challenging less-than-honorable discharges. In the 1958 case of *Harmon* v. *Brucker,*[120] the Supreme Court held that the secretary of the army had exceeded his authority in giving a serviceman with a good record an undesirable discharge because of allegedly subversive activities before his induction and ordered that an honorable discharge be issued. Since then, federal courts have extended their review to less-than-honorable discharges where servicemen were not accorded proper procedural rights under military regulations or the Constitution. In a particularly galling case for the military, a federal court ruled in 1970 that allegations that Private Andy Stapp (founder of the American Servicemen's Union and vigorous critic of the military) had close associations with members of the Communist Party and was a member of the Workers World Party were insufficient grounds for an undesirable discharge since they did not indicate misconduct in the performance of his military duties.[121]

These precedents were significantly expanded during the Vietnam War when federal court review was extended for the first time to servicemen who claimed that they were entitled to be discharged. Such cases involve considerably more interference with the day-to-day operations of the military, since they directly affect military manpower levels. The type of case which the courts were first willing to review involved servicemen refused discharge as conscientious objectors. In 1967, Charles A. Hammond, who had enlisted in the U. S. Naval Reserve four years before when he was seventeen years old, submitted a request for a discharge, stating that he had become a member of the Society of Friends and could no longer participate in good conscience in war in any form. His request was refused and when he failed to attend reserve drills, he was ordered to report for two years active duty. He filed a petition for writ of habeas corpus with the U. S. District Court for Connecticut, asserting that there was no "basis in fact" for the military's finding that he was not entitled to discharge as a conscientious objector, and that he was thus being deprived of his rights to due process and equal protection of the laws under the Constitution. The district court dismissed, but the circuit court held that *Burns* v. *Wilson* and *Harmon* v. *Brucker* were precedents for granting federal court review of a refusal of the military to discharge a serviceman.[122]

The impact of the *Hammond* decision was immediate and dramatic. Four other U. S. circuit courts soon adopted its position and federal district courts around the country began ordering servicemen to be discharged when they found no basis in fact for the military's refusal to discharge them as conscientious objectors. Some courts have extended review to other situations in which military regulations provide for discharge, ordering the discharge of servicemen who have sought discharge because of medical or psychiatric disqualifications, dependency of others upon them, and personal hardship.[123]

The federal courts also expanded review during the Vietnam war to cases in which servicemen claimed they had been improperly inducted or drafted, or, in the case of reservists, improperly activated. Many individuals were ordered discharged because their draft boards failed to follow regulations, denied their constitutional rights in the process of classifying and inducting them, or denied them a deferment without good reason.[124] By the latter part of the war, it was not uncommon for a number of individuals in each group reporting for induction to have their attorneys simultaneously filing writs of habeas corpus for their discharge in the local federal court and for basic training classes to be reduced by court-ordered discharges.

The final critical jump was for federal courts to grant review of military rules, practices, and conduct which were arbitrary or resulted in denial of constitutional rights. The precedent before the Vietnam War was crystal clear that courts should not get involved. However, the deprivation of rights in some cases was simply too great for courts to continue to ignore, and there was a modest break away from this rule. Federal courts began to grant review in cases where the military was shown not to have followed its own regulations, to have grossly abused its discretion, or to have violated constitutional rights. Thus, a serviceman who claimed that he had been assigned to duties for which he was medically unfit obtained a court order that he be given a job which would not require stooping and prolonged standing.[125] The transfer of a serviceman to Vietnam was cancelled by a court where the military had failed to consider that the health of his son would be adversely affected.[126]

Some courts, however, have continued to follow a strict rule of not reviewing duty assignments. A suit brought by a serviceman who claimed he had received orders to Vietnam because of making anti-war statements to a newspaper reporter was dismissed, the court stating that duty assignments of one properly inducted were not reviewable.[127] In *Cortwright* v. *Resor,*[128] suit was brought by a member of the army band at Ft. Wadsworth, New York, who suddenly received orders to Texas after he and other band members had signed a petition calling for immediate withdrawal from Vietnam and some of their fiancees and wives had attempted to march with the band carrying antiwar signs in a Fourth of July parade. The Second Circuit Court of Appeals held that judicial review of duty assignments was appropriate only where the military has clearly exceeded its authority or violated First Amendment rights, while the transfer here may have been justified to avoid disorder or a repeat of the parade incident.

In a highly publicized case, Captain Marcus Arnheiter challenged his removal from the command of a destroyer escort ship as discriminatory.[129] The court refused relief on the grounds that the record showed that his removal was an internal administrative matter involving the judgment of a military commander, which was not reviewable.

Vietnam War suits by servicemen claiming violations of their rights to free speech were among the most difficult for courts because they involved highly controversial conduct that the military considered a threat to the armed forces. Courts were occasionally willing to step in to prevent flagrant violations of rights. For example, in 1969 the fourth circuit found that black soldiers who had organized an antiwar group at Ft. Jackson (known as the "Ft. Jackson 8") were being improperly confined in the stockade pending court-martial because of their views and ordered them released[130]; the court-martial charges, based on their attempts to hold a meeting to discuss the war, were later dropped after adverse publicity and pressure from black congressmen. In the summer of 1973, the D. C. district court declared unconstitutional one of the key Vietnam War antidissent regulations requiring servicemen to obtain permission from their commanders before collecting signatures for a petition.[131] However, suits were unsuccessful in challenging military regulations forbidding public meetings on post to discuss political issues and wearing of hair beyond designated lengths.[132] Reservists who objected to orders to march in a parade in August 1972 for the Veterans of Foreign Wars convention at which Vice-President Agnew was the speaker, on the grounds that it was a prowar political demonstration were denied relief, the judge finding that orders to march in holiday parades were legal.[133]

An interesting case demonstrating the expanded role of federal courts in overseeing the military's personnel practices arose out of a drug abuse program instituted in 1973 by the army in Europe. Designed to identify drug pushers and users, provide users with medical assistance, counselling, and rehabilitation, and eliminate confirmed users from the service, the program sanctioned mandatory inspections of soldiers' property, clothing, and bodies for drugs or indications of drug use.[133] Soldiers in many commands were suddenly faced with mass body searches at 4 A.M., requirements that doors be left unlocked at all times, and inspections of rooms and belongings in their absence, often with the aid of "sniffer dogs" to detect marijuana or drugs.[134] A group of soldiers sued in the District of Columbia federal court, and Judge Gerhard Gesell found a number of the practices unconstitutional, stating:

> The special drug inspections authorized without probable cause are made in a most intrusive manner solely to ferret out drugs and are not analogous to the Army's traditional preparedness inspections. . . . Such distinguishing features as the use of dogs, strip skin examinations and detailed intrusion into a soldier's personal effects take this procedure out of the narrow exemption from traditional Fourth Amendment restrictions that has been carved out for legitimate inspections.[135]

He rejected the military's defense of "military necessity," stating that it "does not embrace everything the military may consider desirable" and concluded that although the drug problem was serious, it was not of "epidemic proportions" such as to warrant ignoring constitutional safeguards.

Despite their reluctance, federal courts have become a significant force for controlling the military. Judges may not have assumed the task of running the military, but they have accepted responsibility for reviewing the legality and constitutionality of a wide variety of military actions. There have been compalints that the imposition of civilian constitutional and legal standards on the military has "dangerously undermined if not subverted law and order and the day-to-day discipline of the Armed Forces."[136] Others argue that the courts' check on arbitrariness in the military and their expansion of servicemen's individual rights will improve morale and efficiency. Federal court remedies for servicemen are still quite limited, and courts will undoubtedly continue to have a difficult time in finding the proper balance between the claims of constitutional protection of servicemen and the institutional demands of the military.

## The Military Mission in a Democratic Society

The mission of the armed forces, according to the traditional view, is to maintain national defense against the possibility of foreign attack. A more realistic view, and one which most contemporary statesmen would have no difficulty in accepting, is that the role of the armed forces, as Harold Lasswell has written, is essentially the "management of violence" within a society.[137] In order properly to manage force within society, good internal control and efficiency within the armed forces are obviously necessary. A poorly disciplined, inefficient military would be a poor manager of force. However, armed forces which have exalted discipline and obedience above all else have all too often dedicated themselves to the interests of the government in power rather than the general welfare, displaying insensitivity to civil liberties and pursuing militaristic values antithetical to democratic ideals.[138] Thus, there is a constant dilemma in a democracy as to how to structure the military so that it will be a disciplined force which serves the interests of the government efficiently and yet does not become a regressive force cut off from and unresponsive to the values and movements of civilian society.

In some ways, the American military seems to be relatively free from the cancer of militarism. Americans have been spared the military plots, coups, and takeovers so prevalent elsewhere. American career military men have generally displayed a sense of professionalism and awareness of the importance of civilian control over the military. Access to the officer level in the American military has not been limited to a privileged economic class, and the military as a whole has been composed of a fairly representative cross-section of racial and economic groups. The high turnover of noncareer men serving a basic term of enlistment has provided a certain citizen-soldier quality which has undercut the closed, separate-society kind of militarism.

Still, in other ways the American military displays troubling tendencies. The military is tightly controlled by the career officer corps, and the high ranks are dominated by graduates of the military academies. Career officers have tended to be estranged from the values and life styles of civilian society. The career military is made up of an undue proportion of white middle-class males, and a disproportionate number come from the south, west, and small-town America. Blacks were almost totally excluded from the officer class of the navy and marine corps until very recently (constituting .9 percent and 1.5 percent respectively, as compared to 6.4 percent and 12.6 percent of the enlisted men in those services) and are underrepresented in the officer class of the army and air force (constituting 3.9 percent and 1.7 percent respectively, as compared to 17 percent and 12.6 percent of the enlisted men in those services).[139] The insularity of military posts, similarity of officer career patterns and experiences, required conformity to traditional values and ideas, and influence of continuous indoctrination programs have contributed to make the career military probably the most conservative single group in America today. Lt. Col. Edward L. King, who retired from the army in 1969 in "opposition to the unnecessary, poorly commanded, no-win war in Vietnam" charges that "organization-man conformity has become the pattern for success in the U. S. Army Officer Corps" producing "unthinking, subservient yes-men who practice deception and concealment in order to cover up any error or failure which, if revealed, could harm either the system or the individual career."[140]

Although the military has not been directly involved in partisan politics, it has played an increasingly important political role since the Second World War. There have been a number of cases of career officers, usually in high ranks, opposing administration policies which they considered insufficiently militant. General MacArthur sent his famous criticism of President Truman's Korean War policies to leaders of the opposition political party. General Edwin Walker established a right-wing indoctrination program for his troops in the early 1960s, and an aide, Major Arch Roberts, was actively involved in right-wing political groups. A significant number of retired generals and admirals have dabbled in right-wing politics.

The precautions taken by the secretary of defense and the joint chiefs in monitoring orders and the like during the last days of the Nixon administration to insure that the military could not be used to block the "constitutional process"[141] may be considered reassuring, although they indicate that the men involved did not discount entirely the possibility of military interference with domestic politics. The military directs enormously expensive information programs at civilians, many of them with a decided political cast.[142] A mandatory program of troop indoctrination has been an integral part of servicemen's lives since the early 1950s. Films, lectures, and classes provide a doctrinaire presentation of information on political issues such as the war, the Communist menace, and military policies. Military men were frequently mustered for politically-oriented parades and other public functions or simply to provide a receptive audience for the president or a member of the administration during the Vietnam War. Finally, the use of the military to spy on tens of thousands of civilians and civilian groups, including members of Congress, because of their opposition to the war or their politics indicates the kind of political role not now unthinkable for the military.

Closely related to the question of militarism and the compatibility of the military with democratic values is the manner in which the military trains and disciplines its men. The military is given great power to in effect remake the men given over to it through enlistment or draft. A Second World War–type of philosophy still seems to predominate in the military: authoritarian, anti-individualistic, and, as Ward Just observed in his book, *Military Men,* "relentlessly anti-intellectual, as distinguished from being anti-brains."[143] The military philosophy of discipline and training is today a hodgepodge of often outdated and sometimes conflicting principles. There is still an attempt to inculcate traditional military values exalting manhood, hardship, and love of war which have little in common with the norms and values of contemporary American society. In basic training, the recruit is still subjected to intentional brutalization which is said to be necessary to make him a soldier; to character building programs which often show little familiarity with modern educational and psychological knowledge; to indoctrination programs which frequently involve such unsophisticated and banal appeals to patriotism and exaltation of war that many recruits do not relate to them; and to competitions designed to develop group consciousness and *esprit de corps* but which often appear patently artificial to today's recruits. There is serious doubt today that these methods and their objectives are either good training methods or consistent with our national objective of maintaining an efficient and responsible military which will preserve, rather than endanger democratic values. The persistence of racial discrimination in job assignments, ratings, promotions, discipline, and military justice, often fostered by career NCOs and lower-level officers despite strong official policies opposing it, has been blamed in part on the insensitivity and group tensions produced by military training. The comment by Paul Meadlo's mother, "I raised him as a good boy and they made a murderer out of him," and the slogan printed on a popular button several years ago, "The Marine Corps Builds Oswalds," express the widespread misgivings about the military's methods of converting young men into soldiers.

An especially anachronistic aspect of the American military today is the officer-enlisted man caste system. A report made by a committee headed by General Doolittle to investigate criticisms of the military after the Second World War found the caste system to be the greatest source of resentment among enlisted men and recommended that the military be "democratized" by doing away with all but functional distinctions in rank.[144] The recommendations were never adopted, and resentment over the injustices resulting from rank continue as an irritant and demoralizing factor in the military. Many enlisted men today, who are products of a more egalitarian civilian society, find the military caste system unbearable. Many others are bitter over the injustices which result—the imbalance in goods and services between officers and enlisted men, the unequal treatment under military justice, and the arbitrariness of officer fiat.

Belatedly, in the late 1960s, the American military began to respond to the dissatisfactions of its personnel by removing some of the more onerous and dysfunctional disciplinary practices (morning reveille, bed check), permitting greater personal and racial identity (longer hair, modified Afro haircuts, and soul music in service clubs), providing more amenities in service life (beer in barracks and a move to individual rooms in future military housing), and granting greater freedom during off-duty time (relaxation of strict off-duty pass regulations).[145] These changes came about because of public criticism, pressure by some congressmen, and military willingness, in the face of serious morale problems, to try something different. These changes also coincided with the realization that the draft was not going to survive Vietnam and that the armed forces were going to have to rely on volunteers—volunteers that could be attracted only if pay and living and working conditions were improved. In the wake of continued disruption in the military, much of it with racial overtones, there have been demands for a return to tighter discipline on the grounds that the military has become too permissive. Nevertheless, many of the changes seemed destined to stay. "A decent life on post," writes Lt. Col. William L. Hauser, who worked on the army reforms in the office of the assistant chief of staff, "is the only alternative to an increased degree of soldier misbehavior and dissipation (especially with higher pay) in the honky-tonks and 'crash pads' of neighboring towns."[146] These personnel reforms were important first steps in establishing room for pluralism in cultural, racial, and individual attitudes and life styles in the military.

It would be wrong, as some critics have been inclined to do, to look at the American military today as a brutalized group of men only trained to kill. Faced with problems not always of its making —racial unrest, drug abuse, generation gaps between young recruits and NCOs, boredom, and identity crises—the military has been making a genuine attempt to find new solutions. After the brief flirtation of policy thinkers with nuclear war strategy in the 1950s and early 1960s, military strategy today primarily relies upon men and what they can or cannot do in relatively conventional warfare.

The American military is becoming increasingly bureaucratized, requiring skilled men who can perform sophisticated technical jobs. Military efficiency in the future is likely to rest primarily on the sort of personnel practices already proved successful in businesses and other government bureaucracies. This will mark a further break from traditional military notions of rigid discipline and obedience.

The volunteer military, which at first would seem ideally suited to both military efficiency and a civilianized atmosphere, carries some risks. It avoids the undesirable compulsion of the draft and the inevitable social and economic inequities which result when not all draft-eligible men are needed to serve. But the volunteer military may not be compatible with democratic values. The expense is considerable, bringing to mind the costly "standing armies" of the eighteenth century which the founding fathers forbade in the Constitution. Some fear that a volunteer military, without the civilian leaven of short-term conscripts, is more likely to be isolated from civilian values and to be used as an unthinking mercenary force for totalitarian ends by the government. The risk is real, and thus there is even more reason to protect individuality and individual rights, guarantee free speech and inquiry among servicemen, avoid authoritarian training and indoctrination, and insure limitations upon arbitrary command.

A reexamination of the function of the military has been going on in recent years which could contribute to a less authoritarian model. Motivated by both the need to find more meaningful occupations for servicemen and the resulting favorable public relations, the military has been increasingly moving into disaster relief, flood and environmental control, and other community projects. Albert D. Biderman, senior research associate of the Social Science Research, has observed that "the military institution suffers from many disabling neuroticisms when it exists in a society and in a world that does not regard combat as one of the most honorable and exalted of human activities," and suggests that the central function of the military be redefined to embrace primarily noncombat objectives.[147] Others have been alarmed at this trend, seeing the military's interest in community projects and emphasis upon education and training of the underprivileged as simply a means to maintain its huge budget and to extend its influence into traditional civilian areas. Any extension of the military into civilian enterprises should probably only come after a decision that civilian agencies cannot handle the job and that the military has been sufficiently restructured to avoid the undesirable aspects of militarism still present today.

Achieving responsiveness from as large and complex a bureaucracy as the military establishment will require not only limitations upon military expansionism, but also changes within the military to insure compatibility with democratic ideals. Several European nations, notably West Germany and Sweden, made such changes in their armed forces after the Second World War. According to the West German concept of the "citizen in uniform," the soldier is entitled to the same basic social and individual rights as a civilian. Soldiers are guaranteed the right to discuss politics and do engage in them freely; there are troop-level grievance boards and a civilian ombudsman to curb arbitrariness and abuse of power[148]; and unnecessary discipline and interference with individual rights have been curtailed. Similar reforms have been introduced in the Swedish armed forces. Order and efficiency are still highly valued in the Swedish and German military forces but the structural changes are an attempt to achieve them without authoritarian methods contrary to democratic ideals.

## Conclusion

The constitutional framework of separation of powers has proved insufficient in itself to check and control the powerful military establishment which has emerged since the Second World War. The Cold War identification of the military with the national interest and the economic and political power derived from massive defense spending and intermittent wars have resulted in a military power base largely insulated from the normal operations of checks and balances within the government. The military has provided relatively well-trained and superbly-equipped armed forces for America, but at tremendous cost, both monetary and social. In the Vietnam War, in which the military served as a partner in 'much of the decision-making, its active role in falsification of information, suppression of dissent, and surveillance of citizens reflected an alarming estrangement from democratic values. Concern over military insularity and abuse of power has led to the development of some new means of checking it, such as greater willingness of the courts to redress denial of rights, expansion of congressional will and resources to monitor the defense budget and military operations, and greater use of ombudsman offices within the department of defense.

But these developments are unlikely to effect basic changes in military accountability and responsiveness unless there is also a substantial reordering of national priorities and significant structural changes in government to reestablish the degree of control intended by the framers of the Constitution. There are hopeful signs that America today, as at the founding of the republic, can find satisfactory mechanisms for controlling the military. The vitality of the critical faculties of the American public, the spirit of free discussion and investigation in the media, the courage of individuals in exposing and challenging abuses of power, and the capacity of citizens' groups, academic institutions, and research institutions for devising creative solutions indicate that America possesses the resources, and hopefully the will, to solve its most serious problem of the postwar period.

# The Design of Institutional Arrangements and the Responsiveness of the Police

*Elinor Ostrom*

The current institutional arrangements for providing police services are based on three designs. In the largest cities, police institutions approximate to a great extent the design recommended by municipal and metropolitan reformers. There, police departments are large, bureaucratized, and professionalized organizations. In the suburban areas surrounding large cities are found by far the largest number of police departments in the country. They are, however, small—too small and unprofessional to function properly, according to many authorities. Rural areas are serviced by county sheriffs and state police, but only a minimum service is needed in such places because of the dispersed population and the relative lack of crime.

Traditional municipal and metropolitan reformers continue to favor the large and professional police departments of great cities. They urge the consolidation of small, suburban departments into a single sizeable department for any one metropolitan region. It is important to note, however, that major charges of unresponsiveness have been levied against police in big cities while few such complaints are heard about suburban or rural police.

In great cities, minority groups in particular complain that police often do not respond to emergency calls. When the police do come, minorities assert, they are liable to descend in large numbers prepared to use immediate and excessive force. Police are also charged with harassment and brutality, and citizens fear retaliation if they file complaints against individual officers. As a result, considerable hostility exists between the police and residents of center-city neighborhoods, who see the police as an army of occupation sent by the wealthy to oppress the poor and disadvantaged. Ghetto residents have little of the suburban sense of the police as public servants who provide essential services for all. Rather, they feel that they get too few of the services they need and too much repression.

Since the charge of unresponsiveness has been lodged against police serving large American cities, it might be well to proceed very cautiously before taking metropolitan departments as the model for others to follow. The problem of how to redesign the institutional arrangements to produce more responsive and effective police services will be the central concern of this essay.

*Definitions.* First, let me make clear what I mean by some of the key terms we will be using. Let us define *responsiveness* as the capacity to satisfy the preferences of citizens. Let us define *institutional arrangements* as decision-making rules used to produce, allocate, and distribute anything valued by individuals. Markets, firms, courts, legislatures, elections, public bureaucracies, and contractual agreements all can be thought of as institutional arrangements designed to produce, allocate, and/or distribute something that people value. The responsiveness of any particular institutional arrangement is the capacity of those who act within the constraints of a set of decision-making rules to satisfy the preferences of others who are dependent upon the institution.

Developing institutional arrangements that will facilitate responsive conduct is a problem of design. Problems of design require for their solution (1) specific performance criteria by which to evaluate the consequences of a design, (2) specific knowledge about the characteristic of the materials involved, and (3) specific knowledge about cause and effect relations in the use of the materials. When the problem is to design institutional arrangements, the first requirement is to decide what result is wanted—in police work, should the criteria of performance be efficiency, justice, or responsiveness? The second requirement is a knowledge about the specific types of events to be produced or exchanged by means of specific institutional arrangements. The third requirement is a general knowledge about the consequences of using different kinds of decision-making rules or institutional arrangements.

Since the design of existing police institutions in large cities is similar to the design recommended by the traditional reform movement, we will first briefly examine the elements of that design.[1] We will ask the following questions: What performance criteria were selected by the reformers? What were their conceptions of the nature of police services? What consequences were presumed to flow from different decision-making rules? Gaining an overview of the basic design, we will then examine the types of consequences resulting from its operation. We can then assess how to redesign police institutions in large cities and elsewhere to increase their responsiveness to the citizens they serve.

## The Reform Design

Efficiency and economy in local government were the performance criteria stressed in the traditional reform literature. Reformers wanted to design institutions to lower the costs of municipal services. It was assumed that large police jurisdictions would realize economies of scale and thus produce services at lower costs than smaller jurisdictions.

Reformers did not wish to design responsive police institutions. Many felt that earlier police institutions had been *too* responsive to particular citizens' interests. They wanted to eliminate the corruption that had pervaded police departments. Citizens' preferences were considered to be based upon private or selfish interests which should be excluded from public decision making. Institutions should serve the general public interest rather than special or private interests.

Recently, reformers recommending the same institutional arrangements have focused somewhat more on such performance criteria as redistribution of wealth and the equitable distribution of service costs to all those who benefit. Metropolitan-wide jurisdictions have been proposed as a means of forcing "rich suburban residents" to help pay for services needed by poorer residents of the central city, as well as for the benefits that suburban residents supposedly receive from the central city.

Proponents of reform considered police services to be similar to all other goods and services normally provided by a city government or by any large business concern. Frequent allusions were made to the economies of scale presumed to exist in the provision of water, sewer and transportation systems. On that analogy, it was assumed that economies of scale could be accomplished in the provision of police services.

Reformers took for granted that a bureaucratic structure approximated an ideal decision-making arrangement for the provision of all urban public goods and services including police services. Hierarchical organization was automatically assumed to be the least costly decision-making arrangement. If all units within any particular city were hierarchically related, the person at the top could presumably give central direction and control to the operation of the department. That official would have the authority and the responsibility for administering the department as a whole. If something went wrong, he would be held responsible and could be removed.

The task of the modern public agency was considered to require the services of professionals. Future public servants should receive extensive training. Well-trained professionals should then be given a high degree of job security to enable them to exercise their professional discretion without fear of being fired by less well-informed citizens or politicians. Internal review procedures were to be preferred to external pressures or influence.

Reformers were successful in gaining acceptance of bureaucratic organization and professionalization of police serving large cities. Most large police departments are hierarchically structured and have adopted quasimilitary discipline. The police chief is officially accountable for all that goes on under him. Police departments have increasingly been staffed by professionals in the sense of specially trained individuals whose career is police service. Recruits in most large police departments are sent first to police academies before assignment. All ranks receive additional training in a wide variety of police techniques. Review of police activities is primarily undertaken by internal police review boards.

*The Consequences of Reform.* A number of studies in large departments have been undertaken recently which provide evidence about
their current operating characteristics. James Q. Wilson, for example, conducted a very relevant study in the Chicago Police Department.[2] He investigated the effect that an increase in professionalization had on the morale of the department's officers and on police
perceptions of citizen respect. He distributed questionnaires to all
sergeants serving in 1960 immediately after Superintendent O. W.
Wilson had taken over a demoralized and poorly run department
with the expressed purpose of increasing its professionalism and
efficiency. A second survey of sergeants was conducted in 1965. Five
years of reform did substantially improve the sergeants' evaluations
of the internal management of their department. However, reform
did not affect the morale of policemen nor their own perceptions of
citizen respect for police. About 60 percent of the sergeants in 1965
indicated that morale was about the same or worse.[3] Police sergeants
continued to feel that citizens lacked respect for police, were uncoop-
erative, and obeyed laws simply from fear of being caught. A dramatic change occurred, however, in the evaluation made by police
sergeants regarding the importance of being liked by the citizens with
whom they had contact. In 1960, 80 percent thought it was important to be liked by the citizens with whom they had contacts. In 1965,
only 60 percent agreed with this statement.[4]

Wilson speculates that a professional police department in a
large city handles its morale problem by downplaying the value of
public opinion. Wilson argues:

> This is a result both of what professional doctrine requires (substituting
> patrol cars for officers walking beats, increasing the size of police
> districts, rotating men among assignments and discouraging police
> involvement in political affairs) and of what the ethos of professional-
> ism assumes (that the impersonal rules of law enforcement are correct
> and appropriate regardless of what a hostile or indifferent citizenry
> may think). . . . A professional force, in principle at least, devalues
> citizen opinion as manifested in personal relations; professionalism, in
> this sense, means impersonalization. Relations with the community are
> no longer handled by the officer's informal contacts—some legitimate,
> some illegitimate—with neighborhoods and individuals but are given
> over to a specialized and bureaucratic agency within the police organi-
> zation.[5]

Wilson concludes that while a police force may be improved because of professionalization, "if at the same time the popular image and authority of the police officer have deteriorated, the two changes may cancel each other out, producing no net gain in police morale and creating a continuing police problem."[6] Police, to maintain their own morale, may have to rely increasingly on bureaucratic rules, their own self-conception of the essential rightness of what they are doing, and a general indifference to the public. This points toward a substantial degree of police "counter-responsiveness" to citizen interests.

A number of studies have documented the growing isolation of large city policemen from the neighborhoods they serve. In eleven of the fifteen large cities in which major riots have occurred, studies by the National Advisory Commission on Civil Disorders report that a majority of the policemen interviewed who served in predominantly black neighborhoods thought adolescents regarded them as enemies.[7] On the other hand, 83 percent of the same police considered storekeepers to be "on their side."[8] Only hostile communication appears to be taking place between police and youth in those areas. One-third of the police reported that they did not know a single important youth leader on their beat well enough to speak to when they saw him. At the same time, 89 percent of the police reported knowing six or more shop owners, merchants, and clerks that well.[9] Further, few police were found who participated in any neighborhood activities where they patrolled or had friends in the area. Black policemen were found to participate more and to know more about the neighborhoods they served. Black police were generally more sympathetic to the problems of individuals living in predominantly black neighborhoods.[10] While black policemen appear to be less isolated than white police in such neighborhoods, the proportion of black patrolmen on most major police forces falls below the proportion of blacks in the population at large. "In no major American city does the police force approximate the ratio of Negroes in the community and at the officer and policy-making levels, the disparities increase."[11] Some critics of professionalized police forces have argued that civil service requirements have long been biased against the employment of blacks and other minority groups and are not related to the achievement of high performance by police.[12]

The growing isolation of police from the communities they serve is also documented by James Q. Wilson, who described a "highly professionalized force" serving 300,000 residents of a "Western City:"

> The city in which they now serve has a particular meaning for only a very few. Many live outside it in the suburbs and know the city's neighborhoods almost solely from their police work. Since there are no precinct stations but only radio car routes, and since they are frequently changed, there is little opportunity to build up an intimate familiarity, much less an identification with any neighborhood. The Western City police are, in a real sense, an army of occupation organized along para-military lines.[13]

Given this isolation, a major problem of large police forces is gaining adequate information about potential and actual offenders. When either the department is small or men are assigned to a regular foot-patrol beat, they begin to know the citizens in their area. Putting men in cars and rotating assignments reduces their level of contact and knowledge. The pattern of crimes subject to arrest "changes with centralization of command and control, since it compels the department to place greater reliance on formal intelligence systems and means of crime solution."[14] Police become more dependent upon information gained from those who have already been arrested and charged with one crime to help in the clearance of other crimes.[15] While the police are dependent upon citizens to provide them with general information about the occurrence of crimes or the whereabouts of suspected offenders, the lack of informal and friendly contacts with citizens living in an area reduces the likelihood of gaining such information.

In a study of the New York Police Department, John H. McNamara focused on one of the major dilemmas faced by large, bureaucratized forces in preparing recruits for duty in the field. The question McNamara posed is whether such a department should "emphasize training strategies aimed at the development of self-directed and autonomous personnel or . . . emphasize strategies aimed at developing personnel over whom the organization can easily exercise control."[16] McNamara found that the New York department had emphasized the second strategy by stressing negative sanctions against patrolmen found in violation of the department's massive, 400-page *Rules and Procedures* and creating an atmosphere of close command supervision over the work of patrolmen. As a consequence, recruits ranked the *Rules and Procedures* handbook their most useful study materials over all others, including the *Penal Code,* the *Code of Criminal Procedures,* lecture notes, and all technical literature. At the same time, 60 percent of the recruits disagreed with the statement, "Patrolmen who rely entirely on the *Rules and Procedures* of the Department are probably excellent police officers."[17] After experience in the field, 80 percent of the patrolmen interviewed agreed with the statement, "It is impossible to always follow the *Rules and Procedures* to the letter and still do an efficient job in police work."[18] However, of patrolmen who had served two years in the field, 55 percent agreed that a "patrolman, for his own good, should never deviate from the provisions contained in the *Rules and Procedures.* "[19]

Thus, in the large New York Police Department, patrolmen judged adherence to internal rules of prime importance not because adherence to rules improved performance but from a fear of internal sanctions for failure to do so. A further consequence of this focus on negative sanctions was a widely shared view by patrolmen with two years experience that *inactivity* is the best means to reduce the risks they faced. "Patrolmen who are always out looking for situations requiring police attention are the ones," the older patrolmen felt, "who usually get into trouble with their supervisors."[20] McNamara speculates that internal discipline "often engendered more concern on the part of the patrolmen with what their supervisors were up to than concern with the problems of the citizenry."[21]

The lack of responsiveness to the needs and preferences of citizens thus induced by the attempt to impose a strict bureaucratic order has not been compensated for by a change in the basic honesty or efficiency of the New York Police Department. The Knapp Commission has uncovered extensive corruption at all levels throughout the department.[22] If anything, the tight bureaucratic controls enabled corrupt practices to continue within the department by reducing exposures to outside investigations. Those responsible for bringing public attention to police corruption were continually threatened with sanctions in efforts to silence their charges. Nor has this lack of responsiveness been compensated for by a decrease in the level and type of police abuses in New York City. Violence against minorities, the use of charges of disorderly conduct and resisting arrest to cover police mistreatment, and the plea bargaining which results have been well documented.[23]

The New York Police Department is not the only large city police force characterized by corruption and police abuses. In a study of Boston, Chicago, and Washington, D. C., observers riding with police officers during a regular shift recorded a wide variety of illegal acts, rule infraction, and police abuse of citizens. The large number of such acts recorded was especially surprising since they occurred when observers were present. As reported by Albert J. Reiss, one in five officers was observed in some form of criminal violation of the law.[24] These violations included, among others, an officer accepting money to alter testimony, an officer receiving money or merchandise from a business, and an officer taking money or property from a deviant or potential offender. Approximately four in ten officers was observed in a serious rule infraction, including drinking on duty, sleeping on duty, neglect of duty, and falsification of reports.[25] It is important to note that the rate of rule infraction varied by the racial composition of the precinct being served. "White officers assigned to non-white precincts had higher rates of rule violation than those in white precincts."[26] Reiss argues that the rate of infraction is related "to the quality of supervision of line officers and the transfer policies of the department."[27] Effective supervision particularly affected the rate of such violations as drinking and sleeping on duty and neglect of duty. Reiss reports that job assignment and transfer policies within a department have the result that:

> officers with the least training and experience are assigned to the highest crime-rate precincts. Officers with the poorest records of performance likewise are transferred to these areas. In American cities today, such police precincts often are nonwhite. . . . Two types of deviant officers were so assigned: those who basically did excellent police work but were against the system, taking every opportunity to show their disregard for it, and those who were both poor police officers and had been sanctioned previously for infractions of the rules. Slum police precinct stations, not unlike slum schools, collect the "rejects" of the system.[28]

While the number of policemen using force judged by observers to be excessive was quite small, 5 percent of all citizens observed in encounters with the police were "openly ridiculed or belittled" and another 5 percent were treated brusquely or in an authoritarian manner.[29] In watching and coding both sides of over 5,000 police-citizen encounters an "inescapable conclusion is that officers are somewhat more likely to be uncivil toward citizens than citizens toward officers."[30]

All in all one would conclude from the studies discussed above, and others reporting similar findings, that police serving very large cities: (1) find themselves in an increasingly hostile environment created at least to some extent by their "professionalism" and removal from contacts with and knowledge of the neighborhoods they serve; (2) discount the importance of public opinion and rely on their own organizationally supported self-conception of the rightness of their behavior; (3) have little communication with young people and other regular citizens, particularly in predominantly black neighborhoods, while maintaining friendly relations with merchants; (4) have difficulty gaining the cooperation of citizens at the time of a crime and have become more dependent on information from paid informants or suspects already arrested; (5) focus excessively on conformance to petty bureaucratic rules and regulations while recognizing that such conformance does not improve performance or efficiency; (6) utilize inactivity and inattention to observed problems as a strategy rather than risk exposure to unpredictable actions by supervisors; and (7) engage to a "significant" extent in illegal activities, major rule infractions, and verbal abuse of citizens.

These behavior patterns add up to the operation of police forces which are not only unresponsive to citizen preferences, but to a large extent have become counterresponsive to citizen preferences and counterproductive for securing the peace and security of the communities they serve.

Since responsiveness was not a primary performance criterion of the traditional reformers, it should not be surprising that police serving large cities should be unresponsive to citizen preferences. If the current design of police institutions produces consequences which meet the performance criteria originally intended by those who propose reforms, one would have to judge the theoretical foundations for that design as basically sound. If such were the case, the question of reform to achieve more responsive institutions would then become one of deciding how new performance criteria could be added to the other elements of the old design. One would retain the reformers' conception of the nature of police services and their analysis of the consequences of utilizing bureaucratic decision rules for the provision of police services.

However, considerable evidence exists that the reformers' design of institutional arrangements for the provision of police services does not lead to greater efficiency and economy in large cities when compared to smaller cities nor to a more equal distribution of law enforcement resources within large cities. Thus, not only are the police departments serving large cities unresponsive to citizen preferences, but they also provide equal or less services at the same or higher costs than are provided in many medium to small cities. (The failure of reform institutions to realize increased efficiency will not be discussed here, since a substantial literature is available which addresses this issue directly.[31]) The basic theoretical underpinnings of the reform design are faulty. A new design based on a different conception of police services and utilizing different kinds of decision rules is necessary to realize greater responsiveness as well as efficiency and redistribution.

## The Problem of Design and the Nature of Police Services

When individuals are engaged in transactions which primarily involve the production and exchange of what are called "private goods," responsive institutional arrangements are relatively easy to design. Private goods and services can be thought of as events which are highly divisible and which can be packaged, contained, or measured in discrete units. The private good or service which one person utilizes or consumes is not available to anyone else. A loaf of bread is a classic example of a private good. The institutional arrangements of a market enable private entrepreneurs to provide private goods under conditions where potential consumers can be excluded from enjoying the benefit unless they are willing to pay the price. The dynamics of a market leads the private entrepreneur to be highly responsive to the preferences of his consumers depending, of course, on their ability to back their preferences with cash for those goods which most closely approximate their preference. If he is not responsive to their preferences, they will go somewhere else. The success of a private entrepreneur in being responsive to consumer preferences can be measured to a large extent by his ability to sell sufficient goods and services to cover costs.

The design of responsive institutional arrangements is a more difficult task when public goods and services are involved. Purely public goods are highly indivisible goods and services where potential consumers cannot easily be excluded from enjoying the benefits.[32] Once public goods are provided for some, they will be available for others to enjoy regardless of who pays the costs. National defense is a classic example of a purely public good. Once it is provided for some individuals living within a particular country, it is automatically provided for all other citizens whether they want it or not and whether they pay for it or not.

In addition to the purely private good and purely public good, there is a continuum in between. Within this continuum, the production or consumption of goods and services may involve spill-over effects or externalities which are not isolated and contained within the transactions between direct beneficiaries. Goods with appreciable spill-overs are similar to private goods to the extent that some effects impinge only on direct participants; but other effects are like public goods and spill over onto others not directly involved. Air pollution which results from producing private goods is an example of a negative spill-over. Most aspects of the production process affect only those directly involved, but the discharge of factory smoke affects others in a wider community. The benefits derived for a neighborhood by the location of a golf course or park is a positive externality. The reduction of a negative externality or the increase of a positive externality have characteristics similar to the provision of a public good.

The provision of public goods or services having appreciable spillovers poses a number of difficulties in the design of institutional arrangements. Since private entrepreneurs cannot exclude beneficiaries, they may have difficulties covering the costs of production. Only private entrepreneurs who will themselves directly benefit from the provision of a public good, or who can organize some form of voluntary association where others share the cost, will be led to produce a public good. Under voluntary provision, consumers of public goods have no incentive to reveal their preferences for the good. Holdouts who refuse to cooperate in covering costs will receive the benefits from the good along with those who pay costs. Beneficiaries will be led to minimize their costs in paying for such a good. Thus, some individuals will remain silent and hope that others will demand and pay for public goods while they quietly benefit and do not have to pay. Reliance on voluntary arrangements for the provision of public goods will lead to no provision or a lower level of provision than affected individuals would prefer.

If individuals wish to have a higher quality of public goods than would be provided under voluntary arrangements, institutional arrangements must be designed where each individual can be compelled to pay his share of the costs. A governmental agency, for example, can be established to provide public goods or services to those living within some political boundaries. Users can be forced to pay for the good through nonvoluntary means such as taxes. However, payments for services are extracted whether citizen consumers like what they receive or not. The lack of *quid pro quo* relations substantially reduces the level of information about user satisfaction routinely transmitted to public agencies as compared with private agencies.

While it is thus possible to provide public goods and services, the resulting institutions will never be as responsive to the preferences of consumers as the institutional arrangements which provide private goods and services under competitive conditions. Elections are substitutes for market mechanisms in registering individual preferences regarding what level of public service should be provided. Other decision mechanisms determine how public goods are allocated, who should pay and how much should be paid. Elections and bureaucratic structures are not as sensitive in revealing user preferences as a market which enables each individual to choose how much he wants from a set of alternative products offered. Some individuals will have a greater voice in articulating preferences within such decision-making structures. The wealthy and the better educated will have an easier opportunity than others (as they have also in a private market). However, the lack of divisibility makes it difficult for any individual to specify exactly what he wants. Further the difficulty in measuring output makes it hard for a public agency to evaluate whether an appropriate level of service is being provided to meet the preferences of those who pay the costs. Consequently, inherent difficulties exist in designing institutional arrangements for the provision of any public good or any good with significant positive or negative spillovers.

*Police Services as Public Goods.* The provision of police services involve some aspects which can be considered as pure public goods and others which involve considerable externalities. When police patrol traffic, most citizens in a jurisdiction benefit from the increase in safety thus provided. This aspect of police work can be thought of as a relatively pure public good. Even when police deal with a problem primarily related to a single family unit, like a family quarrel, other families in the neighborhood receive the indirect benefit of being protected against the chance that a violent conflict in one family will affect others in the neighborhood. Consequently, it must be assumed from the start that inherent difficulties exist in designing responsive institutions for the provision of police services simply because of the public good aspects of police services.

*The Type of Work Involved in Policing.* A second major factor increasing the difficulty of designing police institutions responsive to individual preferences is the specific type of work involved in policing. Police work is largely person to person contact between individual policemen and citizens. Policemen are expected to respond to and handle a wide variety of different problems. Emergency illnesses, family quarrels, burglaries, traffic violations, gang fights in the street, and peaceful political demonstrations are all included within the routine work load. When a policeman responds to a call, he must use discretion in whatever he is called upon to do. Little time is available to ask for instructions from headquarters. Police work is unusual for the amount of discretion which necessarily is placed in the lowest ranks. Even though semimilitary discipline is characteristic, it is difficult for supervisors in a police department to exert effective control over the work of patrolmen.[33]

To compound this problem, police work is frequently dangerous. Policemen must be alert to potential signs of danger. They must learn to be suspicious of all individuals and in all transactions with the public. Interactions which begin in a somewhat low key can suddenly explode into danger. Each policeman knows that his own life may depend upon the support given him by his fellow officers and vice versa. Police also deal with situations where the citizens are apt to manifest their worst, rather than their best, characteristics. Police as a group are known to develop close-knit relations among themselves, to be suspicious of most outsiders, and to be generally cynical about other people.[34] These characteristics, while understandable in light of police work, are hardly the characteristics which lead police to view themselves as public servants responsive to the needs of citizens. Regardless of how police institutions are designed, the character of police work itself will tend to produce clannish, secretive, and cynical individuals who handle large numbers of interactions with citizens with considerable discretion but subject to little control by supervisors.

*The Inter-Dependence of Police and Other Institutional Arrangements.* Whether a police agency is able to provide a desired level of public order depends not only upon its own effectiveness but also on the effectiveness of other institutional arrangements in any community. The degree of security enjoyed by individuals within a community is the result of individuals interacting with one another within a wider set of institutional arrangements. Employment markets, housing markets, welfare programs, educational systems, court systems, community organizations, and the police all affect how individuals will interact with each other.

When individuals in pursuit of opportunities for themselves and their families are able to develop satisfactory arrangements within legal arrangements, little incentive exists to seek illegal means to accomplish their goals. No set of institutional arrangements is ever perfected to the degree that all individuals interact in a productive and lawful manner at all times. However, the more effective are the set of institutional arrangements in enabling individuals to cope with their problems, the less apt individuals will be to adopt strategies outside the limits provided by legal constraints. Thus, the greater the proportion of individuals who are unable to solve basic problems for themselves and their families through legal institutional arrangements, the larger the proportion of individuals who will be motivated to pursue illegal means to solve problems and thus endanger the safety of the community as a whole.

Thus, the type of demands placed on the police will vary to a large extent on the success of other institutional arrangements. If employment markets, housing markets, educational systems, and general governmental mechanisms are working relatively well, fewer individuals will resort to illegal methods for solving problems. However, if the other institutional arrangements are not working well, the number of poor and unemployed within a community will increase and police will face the problem of an increased level of illegal activity. The poor and the disadvantaged may not have sufficient voice within regular political channels to articulate effectively their demands for a change in the way basic institutions are operating. Nonviolent and violent protest may increase as well as the level of crime. Under such circumstances, the wealthy and articulate members of the community may demand that the police devote themselves to protecting their neighborhoods from the poor and the dissatisfied. Such demands may lead to repressive measures by the police and the suppression of the alternative political strategies available to the poor to attempt to alleviate the problems they face. Repressive measures may lead to a vicious circle. The more the police do, the worse things get.

This interdependence of police and other institutional arrangements creates special problems in the design of responsive police institutions. Wealthy and well educated individuals will always have a fairly effective voice in articulating preferences for police services. The problem is how to increase the voice of disadvantaged populations who need a type of police service which will protect them from crime and violence as well as protecting their right to articulate their dissatisfaction with the operations of other institutional arrangements in a society.

*The Influence on the Police of the Type of Community Being Served.*
The design of responsive police institutions is also affected by the nature of the community being served. Of particular concern in the design of police institutions is the relative homogeneity of the com-

munity as measured by such indicators as income, race, religion, and proportion of home owners.

When a population is relatively homogeneous, individuals are more apt to agree on basic values and morals. By mutual agreement, interactions are more likely to stay within agreed-upon standards and the general level of demand upon the police for the maintenance of order is less. However, when a population is relatively heterogeneous, individuals are more apt to disagree on basic values and moral premises. One individual may pursue a strategy that he considers appropriate but that his neighbor considers a threat to his security.

The more heterogeneous the preferences of the individuals being served by the police, the more difficult it is for the police to be responsive. No matter what the police do, someone is unhappy. For example, when the police respond to a complaint about a disturbance in a residential neighborhood, they may provide a service to some residents and a disservice to others. Some people find an empty, quiet street most "orderly." Others prefer a busy, noisy street full of friends and acquaintances. A particular street cannot be empty and busy, quiet and noisy at the same time. Whichever form of "order" is provided, some individuals may perceive the state of affairs as a benefit and others as a cost. Thus, while provision of police services in relatively homogeneous communities will provide joint benefits in the main, the more heterogeneous the community, the more likely the police will impose joint costs or deprivations as well since some individuals will receive "services" which they would prefer to avoid. The perceived citizen hostility which results leads to severe problems of police morale in large and heterogeneous cities.[35]

The inclusion of many activities designed to enforce conventional morality in a heterogeneous community increases the problem of responsiveness still further. When activities which many individuals do not consider immoral are made illegal, the basic calculations of risk and profit of individuals engaged in such activities are significantly changed. When activities, such as gambling, are legal, many potential sellers enter the field and the costs for the consumer are relatively low. By making gambling illegal, many individuals who do not want to risk legal sanctions exclude themselves from rendering such services.

It is an odd paradox that making some activities illegal may actually enhance the opportunities for profit for those willing to run some risks and increase the likelihood for police graft. Such a result does not occur when such activities as driving on the left side of the road, assaulting a person on the street, or robbing a grocery store are made illegal. The creation of a highly profitable business by outlawing activities occurs only when some willing adults have a strong demand for services regardless of their illegality. In such instances, outlawing activities creates a "crime tariff" which protects those who engage in the illegal activity as a business from the entry of too many competitors.[36] It is the protection from competitors which insures high profits. The high profits involved in such "protected" businesses, generate sufficient revenue to enable proprietors to share their profits with police who do not interfere. When this occurs, police become responsive to the managers of illegal establishments in the protection of "organized crime" rather than responsive to a more general population.

*The Problem of Achieving Valid Indicators of Performance.* Another major difficulty in designing responsive police institutions is the task of devising valid indicators of police performance. Without valid indicators of performance it is hard for individuals working within any type of institutional arrangements to be responsive to citizen preferences. Without knowing how well one is doing, it is difficult to know how to improve! Most urban police departments rely on the F.B.I. Crime Index or similar indices as measures of performance. However, the F.B.I. Crime Index is a grossly unreliable and invalid indicator for the following reasons: (1) Many serious crimes, such as narcotics violations, arson, bribery, and fraud are not included in the index; (2) all crimes on the index are weighted equally; (3) many criminal acts are not reported to authorities and are thus not included in the published index; (4) variations in local reporting are extensive and have not been taken into account; (5) there has not been a consistent data base over time; and (6) the distribution of crime among population groupings is not reflected in the index.[37]

The major problem with utilizing any crime index as an indicator of police performance is that it purports to be a measure of crimes committed rather than crimes prevented. Since police attempt to prevent crime, recording the amount of crime committed cannot adequately be interpreted as a measure of the amount of crime prevented. Ideally, what is needed are indicators of what would have happened if the police had not been providing services. That, however, is impossible.

The basic problem is compounded in larger police jurisdictions where problems of control are difficult because of the nature of police work itself. Police administrators in smaller departments can know more about what is going on and can directly coordinate many activities. Police administrators in smaller communities also come into direct contact with many citizens and can gain a more accurate assessment of the success of their department as evaluated by citizens. Police administrators of larger departments are rarely able to interact directly with either their own men or with citizens who are being served. As a result, police administrators in large cities become dependent upon internal statistical reports about the activities of various subunits. In such reports, data is aggregated in ways that lose much essential information about demand and response patterns within the jurisdictions.[38]

Frequently, departments utilize the proportion of reported crimes cleared by arrest as an indicator of performance. However, stress on clearance rates also creates difficulties. Generally, police departments have low success rates in clearing crimes through arrest. Nationwide, only 20 to 25 percent of all crimes are cleared by arrest.[39] "The low success rate in crimes cleared by arrest creates a dilemma for the police administrators in their efforts to maintain a public image of themselves as productive. . . ."[40] This dilemma can easily lead to the manipulation of statistics to create more favorable clearance rates. Clearance rates can be increased, for example, by encouraging known criminals to confess to more than a single crime once they are arrested. Lesser charges may be offered in return.[41] Such an attempt to increase the clearance rates through plea bargaining enables the most hardened criminals to receive lighter sentences than the one-time loser. Some observers have argued that part of the motivation for this activity is to increase the number of "crimes" and "criminals" and thus increase the "need" for police as well as creating crimes which help departments improve their clearance rates.[42]

The general uncertainty relating to performance has led individual policemen to produce as many recorded transactions as possible to increase their own performance ratings.[43] Many traffic officers feel they have an easier job than beat patrolmen since the number of tickets written at the end of the day is a demonstrable product.[44] Beat patrolmen can only attempt to increase their arrest rates. If the activities encouraged by an orientation toward the production of internal statistics to improve performance ratings do not help the police do a better job, continued stress on such statistics is extremely dysfunctional. Police departments always run the risk of fooling themselves about their own productivity while important activities are more or less unrecordable and thus left undone. Multiple measures of police output are needed which are generated from all types of interactions with citizens and are audited for honesty and accuracy.

*A Summary of the Nature of Police Services.* A brief recapitulation of the basic problems involved in designing police institutions which are caused by the nature of police services themselves includes the following points.

1. Because police services have aspects of being public goods:
   a. private entrepreneurs will either not provide such services or will not provide as high a level of services as citizens desire.
   b. recourse to public provision enables a public agency to provide a higher level of financing but the lack of *quid pro quo* transactions reduces information about citizen preferences available to an agency.
   c. citizens can be forced to pay for activities which they perceive as net costs or disservices rather than net benefits or services.
2. Because of the nature of police work itself:
   a. individual policemen working at the lower levels in a hierarchy must utilize considerable discretion.
   b. supervisors cannot be present to control the activities of police officers in most of their activities.
   c. top police administrators, particularly in larger departments, are dependent upon internal reporting mechanisms which may not be very useful regarding activity patterns within the department or citizens' preferences and citizen satisfactions with the services provided.

   d. individual policemen are apt to become cynical, secretive, and suspicious of outsiders and to form close, protective relationships with fellow policemen.

3. Because of the interdependence with other institutional arrangements:

   a. police departments have little control over the causes of crime and thus over the amount of criminal activities occurring within their jurisdiction.

   b. police may be called upon to protect the wealthy and politically effective from the poor and disadvantaged through repressive means.

   c. repressive methods, if utilized, engender such hostility against the police in poor neighborhoods that it is difficult for police to be effective in dealing with security there.

4. If the type of community police serve is heterogeneous:

   a. a single police force cannot simultaneously be responsive to the preferences of all citizens regarding forms of public order.

   b. asking police to enforce morals legislation congruent with the preferences of some but not all residents can lead to a crime tariff and resultant problems of graft within police departments.

5. Because of the difficulty of achieving valid indicators of performance:

   a. police and the public may utilize unreliable and invalid statistics to judge the performance of the department as a whole.

   b. information about the largest proportion of interactions between the police and citizens is either not recorded or not utilized in a regular and meaningful fashion.

   c. individual policemen are motivated to do those activities which are recorded and viewed as productive by supervisors whether or not those activities help or hinder the general job of the police.

   d. police departments may set up vicious circles where the more they do, the worse things become.

## The Problem of Design of Institutional Arrangements for the Provision of Responsive Police Services

Given the nature of police services, it will be difficult to design institutional arrangements to meet any particular set of performance criteria, whatever they might be. Reformers assumed that hierarchy would, by definition, be the most efficient structure for making decisions about the production and allocation of police service. Recent developments in organization theory provide theoretical grounds for challenging the *a priori* assumption that hierarchical organization is always the most efficient decision rule.[45] The empirical findings described above indicate that simple reliance on bureaucratic structure in the management of large-scale police departments has produced pathological consequences, manifesting inefficiencies, corruptions, inequities, and unresponsiveness.

Thus, we must reconsider the design of police institutions which rely primarily on hierarchy. Nor can we place sole reliance on the other simple decision rule—that of a market—since police services have aspects of being public goods and simple market mechanisms will not work.

Hierarchies and markets as structures for decision making achieve control over activities because individuals acting within them are exposed to different forms of risks and opportunities. Hierarchy controls individual behavior through interaction with the behavior of other individuals internal to the organization; and in a hierarchy, subordinates are subject to discipline imposed by superiors. A market controls individual behavior through exposure to the behavior of other individuals external to the organization. Firms not responsive to their markets are liable to suffer financial difficulties.

We need to consider how to design institutions which combine both internal and external control mechanisms.[46] A basic requirement must be the generation of diverse indicators about the day to day operations so that a high level of information is available concerning the consequences of utilizing different mixes of internal and external control mechanisms. It is only through constant evaluation and reevaluation of the performance of police institutions that behavior can be improved in the long run.

*Institutional Arrangements and Performance Criteria.* The selection of performance criteria affects the choice of effective internal and external control mechanisms as well as the type of information essential to evaluate performance. If efficiency were selected as the sole criteria for assessing the performance of police, then internal control mechanisms should be set up to reveal the amount of work each individual is doing. Reward and punishment structures should encourage high levels of activity and discourage low levels of activity. Performance auditing by independent agencies should be included among the external control mechanisms. Information required by both internal and external control mechanisms would include the cost of input units and their relative efficiency in achieving similar performance criteria. Statistical reports on the activity patterns of each division and patrol team within the organization would be needed.

If responsiveness were adopted as the sole criteria, then internal control mechanisms should be rigged to review citizen satisfaction with services performed. Supervisors should visit a random sample of citizens who had interacted with their subordinates to evaluate their satisfaction with services received. Internal reward structures should encourage rapid police responses to citizen calls for service and even-handed treatment of all suspected violators of the law. Internal sanctions should discourage behavior which generated a pattern of citizen complaints. External control mechanisms might also audit a sample of transactions as well as processing citizen complaints. Information required by both internal and external control mechanisms will include the response time for all calls for service, relative satisfaction levels of citizens served, and preferences of citizens concerning the enforcement patterns maintained in their neighborhoods.

However, rarely is only a single performance criteria utilized in the design of institutional arrangements or in the evaluation of the consequences flowing from its operation. Multiple goals present perplexing questions. It is not possible simultaneously to maximize partially conflicting goals. While efficiency and responsiveness are not totally contradictory, the achievement of either of them beyond some level may require the diminution of the other. Thus, police cannot be perfectly responsive to the needs and preferences of all citizens at all times without significantly affecting the efficiency or justice of their operation.

## Towards More Responsive Police Institutions

Given a concern for designing more responsive police institutions which also operate relatively efficiently and maintain a standard of fairness, what type of reforms of current police institutions should be considered? Unfortunately, there is no magic formula for combining institutional arrangements to produce any set of partially competitive performance criteria. One cannot in good conscience specify a "model set of institutions" which can be applied in all types of situations. The best one can do is to sketch some of the elements that would most likely be involved in any effort to increase the responsiveness of police institutions.

It is likely that any desirable system would involve a complex mixture of institutional arrangements. Neither a pure hierarchy nor a pure market will produce the desired results, given the nature of police services. A workable system would most likely rely upon both internal and external control mechanisms. Such mechanisms would need to increase (1) the citizens' voice in articulating their preferences for different types of police services as well as (2) the information generated about system performance. Extensive mechanisms for the evaluation of performance using diverse criteria will be needed. In this way, the individuals affected by institutional arrangements can learn from past behavior and continue to change the institutional mix in light of experience. No design will continue to operate successfully for very long without readjustment in light of new or unanticipated problems.

Such a reformed system would probably involve the establishment of both large and small scale police departments serving the same area.[47] Small units could provide neighborhood patrol services responsive to the preferences of individual neighborhoods while maintaining minimum standards established for a larger area. Large departments could provide specialized services such as crime laboratories, narcotics investigation units, and some aspects of record keeping. Cooperative and contractual arrangements among both large and small units could be developed to establish joint communication services, joint training facilities, cooperative detective units, and cross-deputization to ensure easy movement across jurisdictional boundaries. An increase in the amount of interjurisdictional contracts and agreements would tend in and of itself to generate more information about the performance of the system. Public officials involved in contract negotiation will need to learn about the consequences of the past arrangements.

Post audits conducted by independent agencies of a random sample of contacts between citizens and the police could serve a variety of purposes.[48] First, the accuracy of the reports made by police officers could be assessed, and departments producing invalid reports challenged. Secondly, the satisfaction of citizens with the manner, speed, and methods utilized in responding to their calls for services could be ascertained. Third, the fairness of the methods of apprehending a suspect or stopping a violator of the traffic code could also be assessed.

Regularized procedures enabling citizens to file complaints with an independent agency regarding grievances would also improve the responsiveness of the system.[49] Regular reports could be made concerning the number of cases filed, the findings of the independent agency, and the methods adopted by police departments to reduce the likelihood of future malperformance of police personnel.[50]

Elements of the mix of institutional arrangements adopted to increase responsiveness while also achieving efficiency and fairness would appear to work at cross-purposes. However, this would be necessary, and only reflects the partially conflicting performance criteria. Conflict between individuals associated with different aspects of the mix of decision structures brings attention to the problem of trade-offs between goals. Consequently, the operation of a system of rules designed to accomplish partially competitive goals will, at times, involve high levels of conflict. If the information thus generated is extensive and relatively valid, adjustments can be made in the long run which will approach optimal solutions even though the day to day operation of the system appears chaotic and unorganized.

The question of how current police institutions should be reformed is receiving considerable national attention. Within the last several years, numerous national study commissions have reported on the need to reorganize urban police institutions.[51] With the notable exception of the American Bar Association, most of the study commissions have adopted the efficiency and economy model discussed in the early sections of this paper.[52] The Committee for Economic Development, for example, argues that the "ineffectiveness of the present structure is rooted in the organizational and administrative chaos that characterizes the nation's uncoordinated system of criminal justice. . . ."[53] The committee proposes a complete overhaul of the criminal justice system including the establishment of a strong, centralized department of justice at the state level.

The National Advisory Commission on Criminal Justice Standards and Goals has just urged the consolidation of all police departments employing less than ten men.[54] A large percentage of the $800 million in grant funds offered by the Law Enforcement Assistance Administration to state and local governments is to support plans for reorganization, regionalization, and consolidation of local police departments.

If this unilateral trend toward ever larger police departments continues without the simultaneous creation of smaller units within the larger units, we can expect future police institutions to be even less responsive to citizen preferences than past ones.[55] We may, indeed, be facing the possibility of a long term vicious circle, as the protest engendered by results of previous rounds of centralization leads to still further centralization as a supposed means of increasing the safety of the community.

To avoid this trap, we must learn to understand the operation of complex, and at times, seemingly chaotic, police institutions. We must stop assuming that complex arrangements are automatically inefficient. On the other hand, we need not start assuming that complex institutions are automatically efficient. The critical problem is to develop a reliable theory of institutional design which will enable us to predict the range of likely consequences to flow from the establishment of a particular mix of institutional arrangements for the provision of a particular set of goods and services in a particular environment. Until a more reliable theory of institutional design is developed, further reforms using the traditional ideology are liable to increase the unresponsiveness of urban police institutions.

# Responsiveness and Responsibility: the Anomalous Problem of the Environment

*Lynton K. Caldwell*

The concept of an environmental relationship is easy to state but, beyond that, difficult to manage intellectually. This is because the term *environment* connotes interactions of infinite variety and complexity. There are as many environmental relationships as there are things environed. Even if the definition is confined to environments of human beings, the environment of each individual who lives, or ever has lived, is in a precise sense unique. Moreover, the environmental concept is dynamic; for all environments are in a continuing state of flux although a change may sometimes be so slow as to be imperceptible to the human observer.

Conventional concepts and habits of speech frequently confuse people considering environmental issues. The environment is not merely the physical objects or conditions surrounding or acting upon the environed subject. Although it is conventional to speak of the environment as if it were the objects externally related to an individual or a society, it is, in fact, the relationship between what is environed and the time-space matrix in which it exists that constitutes the true meaning of *environment.* The term implies the relationship. Or should imply it; unfortunately, the interactive relationship between man and his environment is first tacitly assumed and then forgotten in man's interpretation of external reality. There is also, as the French physiologist Claude Bernard observed, an inner environment within the human body, *milieu interieur,* which interacts with, is nourished from, and is sometimes destroyed by elements in the external environment, the *milieu exterieur.*

Social and political problems of the human environment are selected for public attention out of the vastly larger matrix of environmental relationships. Because of the ultimate interconnectedness of all reality, it is not possible absolutely to separate these selected problems from all other aspects of the environment; but it is not necessary to their practical management to do so. Although the development of wise policies to govern man's environmental relationships depends upon an understanding of the chain of consequences following from specific human interactions with the environment, it is not often necessary that these consequences be followed through an infinite sequence of ramifying or subsidiary events. Different environmental interactions entail different sequential chain reactions; but for many circumstances, the practical needs of human society do not require detailed knowledge beyond second, third, or fourth order consequences.

Environmental issues may therefore be perceived selectively and, in a practical sense, may be dealt with selectively even though doing so may at times require far-reaching and detailed examination of complex interactions and relationships. But man's difficulty in understanding environmental relationships is not wholly a factor of the properties of those relationships; it has to do also with the mind and methods with which man attempts to comprehend them. Dynamic environmental relationships are frequently difficult to conceptualize because the human mind is not well adapted to deal with them. Jay W. Forrester observes,

> The human mind is excellent in its ability to observe the elementary forces and actions of which a system is composed. The human mind is effective in identifying the structure of a complex situation. But human experience trains the mind only poorly for estimating the

dynamic consequences of how the parts of a system will interact with one another.[1]

This deficiency applies equally to understanding the behavior of natural and man-made systems and, as Forrester notes, until recently there was no way to estimate their tendencies ". . . except by contemplation, discussions, argument, and guesswork."[2]

There is now hope that sophisticated computer technology can supplement the human mind in the analysis and evaluation of complex, dynamic environmental relationships, project present trends into the future and, by simulating alternative arrangements, enable society to govern its present action in ways conducive to desirable and sustainable environments in the future. Meanwhile, man's understanding of what he is doing to his environment, and what it is doing to him, is less than adequate for his own safety and survival. Yet the direct experience of many ordinary people, the empirical observations of knowledgeable observers, and the verifiable evidence of science have converged to create widespread apprehension over the present and future state of man's environmental relationships. A widespread public apprehension has become a political concern, not only in the United States but in varying degrees throughout the world, this last to a degree which induced the General Assembly of the United Nations to convene the Conference on the Human Environment in Stockholm in June 1972.

But the environment, as we shall presently see, is a peculiar political issue, at least as political issues have been perceived under the systems of political thought dominant since the eighteenth century. And it is strange that environment should be a controversial issue if the issue is in fact survival, as many scientists and some political leaders have now declared it to be. If survival is a universal interest, it could hardly be an adversary issue between contending interests; it would not fit easily into the theory of political alignment propounded by the American *Federalist* or by most political theorists before or after 1788.

*Understanding the Environmental Problem.* The greater number of people do not seem to see survival as the environmental issue. There are many interpretations of the meaning of environment as a political issue and perhaps even more preferences for ways in which environmental problems may be resolved. Sharp differences of opinion may (and do) exist among environmentalists as to goals, strategies, and the underlying causes of environmental degradation. These differences obviously complicate the ability of government to respond to environmental issues.[3]

As with many problems that become political issues, man-environment relationships have two aspects—substantive and procedural. The substantive aspects are those of concept and belief and, sometimes, of verifiable fact. More than most political problems, those concerning the environment appear to be susceptible to scientific verification, although not all of them are at present. For example, there are some scientifically established limits as to the quantities of lead, mercury, carbon monoxide, or other chemical substances that the human body may absorb without injury. The substantive aspects of environmental problems are thus, in many instances, capable of being defined and analyzed by the methods of science; and solutions may often be obtained through the application of science, or science-based technology.

This amenability to scientific verification is increasing not only with respect to environmental problems, but also to those involving bio-medical knowledge. Yet an accurate analysis of the true state of physical conditions and the discovery of demonstrably valid ways of correcting undesirable states of either the environment or human health, do not necessarily influence people's preferences. And moreover, people's professed preferences are not always safe indications of the social, political, or economic prices that they are willing to pay to bring about or maintain more desirable states of affairs. Even when people are agreed regarding the effect of a given state of the environment upon their well-being, they may yet differ on the means for coping with it. This brings us to the procedural aspect of environmental problems, and it is at this point that a peculiarity very widely characteristic of environmental problems complicates political solutions.

It is because of the prevalence of certain peculiar or distinctive characteristics of environmental issues that we have described them as anomalous. Anything that is anomalous presumably deviates from the usual, is exceptional and irregular and does not fit the assumptions and institutional arrangements prevailing in society at a given time. The anomaly of the environment as an issue is perhaps the principal reason for its being unperceived or discounted by many so-called leaders in civic and economic affairs and by political scientists generally throughout the United States and abroad in the years before environmental politics burst out upon the political scene in ways that could no longer be ignored.

Although, in some sense, all political issues embody values, environmental issues are more like religious or ethical questions than the economic-based issues that have been paramount in the thinking of most political analysts since Madison and Marx. The combination of a deeply-held personal ethical value, reinforced by what is believed to be scientific fact, may fuse into a political position not readily open to political compromise or bargaining. It is this fusion of the ethical and the scientific in environmental issues that makes them anomalous in relation to conventional nineteenth and twentieth century politics. Thus the so-called environmentalist or ecological advocate in politics often appears to be an extremist and an intransigent in the eyes of the interest oriented business community, and in the opinion of conventional politicians and social scientists with large personal and professional investments in coalition theory, games, and bargaining as modes of understanding political behavior.

Economic interests obviously weigh heavily in the practical politics of the environment. Nevertheless, economic factors do not simultaneously unite and divide contestants as they do in issues arising between the rich and the poor, between capital and labor, between agriculture and industry, or between rival nations. Economic factors when considered in an ecological context may differ significantly from the way they appear when viewed in relation to the gains and losses of interested individuals. In order to counteract the tendency of environmental issues to transcend traditional class lines, some representatives of the radical left have attacked environmental quality as a diversionist trick of rightists and an evasion of the real issues of poverty and social injustice. And from the extreme right the environmental movement has been viewed as hostile to business, profits, and property.

On a large number of environmental issues, what is perceived as a largely economic question on one side of the argument may not be an economic issue at all on the other side. Labor and management may disagree over the cutting of an economic pie; but over an issue of environmental pollution, the establishment of a wilderness area, or the preservation of a free-flowing river, the contending parties may, at extremes, have no common basis whatever in defining the issue between them other than that they are in fundamental disagreement about what happens to the particular environmental relationship involved. Attempts to apply cost-benefit analysis to an environmental dispute in order to arrive at some common agreement as to the relevant factors may on occasion be effective; but for environmental issues in general, its effectiveness is highly qualified and limited. When the parties are on quite different wavelengths and when the goals sought are quite different and incompatible, the politics of compromise and bargaining finds itself in an uncongenial if not totally negative "environment."

This brings the environment, as a political problem, to its ultimate anomaly: it may be, or appear to be, simultaneously radical and conservative. The man-environment issue is in fact radical in the exact sense of the word—it goes to the roots of man's existence and welfare in the physical world. Its objectives are concerned with the basic conditions of human existence as understood through the biological and behavioral sciences. But the environment as a political issue is concerned with a way of life, an outlook on life—a lifestyle that includes a full range of values and relationships that tend to be oriented to the whole man. Many activists in the politics of environment reject conventional interpretations of human behavior by social and behavioral scientists as being incomplete, abstract, and methodologically biased. In the 1970s in the United States and Western Europe the intellectual leadership of the politics of environment has tended to be critical, even hostile, to prevailing patterns of social and political behavior and social and political priorities. But with only a few exceptions it does not accept the alternative arrangements of the traditional socialist "left" as adequate to the environmental challenge. Thus, in its earlier stages, the politics of the environment has largely been a politics of dissent and often a politics of radical change in priorities, budgets, and institutional arrangements.

On the other hand, the politics of the environment tends to be conservative in a very fundamental sense. It may disapprove of the behavior of the masses as much as of the classes; it may be equally conscious of the unecological behavior of the poor and of the rich; it may be equally critical of environmental degradation caused by socialists and by capitalists. The objective of most environmental protection movements is to stop, reduce, or redirect the impact of man-made change.

The environmental politics of the 1970s is rooted in part in the conservation movement of the earlier decades of the century. In a strictly grammatical, although not popular sense, the movement has preservationist, restorative, and reactionary aspects. The clearly professed objective of a large number of voluntary citizen environmental protection groups is to maintain indefinitely an essentially natural state of the environment over particular and, sometimes, large areas of the country, and to restore other areas or aspects of the environment to something approaching an earlier state of freedom from human spoilation. From the point of view of the corporation executive, who is summoned to a court as a result of an ecologically-inspired public interest law suit, the politics of the environment may seem a radical movement whose proponents preach a philosophy of no economic growth and are more determined enemies of free business enterprise than its traditional adversaries, the labor leaders. (There are labor leaders who sympathize with their long-time corporate adversaries in these views.)

But what may baffle the corporation executive and the labor leader is that many of their environmentalist opponents in no other respect conform to the image of the political radical. The rank and file of the environmental protest movement characteristically cuts across virtually all segments of society, although their greater numbers cluster in the upper middle class. Suburban housewives, physicians, librarians, school teachers, clerical workers, blue collar workers, and, occasionally, representatives of ethnic groups not otherwise distinguished for radical politics may find themselves united in opposition to the capital-labor establishment on environmental issues. Thus, the corporation executive may be surprised to find friends and neighbors and even members of his own family whom he knows to be conservative on nearly all other political issues to be radical on many environmental issues, and to be apparently quite indifferent to the welfare or economic survival of real estate developers, outdoor advertisers, or of public utility vice-presidents responsible for place-ment of power plants and power lines.

On environmental issues, it has not therefore been easy for the politician to anticipate a constituency. It has seldom been possible to divide the issues, or the contending opponents, along conventional party lines. Neither major political party has been able to identify the environmental issues as predominantly its own, and neither party has been able to keep environmental issues from intruding into its own political positions and strategies. The Democratic party might have seized the issue and built it into its public image during the early months of Lyndon Johnson's elected presidency. But Johnson unac-countably abandoned his leadership, perhaps in his preoccupation with the war in Southeast Asia and the effort to assuage and contain civil rights discontent. Leadership in the politics of the environment passed to Congress and was ably led by Senators Jackson, Muskie, and Nelson in the Senate; and by John D. Dingell and John P. Saylor in the House. But even in the Congress, environmental quality lead-ership, although predominantly Democratic, was not wholly so. And when passage of the National Environmental Policy Act became inevitable, the issue was seized by President Nixon, who encountered no insurmountable difficulty in incorporating it into his own political program.

By 1970, the state of the human environment was a problem as well as an issue and had become a high-priority item on the political agenda not only in the United States but in at least half a dozen countries in Western Europe, and was also receiving increas-ing official attention in the Soviet Union and Japan. Recognition that a problem existed was widespread, more widespread than under-standing of what the problem really was. A new set of human cir-cumstances had given rise to a new form of political expression that did not fit traditional political assumptions about the motives of men in politics. By the end of 1971, a substantial body of legislation and administrative regulation had been written not only at the federal level in the United States, but also among at least a third of the states and in many municipalities. Political parties and government had responded to an expressed public concern by taking the first steps toward the assumption of public responsibility for the state of the environment. Public declarations of policy had been made by both

executive and legislative bodies, courts had broadened their interpretation of citizen rights with respect to environmental conditions, and
a large body of statutory law had been enacted, revised, or amended
to cope with mounting environmental problems. The real test of the
responsiveness and responsibility of government to the problems of
the environment would come when officials undertook to translate
these declarations, policies, and laws into action through administrative agencies and the courts.

That the time for testing had arrived became evident early in
1972. The basic environmental quality statute, the National Environmental Policy Act of 1969 (NEPA), had in the preceding two years
of its existence proved to be a powerful instrument for forcing consideration of the environmental effects of federal programs. The act had
been invoked to block construction of the Alaska oil pipeline, the
Cross-Florida Barge Canal, the Tennessee-Tombigbee Canal, and a
large number of electrical generating plants, highway projects, and
other public works near and dear to the hearts of many Congressmen, local politicians, and some highly influential leaders in business
and labor. The provision of the act accomplishing all this was in
Section 102, the environmental impact paragraph, which required
each agency to file a five-point statement regarding the environmental effects of any action "significantly affecting the quality of the
human environment." The adequacy of these statements was open
to challenge in the courts, and for the first time the decision process
in environment-shaping public agencies was opened to broad and
effective public review.

This exposure was generally distasteful to the agencies and was
inherently threatening to jobs, investments, and economic growth.
Efforts to modify or emasculate NEPA were launched in the Ninety-
second Congress, especially with respect to nuclear electrical generating plants. Unlike the Johnson natural beauty campaign of the
mid-1960s, it was clear that environmental quality in the 1970s was
no cosmetic issue. Fundamental policies of population and economic
growth were involved and the conflict between long-standing economic and political assumptions and the new environmental quality
objectives was becoming clear. The environmental problem was becoming a fundamental issue affecting the goals and priorities of
society. To attain a healthful, renewable, stable environment would

require fundamental change in prevailing philosophies in business, labor, agriculture, and government. To attain a quality environment would entail large costs of many kinds. But the ultimate costs of failure to meet these expenses as incurred could mean a higher price for society to pay in the future, if the environmental decline generally perceived within the scientific community were actually in process.

*Institutional Response Capability.* The workings of institutional responsiveness to changing values in society are, at present, largely conjectural—we do not know at what critical mass of political pressure a government will respond and we cannot foresee the nature of its response. Clearly, the relative numbers of people concerned with an issue is not all that makes it political. The relative influence of the individuals concerned, the intensity of their feelings, and the reinforcing or dampening effect of collateral events are all part of the political response; and there are other factors. The environment as a political issue is a social fact, and one of the better ways to understand social facts was stated by Arthur F. Bentley nearly fifty years ago:

> The social fact which we can hold before us to classify and study presents itself as a cross-sectional and groupal activity resting in many man-lives, and nowhere else: not capable of definition in terms of any one life or summation of separate lives: never instantaneously existing but always defined in a period of time: not losing its observational singleness of fact because the lives in which it rests are, if individually defined, found in separate regions of space: always involving past and future man-society references.[4]

But the interpretation of this social fact, its weighting relative to other facts, and the probabilities for its enlargement or diminution remain practical problems for politicians. Few reliable predictions can realistically be expected from the present state of social science research. Nevertheless, some practical strategies must be found by the society's official decision makers for dealing with environmental problems as they come to public attention.

The environmental issue did not arise in isolation from other issues and conditions in society. As Bentley observed, "the very definition of each activity involves other activities and is made in terms of representativeness with reference to them, all governmental and opinionative activities of society being capable of being brought fully and with heightened meaning under such definition."[5] Following Bentley's reasoning, the question logically follows: Of what more comprehensive issues or trends is the social fact of popular anxiety over the state of the environment "representative"?

In brief, what etiological or conditioning causes have given rise to the environmental quality movement? At this time, no answers are available that are in any sense "scientific." We are still dealing in hypothesis and conjecture. But it is possible to apply Bentley's method, in part, by identifying certain other collateral and conditioning social facts which by the test of strong inference would be significant factors to be considered in any adequate and verifiable interpretation of the environmental quality movement and the politics of the environment.

It is hard to think of any political issues or conflicts that are not, for some of the parties involved, politics of discontent. The politics of the environment represents a compounding of discontents concerning a number of related developments in society. It may be argued that *environment* is representative of a broad range of discontents in society, many of which are beyond the influence or control of the individual, or even of relatively large organized groups. Environmental problems, however, have the advantage of being tangible. For many of them there are technically feasible solutions, and they appear to be more amenable to public action than do the problems of war, crime, race, and inflation. Environmental discontents in North America and Western Europe represent frustrations of the expectations of economically upward mobile populations in technologically-advanced societies. The core of discontent appears, as might be expected, in an expanding middle class whose expectations of the "good life" are being nullified by unforeseen consequences of growth, development, and affluence.

Reinforcing the environmental quality movement has been a growing disillusionment among the more educated and literate individuals with the consequences of "progress," and with the impact of science and technology upon the conditions of existence—not only of their own existence, but of others of whom they have increasing knowledge in an information-filled world. Disappointment, or disillusionment, is evident in poetry, drama, painting, and science fiction, and in political demands for reassessing the uncritical pursuit of technology and for the reallocation of public resources applied to science and technology. This disappointment has not merely been a philosophical reaction of the more thoughtful and sensitive individuals of society; it has been a mass reaction to direct and personal discomfort—for example, from atmospheric pollution, rising levels of noise, and increasing inconvenience and irrationality in public transportation. One disillusioned observer is reported to have said, "The future isn't what it used to be."

The discontents of the present and the impeding hazards of the future are increasingly being seen, not as inevitable workings of nature, but of human behavior and of institutional arrangements. They can be corrected only insofar as man brings his own behavior under control and directs it toward attaining or maintaining more preferable environmental states.

Unfortunately, the attitudes, habits, and institutions that society brings to this task are the very ones that historically have helped create increasingly unsatisfactory environmental conditions. The state of the environment has become a political issue largely because public dissatisfactions were not being adequately answered by existing institutional arrangements, which, of course, were not designed to answer such complaints. If there is one social fact seemingly confirmed by a large number of independent observations, it is that human institutions are resistant to rapid change, particularly in directions which are inconsistent with the values and objectives by which they have historically been guided. Thus, attack upon the ecological problems of the human environment has almost everywhere also become an attack upon the behavior of government itself and has led to demands for changes in both the machinery of government and in the procedures for activating it.

Throughout nearly all Western society, the structure of government and its procedures have been heavily influenced by industrial and democratic revolutions of the nineteenth century. Governments almost everywhere have been structured to serve the wishes of economic producers, whether socialist or capitalist. Almost nowhere has government been designed to respond to consumer-interest, value-oriented, science-based issues. Human institutions generally are structured as if time, social circumstances, and technology remained relatively unchanged. Therefore, it is unrealistic to expect public agencies to respond to a sudden upsurge of public discontent, even when that discontent represents a much more deep-seated and pervasive set of disconcerting influences.

Environmental discontents, moreover, have become most evident in Western mass democracies whose governments are controlled through complex processes of consensus formation and by constitutional and statutory provisions, seldom modified or adapted to keep pace with technological and attitudinal change. The nongovernmental institutions in Western societies, even under socialist governments, have been based upon the propositions and expectations of nineteenth century experience; and they reflect widespread desires for exploitation of resources, domination of the natural environment by man, and an ever-expanding economy. The guiding assumptions of nineteenth century industrial society have been narrowly economic, and neither government nor the dominant industrial-commercial institutions respond readily or effectively to nonmonetary values except in marginal or incidental ways.

A market economy is by definition a bargaining economy, and it is against its very nature to cope with nonnegotiable demands or with ultimatums for unilateral change without compensatory consideration. Industry has wanted at most to bargain over how much carbon monoxide may be emitted into the atmosphere or how much mercury may be dumped into public waterways, but the concerned environmental reformer is not inclined to bargain over the extent to which he should be poisoned. It is logically inconsistent to bargain over the extent to which wilderness areas may be used for mass recreation or commercial purposes. Environmental complaints more often seem appropriate to police action than to bargaining; and societies in which there is widespread popular aversion to policing may experience considerable political frustration in trying to cope with environmental issues.

The consequence of this incompatibility between circumstances and institutions, between the perceived tasks of governmental agencies and the perceived needs of increasingly dissatisfied individuals, has been an apparent unresponsiveness of government to environmental values. Both unhappy citizens and harried administrators have sought ways to avoid situations of mutual frustration. One method has been to define the environmental issue in relatively circumscribed ways, making it easier to deal with through conventional institutions and procedures. The effort is in fact to make the environmental problem less anomalous. The most common example of this approach has been to define the environmental issue as "pollution."

Although pollution is hardly a scientific term, its incidence may be defined in scientifically measurable ways, as for example through a count of percentage points of bacteria, nitrates, or mercury in drinking water, or of particulate material or gases in the atmosphere. On these issues of environmental pollution it has not been too difficult to adapt traditional modes of public action, including police power and the redefinition of the rights of citizens to sue for redress in the courts, and to bring the force of public dissatisfaction to bear upon many of the culprits. The establishment and financing of sewage and other waste treatment systems can be undertaken along lines already established for the construction of public works generally—including highways, canals, and airports—with federal aid, user taxes, and application where necessary of powers of eminent domain. Beyond statutory and judicial modifications, the environmental pollution issue lends itself to direct action by angered citizens, including demonstrations, boycotts, picketing, counteradvertising, and even attacks upon property such as billboards (visual pollution). Note, for example, the exploits of an ecological activist, "The Fox," in the western suburbs of Chicago, who resorted to extralegal methods of punishing polluters by stopping up illegally polluting smoke stacks and sewage outfalls, and dumping cans, bottles, and other refuse on the carpeted outer offices of the executives of polluting corporations.

But pollution is not the sum total of environmental issues; and when one moves beyond pollution into questions of land use policy, for example, the matter becomes less simple, scientific evidence less persuasive (although no less valid), public opinion more divided, and the public laws, statutes, and traditional assumptions less amenable to incremental reform.

The ability of governmental institutions to respond is limited by the purposes for which the institutions were created and the political milieu in which they exist. Pollution abatement is, in principle, a traditional function of government. Novel problems of pollution control can be more easily dealt with through conventional politics than can the need to reduce energy consumption, to prevent development of unoccupied land, or to redirect expenditures on public works. Responding to the more comprehensive theories of environmental policy and administration, usually linked to advocacy of a no-growth steady-state society, appears beyond the capacity of any existing governmental structure.

It is not surprising that popular concern over environmental issues has developed more rapidly than institutional means for effective response. Such a lag is a normal social phenomenon. But the problem is accentuated by uncertainty about just what types of institutional changes are required to cope with the diverse range of environmental problems. The logical institutional answer to most environmental difficulties points toward comprehensive public planning and control of man's activities affecting his environment. This solution has not been politically attractive to the American electorate, and even if it were, only if it were based on a strong, operational, ecological philosophy would it lead to desired results. The Soviet Union, for example, has the basic institutional means for comprehensive environmental control but, at least until now, has given the matter relatively low priority.

*The Dichotomy of Responsiveness-Responsibility.* At this point, it may be useful to summarize some of the more commonly acceptable propositions regarding the responsiveness of government to social pressures and the extent to which such response is consistent with various concepts of public responsibility. It should be clear that responsiveness and responsibility refer to quite different modes of behavior which may or may not be compatible. The actions of government may be viewed by their authors and by some sectors of the public as highly responsible, and yet be utterly unresponsive to certain strongly-voiced demands in society. Conversely, governments that attempt to respond to a wide range of rapidly changing public demands may, in fact, be held irresponsible, depending upon the criteria of responsibility.

It is difficult to imagine an issue of responsiveness and responsibility in which time is not a significant factor, and this is particularly true for environmental issues. The time-lag in institutional adaptability, particularly in large bureaucratic hierarchies governed by rules and regulations, almost ensures a time-lag in responsiveness to social needs and demands. On the other hand, responsiveness of government to contemporary popular opinions and desires may, in a broad time context, be irresponsible. Forrester's observation, that the human intellect finds it hard to foresee the future consequences of present actions, appears to be confirmed by the historical record. And, at least at the present day, it is not clear that any particular form of social or political organization enjoys an advantage over others in detecting error in its policies and in accurately estimating the ramifications of present actions. The claims of Marxists that their system is self-correcting do not seem to be empirically confirmed; and whatever opportunities pluralist free enterprise democracies may have for devising self-correcting institutions, no more than a random and partial beginning has been made on the project.

The Council of Economic Advisors [1946–.] and the Council on Environmental Quality [1970–.] in the government of the United States are, in some respects, institutions intended to identify and to propose corrections for certain types of economic and environmental error. But, in fact, the political and institutional restraints on these agencies severely limit their usefulness in detecting and correcting error. There is now a growing body of data on cybernation, feedback, and control available to governments and large technical structures (industrial corporations, for example) to apply toward goal attainment and the avoidance of error. But cybernetic methodology may be deceptive and lead to miscarriage as readily as to the intended goal if inappropriate signals are received and acted upon, or if appropriate signals are misinterpreted and misapplied. And in plain speech, there is the old computer warning—GIGO, garbage in, garbage out.

On environmental issues, the signals are frequently very numerous, of greatly varied intensity, and part of a total relevant field which is seldom adequately mapped. The information available to guide the public decision maker is often incomplete, sometimes contradictory, seldom in a form that meets his needs, and almost always changing. In consequence, he is inclined to fall back on traditional, empirical tests of truth and wisdom, and to be guided foremost by

what he believes to be the probable consequences which he personally will experience as a result of action taken.

To whom, then, does the public decision maker respond: why,
when, and how? In the conventional view, public officials, particularly elected ones, respond primarily to whoever they believe can
significantly affect their political futures. This includes organized
popular groups who are able, ready, and willing to vote for or against
them on a particular issue, and who have more than an even chance
of affecting the outcome of an election. The politician also listens to
representatives of groups whom he believes command active popular
support. It is also highly probable that public officials will be especially responsive to those to whom they may be personally indebted
and on whom they may be dependent, especially if these clients or
patrons are able and willing to enforce whatever obligations he may
owe them.

None of these interests or relationships are indefinitely stable,
however, and the political response appears to depend upon the
politician's assessment of how the weight of influence is shifting. The
politician may shift from inaction to action or to alternative plans
if he surmises that failure to change may be hazardous to his political
health. A case in point is surely the response of President Nixon to
the National Environmental Policy Act of 1969 (PL 91–190). Progress of this legislation through the Congress had been opposed by
the White House staff and the Bureau of the Budget. The president
had, in May 1969, set up his own cabinet-level environmental council; and his science advisor, Dr. Lee DuBridge, had declared a statutory environmental council to be unnecessary when the president
had already taken appropriate action at the highest levels. Neither
the president nor the Republican party, as indicated by party plat-
forms and identification of issues by the leadership, regarded the
environmental issue as a matter of important public concern. Within
the Nixon administration, the view seems to have been widely prevalent that environmental quality legislation would open the door to
new big public spending contrary to its established fiscal principles,
would lead to new forms of interference by government with business, would slow economic growth, and would garner few new votes
among the mass of the electorate. Passage of the National Environmental Policy Act, and perhaps a reading of public opinion polls,

appears to have changed the White House perspective; President Nixon embraced the legislation as his own and made its signing his first official act of 1970. He then proceeded to give the environmental issue a priority and high-level official support that could hardly have been predicted from the previous record of his administration.

But by embracing the environmental quality movement, the administration did not thereby cancel its commitment to economic growth and to particular techno-economic programs, like the development of supersonic transport. Moreover, given the traditional client-oriented structure of the federal administrative establishment, some members of the administration (frequently the Secretary of Commerce, for example) have leapt to defend commerce and industry when these interests came under attack by environmental action groups. The administration faced the problem of any democratically-constituted government in a pluralistic society: It somehow had to respond to diverse and not always compatible interests without appearing to be utterly inconsistent and unprincipled in its public posture or to disregard the public interest.

Conventional and readily available methods exist for satisfying almost everybody, at least part of the time. Official action may be shaded to accommodate various groups at various times. This leads to a strategy of alternately pleasing and displeasing each group, but keeping all of them from becoming irreparably alienated. This is often accomplished by holding out the possibility that administrative support will finally come down positively and unequivocally on the side desired by each intending group. To some extent, this appears to have been the earlier strategy of the Nixon administration in responding to conflicting attitudes toward environmental policy: Vice-President Agnew and Secretary of Commerce Stans decrying environmental extremists, but the Council on Environmental Quality, Secretary of Interior Morton, and Environmental Protection Agency Administrator Ruckelshaus acting in support of environmental quality measures, even to the extent of displeasing certain powerful economic interests believed to have been substantial contributors to the Republican party treasury.[6]

A second and more sophisticated strategy, less readily available and more difficult to implement, would be to develop an integrative policy that would broaden the administration's base of support and enable it to, in fact, satisfy a very wide spectrum of political differences and demands.

During President Nixon's second term, administration strategy shifted noticeably away from environmental quality concerns and toward economic priorities.[7] The energy crisis of 1973–74 provided opportunity for a broader attack upon environmental programs, for example in renewed demands for mass use of pesticides and for rescinding the administration's ban on the poisoning of predators on public lands. But in fairness to the federal executive, it should be noted that federal courts appeared ambivalent in upholding governmental action in the face of pleas for protection of property rights and maintenance of jobs that were alleged to be threatened by environmental protection measures.[8]

Closely related to the integrating formula is the search for a technological fix that would engineer the source of controversy out of existence and thus obviate the need for political action. For example, technological innovations to eliminate automobile exhaust emissions or sulfur dioxide from stack emissions would be ideal solutions to environmental problems, provided they did not create equally troublesome new ones. Unfortunately, technological fixes rarely fix everything. A basic physical proposition, amply illustrated by systems theory and the science of ecology, is that it is never possible to do just one thing. Thus a new pollution-free form of energy could have a disastrous effect upon important factors of an economy, if the technological innovation arrived more rapidly than the adjustments necessary to accommodate it.

It is thus easier to say when government is being responsive than when it is behaving responsibly. In everyday life, the responses of public officials, as Arthur Bentley observed, are always to individuals, to aggregations of individuals perhaps, but never really to abstract concepts or to problems. Concepts of responsibility do of course influence how and to whom government officials respond. Modern concepts of responsibility are strongly conditioned by the prevailing historicity of our culture, a belief that all events occur on a continuum of time. Generations of individuals extend from past into future time, and today is yesterday's future and tomorrow's past. Concepts, such as society and the state, organize the official's perception of how individuals are aggregated. Given the prevailing perceptions in Western society regarding time and the future, the public official would be held to have behaved irresponsibly on environmental and similarly time-related issues, unless he responded to what he (and often many others) believed would be the needs and demands of individuals in the future.

*Responsiveness as a Political Problem.* The essence of the dichotomy of responsiveness-responsibility, therefore, is that the politician's survival depends upon his action in the present, but that action must, if it is to serve him well, respond to considerations of the future. The dominant elements of his constituency may demand a specified quality of future environment and, in any age of rapid change, that future may be very near at hand—within his own expected political lifetime. A future-oriented politics therefore greatly needs reliable techniques for forecasting and prediction. It also needs a greatly increased interchange of information and ideas between public decision makers, knowledge producers (scientists, broadly defined), and as many of the body politic as must be reached to achieve public goals. This number is not uniform for all issues, but includes the entire politically active adult population on the broader issues of social policy.

The cardinal moral problem for a politician truly concerned with the human condition is therefore how to respond to the pressures of the day without behaving irresponsibly toward future society. The informed and conscientious public personality can hardly avoid emotional conflict in trying to cope with this problem. Men have therefore sought to reduce the psychic (and physical) hazards of personal responsibility by institutionalizing, first, the obligation to respond, and second, the responsibility for the acts of individuals in public office. Thus, we speak of the White House, the Department of the Interior, the TVA, or the Forest Service, as if these institutions were living realities; and, in our laws, we distinguish between acts performed in an official capacity and those of a personal nature.

Another method of simplifying the problem of administrative response to conflicting popular demand is mandatory law or custom. Administrative agencies at all levels of government may be required by law to give preference to certain clients or interests. There are convenient federal traditions in U. S. political behavior by certain officials of one political level of government toward certain officials of other levels, as when presidents decline to authorize federal action within a state which is obnoxious to the governor or to the congressional delegation. This convention is convenient when presidents have invoked it as an excuse for not doing things which they did not particularly want to do; but it can be ignored when, for whatever reason, the president wishes to act regardless of the expressed wishes of local officials. At least in the past, federal administrations have tended to defer to state and local authorities on environmental issues; but this deference has in the main not extended to the interpretation or enforcement of other federal action, notably in civil rights legislation.

When issues and conflicts cross governmental boundaries, responsiveness of state and local government is frequently brought into question. The courts and the federal executive have usually refused to consider the representativeness of state and local officials as a legitimate matter of debate. (Again, the civil rights issues may offer exceptions. The difference may be that the representation of particular identifiable groups of individuals has been involved in most civil rights disputes.) Popular democracies are almost inherently people-oriented rather than problem-oriented. In multiethnic or multiracial societies *people* tend to be one of the major social and political problems and hence a major issue in public affairs. Environmental problems almost invariably are people problems, but have not always been formulated in ways that make this clear.

Paradoxically, modern societies have simultaneously become more complex and more varied and more homogenized and interdependent. These apparently contradictory trends can become very frustrating when political decision makers must take action that cannot possibly be in the interest of all their constituents. As governmental intervention is required increasingly to mediate and adjust differences and incompatibilities in society, society itself inevitably becomes more political. Demands are now being made on government by many social groups that have never done so before or that were formerly weak but now have become politically significant. The environmental action groups belong in this respect to a larger number of activists seeking various kinds of redress from conventional institutional policies and procedures.

As we have previously noted, the institutions to which these protest groups appeal have seldom been structured, authorized, or conditioned to make the desired response. There are no institutions in the United States capable of satisfying a demand for comprehensive land-use management, for example. Demands are, therefore, often taken or find their way to inappropriate institutions which respond with unsatisfactory answers. The protestors' frustrations with environmentally damaging activities of public works agencies like the United States Corps of Engineers or the Soil Conservation Service are illustrative. Attempts to persuade these bodies to abandon or alter their missions are consistently resisted on the argument that the agencies are merely carrying out their congressional charter. The authorizing congressional committees (Public Works, Agriculture, etc.) are not set up to consider environmental quality and are not easily subjected to organized pressure by noneconomic environmental groups. But reform of congressional committee structure seems impractical in the short run when the object is to stop construction of an unwanted dam.

Complaints that government is unresponsive must therefore be examined in context if their meaning is to be understood. Once an issue is raised, failure by government to respond may be considered a kind of negative response. More frequently, however, the complaint of unresponsiveness really means that government is responding to what the complainant views as the wrong interests, values, or priorities.

In an abstract, theoretical way, the responses of government may be divided between those primarily directed toward problems and those primarily directed toward interests. But, of course, almost every problem involves differences among interests. A political problem does not arise until the political decision makers are confronted by a difficulty which does not automatically provide its own solution. Problems are invariably identified and propounded by people. They emerge when something must be done about them; until then, they are merely circumstances or events.

It follows that an unknown number of problems may be latent in society, unrecognized and undefined. Scientific inquiry may reveal a seemingly endless sequence of circumstances, tendencies, or potentialities that affect human values and interests. The significance of many of these findings is not readily apparent, but some afford grounds for concern. People, and especially the more literate and better educated, are continually barraged with warnings and alarms. The Food and Drug Administration has found carcinogenic herbicidal residues on cranberries, mercury in swordfish, and DDT in milk. The air in large cities is contaminated by lead, asbestos, carbon monoxide, and many other harmful compounds and residuals. An energy crisis is dragging on, population projections point toward a world of rising tensions and falling living standards, and radioactive disaster from several possible sources remains a constant threat.

The majority of these threats and alarms are environmental. Some may be at times misinterpreted or exaggerated, but most reflect valid scientific findings. Among these, some percentage will almost certainly become problems that government will have to deal with. But if traditional adversary methods are employed—that is, public policy is shaped by the pressures of contending groups—the results may prove to be unsatisfactory to all parties concerned and the problem remain unsolved.

The logic of the quandary posed for public officials by the accelerating flow of problem-creating information would indicate that processes of government should be restructured for problem-solving. But public agencies are not scientific laboratories, and few environmental problems can be so precisely and objectively defined as to be resolved solely upon the basis of objective evidence. Moreover, few problems can be contained or delimited in a given time period or space. Nothing remains certain except the prospect of change —often for the worse. The status of long-standing habits may be changed almost overnight by an opinion of the United States Supreme Court, or an announcement by the surgeon general, or by a committee report of the National Academy of Sciences. The large number of changes, their erratic and unpredictable advent, and their frequently unforeseeable ramifications upset large sectors of the population, resulting in a generalized state of irritability and discontent permeating society, although differing among individuals and groups over time and in intensity.

Political responsiveness today and in the future cannot be realistically defined unless these factors of knowledge and change are taken into account. Traditional political theory, including democratic theory, is too simplistic to afford meaningful answers to questions of how "responsiveness" in the kind of society in which we now live is to be understood and implemented in the public interest. Implementation implies new or improved machinery for determining what government should do and how action should be taken. Under emerging circumstances, fact finding becomes the appropriate first response of government to most problems, but with procedures that would make for a broad public understanding of the issues involved and of probable outcomes of alternative courses of action.

## Must "Responsibility" Be Redefined?

It should be evident from reading of this essay and others in this volume that the responsiveness of public institutions to a democratic electorate in a pluralistic society is anything but simple. To be responsive may or may not be consistent with responsibility; and responsibility out of context is a highly abstract concept. If the governors of society are responsible to the governed individuals in the aggregate and over a period of time, the issue of public responsibility is not so much to whom government is responsible but rather for what.

The notion of responsibility implies the existence of goals, values, and outcomes which a society or its official representatives have postulated as the purposes of government. In large, complex, and diverse societies like that represented by the United States of America, general consensus on the purposes of government has been obtained only by stating those ends at high levels of abstraction. Historically this has permitted the purposes of government, as articulated in the Constitution, to be interpreted and reinterpreted by political action to mean what the politically dominant forces at any given time wish them to mean. In the United States, this interpretation has been largely the work of the least responsible of political institutions, namely the judiciary. The courts were not designed to solve complex social problems. They are not effective instruments for comprehensive planning. In a strict sense, the opinions of the courts relate only to the cases and controversies coming before them, and it is often only by inference, drawn from a series of related court decisions, that a broad public policy emerges. The courts have no way of assuming responsibility for implementing the policies that they may declare. They may reiterate and reinforce their judicial policy making as new cases come before them; but until or unless further specific issues for adjudication are brought before them, they are juridically unconcerned with the situation their decision making creates.

The courts act most legitimately and most responsibly within a frame of reference established by informed legislative action. To the extent that such action exists, the courts have less occasion for policy making. This is especially true if legislative action is based upon a careful and comprehensive assessment of all of the factors involved in an issue; in other words, if the issue lends itself to scientific objectivity. Clearly, not all public issues do but many pertaining to the quality of the environment may. Moreover, as environmental sciences formerly conspicuously neglected begin to develop in breadth and sophistication, the knowledge-base for public action will be broadened. To the extent that environmental policies may be objectively stated, to the extent that cause and effect relationships are demonstrable and the rationality of a policy is clear, the role of the judiciary in environmental politics may be diminished or largely confined to determining whether procedural safeguards against arbitrary or dishonest administration have been observed. The *if* is a very large *if;* but if substantial advances in environmental science occur in the years ahead, we might logically expect a shift in adjudicative procedures away from less responsible courts of law into more responsible administrative agencies.

The current enthusiasm for judicial settlement of environmental disputes and for the defense of environmental rights through litigation reflects a profound and widespread distrust of the responsiveness and responsibility of administrative agencies. It is at least plausible that environmental litigation is taking up the slack caused by the inevitable slowness of the public bureaucracy to reorient itself to the new public awareness and concern with the environment. The enactment of statutes, the authorization of implementing appropriations, the actual appropriation of adequate funds, the budgeting of those funds, the establishment of new programs and agencies, the staffing of those agencies, and the adoption of effective policies and procedures—the process stretches from months into years and may well run into decades. But the application of high-powered technologies to the environment may require only hours or minutes. Chain saws may fell redwoods and bulldozers obliterate sand dunes in less time than it takes to hold a public hearing on a proposed new environmental quality act. Until the politically dominant forces of society are prepared to give the administrators power to take direct preventive action in support of clearly articulated and sanctioned public standards, resort to the courts of law will be the practical recourse when sudden irreversible damage to the environment is threatened.

The United States and more than half a dozen other Western countries are now officially committed to maintain and, if possible, to restore the qualities of their physical environments, both natural and manmade. In a number of countries, especially in the United States, this commitment has been written into a body of law that is as unequivocal as any that deals with large, complex, and dynamic issues. In nearly all of these countries, and notably in the United States, Canada, Sweden, France, and the United Kingdom, structural changes in administrative organization have been made in order to cope with the type of complex, interrelating issues that management of the environment presents. Whether these structural changes will be sufficient is yet to be seen. But there is reason to believe that they are merely the first steps toward major reorientations in the public service. Greater changes may be necessary if society through government is to cope with the problems created by its own, largely inadvertent, evolution.

"Environment" belongs to a set of future-oriented issues for which a new politics, or at least a new emphasis in politics, may be required. This politics would probably have little similarity to that of the eighteenth and nineteenth centuries with its conventional range from left to right; and the terms *radical, liberal,* and *conservative* will have little of the meaning they now carry in popular usage. The logical tendency of this politics would be toward problem solving and the use of science and science-based technology in the development and execution of public policies. This development implies no upswell of popular enthusiasm for science, and it does not require the embrace of a scientific mystique by political leaders. It will probably come about because no other way will be found to reconcile the popular desire for a responsive government with public action that is truly responsible.

At some point, this new kind of politics may be expressed through the sudden appearance of a new sociopolitical ideology. After a century of change unprecedented in human history, the world may be ready for some new political concepts, if there are any still undiscovered. No really new or compelling political ideology has emerged since Marxism—a mid-nineteenth century doctrine, many of whose propositions have already been empirically demonstrated to have been inadequate and which, in any case, was based upon expectations that present knowledge and historical experience have shown to be ill-founded. Perhaps the present debate over priorities in public policy is evidence of the inadequacy of prevailing political doctrine and indicates a search for a rationale for public policy more effectively related to emerging needs than any we now have.

This restructuring of political concepts, if and when it occurs, would be one of those so-called quantum leaps or hierarchical restructurings which characterized scientific and ideological revolutions in the past. But such events occur only when their time has come, and that time is necessarily heralded by the unobtrusive appearance of new approaches, procedures, attitudes, and assumptions within the interstices of the dominant sociopolitical system. A predictive political science should be able to spot incremental factors in today's society accumulating toward a point in time and under circumstances indicating that they could reach a critical mass. At that time, a fundamental restructuring of politics would occur, although the extent of change, actual or apparent, might depend on how far incremental changes had proceeded during the preceding years.

In summary, contemporary man's efforts to cope with environmental problems that he creates for himself will probably result in far greater changes in his political behavior and in his governmental institutions than most observers now suspect. It is easier to make the case that fundamental changes will occur and to estimate their general nature and direction than to forecast more specifically how far and how fast the new politics will move. Nor is it clear what it will mean with respect to a large number of existing laws, relationships, and practices in society. It does seem plausible that the needs and desires that bring this politics into existence will make it problem-oriented and that, to this extent, it will differ substantially from the politics of the right, left, and center that have dominated Western societies for more than a hundred years. There may well be political divisions under this new politics, for certainly many of the old values, issues, and contentions will remain. But how they may be reformulated under the conditions of the future cannot be foreseen. There has not yet been enough time to demonstrate the respective survival capabilities of mono-party, bi-party, or multi-party political systems; and, of course, political party structure is not the only factor that may account for the survival and demise of any particular political regime.

Within the configuration of present society in the United States and Western Europe it is hardly possible to predict with assurance who would be hurt and who would be helped by politics responsible to the ecological well-being of society. Everyone would be affected and certainly the relative positions of certain groups and occupations in the socioeconomic structure would change. Nevertheless, the probability is that, in the long run, the changes would be very fundamental, because an ecologically responsible society logically will function as a steady state. Social dynamics will be expressed in replacement and innovation rather than in the type of expansion that has powered virtually all Western societies for the past five hundred years. No one familiar with the biological, behavioral, or social science implications for a homeostatic society can doubt that it would be very different from anything that Americans have known historically. But in a finite world, a society whose dynamism operates in substantially a steady state appears to be the most desirable of possible outcomes. The prospects for this type of society, seen from the viewpoint of American traditions in mid-twentieth century, may seem unappealing to many people, but the alternatives would almost certainly appear to be less attractive.

# Notes

### Introduction

1. These abuses can, for convenience, be listed in four categories: (1) Conspiracy to obstruct justice in covering up the original Watergate break-in, for which White House Counsel John Dean among others pleaded guilty and for which other top presidential advisors such as H. R. Haldeman and John Ehrlichman were indicted by a federal grand jury. (2) Manipulating the agencies of the federal bureaucracy for partisan purposes. It has been alleged that improper use of, or approach to, the CIA, FBI, Securities and Exchange Commission, and Internal Revenue Service was encouraged by members of the administration. John Mitchell and Maurice Stans, former cabinet members and major figures in President Nixon's reelection campaign were indicted on such charges and a number of major corporations pled guilty to making illegal campaign contributions, gifts they felt necessary to keep up with their major competitors. (3) Tampering with civil rights and the legal system. The charges here include implementing an admittedly illegal domestic surveillance scheme (rescinded after five days), wiretapping, burglarizing the office of Daniel Ellsberg's psychiatrist, and an unethical approach to the judge presiding in the Pentagon Papers Case. (4) The president's personal financial manipulations which led both the IRS and the Joint Congressional Committee on Internal Revenue Taxation to rule that he owed in excess of $450,000 in back taxes plus interest.

2. See, inter alia, Louis Harris, *The Anguish of Change* (Norton, 1973), esp. ch. 3.

3. As reported in Subcommittee on Intergovernmental Relations, Senate Committee on Government Operations, *Confidence and Concern: Citizens View American Government. A Survey of Public Attitudes* (Government Printing Office, 1973).

### The American Presidency

1. Quoted in *Time,* October 23, 1972.

2. Gilbert Steiner, *The State of Welfare* (Washington, D. C.: the Brookings Institution, 1971), 79.

3. *The President's Commission on Income Maintenance Programs,* 1969.

4. Steiner, op. cit., 329.

5. Joe Fagin, "Poverty: We Still Believe That God Helps Those Who Help Themselves," *Psychology Today,* 6: 6 (November 1972), 101–11.

6. For an extended discussion of the relationship between differing ideological perspectives and the nature of public programs, see David Gordon, ed., *Problems in Political Economy* (Lexington, Mass.: D. C. Heath, 1971).

7. John Kenneth Galbraith, *The Affluent Society,* 2nd ed. (Boston: Houghton Mifflin, 1969), 94.

8. Joel Schwartz and David Tabb, "Social Welfare," *American Behavioral Scientist,* 15: 5, May–June 1972, 645–63.

9. September 16, 1972.

10. Herbert L. Packer, "Law and Order in the Seventies," *The New Republic,* January 10, 1970, 12.

11. *Time,* December 5, 1969.

12. The following litany is based on editorials in *The New Republic* for July 18, 1970.

13. New York: Universe Books, 1971.

14. We have paraphrased the words of John Osborne, "More Than Ever," *The New Republic,* November 18, 1972, 18.

15. The most ambitious (but also controversial) effort to analyze the impact of an incumbent's personality (style, world view, and character) on his performance in the White House is that of James D. Barber, *The Presidential Character* (Englewood Cliffs, N. J.: Prentice Hall, 1972).

### Congress: After Watergate, What?

I acknowledge with gratitude the perceptive and useful commentary of my colleague Jeff Fishel on an earlier draft of this paper.

1. On the oil depletion allowance, see "Industry Has Strong Friends on Finance Committee," *Congressional Quarterly Weekly Report,* September 26, 1969, 1787–95. The energy "crisis" (or "problem") has renewed interest in reducing the allowance.

2. This statement, of course, is an overgeneralization. Many legislators have been energetic and effective workers for social change and reform. As an institution, however, Congress has not distinguished itself by its novel solutions to major policy problems. Except for the early New Deal and the

legislative innovations of 1964–65, the past four decades have seen more caution than action.

3. We must recognize that much reform is "politically" inspired, that is, it seeks to bring about desired policy outcomes by altering the hindering institutions. Thus, in the 1930s frustrated liberals criticized the Supreme Court and urged "packing" it to circumvent the conservative decisions of the "nine old men"; by the 1960s the same liberals were among the stoutest defenders of the Warren Court. Similarly, the same persons who defended an "internationalist" president, Dwight Eisenhower, against crippling attacks like the Bricker amendment became a scant two decades later the chief proponents of a congressional revival designed to impose limits on "militaristic" Presidents Lyndon Johnson and Richard Nixon.

The present essay attempts to avoid such politically-inspired reform; rather I want to focus on changes that could be initiated to bring about one or another vision of what Congress should become in the years ahead.

4. As this essay is written, the unfolding tale of executive malfeasance, known popularly as Watergate but in reality extending far beyond one singular burglary, seems about to inspire Congress to reassert a countervailing power to the chief executive, especially in foreign policy where the president has long ruled supreme.

5. Richard Nixon's argument was that his 1972 reelection margin, over 60 percent of the two-party vote, constituted a "mandate" both approving his conduct during his first term and giving him carte blanche during his second. He believed that he had been both efficient (solved problems) and representative of the majority of Americans (responsive) and, in consequence, was reelected to continue such service.

6. Needless to say, this last possibility is the most likely outcome of any reform impetus. Congress is not likely to give up willingly anything it considers its legitimate prerogative, and the issue, realistically, is how to combine legislative functions most effectively, how to organize Congress most efficiently, so that the observer-critic's vision can be most closely approximated.

7. Much of what follows is drawn, without presentation of full supporting data, from my *Congressional Politics* (McGraw-Hill, 1973). The positions enunciated are hardly radical; for verification of them the reader may wish to consult the leading texts in the field: Malcolm E. Jewell and Samuel C. Patterson, *The Legislative Process in the United States,* 2nd ed., (Random House, 1973) and William J. Keefe and Morris S. Ogul, *The American Legislative Process,* 3rd ed. (Prentice-Hall, 1973).

8. Some of these seemingly inconsequential changes, the breach of the seniority *principle* (not yet the practice) for example, contain the poten-

tial for great change. It is still too early to tell whether these seeds of change, already planted, will slowly take root, or whether the disclosures of the Watergate scandals will lead to a sudden growth in reform sentiment.

9. On this point, see Nelson W. Polsby, "The Institutionalization of the House of Representatives," *American Political Science Review* 15 (1968), 144–68.

10. For instance, see John W. Kingdon, *Candidates for Office* (Random House, 1968), David A. Leuthold, *Electioneering in a Democracy: Campaigns for Congress* (Wiley, 1968), and Jeff Fishel, *Party and Opposition* (McKay, 1973), ch. 5.

11. This too is an overgeneralization. There is a growing body of literature (see esp. Richard F. Fenno, Jr., *Congressmen in Committees,* Little, Brown, 1973) describing the variation in organizational and decision-making patterns among committees. In addition, events or changes in personnel may alter committee patterns. All that is suggested here is that autonomous committees with relatively powerful chairmen are the more common situation.

12. For a description and discussion of the strategic importance of the rules, see Lewis A. Froman, Jr., *The Congressional Process: Strategies, Rules, and Procedures* (Little, Brown, 1967).

13. The Great Depression and the Hoover administration's lack of success in coping with it, led voters to turn to Franklin Roosevelt and the Democrats in large numbers in the elections of 1932, 1934, and 1936. The singular combination of the assassination of John F. Kennedy and the 1964 Republican debacle with Barry Goldwater gave Democrats a genuine working majority in Congress for a brief period during the mid-1960s.

14. When the president sought to eliminiate OEO informally by appointing as its director a man committed to dismantling the agency, the Senate took the executive to court and won a decision from a lower Federal Court holding that the OEO Director was in office illegally and barring him from further direction of the agency's affairs.

15. In these private sessions, the committee goes over a bill line-by-line, often amending it substantially in order to produce the final version on which the full committee or the entire chamber will be asked to act.

16. Chairman Wilbur D. Mills (D., Ark.) of the House Ways and Means committee personally held off adoption of the principle of national health insurance for the elderly. When, and only when, Mills became convinced of the need for such a program and steered an acceptable bill through his committee did Medicare become law. See Theodore R. Marmor, *The Politics of Medicare* (Aldine, 1973).

17. Lewis A. Dexter, "Congressmen and the Making of Military

Policy," in Robert L. Peabody and Nelson W. Polsby (eds.), *New Perspectives in the House of Representatives* (Rand McNally, 1963), 305–24. On the general weakness of Congress in military affairs, see also Samuel P. Huntington, *The Common Defense* (Columbia University Press, 1961).

18. Raymond H. Dawson, "Congressional Innovation and Intervention in Defense Policy: Legislative Authorization of Weapons Systems," *American Political Science Review* 56 (1962), 42–57.

19. Richard E. Neustadt, *Presidential Power* (Wiley, 1960), esp. chs. 3–5.

20. The president, of course, does not personally make all these contacts and engage in all such negotiations. He has a large liaison staff, in his own White House office and in the executive departments, at his disposal; the liaison organizations assist the president in persuading congressmen to go along with his policy proposals; they serve as a chief communications device by which presidential-legislative accommodations are worked out. On liaison, see Abraham Holtzman, *Legislative Liaison: Executive Leadership in Congress* (Rand McNally, 1970).

The lobbying efforts of the executive branch may not always be in support of the president's programs, though most often they seem to be at least nominally. The agencies may ask Congress to depart from official executive requests because they do not feel satisfied with the authority or funds requested for them. Some bureaus, the Army Corps of Engineers for instance, may develop such close ties to Congress that they become virtually immune from executive control.

21. For evidence suggesting that lobbyists have less clout than generally believed, that they are often understaffed and inadequately financed, and that they seek to avoid "pressure tactics" and the "hard sell," see Lester Milbrath, *The Washington Lobbyists* (Rand McNally, 1962), Raymond A. Bauer et al., *American Business and Public Policy,* rev. ed. (Atherton, 1972), and Lewis A. Dexter, *How Organizations Are Represented in Washington* (Bobbs-Merrill, 1969).

22. This stress on the supportive rather than the aggressive tactics of interest associations does not mean that other, more traditional techniques of influence are not used. Groups do hire intermediaries, influential constituents of the legislators, to express group sentiments; some do get involved in elections to reward their friends and punish their enemies; others do engage in public relations campaigns intended to bring the weight of public opinion to bear on target congressmen. Occasionally, as recent convictions amply demonstrate, groups do resort to bribery. Yet, and this is the central point, it seems clear that these tactics are relatively costly and inefficient. Direct communication is more effective and is preferred.

23. It is clear that people with better educations and incomes and with more leisure time communicate more often and are an atypical sample of constituents.

24. This point should not be overemphasized. As noted, electoral uncertainties do compel congressmen to worry about possible constituent reactions and this introduces some link between governor and governed. Here, I note that this linkage is probably stronger than empirically necessary. Legislators need not worry about most single acts; rather they need chiefly to cultivate the impression among their constituents that they are alive, well, and most important, working hard for the state or district.

25. See Angus Campbell, Philip E. Converse, Warren E. Miller, and Donald E. Stokes, *The American Voter* (Wiley, 1960) and the same authors' *Elections and the Political Order* (Wiley, 1966). One study found that in any off-year congressional election only 7 percent of those polled gave issue-related reasons to explain their votes. See Donald E. Stokes and Warren E. Miller, "Party Government and the Salience of Congress," *Public Opinion Quarterly* 26 (1962), 530–46.

26. See, inter alia, David E. RePass, "Issue Salience and Party Choice," *American Political Science Review* 65 (1971), 389–400; Gerald M. Pomper, "From Confusion to Clarity: Issues and American Voters, 1956–1968," ibid., 66 (1972), 415–28; and Richard W. Boyd, "Popular Control of Public Policy: A Normal Vote Analysis of the 1968 Election," ibid., 66 (1972), 429–49.

27. A recent study finds that, in the 1966 off-year House elections to select the 90th Congress (1967–68), losing candidates bore a striking ideological similarity to the winners. That is, had the defeated nominees actually won, the resulting House would have been slightly more liberal in foreign policy but slightly more conservative in the domestic sphere. To be sure, if the national electorate had been moved sharply in one direction, along party or liberal-conservative lines, the resulting heavily Democratic or liberal (or Republican or conservative) Congress would have been far different from the 90th Congress actually elected. But such unidimensional swings in partisan or ideological preferences, affecting virtually all electoral districts, are unknown in American politics. See John L. Sullivan and Robert E. O'Connor, "Electoral Choice and Popular Control of Public Policy: The Case of the 1966 House Elections," *American Political Science Review* 66 (1972), 1256–68. On the incumbent-challenger relationships, see also Fishel, op. cit.

28. In 1972, only thirteen incumbents were defeated. There were sixty-nine freshmen in the House seated in January 1973, but many were of the same party and point of view as the retiring member whom they replaced.

29. For data on this point, see Charles O. Jones, "Inter-party Competition for Congressional Seats," *Western Political Quarterly* 17 (1964), 461–76.

30. The exception, of course, was the 1964 election when the Republican presidential debacle swept in an abnormal number of liberal Democrats, about half of whom were defeated in 1966.

31. The discussion of reformist perspectives must necessarily be over-simplified. The effort here is to identify major points of view, but it must be recognized that multiple variations exist on each theme which space limitations prevent being differentiated here.

32. For arguments supporting a strong or dominant presidency, see Robert A. Dahl, *Congress and Foreign Policy* (Harcourt, Brace & World, 1950), Walter Lipmann, *The Public Philosophy* (Little, Brown, 1954), and Clinton Rossiter, *The American Presidency,* rev. ed. (Harvest Books, 1960). On the responsible party idea, see James McGregor Burns, *Congress on Trial* (Harper, 1949) and *The Deadlock of Democracy* (Prentice-Hall, 1963); The Committee on Political Parties of the American Political Science Association, *Toward a More Responsible Two-Party System* (Rinehart, 1950), and David Broder, *The Party's Over* (Harper and Row, 1972). On the latter notion, cf. also Evron M. Kirkpatrick, "Toward a More Responsible Two-Party System: Political Science, Policy Science, or Pseudo-Science?" *American Political Science Review* 65 (1971), 965–90, and Gerald M. Pomper, "Toward a More Responsible Two-Party System? What, Again?" *Journal of Politics* 33 (1971).

33. David Butler, "American Myths About British Parties," *Virginia Quarterly Review* 31 (1955), 45–56 and Robert T. McKenzie, *British Political Parties* (Praeger, 1964), suggest that, in fact, British parties scarcely resemble the image of them that the responsible party school holds.

34. The Republican procedure called for a caucus vote on the committee-on-committees' recommendation, a suggestion that need not follow the seniority principle. The Democrats adopted a plan, sometimes called a "Kamikaze system," whereby ten committee members could force a vote in caucus on their chairman. The need to stand up against a powerful chairman served to deter challengers, but there was one vote in the Democratic caucus. Liberals on the District of Columbia Committee sought to oust Chairman John L. McMillan (S. C.), objecting to his long opposition to home rule for Washington, D. C., but lost on a 126–96 caucus vote. Whether this substantial challenge contributed to McMillan's defeat in his district's 1972 primary is a moot point. In 1973 the Democrats went one step further; they determined that the full caucus should vote on each chairmanship, and if one-fifth of the members so desired, by secret ballot.

In practice, however, all decisions followed seniority, with negative votes against the senior man ranging from two to forty-nine and in no instance reaching one-third of those cast. There were two challenges within the Republican conference in 1973, but the seniors retained their chairs by three-to-one margins.

35. For instance, new rules might eliminate or curtail the "morning hour," when Senators make short speeches and handle miscellaneous chores not immediately related to lawmaking; the practice of insisting that the *Journal* be read in full; and the dilatory use of repeated quorum calls. The present rules, especially in the Senate, provide many opportunities for diversion and delay, and their elimination would enhance the majority's ability to move its desired legislation ahead.

36. Filibusters can begin at many points: on the motion to take up (begin consideration of) a bill, on amendments, on passage, and on acceptance of conference report. It has been proposed to make the motion to consider nondebatable, thus removing one opportunity to talk a bill to death.

37. The Voting Rights Act of 1970 is typical of the successful operation of the strategy. Congress appended to the bill a provision granting eighteen-year-olds the right to vote despite President Nixon's declaration that such a change required a constitutional amendment. He signed the measure with considerable reluctance and sought an early court test of the constitutionality of changing the voting age by statute. As noted above, the legal end to American military involvement in Southeast Asia came about in 1973 as a result of a partially successful application of the strategy.

38. There is, most certainly, some doubt about whether the electorate as presently constituted can muster the central concern with the substance of political issues necessary to hold Congress accountable. We will return to this problem below.

39. James Burnham, *Congress and the American Tradition* (Regnery, 1959) presents the classic exposition of this view. See also Alfred de Grazia, *Republic in Crisis: Congress against the Executive Branch* (Federal Legal Publications, 1965).

40. Even the few contemporary critics who do urge genuine congressional domination are at a loss about how to proceed. The president, building on his constitutional power as commander in chief as well as on considerable precedent, has become too strong, too essential, to challenge seriously; the federal government has become too large, too involved in too many areas, to strip of all its authority and responsibility. Burnham, op. cit., proposes, in effect, to dismantle the federal apparatus, turning most of its present duties over to the states and localities. Most observers, how-

ever, find this idea unrealistic. The Nixon administration's various revenue sharing proposals, a short step toward a reallocation of authority if not of funding sources within the federal system, found only modest support even among direct recipients of the money.

41. Such diffusion of authority is highly compatible with the congressmen's career aspirations. In a stable institution like Congress, many lawmakers covet long-term service; they seek reelection regularly. Thus, structural and procedural changes which serve to open access to power, even over small segments of legislative business, allow legislators to make a mark, to find a niche earlier in their congressional service.

42. The fears regarding reapportionment seem largely to have been misplaced. Now that the dust of the *Baker v. Carr* and *Wesberry v. Sanders* decisions has settled, it appears that the dozen or so seats lost by rural areas in the House of Representatives wound up controlled by suburban conservatives rather than by urban liberals. The impact of court-enforced reapportionment to date has been minimal. Should the courts proceed to encourage or demand creation of districts to assure minorities—blacks in central cities, for instance—representation in Congress, the fears of the pro-Congress forces might be realized. It is highly unlikely that the present "Nixon-Burger" Supreme Court will move in this direction.

43. The prospect that party leadership might dominate the committee assignments might be more real when the same party controls the White House and Congress; the leaders might be tempted to work to place presidential loyalists in important assignments under such circumstances. Controlling committee action through manipulating the leadership of committees would, of course, tend to centralize power in the House.

44. A House Select Committee on Committees (the Bolling Committee) has reported a resolution (H. Res. 988) that would automatically assign one-third of a committee's staff to the minority. The Select Committee's *Hearings* and *Panel Discussions,* 3 vols. (Government Printing Office, 1973) constitute a mine of information about and proposals for committee reform.

45. The newly enlarged Steering Committee in 1973 did manipulate the membership of the Finance Committee, adding liberals in what appeared to be an effort to weaken the position of the committee's chairman, Russell Long (D., La.).

46. These reformers also have reservations about broad delegations of authority for executive control of foreign trade policy, holding that Congress should determine tariff levels on its own initiative.

47. It is encouraging to observers favoring a strengthened legislature that Congress has undertaken serious and comprehensive budget reform rather than resorting to minor adjustments in current practice.

48. Such calculations about the relationship between revenues and expenditures are extraordinarily difficult and complex. For one thing, agencies, especially in the Defense Department, with the approval of the appropriate committee, subcommittee, or ranking member thereof, can "re-program" funds, that is, spend them in ways other than those for which they were originally appropriated. For another, money is often "in the pipeline," that is, appropriated but unspent, at any given point and a cut in subsequent appropriations will not affect programs until unspent funds are exhausted. Finally, agencies may spend via the "backdoor"—through borrowing, permanent appropriations, or mandatory spending—which is beyond the legislature's annual appropriations power. For a useful summary of the problems of present budgetary practice, see *Congressional Quarterly Weekly Report,* April 28, 1973, 1013–18.

49. The new Budget Act moved to curb "backdoor" spending, requiring that funds for new expenditures be authorized annually. The impact of this, of course, is to enhance congressional control.

50. Note that these anti-impoundment provisions tip the balance of power in the legislature's direction: either house can require spending of appropriated funds but both must agree to rescinding enacted appropriations.

51. For a cogent discussion of Congress' information problems and some proposed remedies, see John S. Saloma III, *Congress and the New Politics* (Little, Brown, 1969).

52. Attorney General Richard Kleindienst, presumably on behalf of the Nixon administration, may have encouraged congressional action. Appearing before a Senate committee, Kleindienst asserted an extraordinarily broad view of the privilege, claiming that the president could prohibit any or all of the more than two-and-one-half million employees of the executive branch from appearing before Congress or even supplying documentary information. There is no evidence that any administration will insist on Kleindienst's view, but many members of the legislature are concerned over this potentially very large increase in the executive's authority to withhold data.

53. There is no real quarrel about the desirability of some form of executive privilege; most observers agree that national security matters, unsubstantiated accusations, and communications between the president and his advisers comparable to lawyer-client or doctor-patient communications may need to be kept from public scrutiny. One item at issue is whether communications, even those to which the president was a party, relating to nonconstitutionally mandated duties, e.g., election campaigns, are protected. While it surely hastened Richard Nixon's departure from office, the

8–0 Supreme Court decision in *United States* v. *Nixon* (1974) failed to resolve the issue. The Court held that executive privilege exists but must give way in criminal proceedings. The exact scope of the privilege remains undefined.

54. On some of these notions, see James A. Robinson, "Decision Making in Congress," and Charles R. Dechert, "Availability of Information in Congressional Operations," in de Grazia (coord.), op. cit., 259–94 and 167–211.

55. On data systems for Congress, see Kenneth Janda, "Information Systems for Congress," in de Grazia (coord.), op. cit., 415–56 and *Information Retrieval: Applications in Political Science* (Bobbs-Merrill, 1968). Cf. also, Saloma, op. cit. Perhaps the seemingly successful House use of an electronic voting system, which has saved considerable amounts of time, may encourage the legislators to try other forms of computer assistance.

56. The House Select Committee on Committees Reform Amendments of 1974, if passed, might well serve to make the lower chamber both more efficient and more responsive. See the committee's *Report* (Washington, 1974).

57. It is probable that the Impeachment and Watergate hearings received extensive coverage, including live telecasting of their sessions, because they impinged directly on the president and his inner circle in the White House.

58. Under House rules, a device known as the Committee of the Whole House on the State of the Union is used. The Speaker need not preside; a quorum is 100, not the 218 required when the House sits formally; and the preliminary consideration of legislation is facilitated. Voting in this committee is by voice vote, standing vote where the presiding officer counts the "yeas" and then the "nays" as each group in turn rises, or teller vote where each group comes forward in the chamber to be counted as they pass between tellers. When the Committee of the Whole concludes preliminary consideration, it "rises," the Speaker resumes the chair, and a quorum reverts to 218. The House then acts to review—ratify or reject—decisions taken in the Committee of the Whole.

59. Jeff Fishel has suggested that the view presented here is too pessimistic. He argues, with some justice, that in some constituencies some groups (e.g., the National Committee for an Effective Congress) can "intervene selectively" to promote particular candidates. Without denying the point, it remains true that such activities, even if successful, have only marginal impact on the overall accountability of Congress.

60. Needless to say, the mere nomination of his opponent, a man seemingly cavilier in his willingness to push the nuclear button and openly

opposed to many fixtures of the welfare state—Social Security, Medicare, and the Tennessee Valley Authority, for instance—should have brought terror to the hearts of the liberal executive supremicists. The electorate's decisive rejection of this nominee, in keeping with the executive domination view of accountability, only postponed the final undermining of the executive supremacy position.

61. Ironically, the plan was rescinded only when FBI Director J. Edgar Hoover, long the *bete noire* of the liberal establishment, refused to acquiesce in it. Indeed, Hoover's opposition to the plan seems to have stemmed more from bureaucratic infighting than from civil libertarian concerns.

62. As a practical matter, the kinds of changes necessary to implement a presidential supremacy arrangement, especially with responsible parties, would require amending the Constitution and many statutory revisions. Congress is hardly to be expected to enact the dissolution of its own claims to influence policy making.

63. Again (see note 53 above), not all legislative activity can or should go on in public. What is important is that the public be in a position to find out what has been done and who supported what actions. The use of secrecy to enable a lawmaker to take both sides of the same question, to pursue the strategy of legislative obfuscation, should be eliminated in the name of increasing the potential for meaningful accountability. Equally important is that rubrics like "executive privilege" or "national security" not be used to prevent Congress or the public from discovering information they are entitled to know.

64. One of the chief reasons that discharge petitions, requiring 218 signatures, a majority of the full House, are seldom used is the reluctance of rank-and-file members to risk the wrath of powerful chairmen by signing them. If easier discharge requirements are coupled with a relaxation of the chairman's control over his committee, as has also been proposed above, the prospect of getting a vote on legislation will be increased.

65. These majorities would, of course, be similar to those found at present—shifting from issue to issue and created in consequence of negotiation.

66. The costs would be in responsiveness. The authorizing and appropriating bodies might be unable to account for all interests under the budgetary ceiling imposed by the joint resolution embodying the total congressional budget. Yet multiple interests would have ample opportunity to be heard during the formulation of the overall budget and to compete within the various committees for a larger share of the funds allocated to any particular budgetary subcategory.

67. See Roger Davidson, et al., *Congress in Crisis: Politics and Congressional Reform* (Wadsworth, 1966), 59–63.

68. For many other examples and a discussion of conflict of interest in the contemporary Congress, see Robert Sherrill, "Why We Can't Depend on Congress to Keep Congress Honest," *New York Times Magazine,* July 19, 1970.

69. Members of the House publicly reveal from what businesses they receive more than $1,000 annual income or in which their holdings are valued at $5,000 or more, *if* the source of income was engaged in *"substantial"* business with the federal government or was under federal regulation: they also report their connections with organizations from which they received an income of $1,000 or more. The public disclosures of senators are limited to lecture fees and honoraria; all fees are to be reported. Congressmen also file additional data, but these remain sealed and are opened only in extraordinary circumstances.

70. The voters do seemingly respond to charges of unethical conduct on occasion. In 1966 charges that Senator A. Willis Robertson (D., Va.), Chairman of the Senate Banking and Currency Committee, was too close to banking interests may have contributed to his defeat. Robertson sponsored legislation to provide an exemption from the antitrust laws for two banks which desired to merge; the bank responded by sending out letters urging stockholders to give their "thanks" to Robertson, presumably in the form of campaign contributions. Two years later, Sen. Edward Long (D., Mo.), was retired from office following *Life* magazine's report that he had received substantial sums from the Teamsters Union for "referral fees."

71. For instance, the New York City Bar Association has proposed (*Congress and the Public Trust,* Atheneum, 1970) a blanket prohibition, effective six years after election, of the practice of law by sitting legislators and on the practice of members' law firms representing clients that the members cannot serve. Others seek a post employment ban, like that imposed on former executive employees, on exlegislators' dealings with the federal government. For a summary of many of these issues of ethics, see Robert S. Getz, *Congressional Ethics* (Van Nostrand, 1966).

72. David Mayhew (*Party Loyalty Among Congressmen,* Harvard University Press, 1966) suggests that Democrats in the House of Representatives derive considerable party cohesion from such a frame of mind. Each faction of the party seems ideologically flexible and quite prepared to provide support for their colleagues on matters of concern to the latter in return for backing on items of importance to itself. Such a habit, not found among House Republicans, would be difficult to break.

73. As noted, the comprehensive approach to budget reform is en-

couraging. Far more important, however, is the degree to which congressional determination survives in the Ford and subsequent administrations. Only if Congress concludes that the importance of improving its position transcends the Nixon scandals will the vision of a reinvigorated legislature be realized.

## The Supreme Court Nine

1. John Locke, *Second Treatise on Civil Government* (Chicago: Henry Regnery Co., 1955), 69, para. 87.

2. *Roe* v. *Wade,* 410 U. S. 113 (1973); *Doe* v. *Bolton,* 410 U. S. 179 (1973).

3. George Gallup, *Gallup Opinion Index* (Princeton, New Jersey: Gallup International, Report No. 26) August 1967, 15–21 at 15. Cf. surveys for July 1968, 25 and July 1973, 14.

4. Gallup, Report No. 26, op. cit., 21.

5. Joel Feinberg, *Doing and Deserving, Essays in the Theory of Responsibility* (Princeton: Princeton University Press, 1970); Carl Friedrich, *Responsibility,* Nomos 3 (New York: Atherton Press, 1960); Morris Ginsberg, *On Justice in Society* (Ithaca: Cornell University Press, 1965); H. L. A. Hart, "The Ascription of Responsibility and Rights," *Proceedings of the Aristotelian Society,* 49:171–94 (1948/49); J. Roland Pennock, "Responsiveness, Responsibility and Majority Rule," *American Political Science Review* 56:790–807 (Sept. 1952); Moira Roberts, *Responsibility and Practical Freedom* (London: Cambridge University Press, 1965).

6. Herbert Wechsler, "Toward Neutral Principles of Constitutional Law," 73 *Harvard Law Review* 1 (1959).

7. *Brown* v. *Board of Education* 347 U. S. 483 (1954); *Smith* v. *Allwright,* 321 U. S. 649 (1944); *Shelley* v. *Kraemer,* 334 U. S. 1 (1948); see Louis Pollack, "Racial Discrimination and Judicial Integrity: A Reply to Professor Wechsler," 108 *University of Pennsylvania Law Review* 1 (1959). A more recent contribution to this debate was made by Jan Deutsch, "Neutrality, Legitimacy and the Supreme Court; Some Intersections between Law and Political Science," 20 *Stanford Law Review* 169–201 (January 1969).

8. Eugene V. Rustow, *The Sovereign Prerogative* (New Haven: Yale University Press, 1962), 22–44.

9. Phillip Kurland, *Politics, The Constitution, and the Warren Court* (Chicago: University of Chicago Press, 1970).

10. *Brown* v. *Board of Education* 347 U. S. 483 (1954); 349 U. S. 294 (1955).

11. *Abbington School District* v. *Schempp,* 374 U. S. 203 (1963).

12. *South Carolina* v. *Katzenbach,* 383 U. S. 301 (1966).

13. *Escobedo* v. *Illinois,* 378 U. S. 478 (1964); *Miranda* v. *Arizona,* 384 U. S. 436 (1966).

14. *Mapp* v. *Ohio,* 367 U. S. 643 (1961).

15. Phillip Kurland, "Toward a Political Supreme Court," 37 *University of Chicago Law Review* 19, (Fall 1969). Cf. Edward N. Beiser, "Lawyers Judge the Warren Court," 7 *Law and Society Review* 139–49 (Fall 1972).

16. Alexander Bickel, *The Supreme Court and the Idea of Progress* (New York: Harper and Row, 1970).

17. Ibid., 94.

18. Herbert Wechsler, *Principles, Politics and Fundamental Law* (Cambridge, Mass.: Harvard University Press, 1961) xiii–xiv.

19. Oliver Wendell Holmes, "The Path of the Law," 10 *Harvard Law Review* 457 (1897).

20. Quoted by J. D. Hyman, "Concerning the Responsibility and Craftsmanship of the Judge," 14 *Buffalo Law Review* 347 (Spring 1965).

21. *Mapp* v. *Ohio,* 367 U. S. 643 (1961) [Fourth Amendment search and seizure], overruling *Wolf* v. *Colorado* 338 U. S. 25 (1949); *Malloy* v. *Hogan,* 378 U. S. 1 (1964) [Fifth Amendment right to silence], overruling *Twining* v. *New Jersey,* 211 U. S. 78 (1908); *Benton* v. *Maryland,* 395 U. S. 784 [Fifth Amendment bar against double jeopardy], overruling *Palko* v. *Connecticut,* 302 U. S. 319 (1937); *Gideon* v. *Wainwright,* 372 U. S. 335 (1963) [Sixth Amendment right to counsel], overruling *Betts* v. *Brady,* 316 U. S. 455 (1942); *Pointer* v. *Texas,* 380 U. S. 400 (1965), [Sixth Amendment right to confront adverse witnesses]; cf. *West* v. *Louisiana,* 194 U. S. 258 (1904); *Klopfer* v. *North Carolina,* 386 U. S. 213 (1967) [Sixth Amendment speedy trial requirement]; *Washington* v. *Texas,* 388 U. S. 14 (1967) [Sixth Amendment right to compulsory process for defense witnesses], affirming on constitutional grounds the overruling of *United States* v. *Reid,* 12 How. 461 (1865); *Duncan* v. *Louisiana,* 391 U. S. 145 (1965) [Sixth Amendment jury trial right], overruling *sub silentio Maxwell* v. *Dow,* 176 U. S. 581 (1900); *Robinson* v. *California,* 370 U. S. 660 (1962), [Eighth Amendment bar against cruel and unusual punishment].

22. *Benton* v. *Maryland,* 395 U. S. 784 (1969).

23. "Proceedings in Memory of Justice Brandeis," 317 U. S. ix, xiv (1942).

24. *United States* v. *Carolene Products,* 304 U. S. 144, n4 (1938).

25. Gerald Garvey, *Constitutional Bricolage* (Princeton, New Jersey: Princeton University Press, 1971), 140.

26. *Kovacs* v. *Cooper,* 336 U. S. 77 at 90 (1949).

27. Martin Shapiro, *Freedom of Speech* (Englewood Cliffs, N.J.: Pren-

tice Hall, 1966), chap. 1, and his "The Supreme Court, Politics, and Neutral Principles," 31 *George Washington Law Review* 587 (Mar. 1973); Fred Rodell, "Review of Kurland's *Politics, The Constitution, and the Warren Court,"* 49 *Texas Law Review* 949–52 (1971).

28. Adolph A. Berle, *The Three Faces of Power, The Supreme Court's New Revolution* (New York: Harcourt, Brace and World, 1967).

29. *Marbury* v. *Madison,* 1 Cranch 137 (1803).

30. See M. Kent Jennings and Harmon Zeigler, "Response Styles and Politics," 15 *Midwest Journal of Political Science* 290 at 294 (May 1971); Amitai Etzioni, "Responsiveness and Flexibility Defined," *The Active Society* (New York: The Free Press, 1968), 504–506; and Neil N. Snortland and John E. Stanga, "Neutral Principles and Decision-Making Theory: An Alternative to Incrementalism," 41 *George Washington Law Review* 1006–1032 (Jul. 1973).

31. James Coleman, "Conflicting Theories of Social Change," 14 *American Behavioral Scientist* 633–50 (May–June 1971).

32. 42 U.S.C. 1983.

33. John Sprague, *Voting Patterns of the United States Supreme Court* (Indianapolis: Bobbs-Merrill, 1968), 70–85.

34. Richard Richardson and Kenneth Vines, *The Politics of Federal Courts* (Boston: Little, Brown, 1970), 127.

35. *Harris* v. *New York,* 401 U. S. 222 (1971); cf. *Miranda* v. *Arizona,* 384 U. S. 436 (1965); *Mahan* v. *Howell,* 410 U. S. 315 (1973); cf. *Reynolds* v. *Sims,* 377 U. S. 533 (1964); *Miller* v. *California,* 413 U. S. 15 (1973); cf. *Roth* v. *United States,* 354 U. S. 476 (1957).

36. The governing constitutional principles in the area of abortion policy are largely set out or clarified in *Roe* v. *Wade,* 410 U. S. (1973); the death penalty in *Furman* v. *Georgia,* 408 U. S. 238 (1972); national security warrantless eavesdropping in *United States* v. *United States District Court,* 407 U. S. 297 (1972).

37. Abe Fortas, "Equal Rights—For Whom?" James Madison lecture, (New York University Law School, 1967), private printing, 3.

38. Berle, op. cit., vii.

39. *Gitlow* v. *New York,* 268 U. S. 652 (1925), see note 21 above.

40. Robert Dahl, *Pluralist Democracy in the United States* (Chicago: Rand McNally, 1967), 143–70 at 163.

41. Rexford Tugwell, *A Model for a United Republic of America* (Palo Alto, California: James Freel and Associates, 1970).

42. Theodore Lowi, *The End of Liberalism* (New York: W. W. Norton, 1969), chap. 10.

43. Berle, op. cit., 61.

44. Study Group, Paul Freund, chairman, *Report of the Study Group on the Case Load of the Supreme Court* (Washington, D. C.: Federal Judicial Center, 1972).

45. International Commission of Jurists, *The Rule of Law and Human Rights* (Geneva: International Commission of Jurists, 1966), 16–19.

46. *Orlando* v. *Laird, cert denied,* 404 U. S. 869 (1971); comparably unsuccessful in securing a hearing were: *Holtzman* v. *Schesinger,* U. S. (1974). *Massachusetts* v. *Laird, original* 400 U. S. 886 (1970); *Holmes* v. *United States,* 391 U. S. 936 (1968); *Hart* v. *United States,* 391 U. S. 956 (1968); *McArthur* v. *Clifford,* 393 U. S. 1002 (1968); *Katz* v. *Tyler,* 386 U. S. 942 (1967); *Mitchell* v. *U. S.,* 386 U. S. 972 (1967); *Mora* v. *McNamara,* 389 U. S. 934 (1967). Judge John Frank has aptly identified the four elements associated with such a judicial hands-off policy: "the need of a quick and single policy," "judicial incompetence," the "clear prerogative of another branch of government," and "avoidance of unmanageable situations." J. P. Frank, "Political Questions," in Edmond Cahn, ed., *Supreme Court and Supreme Law* (Bloomington: Indiana University Press, 1954), 36–47.

47. 28 U.S.C. 2201. Cf., *United States* v. *Nixon, President of the United States,* 94 S. Ct. 3090 (1974).

48. *Katzenbach* v. *Morgan,* 384 U. S. 641 (1966), limitations on congressional power specified in note 10; *Oregon* v. *Mitchell,* 400 U. S. 112 (1970), qualifications on broad congressional powers, at 128–29, note 11. See the analysis of Archibald Cox, "The Role of Congress in Constitutional Determinations," 40 *University of Cincinnati Law Review* 199–261 (Summer 1971).

49. Civil Rights Commission, *Racial Isolation in the Public Schools* (Washington, D. C.: Government Printing Office, 1967), 187. Cf., *Milliken, Governor of Michigan* v. *Bradley,* 94 S. Ct. 3112 (1974).

50. Walter F. Murphy and Joseph Tanenhaus, "Public Opinion and the United States Supreme Court," 2 *Law and Society* 357–76 (May 1968).

51. *New York Times Co.* v. *United States,* 403 U. S. 713 (1971).

52. "Nominations of Abe Fortas and Homer Thornberry," *Hearings before the Committee on the Judiciary,* U. S. Senate, 90th Cong., 2d Sess., 132 (1968).

53. Glendon Schubert, *Judicial Policy Making* (Chicago: Scott, Foresman, 1965), 149–53.

54. E.g., Stephen L. Wasby, *The Impact of the United States Supreme Court* (Homewood, Illinois: The Dorsey Press, 1970).

55. *Lombard* v. *Louisiana,* 373 U. S. 267 (1963); *Peterson* v. *Greenville,* 373 U. S. 244 (1963); *Griffen* v. *Maryland,* 378 U. S. 130 (1964).

## The Federal Bureaucracy: Responsiveness to Whom?

1. Harrison Wellford, "Agribusiness: Overkill on the Farm," *Washington Monthly* (September 1971), 28–37.

2. *The Ralph Nader Study Group on Air Pollution: Vanishing Air,* John Esposito, project director (New York: Grossman Publishers, 1970), 152–81.

3. James Turner, *The Chemical Feast* (New York: Grossman Publishers, 1970), 88–92.

4. Donald Allen Schon, *Beyond the Stable State: Public and Private Learning in a Changing Society* (London: Maurice Temple Smith, 1971), 32.

5. Lee Loewinger, "The Administrative Agency as a Paradigm of Government—A Survey of the Administration Process," *Indiana Law Journal,* 40:3 (Spring 1965), quoted in Leo J. Fritschler, *Smoking & Politics* (New York: Appleton-Century-Croft, 1969), 94.

6. There exists a considerable dialogue in political science over whether or not bureaucracy is, or can be, responsible. For reasons we shall set forth, we feel this is the wrong question to address. See Carl J. Friedrich and Edward S. Mason, eds., *Public Policy: 1940* (Cambridge: Harvard University Press, 1940). Herman Finer, "Administrative Responsibility in Democratic Government," *Public Administration Review* 1 (1941). For a discussion of the confusion surrounding terms like *responsibility* and *responsiveness,* see Norman John Powell, *Responsible Bureaucracy in the United States* (Boston: Allyn & Bacon, 1967, especially 6–8). Also J. Roland Pennock, "Responsiveness, Responsibility, and Majority Rule," *The American Political Science Review* 46 (1952), 791–92.

7. Samuel P. Huntington, *Political Order in Changing Societies* (New Haven: Yale University Press, 1968), and Richard Neustadt, *Presidential Power* (New York: Wiley, 1960).

8. For an insight into how the bureaucracy defies the president on foreign policy, see Graham Allison, *Essence of Decision* (Boston: Little, Brown, 1970).

9. For examples see Aaron Wildavsky, *The Politics of the Budgetary Process* (Boston: Little, Brown), 66–72. Harold Seidman, *Politics, Position and Power* (New York: Oxford University Press, 1970), ch. 2.

10. For the concept of policy subsystem see J. Leiper Freeman, *The Political Process* (New York: Random House, 1965); or Lee J. Fritschler, op. cit.

11. Sidney Baldwin, *Poverty and Politics: The Rise and Decline of the*

*Farm Security Administration* (Chapel Hill: University of North Carolina Press, 1968).

12. By *consensus-legitimacy pattern* we mean the distribution of positive and negative sentiment regarding an agency's purpose, means of accomplishment, and claim on resources. Agencies strive for and eventually must have a positive margin, a consensus among "relevant others," as to its legitimacy.

13. James Turner, *The Chemical Feast,* op. cit.

14. Samuel Huntington, "The Marasmus of the ICC: The Commission, the Railroads and the Public Interest," 61 *Yale Law Journal* 467, 1952. Also Walton Hamilton, *The Politics of Industry* (New York: Alfred Knopf, 1957), 34.

15. For an example of frantic and largely futile efforts to establish objective criteria, see Louis L. Jaffe, "The Scandal in TV Licensing" in Samuel Krislov and Lloyd Musolf, eds., *The Politics of Regulation* (Boston: Houghton-Mifflin, 1964).

16. Theodore Lowi developed these categories for use in analyzing policies. See his "American Business, Public Policy, Case Studies and Political Theory," *World Politics* 16 (July 1964), 677–715. Most of his work with these categories has dealt with the legislative and presidential politics of these policies. We are focusing on their administrative or bureaucratic politics. Robert Salisbury and John Heinz have developed a fourth category: self-regulative to cover a regulative agency captured and controlled by clients. We will not use it here because its responsiveness pattern is self-evident. See their "A Theory of Policy Analysis and Some Preliminary Applications," in *Policy Analysis in Political Science,* edited by Ira Sharkansky (Chicago: Markham, 1970, ch. 3). In later work, Lowi has discussed a constituency policy which we are not able to utilize here. See his "Four Systems of Policy, Politics and Choice," *Public Administration Review* 33:4, 1972.

17. Another question is often raised by the groups subject to regulation: Is due process being followed in allocating these values? This important question is often a rhetorical smokescreen for delaying a deprivation. See E. R. Quesada, "The Pressures Against Air Safety," in Samuel Krislov and Lloyd Musolf, ed., op. cit. Though an important question, it is not particularly relevant in distinguising between the categories posited here.

18. See Marver Bernstein, *Regulating Business by Independent Commission* (Princeton: Princeton University Press, 1955), 74–95.

19. Peter Bachrach and Morton Baratz, *Power and Poverty: Theory and Practice* (New York: Oxford University Press, 1970).

20. Harold Wolman, *Politics of Federal Housing* (New York: Dodd, Mead, 1971), 143–44.

21. See Alan Lupo, Frank Colcord, and Edmund Fowler, *Rites of Way: The Politics of Transportation in Boston and the U. S. City* (Boston: Little, Brown, and Company, 1971); Thomas Morehouse, "The 1962 Highway act: A Study in Artful Interpretation," *Journal of the American Institute of Planners* 37:3, May 1969, 160–68.

22. David Rogers, *110 Livingston Street, Bureaucracy and Politics in NYC Schools* (New York: Vintage, 1969), 267.

23. Stanley Turrenberg, *Manpower Challenges of the 1970's: Institutions and Social Change* (Baltimore: Johns Hopkins Press, 1970).

24. For a definition of professionalism see Robert S. Friedman, "Professionalism: Expertise and Policy Making" (New York: General Learning Press, 1971). For data on its increase in federal service see Franklin P. Kilpatrick, Milton C. Cummings, Jr., and M. Kent Jennings, *The Image of the Federal Service* (Washington: Brookings Institution, 1964), 41; The University-Federal Agency Conference on Career Development, Princeton University, November 1961, *Working Papers* (Washington: U. S. Civil Service Commission, 1961), 2–4. For other general discussions of the trend see Frederick C. Mosher, *Democracy and the Public Service* (New York: Oxford University Press, 1968), 103; and Seidman, *Politics, Position and Power,* op. cit., 124–35.

25. James Turner, *The Chemical Feast,* op. cit., 97–106.

26. Richard A. Cloward and Francis F. Piven, *Regulating the Poor: The Functioning of Public Relief* (New York: Pantheon, 1971).

27. Mosher, *Democracy and the Public Service,* op. cit., 210.

28. Seidman, *Politics, Position and Power,* 107–22.

29. In most cases basic characteristics desired are written into Civil Service applicant requirements or are pursued by a winnowing of a list of qualified applicants. As any good personnel manager knows, there are a variety of ways of working down a list past the top or top three applicants.

30. See Gary L. Wamsley, *Selective Service and a Changing America* (Columbus: Chas E. Merrill, 1970), 73–82.

31. See H. Kaufman, *The Forest Ranger—A Study in Administrative Behavior* (Baltimore: Johns Hopkins Press, 1960).

32. Francis Fielder and Godfrey Harris, *The Quest for Foreign Affairs Officers—Their Recruitment and Selection* (New York: Carnegie Endowment for International Peace, 1966).

33. Ross B. Talbot and Don F. Hadwiger, *The Policy Process in American Agriculture* (San Francisco: Chandler, 1968), 237.

34. Seidman, *Politics, Position and Power,* op. cit., 14.

35. Wildavsky, *Politics of the Budgetary Process,* op. cit., 172.

36. Allison, *The Essence of Decision,* op. cit., 78–100.

37. Alan Altshuler, *City Planning Process* (Ithaca: Cornell University Press, 1965); Lupo, Colcord, Fowler, *Rites of Way,* op. cit.; Morehouse, "The 1962 Highway Act. . . ," op. cit.

38. National Commission on Urban Problems, *Building the American City* (Washington, D. C.: GPO, 1968), 94–103.

39. Speech of FHA Commissioner Philip Brownstein, October 23, 1967, reprinted in U. S. Cong., House, Committee on Banking and Currency, *Real Estate Settlement Costs, F.H.A. Mortgage Foreclosures, Housing Abandonment, and Site Selection Policies,* Hearing Before the Subcommittee on Housing, 92d Congress, 2nd Session, Feb. 1972, 265–67.

40. Ibid. (Emphasis added)

41. For detail on the FHA housing scandals, see: House Banking Committee Hearings on *FHA Mortgage Foreclosures,* 92d Congress, 2d Session; U. S., Congress, House, Committee on Government Operations, *FHA Defaults: Detroit Report,* 92d Congress, 2d Session; William Lilley and Timothy B. Clark, "Federal Programs Spur Abandonment of Housing in Major Cities," *National Journal,* January 1, 1972.

42. Robert Fellmeth, Edward Cox and Harrison Wellford, "How Ralph Nader, Tricia Nixon, the ABA, and Jamie Whitten Helped Turn the FTC Around," *The Washington Monthly,* October 1972, 5–13.

43. Stephen K. Bailey and Edith K. Mosher, *ESEA: The Office of Education Administers a Law* (Syracuse: Syracuse University Press, 1968).

44. Seidman, *Politics, Position, and Power,* op. cit., 133 (emphasis added).

### The Political Responsiveness of the American States and Their Local Governments

1. Presidential Message to Congress, February 7, 1972. Quoted from text of message in *Congressional Quarterly Weekly Report,* 30 (February 12, 1972), 292.

2. United States Senate Committee on Government Operations, Subcommittee on Intergovernmental Relations, *Confidence and Concern: Citizens View American Government* (Washington: United States Government Printing Office, 1973), I:42–43.

3. Theodore Lowi, *The End of Liberalism* (New York: W. W. Norton, 1969), 305–306.

4. For discussions of similar definitions of political responsiveness,

see Harold F. Gosnell, *Democracy: The Threshold of Freedom* (New York: The Ronald Press, 1948), 130–41; Hanna F. Pitkin, *The Concept of Representation* (Berkeley: University of California Press, 1967), 209–40; and Paul E. Peterson, "Forms of Representation: Participation of the Poor in the Community Action Program," *American Political Science Review* 64 (June 1970), 491–94.

5. Arthur H. Samish and Bob Thomas, *The Secret Boss of California: The Life and High Times of Art Samish* (New York: Crown Publishers, 1971), 32.

6. Mike Royko, *Boss: Richard J. Daley of Chicago* (New York: E. P. Dutton, 1971), 46.

7. See Ronald E. Weber, *Public Policy Preferences in the States* (Bloomington: Indiana University Institute of Public Administration, 1971), 94–99.

8. For a full discussion of how responsiveness is measured, see William R. Shaffer and Ronald E. Weber, *Policy Responsiveness in the American States* (Beverly Hills: Sage Professional Papers in Administrative and Policy Studies, 1974).

9. Advisory Commission on Intergovernmental Relations, *State-Local Finances: Significant Features and Suggested Legislation, 1972 Edition* (Washington: U. S. Government Printing Office, 1972), 150–59.

10. Advisory Commission on Intergovernmental Relations, *Urban America and the Federal System* (Washington: U. S. Government Printing Office, 1969), 90; and Advisory Commission on Intergovernmental Relations, *State Action on Local Problems: 1971* (Washington: U. S. Government Printing Office, 1972), 3–4.

11. The three measures of malapportionment most often used are reported in Manning J. Dauer and Robert G. Kelsay, "Unrepresentative States," *National Municipal Review* 44 (December 1955), 571–75, 587; Paul T. David and Ralph Eisenberg, *Devaluation of the Urban and Suburban Vote* (Charlottesville: University of Virginia Bureau of Public Administration, 1971); and Glendon Schubert and Charles Press, "Measuring Malapportionment," *American Political Science Review* 58 (June 1964), 302–27.

12. Malcolm E. Jewell, "Political Patterns in Apportionment," in Malcolm E. Jewell, ed., *The Politics of Reapportionment* (New York: Atherton Press, 1962), 18–19.

13. See the results of the following studies: Herbert Jacob, "The Consequences of Malapportionment: A Note of Caution," *Social Forces* 43 (December 1964), 256–61; Thomas Dye, "Malapportionment and Public Policy in the States," *The Journal of Politics* 27 (August 1965), 586–601; Richard Hofferbert, "The Relation Between Public Policy and Some Struc-

tural and Environmental Variables in the American States," *American Political Science Review* 60 (March 1966), 73–82; and David Brady and Douglas Edmonds, "The Effects of Malapportionment on Policy Output in the American States," The Laboratory of Political Research, Report No. 3, Department of Political Science, University of Iowa.

14. Shaffer and Weber, *Policy Responsiveness in the American States.*

15. *Baker* v. *Carr,* 369 U. S. 186 (1962), and *Reynolds* v. *Sims,* 377 U. S. 533 (1964).

16. For a complete breakdown on state legislative reapportionment in the first years after the U. S. Supreme Court decisions, see William J. D. Boyd, ed., *Apportionment in the Nineteen-Sixties* (New York: National Municipal League, 1967).

17. For a discussion of reapportionment activities after the 1970 census, see *Reapportionment in the States* (Lexington: Council of State Governments, 1972), and *Reapportionment in the Seventies* (Lexington: Council of State Governments, 1973).

18. *Mahan* v. *Howell* (35 L. Ed. 2d 320). This decision was reaffirmed later in the same term in the cases of *Gaffney* v. *Cummings* (37 L. Ed. 2d 298) and *White* v. *Register* (37 L. Ed. 2d 314).

19. See particularly, William deRubertis, "How Apportionment with Selected Demographic Variables Relates to Policy Orientation," *Western Political Quarterly* 22 (December 1969), 904–20; Bret Hawkins and Cheryl Whelchel, "Reapportionment and Urban Representation in Legislative Influence Positions: The Case of Georgia," *Urban Affairs Quarterly* 3 (March 1968), 69–80; and Richard Lehne, *Reapportionment of the New York Legislature: Impact and Issues* (New York: National Municipal League, 1972).

20. Shaffer and Weber, *Policy Responsiveness in the American States.*

21. For an excellent critique of existing studies and suggestions on how to better study the problem, see William E. Bicker, "The Effects of Malapportionment in the States—A Mistrial," in Nelson W. Polsby, ed., *Reapportionment in the 1970's* (Berkeley: University of California Press, 1971), 151–208.

22. O. Glenn Stahl, *Public Personnel Administration,* 5th Ed. (New York: Harper and Row, 1962), 37.

23. Advisory Committee on Merit System Standards, Department of Health, Education and Welfare, *Progress in Intergovernmental Personnel Relations* (Washington: U. S. Government Printing Office, 1969), 17.

24. For a ranking of the states on salary and fringe benefits, see Ira Sharkansky, "State Administrators in the Political Process," in Herbert Jacob and Kenneth N. Vines, eds., *Politics in the American States: A Comparative Analysis,* 2nd Ed. (Boston: Little, Brown, 1971), 264.

25. For extensive discussions of legislative reform, see *Modernizing State Government* (New York: Committee for Economic Development, 1967), 32–44; John Burns, *The Sometime Governments* (New York: Bantam Books, 1971); and The Citizens Conference on State Legislatures, *State Legislatures: An Evaluation of their Effectiveness* (New York: Praeger Publishers, 1971).

26. Burns, *The Sometime Governments,* 51.

27. The Citizens Conference on State Legislatures, *State Legislatures: An Evaluation of their Effectiveness,* 77.

28. Leonard G. Ritt, "State Legislative Reform: Does It Matter?" *American Politics Quarterly* 1 (October 1973), 499–510.

29. Shaffer and Weber, *Policy Responsiveness in the American States.*

30. For a theoretical discussion of revenue elasticity, see Werner Z. Hirsch, *The Economics of State and Local Government* (New York: McGraw-Hill, 1970), 72–77.

31. They have elasticity coefficients hovering around 1.0, meaning that for every one unit change in income, a one unit change will occur in revenue from the tax.

32. The above information was digested from Table 9 in A.C.I.R., *State-Local Finances, 1972 Edition,* 23–24.

33. *Earmarked State Taxes* (New York: Tax Foundation, Inc., 1965), 19.

34. Advisory Commission on Intergovernmental Relations, *Measuring the Fiscal Capacity and Effort of State and Local Areas* (Washington: U. S. Government Printing Office, 1971), 126–27.

35. Kenneth E. Quindry, *State and Local Revenue Potential 1970* (Atlanta: Southern Regional Education Board, 1971).

36. Computed from data presented in Quindry, *State and Local Revenue. . . .*

37. *State Government News* 17 (January 1974), 8.

38. For a full compilation of state elective administrative officials, see *The Book of the States, 1972–73,* Vol. 19 (Lexington: The Council of State Governments, 1972), 152–53.

39. For a representative reform proposal, *see Modernizing State Government,* 20–21.

40. For a discussion of the governors' views on the subject of reorganization, see Thad Beyle, "The Governor's Formal Powers: A View from the Governor's Chair," *Public Administration Review* 28 (November–December 1968), 540–45. On recent reorganization activities, see *Reorganization in the States* (Lexington: The Council of State Governments, 1972).

41. *Reorganization in the States,* 5–7.

42. William Watts and Lloyd A. Free (eds.), *State of the Nation* (New York: Universe Books, 1973), 299.

43. *Louisville Courier-Journal,* July 5, 1973, A19.

## Accountability and Responsiveness of the Military Establishment

1. "Farewell Radio and Television Address to the American People," Jan. 17, 1961, *Public Papers of the Presidents of the U. S., Dwight D. Eisenhower, 1960–61,* 1035, 1038.

2. Shoup, "The New American Militarism," *Atlantic Monthly* (April 1969), 54.

3. Myers v. U. S., 272 U. S. 52, 293 (1926) (Brandeis, J., dissenting).

4. *Writings of Abraham Lincoln* (Lapsetz ed., 1905), 2:52.

5. Hamilton, Jay, and Madison, "Federalist Paper 69," *The Federalist* (Modern Library ed., 1937), 448.

6. 1 Cranch 137, 2 L. ed. 60 (1803).

7. U. S. Constitution, Art. I, sec. 8, cl. 15.

8. *Id.* at cl. 16.

9. W. Millis, *Arms and Men* (1956).

10. But see Kneedler v. Lane, 45 Pa. 238 (S. Ct. Pa. 1863) holding act constitutional.

11. Selective Draft Law Cases, 245 U. S. 366 (1918).

12. Hart v. U. S., 391 U. S. 956 (1968); Holmes v. U. S., 391 U. S. 936 (1968); Mitchell v. U. S., 386 U. S. 972 (1967).

13. Youngstown Sheet and Tube Co. v. Sawyer, 343 U. S. 579, 642 (1952).

14. II Farrand, *The Records of the Federal Convention of 1787,* 318 (1911).

15. Emerson (Legislative Assistant to Senator Barry Goldwater), "War Powers: An Invasion of Presidential Prerogative," 58 American Bar Assoc. Journal 809, 810 (1972).

16. See Report of the Senate Committee on Foreign Relations to Accompany S. Res. 187, Report No. 797, 90th Cong., 1st Sess. 8–12 (1967).

17. *Id.* at 9.

18. U. S. Congress, Joint Committee on Printing, I *Compilation of Messages and Papers of Presidents* (J. Richardson ed. 1897) 314.

19. Letter from J. Adams to J. Salazar, Aug. 6, 1824, quoted in *The Record of American Diplomacy* (R. Bartlett ed. 1954), 185.

20. Mora et al. v. McNamara, 389 U. S. 934 (1967).

21. Massachusetts v. Laird, 451 F. 2d 26 (1st Cir. 1971); Orlando & Berk v. Laird, 443 F. 2d 1039 (2d Cir. 1971).

22. Holtzman v. Schlesinger, 361 F. Supp. 544, 553 (E.D.N.Y. 1973), *stay granted,* 94 S. Ct. 11, *rev'd,* 484 F. 2d 1307 (2d Cir. 1973), *cert. denied,* 94 S. Ct. 1935 (1974).

23. The cut-off was attached to a $3.3 billion supplemental appropriations bill after the president agreed to a compromise that would not cut off funds for another six weeks. *N. Y. Times,* June 30, 1973, 1.

24. Pub. L. 73–148 (Nov. 7, 1973).

25. *N. Y. Times,* Nov. 8, 1973, 1, 20.

26. See M. McDougal & F. Feliciano, *Law and Minimum Public Order: The Legal Regulation of International Coercion* 350–53 (1961) for analysis of seven functions involved in the decision about the use of sanctions, in a number of which one could find the military playing a key role today—intelligence gathering, promotion (i.e., recommendation of policy), prescription (i.e., promulgation of norms), invocation (i.e., provisional application of norms), application, termination (i.e., ending prescription), and appraisal.

27. S. Huntington, *The Soldier and the State* 348 (1957).

28. See III *Pentagon Papers* (Gravel ed. 1971) 206–38, 315–21, 334–36, 426–30, 450–52, and accounts in D. Halberstam, *The Best and the Brightest* (1972); T. Hoopes, *The Limits of Intervention* (1969).

29. See U.N. Resolution 2162 B (XXI), Dec. 5, 1965 (declaring the 1925 Protocol for the Prohibition of the Use in War of Asphyxiating, Poisonous or Other Gases and of Bacteriological Methods of War, to which U. S. is not a party, to be customary international law binding on all states); U.N. Resolution A/2603, Dec. 16, 1969 (declaring contrary to international law use of "any chemical agents or warfare—chemical substances, whether gaseous, liquid or solid—which might be employed because of their direct toxic effects on man, animals, or plants").

30. See, e.g., accounts in Halberstam, *The Best and the Brightest,* note 28 above.

31. Hyman, "The Governance of the Military," 406 *The Annals of the American Society of Political and Social Sciences* 38, 45 (1973).

32. *Time,* May 6, 1974, 34.

33. E. Hughes, *The Living Presidency* (1974).

34. *Washington Post,* Sept. 7, 1973, 1.

35. *Id.*

36. *N. Y. Times,* Jan. 13, 1974, 1. See also *N. Y. Times,* Aug. 7, 1973, 20, concerning use of presidential authority to force promotion

of a lieutenant colonel on staff of domestic advisor John Ehrlichman.

37. R. Sherrill, "L. Mendel Rivers: King of the Military Mountain," 210 *The Nation* (Jan. 19, 1970), 40.

38. W. McGaffin & E. Knoll, *Scandal in the Pentagon: A Challenge to Democracy* 93–4 (1969).

39. T. Coffin, *The Armed Society: Militarism in Modern America* (1968), 20.

40. *N. Y. Times,* Jan. 14, 1974, 1; Jan. 19, 1974, 1.

41. Halperin, "The President and the Military," 50 *Foreign Affairs* 310, 313 (1972).

42. Sheehan, "Influence of Joint Chiefs is Reported Rising," *N. Y. Times,* June 30, 1969, 1.

43. *N. Y. Times,* June 14, 1972, 1, 20.

44. *N. Y. Times,* June 22, 1972, 4.

45. *Louisville Courier-Journal,* Sept. 16, 1972, 20.

46. *N. Y. Times,* Oct. 20, 1972, 1.

47. *N. Y. Times,* July 18, 1; Sept. 11, 1973, 1.

48. *N. Y. Times,* Sept. 11, 1973, 1. See also *N. Y. Times,* Aug. 21, 1973, 1.

49. *N. Y. Times,* July 24, 1973, 1.

50. U. S. Constitution, Art. I, Sec. 8, Cl. 12.

51. McGaffin & Knoll, *Scandal in the Pentagon, supra* note 38, at 92.

52. Congressional Quarterly, *The Power of the Pentagon: The Creation, Control and Acceptance of Defense Policy by the U. S. Congress* (1972), 3.

53. McGaffin & Knoll, *Scandal in the Pentagon, supra* note 38, at 90.

54. *Id.* at 97.

55. Pub. L. 93–344 (July 12, 1974); 88 Stat. 297.

56. Congressional Quarterly, *The Power of the Pentagon, supra* note 53, at 9.

57. *Id.* at 5.

58. Sherrill, "L. Mendel Rivers," *supra* note 37, at 41–2.

59. See McGaffin & Knoll, *Scandal in the Pentagon, supra* note 38, at 61–80; R. Lapp, *Arms Beyond Doubt: The Tyranny of Weapons Technology* 35–56 (1970).

60. Congressional Quarterly, *The Power of the Pentagon, supra* note 53, at 5.

61. *Id.*

62. J. Raymond, *Power at the Pentagon* 297 (1964).

63. Lapp, *Arms Beyond Doubt, supra* note 59, at 57–89.

64. A. Yarmolinsky, *The Military Establishment: Its Impacts on American Society* (abridged ed. 1973) 51–2.

65. Quoted in *id.* 53 (1971).

66. R. Lapp, *Arms Beyond Doubt: The Tyranny of Weapons Technology* (1970), *The Weapons Culture* (1968).

67. J. Galbraith, "How to Control the Military," *Harper's* (June 1969), 31.

68. F. Cook, *The Warfare State* (1962).

69. S. Melman, *Pentagon Capitalism: The Political Economy of War* (1970).

70. Congressional Quarterly Weekly Report, May 1, 1968, 1063.

71. Yarmolinsky, *The Military Establishment, supra* note 64, at 208–9; C. Mollenhoff, *The Pentagon: Politics, Profit, and Plunder* 298–312 (1967).

72. See McGaffin & Knoll, *Scandal in the Pentagon, supra* note 38, at 17; Yarmolinsky, *The Military Establishment, supra* note 64, at 235.

73. *N. Y. Times,* Nov. 12, 1973, 8.

74. "The Military-Industrial Job Hoppers," *Business Week* 51 (Jan. 15, 1972).

75. See *N. Y. Times,* July 15, 1972, 8; Dec. 18, 1972, 7; Dec. 26, 1972, 32 (ed); Jan. 6, 1973, 17. See generally R. Kaufman, *The War Profiteers* (1971). See also *N. Y. Times,* Feb. 18, 1972, 70 (charge that four congressmen and senators pressured navy on behalf of Avondale Shipyards in contract dispute).

76. *N. Y. Times,* Dec. 20, 1972, 25.

77. See Lapp, *Arms Beyond Doubt, supra* note 59, at 162; McGaffin & Knoll, *Scandal in the Pentagon, supra* note 38, at 83–4; *N. Y. Times,* Sept. 20, 1973.

78. *N. Y. Times,* Dec. 23, 1972, 1; Aug. 15, 1974, 21.

79. The Pentagon reported spending $24.8 million on public affairs in fiscal year 1973, but a General Accounting Office report showed another $24 million was spent on "promotional" activities in violation of the $28 million ceiling set by Congress in 1970. *N. Y. Times,* Aug. 6, 1973, 27.

80. Congressional Quarterly, *The Power of the Pentagon, supra* note 52, at 5.

81. McGaffin & Knoll, *Scandal in the Pentagon, supra* note 38, at 94–5.

82. Reservists Committee to Stop the War v. Laird, 323 F. Supp. 833 (D.D.C. 1971), *aff'd, without opinion* (D.C. Cir. 1972), *rev'd sub nom.,* Schlesinger v. Reservists Committee to Stop the War, 94 S. Ct. 2925 (1974).

83. Quoted in Hearings on H.R. 2498 Before a Special Subcommittee of the House Committee on Armed Services, 81st Cong., 1st Sess. 780 (1949).

84. 10 U.S.C. § § 801–940 (1970).

85. See West, "A History of Command Influence on the Military Judicial System," 18 U.C.L.A. Law Review 1 (1970); Remcho, "Military Juries: Constitutional Analysis and the Need for Reform," 47 Indiana Law Journal 193 (1972); Willis, "The Constitution, the United States Court of Military Appeals and the Future," 57 Military Law Review 27 (1972); Sherman, "The Civilianization of Military Law," 22 Maine Law Review 3 (1970).

86. 71 U. S. (4 Wall.) 2 (1866).

87. But see, Arts. 32 & 43, UCMJ (providing for thorough pretrial investigation in general courts-martial, and informal investigation in special and summary courts-martial) and Art. 25(c)(1)(permitting enlisted man to request that 1/3 of court members be enlisted men).

88. U. S. ex rel. Toth v. Quarles, 350 U. S. 11 (1955).

89. Reid v. Covert, 354 U. S. 1 (1957); Kinsella v. U. S. ex rel. Singleton, 361 U. S. 234 (1960); McElroy v. U. S. ex rel. Guagliardo, 361 U. S. 281 (1960); Grisham v. Hagan, 361 U. S. 278 (1960).

90. 395 U. S. 258 (1969).

91. Compare U. S. v. Rose, 19 U.S.C.M.A. 3, 41 C.M.R. 3 (1969) with Cole v. Laird, 468 F. 2d 829 (5th Cir. 1972).

92. 346 U. S. 137 (1953).

93. Broussard v. Patton, 466 F. 2d 816 (9th Cir. 1972); Kennedy v. Commandant, 377 F.2d 339 (10th Cir. 1967).

94. Robb v. U. S., 456 F. 2d 768 (Ct. Cl. 1972); Kaufmann v. Secretary of the Air Force, 415 F. 2d 991 (D.C. Cir. 1969).

95. See, e.g., In re Stapley, 246 F. Supp. 316 (D. Utah 1965); Ashe v. McNamara, 355 F. 2d 277 (1st Cir. 1965).

96. The military appeal courts are made up of the intermediate Courts of Military Review in each service composed almost entirely of military legal officers and the ultimate Court of Military Appeals composed of three civilian judges appointed to fifteen-year terms by the president.

97. See H. Moyer, *Justice and the Military* 233–665 (1972).

98. Daigle v. Warner, 348 F. Supp. 1074 (D. Hawaii 1972), holding the Supreme Court's decision that a defendant is entitled to legally trained counsel at a trial where confinement is possible in Angersinger v. Hamlin, 407 U. S. 25 (1972), applies to summary courts-martial. The decision was later reversed. See note 100, *supra.*

99. DAJA-MJ 1972/12338.

100. Compare Daigle v. Warner, 490 F. 2d 358 (9th Cir. 1973) (5th and 6th Amendments do not apply to courts-martial and there is no constitutional right to counsel in summary courts-martial) with Betonie v. Sizemore, 43 LW 2045 (5th Cir. July 5, 1974) (summary court martial without counsel deprives defendant of constitutional right under 6th Amendment).

101. U. S. v. Alderman, 22 U.S.C.M.A. 298 (1973).

102. Article 133, UCMJ.

103. Article 134, UCMJ.

104. Avrech v. Secretary of the Navy, 477 F. 2d 1237 (D.C. Cir. 1973).

105. Levy v. Parker, 478 F. 2d 772 (3d Cir. 1973).

106. Secretary of the Navy v. Avrech, 94 S. Ct. 3039 (1974); Parker v. Levy, 94 S. Ct. 2547 (1974).

107. 94 S. Ct. at 2574–5.

108. Stolte & Amick v. Laird, 353 F. Supp. 1392 (D.D.C. 1972).

109. *Id.* at 1403.

110. See Report of the Task Force on the Administration of Military Justice in the Armed Forces, Vol. I.

111. Public Law No. 90–632 (Oct. 24, 1968).

112. Bayh, S. 1127, 92d Cong., 1st Sess. (1971); Hatfield, S. 4168–4178, 91st Cong., 2d Sess. (1970); and Bennett, H.R. 291, 93rd Cong., 1st Sess. (1973).

113. See Everett, "The New Look in Military Justice," 1973 Duke Law Journal 649, 661–63.

114. See Hodson, "Courts-Martial and the Commander," 10 San Diego Law Review 51 (1972); Westmoreland, "Military Justice—A Commander's Viewpoint," 10 American Criminal Law Review 5 (1971).

115. 395 U. S. at 265 (1969).

116. See Sherman, "Military Justice without Military Control," 82 Yale Law Journal, 1398 (1973).

117. Carlson v. Schlesinger, 364 F. Supp. 626, 639 (D.D.C. 1973).

118. The Congressional Black Caucus Report, Racism in the Military: A New System for Rewards and Punishments, 118 Cong. Rec. E 8674–8688 (Oct. 14, 1972); ACLU Board Resolution 7, Special Committee on Military Rights (1974).

119. Orloff v. Willoughby, 354 U. S. 83, 94 (1953).

120. 355 U. S. 579 (1958) (per curiam).

121. Stapp v. Resor, 314 F. Supp. 475 (S.D.N.Y. 1970).

122. Hammond v. Lenfest, 398 F. 2d 705 (2d Cir. 1968).

123. See, e.g., U. S. ex rel. Kempf v. Commanding Officer, 339 F. Supp. 320 (S.D. Io. 1972); Townley v. Resor, 323 F. Supp. 567 (N.D. Cal. 1970); Ottman v. Laird, 3 SSLR 3540 (E.D. Wis. 1970). But see Silverthorne v. Laird, 460 F. 2d 1175 (5th Cir. 1972).

124. See, e.g., U. S. ex rel. Wilkerson v. Commanding Officer, 286 F. Supp. 290 (S.D.N.Y. 1968); Lewis v. Secretary of the Army, 402 F. 2d 813 (9th Cir. 1968); Magaro v. Cassidy, 2 SSLR 3677 (5th Cir. 1970); Powers v. Powers, 400 F. 2d 438 (5th Cir. 1968).

125. Patterson v. Commanding Officer, 321 F. Supp. 1080 (W.D. La. 1971).

126. Bluth v. Laird, 435 F. 2d 1065 (4th Cir. 1970).

127. Saunders v. Westmoreland, 2 SSLR 3157 (D.D.C. 1969).

128. 447 F. 2d 245 (2d Cir. 1971).

129. Arnheiter v. Chaffe, 435 F. 2d 691 (9th Cir. 1970).

130. U. S. ex rel. Chaparro v. Resor, 412 F. 2d 443 (4th Cir. 1969).

131. Carlson v. Schlesinger, *supra* note 105.

132. See, e.g., Yahr v. Resor, 431 F. 2d 690 (4th Cir. 1970), *on remand,* 339 F. Supp. 964 (E.D.N.C. 1972); Dash v. Commanding General, 307 F. Supp. 849 (D.S.C. 1970), *aff'd,* 429 F. 2d 427 (4th Cir. 1970); Schneider v. Laird, 453 F. 2d 345 (10th Cir. 1972); Doyle v. Koelbl, 434 F. 2d 1014 (5th Cir. 1970); Anderson v. Laird, 437 F. 2d 912 (7th Cir. 1971).

133. Jones v. Secretary of Defense, 346 F. Supp. 97 (D. Minn. 1972).

133. USAREUR Circular 600–85 (Sept. 10, 1973).

134. *N. Y. Times,* Jan. 11, 1974, 1.

135. Committee for G.I. Rights v. Callaway, 370 F. Supp. 934, 939 (D.D.C. 1974). The army obtained a stay of the order pending appeal.

136. R. Heinl, "The Collapse of the Armed Forces," *Armed Forces Journal* (June 7, 1973).

137. H. Lasswell, *The Garrison State* (1937).

138. See A. Vagts, *A History of Militarism* (1937), 13–17.

139. Statistics from Department of Defense, June 30, 1972, published in Griggs, "Minorities in the Armed Forces," *Race Relations Reporter* (July 1973), 9, 10.

140. King, "Making It in the U. S. Army," *New Republic* (May 30, 1970), 19.

141. *N. Y. Times,* Aug. 25, 1974, 1.

142. See J. Swomley, *The Military Establishment* (1964), 113–28, 177–98.

143. W. Just, *Military Men* (1971).

144. "The Doolittle Report," S. Doc. No. 196, 79th Cong., 2d Sess. 7 (1949).

145. See, e.g., "The New Army: A Ft. Benning Brigade of Volunteers Indicates Nixon Plan Will Work," *Wall Street Journal,* Nov. 13, 1972, 1; "Humanizing the U. S. Military," *Time,* Dec. 21, 1970, 16.

146. Hauser, "The Impact of Societal Change on the U. S. Army," 1 *Parameters* (Winter 1972), 9, 12.

147. Biderman, "What Is Military?" in *The Draft* (S. Tax, ed. 1969), 135.

148. The report of the Senate Watergate Committee recommended legislation to establish a permanent office of public attorney to inquire into complaints concerning federal departments and to prosecute when there is a conflict of interest in the executive branch. *N. Y. Times,* July 14, 1974, 1.

### The Design of Institutional Arrangements and the Responsiveness of the Police

I acknowledge the support of the Center for Studies of Metropolitan Problems, National Institute of Mental Health, Grant No. MH 19911–02. The comments of Vincent Ostrom, Dennis Smith, and Donald Zauderer on an earlier draft of this paper are appreciated.

1. *The Georgetown Law Journal* of Spring 1970 was devoted to a symposium on reform of metropolitan governments. For extensive citations to the reform literature, see Elinor Ostrom, "Metropolitan Reform: Propositions Derived From Two Traditions," *Social Science Quarterly* 53 (December 1972), 474–93.

2. James Q. Wilson, "Police Moral, Reform, and Citizen Respect: The Chicago Case," in *The Police: Six Sociological Essays,* ed. by David J. Bordua (New York: John Wiley, 1967), 137–62.

3. Ibid., 146.

4. Ibid., 147.

5. Ibid., 159–60, Wilson's emphasis.

6. Ibid., 161.

7. Peter H. Rossi, Richard A. Berk, David P. Boesel, Bettye K. Eidson and W. Eugene Groves, *Between White and Black. The Faces of American Institutions in the Ghetto.* A supplemental study for the National Advisory Commission on Civil Disorders (New York: Frederick A. Praeger, 1968), 106.

8. Idem.

9. Ibid., 113.

10. Idem.

11. Curtis J. Berger, "Law, Justice and the Poor," in *Urban Riots: Violence and Social Change,* ed. by Robert H. Connery (New York: Random House, 1968), 59.

12. Allan Altshuler, *Community Control: The Black Demand for Par-*

*ticipation in Large American Cities* (New York: Pegasus Books, 1970), 156.

13. James Q. Wilson, "The Police and the Delinquent in Two Cities," *City Politics and Public Policy,* ed. by James Q. Wilson (New York: John Wiley, 1968), 190.

14. Albert J. Reiss and David J. Bordua, "Environment and Organization: A Perspective on the Police," in *The Police: Six Sociological Essays,* ed. by David J. Bordua (New York: John Wiley, 1967), 43.

15. See Jerome H. Skolnick and J. Richard Woodworth, "Bureaucracy, Information and Social Control," in *The Police: Six Sociological Essays,* ed. by David J. Bordua (New York: John Wiley, 1967), 104–12.

16. John H. McNamara, "Uncertainties in Police Work: The Relevance of Police Recruits' Backgrounds and Training," in *The Police: Six Sociological Essays,* ed. by David J. Bordua (New York: John Wiley, 1967), 251.

17. Ibid., 240.

18. Ibid., 241.

19. Idem.

20. Ibid., 249.

21. Ibid., 238–39.

22. See Commission to Investigate Allegations of Police Corruptions and the City's Anti-Corruption Procedures, *Commission Report* (New York: The Fund for the City of New York, 1972).

23. Paul Chevigny, *Police Power: Police Abuses in New York City* (New York: Random House, 1969).

24. Albert J. Reiss, *The Police and the Public* (New Haven: Yale University Press, 1971), 156.

25. Ibid., 164.

26. Ibid., 167.

27. Idem.

28. Ibid., 167–68.

29. Ibid., 142.

30. Ibid., 144.

31. See Elinor Ostrom, William Baugh, Richard Guarasci, Roger Parks, and Gordon Whitaker, "Community Organization and the Provision of Police Services," *Sage Professional Papers in Administrative and Policy Study* (Beverly Hills, California, 1973); Elinor Ostrom and Gordon P. Whitaker, "Does Local Community Control of Police Make a Difference? Some Preliminary Findings," *American Journal of Political Science* 17 (February 1973), 48–76; Elinor Ostrom and Roger B. Parks, "Suburban Police Departments: Too Many and Too Small?" in *The Urbanization of the Suburbs,* ed. by Louis H. Masotti and Jeffrey K. Hadden, *Urban*

*Affairs Annual Reviews* 7 (Beverly Hills: Sage Publishers, 1973), 367–402.

32. See Paul A. Samuelson, "The Pure Theory of Public Expenditure," *The Review of Economics and Statistics* 36 (November 1954), 387–89; Robert Bish, *The Public Economy of Metropolitan Areas* (Chicago: Markham Publishing, 1971); Robert Bish and Vincent Ostrom, *Understanding Urban Government* (Washington, D. C.: American Enterprise Institute, 1973).

33. Jerome Skolnick, *Justice Without Trial* (New York: John Wiley, 1967).

34. Arthur Niederhoffer, *Behind the Shield: The Police in Urban Society* (New York: Doubleday, 1969).

35. James Q. Wilson, "Police Morale, Reform and Citizen Respect: The Chicago Case," *The Police: Six Sociological Essays,* ed. by David J. Bordua (New York: John Wiley, 1967), 137–63.

36. Herbert L. Packer, "The Crime Tariff," *The American Scholar* 33 (1964), 551–57.

37. For a discussion of these problems see Elinor Ostrom, "Institutional Arrangements and the Measurement of Policy Consequences: Applications to Evaluating Police Performance," *Urban Affairs Quarterly* 6 (June 1971), 447–76.

38. See Roger B. Parks, *Measurement of Performance in the Public Sector: A Case Study of the Indianapolis Police Department* (Bloomington, Indiana: Indiana University, Department of Political Science, Studies in Political Theory and Policy Analysis, 1971).

39. Albert J. Reiss and David J. Bordua, op. cit., 35.

40. Ibid.

41. See Jerome Skolnick, op. cit.

42. See Hallock Hoffman, "Policing," *The Center Magazine* 1 (May 1968), 63.

43. Cantrill indicates that in Philadelphia, "presently the means, rather than the end results are measured against a man. The policeman given the highest performance rating is one who turns in the greatest *quantity* of 'activity'—reports of various kinds, arrests, tickets written. A policeman would develop greater skills and earn more public respect if it was the end result of his work which was scrutinized by his superiors." John Cantrill, "From the Other Side of the Badge," *Columns* 4 (March 1972), 16.

44. John A. Gardiner, "Police Enforcement of Traffic Laws: A Comparative Analysis," in *City Politics and Public Policy,* ed. by James Q. Wilson (New York: John Wiley, 1968), 157.

45. See Gordon Tullock, *The Politics of Bureaucracy* (Washington,

D. C.: The Public Affairs Press, 1965); William A. Niskanen, Jr., *Bureaucracy and Representative Government* (Chicago: Aldine-Atherton, 1971); and Oliver E. Williamson, "Hierarchical Control and Optimum Firm Size," *Journal of Political Economy* 75 (April 1967), 123–238.

46. Robert A. Dahl also argues that "no system of *internal* control negates the need for a system of *external* controls that compel or induce those who exercise authority within the enterprise, whether these managers are chosen by and are accountable to stockholders, workers, or the state, to employ their power and resources for jointly beneficial purposes rather than for exploiting consumers." "The City in the Future of Democracy," *American Political Science Review* 61 (1967), 962.

47. For an argument that small scale institutions need to be created within large scale institutions, see Irving Louis Horowitz, " 'Separate but Equal': Revolution and Counter-Revolution in the American City," *Social Problems* 17 (Winter 1970), 294–312; Charles Press, "The Cities Within a Great City: A Decentralist Approach to Centralization," *Centennial Review* 7 (1963); Kenneth E. Marshall, "Goals of the Black Community," in *Governing the City: Challenges and Options for New York City,* ed. by Robert H. Connery and Demetrios Caraley (New York: Frederick A. Praeger, 1969), 193–205; Robert Dahl, "The City in the Future of Democracy," *American Political Science Review* 61 (December 1967), 953–70; Dale Rogers Marshall, "Metropolitan Government: Views of Minorities," in *Minority Perspectives,* ed. by Lowden Wingo (Washington, D. C.: Resources for the Future, 1972), 9–30.

48. The St. Louis Police Department has been a pioneer in this regard. An external audit of a sample of all cases is conducted regularly in an effort to maintain a reliable system of records. See Arthur C. Meyers, Jr., "Statistical Controls in a Police Department," *Crime and Delinquency* 8 (January 1962).

49. This is similar to a proposal made by Albert J. Reiss, op. cit.

50. One might even want to consider a fine system like that proposed by Judge Tim Murphy of the Superior Court of Washington, D. C., in the following statement: "I have never heard of a policeman who has been subjected to disciplinary sanctions within a police department because he had made an illegal search or an illegal arrest. I would like to suggest a way you can stop bad arrests and bad searches relatively quickly—and I am not talking now about the marginal instances about which we could argue all night as to whether there was probable cause; I am talking about kicking down the door and ransacking a place just for the hell of it. I suggest that on simple application by the aggrieved person, where a judge has thrown the case out or the United States Attorney has declined to prosecute

because of an illegality, the aggrieved person collect two hundred and fifty dollars to be taken out of police operating funds. As soon as the chief sees that a precinct cost the police fund five thousand dollars in fines last week, he will stop the bad arrests. The buck pays off." "The Police," *The Center Magazine* 3 (May–June 1971), 17.

51. See, for example, President's Commission on Law Enforcement and the Administration of Justice, *The Challenge of Crime in a Free Society* (Washington, D. C., 1967); Task Force on the Police, *Task Force Report: The Police* (Washington, D. C., 1967); National Commission on Urban Problems, *Building the American City* (Washington, D. C., 1968).

52. Advisory Committee on the Police Function of the American Bar Association, *The Urban Police Function,* tentative draft (New York: Institute of Judicial Administration, 1972).

53. Committee for Economic Development, *Reducing Crime and Assuring Justice* (New York: Committee for Economic Development, 1972), 7.

54. See discussion in *New York Times,* January 15, 1973, 16.

55. For a discussion and analysis of this trend see Richard A. Cloward and Frances Fox Piven, "The Urban Crisis and the Consolidation of National Power," in *Urban Riots,* ed. by Robert H. Connery (New York: Random House, 1968).

## Responsiveness and Responsibility: the Anomalous Problem of the Environment

1. *World Dynamics* (Cambridge, Massachusetts: Wright-Allen, 1971), 15.

2. Ibid.

3. I have analysed the environmental policy issue in greater detail in an essay entitled "Political Science," in *Interdisciplinary Environmental Approaches,* edited by Albert E. Utton and Daniel H. Henning (Costa Mesa, California: Educational Media Press, 1974), 5–18.

4. *Relativity in Men and Society* (New York: G. P. Putnam's Sons, 1926), 206–207.

5. Ibid., 207–208.

6. Rowland Evans and Robert Novak, "Politics Influencing Environmental Fight," *Daily Herald-Telephone,* Bloomington, Indiana (December 31, 1971).

7. Les Gapay, "Train's Troubles: Energy Crisis Widens Gap Between Nixon, Environment Aide," *The Wall Street Journal* (March 22, 1974).

8. Note court decisions having the effect of invalidating land-use and urban growth controls by Petaluma, California, restoring impounded funds for the Cross-Florida Bays Canal, and reopening the Reserve Mining Company plant on Lake Superior initially closed by a federal judge for violation of pollution control measures. But cf. Cynthia Brucato, "Minnesota May Have an Answer to Environmental Control vs. the Breadline," *Environment Midwest* (July 1974), 8–9.

# Index